YOUR
ASTROLOGY
GUIDE
2009

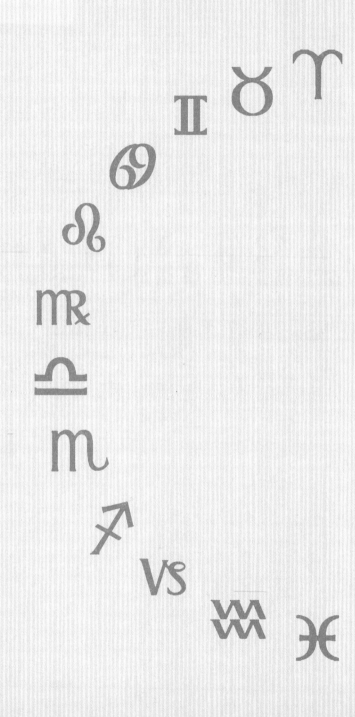

YOUR
ASTROLOGY
GUIDE

2009

RICK LEVINE & JEFF JAWER

STERLING

New York / London
www.sterlingpublishing.com

STERLING and the distinctive Sterling logo are registered
trademarks of Sterling Publishing Co., Inc.

10 9 8 7 6 5 4 3 2 1

Published by Sterling Publishing Co., Inc.
387 Park Avenue South, New York, NY 10016
© 2008 by Sterling Publishing Co., Inc.
Text © 2008 Rick Levine and Jeff Jawer

Distributed in Canada by Sterling Publishing
c/o Canadian Manda Group, 165 Dufferin Street
Toronto, Ontario, Canada M6K 3H6
Distributed in the United Kingdom by GMC Distribution Services
Castle Place, 166 High Street, Lewes, East Sussex, England BN7 1XU
Distributed in Australia by Capricorn Link (Australia) Pty. Ltd.
P.O. Box 704, Windsor, NSW 2756, Australia

Sterling ISBN 978-1-4027-5023-6

For information about custom editions, special sales, premium and
corporate purchases, please contact Sterling Special Sales
Department at 800-805-5489 or specialsales@sterlingpublishing.com.

TABLE OF CONTENTS

ACKNOWLEDGMENTS

Many people continue to contribute to this annual book, both in conception and in production. Some have been with us from the start; some have only recently joined the team. First of all, our heartfelt thanks to Paul O'Brien, whose creative genius behind Tarot.com led us to this project. Paul is our agent, our friend, and his vision opened the doors to make this book possible. On the production side, we are grateful for our editor, Gail Goldberg. Her ability to clarify concepts, untangle sentences, and sharpen our words is matched by her commitment to presenting astrology in an intelligent light. We appreciate her energetic Mars in efficient Virgo; her persistent attention to detail continues to challenge us to write better books. Of course we are very grateful to Michael Fragnito, editorial director at Sterling Publishing, for his initial vision of what this book could be, his tireless support for the project, and his trust in our work. Barbara Berger, Sterling's supervising editor on this book, has shepherded the project with Taurean persistence and good humor under the ongoing pressures of very tight deadlines. We thank Laura Jorstad for her refinement of the text, and project editor Mary Hern for her careful guidance. We are thankful to Marcus Leaver, Jason Prince, Jeremy Nurnberg, Karen Nelson, Elizabeth Mihaltse, Rebecca Maines, and Rachel Maloney at Sterling. Thanks go to Bob Wietrak and Jules Herbert at Barnes & Noble, and whoever said yes in the beginning. We appreciate 3+Co and Asami Matsushima for the original design; and thanks for the art and ideas from Jessica Abel and the rest of the Tarot.com team. Thanks, as well, to Tara Gimmer and company for the author photo.

Rick: I am indebted to a truly great writing partner. Thank you, Jeff, for showing up with a combination of unwavering reliability, solid astrology, and the willingness to keep pushing the envelope of creativity. My deep appreciation also goes to Gail Goldberg, editor extraordinaire, who doesn't ever let us take the easy way out. Her steadfast commitment to making a difference through what we say in these annuals has made each of them better. And, of course, we are blessed with readers who are hungry for valid astrology information that is based on hope rather than fear. We are here because of you.

Jeff: Thanks, Rick, for the consistently high quality of your astrology, your writing, and the great gift of your friendship. I have special thanks for Gail Goldberg who served this book and its readers with uncommon dedication and skill. Thanks, too, to my live-in inspirations: my wife, Danick, whose music fills our home with creativity, and my daughters, Laura and Lyana, whose joyous discoveries of life fill me with hope for the future.

INTRODUCTION

YOU ARE THE STAR OF YOUR LIFE

The more you learn about yourself, the better able you are to wisely use the energies in your life. For more than 3,000 years, astrology has been the sharpest tool in the box for describing the human condition. Used by virtually every culture on the planet, astrology continues to illuminate the link between individual lives and planetary energies and cycles.

The purpose of this book is to help you take a more active role in creating your present and, by extension, your future by showing you how to apply astrology's ancient wisdom to today's world. Our aim is to facilitate your day-to-day journey by revealing the turns in the road of life and describing the best ways for you to navigate them.

Astrology's highest use is to enable you to gain knowledge of yourself and perspective of your surroundings. It is common to go through life feeling blown about by forces beyond your control. Astrology can help you see the changing tides within and outside you. By allowing you to recognize the shifting patterns of mood and circumstance at work in your life, it helps you to stay centered and empowered. As you follow along in this book, you will grow to better understand your own needs as well as the challenges and opportunities you encounter.

In *Your Astrology Guide: 2009*, we describe the patterns of your life as they are reflected in the great cycles of the sky above. We do not simply predict events, although we give examples of them throughout the book. Rather, we are reporting the planetary energies—the cosmic weather in which you are living—so that you understand these conditions and know how to use them effectively. The power, though, is not in the stars, of course, but in your mind, your heart, and the choices that you make every day. Regardless of how strongly you are buffeted by the winds of change or bored by stagnation, your mind has many ways to see any situation. Learning about the energies of the Sun, Moon, and planets will both sharpen and widen your perspective. Thousands of years of human experience have proven astrology's value; our purpose is to show you how to enrich your life with it.

The language of astrology gives the gift of awareness, not a rigid set of rules. It works best when blended with common sense, intuition, and self-trust. This is your life, and no one knows how to live it as well as you. Take what you need from this book and leave the rest. Think of the planets as setting the stage for the year ahead, but it is you who are the writer, director, and star of your life.

ABOUT US

We were practicing astrology independently when we joined forces in 1999 to launch StarIQ.com. Our shared interest in making intelligent astrology available to as wide an audience as possible led to StarIQ, as well as a relationship with Tarot.com and the creation of this book. While we have continued to work independently as well, our collaboration has been a success and a joy as we've made our shared goals a reality, and we plan for it to continue long into the future.

RICK LEVINE

I've always wanted to know the answers to unanswerable questions. As a youth, I studied science and mathematics because I believed that they offered concrete answers to complex questions. I learned about the amazing conceptual breakthroughs made by modern man due to the developing technologies that allowed us to peer into the deep reaches of outer space and also into the tiniest subatomic realms. But as I encountered imaginary numbers in higher mathematics, along with the uncertainty of quantum physics, I began to realize that our modern sciences, as advanced as they are, would never satisfy my longing to understand my own individual life or the world around me. I learned that our basic assumptions of time and space fall apart at both ends of the spectrum—the very big and the very small. I became obsessed with solving the puzzle of the cosmos and discovering its hidden secrets.

As a college student at the State University of New York at Stony Brook in the late sixties, I studied psychology and philosophy, and participated in those times as a student of the universe. I read voraciously and found myself more interested in the unexplainable than in what was already known. As a psychology student, I was less concerned with running rats through mazes than with understanding how the human mind worked. I naturally gravitated to the depth psychologies of Sigmund

Freud and Carl Jung. Additionally, the life-altering information coming from the humanistic psychology movement presented me with an academic framework with which to better understand how human potential could be further developed. I knew then and there that human consciousness was expanding and that I wanted to be a part of this evolutionary process. In this environment, I first encountered the writings of R. Buckminster Fuller. He appealed to my scientific mind-set, but blessed me with new ways to view my world. In the early 20th century, Albert Einstein had clearly demonstrated that energy is simply the transformation of light into mass and mass into light—but that was just an intellectual concept to me.

Bucky Fuller, however, went on to establish a scientific language to describe the relationships between mass and light, particles and waves. His incredible geodesic domes are merely representations of what he discovered. I began to understand that what we can see is but a faint shadow of the knowable universe. I learned that everything vibrates. There are no things out there, just different frequencies of vibration—many of which are so fast that they give us the illusion of a solid world. Even something as basic as the color green or red is merely a label for certain frequencies of light vibration.

This was my world when I first discovered that astrology was more than just a parlor game. Already acquainted with the signs of the zodiac, I knew that I was an impulsive Aries, a pioneer, and an independent thinker. I noticed how my friends and professors fit their sun signs. Then, I was astounded to learn that Jung's *Analytical Psychology of Four Types* was based upon the astrological elements of fire, earth, air, and water. And I was amazed to discover that a great scientist, such as Johannes Kepler—the Father of Modern Astronomy—was himself a renowned astrologer. The more I read, the more I realized that I had to become an astrologer myself. I needed to know more about astrology and how it works. Now, nearly 40 years later, I know more about astrology—a lot more—with still so much to learn.

Astronomers have their telescopes, enabling them to see things *tele*, or far away. Biologists have microscopes to see what is *micro*, or small. We astrologers have the horoscope, extending our view of the *horo*, or hour. For more than three decades, I have calculated horoscopes—first by hand, later with computer—and have observed the movement of time in its relationship to the heavenly bodies. I have watched the timing of the transitions in my own life and in the lives of my family, friends, and clients. I have been privileged to see, again and again, the unquestionable harmony between the planetary cycles and our individual lives.

I am proud to be a part of an astrological renaissance. Astrology has become increasingly popular because it fulfills our need to know that we are a part of the cosmos, even though modern culture has separated us from nature. It is not man versus nature. We are nature—and our survival as a species may depend on humanity relearning this concept. I take my role as an astrologer very seriously as I use what I have learned to help people expand their awareness, offer them choices, and educate them on how to cooperate with the cosmos instead of fight against it. I contributed to reestablishing astrology in academia as a founding trustee of the Kepler College of Astrological Arts and Science (Lynnwood, Washington). I maintain an active role in the international community of astrologers as a member of the International Society for Astrological Research (ISAR), the National Council for Geocosmic Research (NCGR), the Association for Astrological Networking (AFAN), and the Organization for Professional Astrology (OPA).

In 1999, I partnered with Jeff Jawer to create StarIQ.com, an innovative astrology Web site. Since then Jeff and I have been working together to raise the quality of astrology available to the public, first through StarIQ.com and, later, through our partnership with Tarot.com. It continues to be a real privilege and thrill to work with Jeff and to now offer the fruits of our labors to you.

JEFF JAWER

I've been a professional astrologer for more than 30 years. Astrology is my career, my art, and my passion. The excitement that I felt when I first began is still with me today. My first encounter with real astrology was in 1973 when I was going through a painful marriage breakup. All I knew about astrology at the time was that I was a Taurus, which didn't sound very exciting to me. "The reliable Bull is steadfast and consistent," I read. "Not given to risk taking or dramatic self-expression, Taurus prefers peace and comfort above all." Boring. Fortunately, I quickly discovered that there was more to astrology—much more.

An amateur astrologer read my chart for me on my 27th birthday, and I was hooked. I bought the biggest astrology book I could find, began intensive study, found a teacher, and started reading charts for people. Within a few months, I changed my major at the University of Massachusetts at Amherst from communications to astrology under the Bachelor's Degree with Individual Concentration program. There were no astrology classes at the university, but I was able to combine courses in astronomy, mythology, and psychology, with two special seminars on the history of astrology, to graduate in 1975 with a B.A. in the history and science of astrology. In 1976, I moved to Atlanta, Georgia, the only city in the United States with a mandatory examination for professional astrologers. I passed it, as well as the American Federation of Astrologers' professional exam, and served twice as president of the Metro Atlanta Astrological Society and as chairman of the City of Atlanta Board of Astrology Examiners.

For several years, I was the corporate astrologer for International Horizons, Inc., a company that sold courses on English as a second language in Japan. The owner had me research the founding dates of banks he was interested in acquiring so that I could advise him based on their charts. Later, he and I created Astro, the world's first electronic astrology calculator. In 1982, I was one of the founding members of the Association for Astrological Networking (AFAN), an organization that plays a major role in defending the legal rights of astrologers. AFAN joined with two other organizations, the International Society for Astrological Research (ISAR) and the National Council for Geocosmic Research (NCGR), to present the first United Astrology Congress (UAC) in 1986. UAC conferences were the largest astrology events in North America for more than a decade. I served on the UAC board for four years.

I began teaching at astrology conferences in the late 1970s, and there I met many of the world's leading astrologers, many of whom are my friends to this day. I have taught at dozens of conferences and local astrology groups around the United States. I have lectured at the World Astrology Congress in Switzerland four times, as well as in Holland, France, England, Belgium, Spain, Germany, Canada, Brazil, and Australia. However, the most important time for me personally was the two years I spent teaching for the Network of Humanistic Astrologers based in France. There I met my wife, Danick, in 1988. Her double-Pisces sensitivity has added to my work and my life immeasurably.

Counseling individual clients is the core of my professional life, as it is for most astrologers, but writing about astrology has always been important to me. I've written hundreds of articles for journals, magazines, books, Web sites, and newspapers ranging from the monthly calendar for *The Mountain Astrologer* to sun-sign forecasts for *CosmoGIRL!* magazine. Currently, I write "LoveScopes" (a weekly sun-sign romance horoscope), the "New Moon Report," and other specialized material for Tarot.com, AOL, and StarIQ.com. I've also been employed in the astrology industry as director of public relations for Matrix Software and vice president of Astro Communication Services, two of the field's oldest companies. Rick and I founded StarIQ in 1999, the beginning of our professional collaboration. We produce a daily audio forecast called *Planet Pulse*, and *StarTalkers*, a weekly radio broadcast. Early in my career, I contributed to pioneering the field of experiential astrology, also called astrodrama. It's been a great adventure to combine theater games, psychodrama, Gestalt techniques, visualization, movement, art, and sound to bring astrology to life in workshops around the world. To experience astrology through emotions and in the body, rather than by the intellect alone, can ground one's understanding of the planets and signs in a very useful way.

Think about Venus, for example. She's the goddess of love, the planet of beauty and attraction. What if you need more sweetness in your life? Imagine how Venus walks. Now, get up and do your own Venus walk to the kitchen. Feel in balance and graceful as your feet embrace the floor and as your hips sway. Be Venus; invite her presence to you. Glide, slide, and be suave; you're so beautiful. Remember this walk if you're feeling unloved and, the next thing you know, Venus will arrive. Each planet is different, of course, according to its unique character. You'll learn another dance from responsible Saturn—a slower march across the floor, head upright, shoulders back—steady and straight, but not too stiff. Try that one for self-discipline.

Astrology describes the energy of time, how the quality of Tuesday afternoon is different from Wednesday morning. Seeing when and where patterns arise in your life gives you clearer vision and a better understanding of the choices that are open to you. The rich language of astrology makes a cosmic connection that empowers you and rewards the rest of us as you fulfill more and more of your potential.

ASTROLOGY'S ORIGINS

Astrology is as old as time. It began when events in the sky were first observed to affect events here on Earth. The turning of day into night, the rising and falling of the tides with the Moon's cycles, and the changing seasons were watched by humanity long before written history, even at the very dawn of human civilization. Ancient Egyptians tracked the star Sirius to predict the flooding of the Nile River, which was essential to their agriculture. Babylonians, Mayans, Hindus, Chinese, and virtually every other group of people on the planet have practiced a form of astrology. Part science, part religion, calendar, mythology, and almanac, astrology remains the most comprehensive and coherent system for understanding life on this planet.

In the 2nd century AD, Claudius Ptolemy codified astrology, based on its origins in Mesopotamia and development in classical Greece. Astrology was an essential part of the scientific and philosophical evolution that gave birth to Western civilization. Another major path of development occurred in India, where Vedic astrology remains an integral part of the culture. Astrology was originally used to address collective concerns such as climate and warfare. It was rarely applied to the lives of individuals, except for rulers whose fates were considered tied to those of the nation. Astrology is still applied to public concerns, especially in the burgeoning field of financial astrology, which is used for stock market forecasting. Today, however, the vast majority of astrology is applied to the lives of individuals through personal consultations, computer-generated reports, horoscope columns, books, and the Internet.

The importance of astrology has risen, fallen, and risen again in the Western world. Through the Renaissance and the Elizabethan period, astrology was part and parcel of daily life. Shakespeare's numerous references to it are just one indicator of its wide acceptance and popularity in his time. However, the rationalism of René Descartes and his followers took hold in philosophical circles and demanded that modern science exclude anything that cannot be proven according to its methods. Astrology was banished from academia in 1666, and it remained outside the intellectual mainstream for almost 300 years. Modern astrology began its rebirth in the early part of the 20th century largely due to the work of Alan Leo, the father of sun-sign astrology. A second, and larger, wave of interest grew out of the counterculture movement of the 1960s when interest in metaphysics and Eastern religions also gained momentum. The brilliant works of the Swiss psychologist Carl Jung and French-American astrologer Dane Rudhyar inspired a new generation of astrologers, including the authors of this book.

ASTROLOGY TODAY: EMPOWERMENT

Thanks to Jung, Rudhyar, and many other brilliant minds, modern astrology has largely separated itself from the fatalism of the past when, for example, the sighting of an approaching comet meant the king would die and nothing more. Today's astrology is, as Rudhyar wrote, "person-centered," with the focus on individual choice and personal growth rather than the simple prediction of events. In fact, while we do write about events in this book, we spend more time describing energy patterns and emotions for several reasons.

First, you're a unique individual. You may share characteristics and tendencies with fellow members of your sun sign, but you will experience them in your own way. In addition, you have a personal birth chart in which the positions of the Moon, planets, and other factors distinguish you from the other members of your sun-sign clan. Analyzing how all the planets and signs interact in a person's chart is the foundation of a personal consultation with a professional astrologer or a detailed custom report like those available at http://www.tarot.com/astrology/astroprofile.

ENERGY, EVENTS, AND EMOTION

At its essence, astrology describes energy. Energy can take many forms; it can be an event, emotion, or attitude. We suggest the possible outcomes of astrological events in this book, but they are examples or models of how the planetary energies might be expressed. Each person is going to experience these patterns in his or her own unique way. We have learned that it is more helpful to understand the underlying energy patterns of events than it is to describe them. You may not be able to change the world outside you, but you have an enormous range of choice when it comes to your thoughts and attitudes.

We are here to assist you with ideas and information rooted in history and woven into the cloth of our culture. We recognize and honor you as the center of your life. This book is not a collection of ideas that are foreign to your nature, but a recollection of human experiences that exist within all of us. Whether you know their meanings or not, all the signs and planets live within you. They are part of your human heritage, a gift of awareness, a language not meant to label you and stick you in a box, but a treasure map to yourself and the cosmos beyond. It is a glorious journey we all share. May your way be filled with light this year and in the years to come.

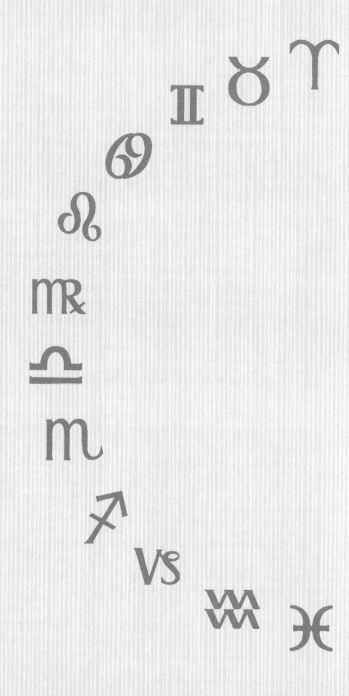

PART 1
2009
ASTROLOGY
& YOU

HOW TO USE THIS BOOK

ASTROLOGY BASICS

WHAT'S YOUR SIGN?

In this book, we present a view of the year ahead for each sun sign. Your sign is based on the Sun's position at the moment of your birth. As most people know, the Sun travels through the twelve signs of the zodiac over the course of a year. However, the Sun doesn't change signs at the exact moment on the same date every year. If you were born within two days of the cusp (the end or beginning) of a sign, a more exact calculation may be required to determine your sun sign. So, if you are uncertain about your sign, consult an astrologer or get a free copy of your birth chart from http://www.tarot.com/astrology/astroprofile to determine the correct one. In addition to giving you the exact position of the Sun at the moment of your birth, an individual birth or natal chart includes the positions of the Moon and planets as well, which provides a much more detailed astrological view of your life. This information is used in private consultations and computer-generated astrology reports. The sun sign does not tell your entire astrological story. But it is powerful enough to light up your consciousness with ideas that can change your life.

For those of you who have your astrology chart, in addition to reading the chapter in this book on your sun sign, you will also want to read about your moon and rising signs as well. Your intuition will guide you as you integrate the information.

TRANSITS

The information presented in this book is based on the relationship of the planets, including the Sun and the Moon, to the twelve signs of the zodiac in 2008. The movement of the planets in their cycles and their geometric relationship to one another as they interact are called **transits**; they are the primary forecasting tool for astrologers.

As planets enter into specific relationships with one another, astrologers consider the astrological events that occur. For example, when the Sun and the Moon align in a certain way, an event called an **eclipse** occurs. As you read this book, many of you will study more than one sign, whether you are checking up on someone you know or on your own moon or rising sign. You will notice that certain dates are often mentioned repeatedly from sign to sign. This is because major planetary events affect everyone, but some more than others, and in different ways.

For example, in 2008, there is a New Moon Eclipse in Pisces on March 18. Everyone will feel the power of the eclipse, but their reactions will differ. It will be felt most immediately by Pisces and its opposite sign, Virgo. Since this particular eclipse is stressed by Pluto, it will also be challenging for Scorpios, the sign ruled by this planet. The cosmic weather rains on all of us; the water can be parted in twelve ways, each a door to a sign, a Self, another aspect of being human.

RULING OR KEY PLANETS

Every sign is associated with a key or ruling planet. There is an affinity between signs and their planetary rulers—a common purpose that connects them, like lungs with breathing or feet with walking. In astrology's early days, the Sun (Leo) and the Moon (Cancer) ruled one sign each, and the rest of the known planets—Mercury, Venus, Mars, Jupiter, and Saturn—ruled two. However, in the modern era, new planets have been discovered and astrology has evolved to reflect this. The discovery of Uranus in the late eighteenth century coincided with revolutions in the United States and France, triggered a technological revolution that's still going on today, and transformed astrology's traditional rulership system. Radical Uranus was assigned to rule inventive Aquarius, while its old ruler, Saturn, took a step back. Neptune, discovered with photography sixty-five years later, became the ruler of Pisces, nudging Jupiter into the background. And if Pluto hasn't purged Mars from Scorpio, it's certainly taken the dominant role in expressing this sign's energy.

We mention ruling planets quite a bit in the book as we track the cycles of a given sign. The sign Aries, named for the Greek god of war, is ruled by Mars, the Roman name for the same god. Transits of Mars, then, play a leading role in the forecasts for Aries. Venus is used in the same way in the forecasts for Taurus. For double-ruled Scorpio, Aquarius, and Pisces, we take the traditional and modern planetary rulers into account. The planets and the signs they rule are further discussed later in this section.

ELEMENTS

The four astrological elements are fire, earth, air, and water. The action-oriented fire signs—Aries, Leo, and Sagittarius—are warm and dynamic. The sense-oriented earth signs—Taurus, Virgo, and Capricorn—are practical and realistic. The thought-oriented air signs—Gemini, Libra, and Aquarius—are logical and sociable. The emotion-oriented water signs—Cancer, Scorpio, and Pisces—are intuitive and instinctual. Signs of the same element work harmoniously together. In addition, fire and air signs work well together, as do earth and water.

INGRESSES

An **ingress** is the entry of a planet into a new sign. The activities and concerns of the planet will be colored by that sign's energy. For example, when the communication planet Mercury enters Leo, the expressive qualities of that sign tend to make for more dramatic speech than in the previous sign, self-protective Cancer. When Mercury leaves Leo for detail-oriented Virgo, thoughts and words become more precise. Each planet has its own unique rhythm and cycle in terms of how long it takes that planet to move through all the signs. This determines how long it stays in one sign. The Moon, for example, flies through a sign in two and a half days, while Uranus takes seven years.

HOUSES

Your natal chart is divided into twelve astrological houses that correspond to different areas of your life. This book uses solar houses that place your sun sign in the 1st House. In this system, when a planet enters a new sign, it also enters a new house. Thus, the effect of a planet's ingress into a particular sign depends also on which house of the sign in question it's entering. For example, for a Gemini sun sign, Gemini is its own 1st House, followed by Cancer for the 2nd, Leo for the 3rd House, and so on. If you are a Taurus, your 4th House is Leo. As a Scorpio, your 8th House is Gemini. If this is confusing, don't worry about counting houses; we do it for you. The influence of an astrological event differs considerably based on which house of a sign it falls in.

You'll notice that there are many different, but related, terms used to describe each house, sign, and planet. For example, Mars is called feisty, assertive, impatient, or aggressive at different times throughout the book. Also, we use different house names depending on the emphasis we perceive. You'll find the 4th House described as the 4th House of Home and Family, the 4th House of Security, and the 4th House of Roots—all are valid. We change the descriptions to broaden your understanding, rather than repeat the same limited interpretation over and over. Later in this section is a brief description of all the houses.

ASPECTS

Aspects are geometrically significant angles between planets and a key feature of any astrological forecast. A fast-moving body like the Moon will form every possible aspect to every degree of the zodiac during its monthly orbit around the Earth. The Sun will do the same in a year, Mars in two years, Jupiter in twelve. The slower a planet moves, the less common its aspects, which makes them more significant because their effect is longer. A lunar aspect lasts only a few hours, and one from Mercury a day or two, but a transit like the Jupiter-Neptune square that occurs three times this year can last for a week or two or more.

The qualities of the two planets involved in an aspect are important to its meaning, but so is the angle between them. Soft aspects like **sextiles** and **trines** grease the cosmic wheels, while hard ones like **squares** and **oppositions** often reflect bumps in the road. **Conjunctions**, when two planets are conjoined, are arguably the most powerful aspect and can be easy or difficult according to the nature of the planets involved. To learn more about the nature of the aspects, turn to the next chapter.

The effect of an aspect on each sun sign is modified according to the houses of that sign where the planets fall. A Venus-Mars trine from Cancer to Scorpio is the harmonious expression of Venus's desire for security with Mars's instinct to protect. They are both in water signs, thus compatible. And if you are a Pisces, Venus in Cancer is in your 5th House and Mars in Scorpio is in your 9th, stirring romance and adventure. Alternatively, if you are a Gemini, Venus in Cancer is in your 2nd House and Mars in Scorpio is in the 6th. Applying the cozy relationship of a trine to Gemini's chart gives the interpretation that there will be a comfortable flow in the practical realms of money and work.

RETROGRADES

All true planets (i.e., excluding the Sun and Moon) turn **retrograde** from time to time. This means that the planet appears to go backward in the zodiac, revisiting recently traveled territory. As with other planetary phenomena, astrologers have observed specific effects from retrogrades. The days when planets turn from direct, or forward, motion to retrograde and back again are called **stations** (because the planet appears to be stationary). These are significant periods that emphasize the energy of the stationing planet.

A retrograde station, when backward motion begins, indicates the beginning of a relatively introspective cycle for that planet's energy. At a direct station, the energy that has been turned inward during the retrograde period begins to express itself more overtly in the outer world once again. Retrogrades can cause certain aspects to occur three times—first forward, then retrograde, then forward again. These triple events can be like a play that unfolds in three acts. The first aspect often raises an issue that's reconsidered or adjusted during the second transit and completed during the third.

LUNATIONS AND ECLIPSES

New Moons, Full Moons, and eclipses are important astrological events. These aspects involving the Moon are called **lunations**. Every month the Sun and Moon join together at the New Moon, seeding a fresh lunar cycle that affects us each in a personal way. The New Moon in the partnership sign of Libra sparks relationships, while the New Moon in the resource sign of Taurus brings attention to money. Two weeks later, the Moon opposes the Sun at the Full Moon. This is often an intense time due to the pull of the Moon in one direction and the Sun in another.

The Full Moon in Cancer, for example, pits the need (Moon) for inner security (Cancer) against the Sun in Capricorn's urge for worldly recognition. The Full Moon can be stressful, but it is also a time of illumination that can give rise to greater consciousness. At the Full Moon, instead of seeing yourself pulled apart by opposing forces, it helps to imagine that you're the meeting point where the opposition is resolved by a breakthrough in awareness.

Planets that form significant aspects with the New or Full Moon play a key role in shaping their character. A New Moon square Jupiter is challenged by a tendency to be overexpansive, a negative quality of that planet. A Full Moon conjunct Saturn is bound in seriousness, duty, or doubt symbolized by this planet of necessity.

Eclipses are a special class of New and Full Moons where the Sun and Moon are so close to their line of intersection with the Earth that the light of one of them is darkened. The shadow of the Moon on the Sun at a Solar Eclipse (New Moon) or of the Earth on the Moon at a Lunar Eclipse (Full Moon) makes them memorable. They work, in effect, like super New or Full Moons, extending the normal two- to four-week period of these lunations to an influence up to six months before or after the eclipse. An eclipse will affect each person differently, depending on where it falls in a chart. But they can be unsettling because they usually mark the ends of chapters in one's life.

HOW THIS BOOK IS ORGANIZED

In this book, we take a look at what 2009 holds in store for each of the twelve signs. We evaluate each sign according to the transits to it, its ruler, and its solar houses. The chapter on each sign begins with an overview of the year for the sign. Here we suggest some of the key themes that the sign will encounter in 2008 in general as well as in specific areas of life: love, career, money, health, home, travel, and spirituality. Each of these areas is identified with an icon, as shown at the top of the next page, for easy reference.

The overview is followed by a month-by-month analysis of all of the most important astrological events for that sign. This will enable you to look at where you are as well as what may be coming up for you, so that you can best make choices about how you'd like to deal with the planetary energies at work.

KEY TO ICONS IN OVERVIEW SECTIONS FOR EACH SIGN

LOVE AND RELATIONSHIPS

CAREER AND PUBLIC LIFE

MONEY AND FINANCES

HEALTH AND VITALITY

HOME AND FAMILY

TRAVEL AND HIGHER EDUCATION

SPIRITUALITY AND PERSONAL GROWTH

TIMING, KEY DATES, AND SUPER NOVA DAYS

The monthly forecast for each sign includes a description of several Key Dates that month. (Eastern time is used throughout the book.) We provide some likely scenarios of what may happen or how someone born under the sign might experience the planetary effects at the time of the Key Dates. It is wise to pay closer attention to your own thoughts, feelings, and actions during these times. Certain Key Dates are called Super Nova Days because they are the most intense energetic periods, positive or negative, of the month.

Note that the exact timing of events, and your awareness of their effects, can vary from person to person, sometimes coming a day or two earlier or arriving a day or two later than the Key Dates given.

The period of influence of a transit from the Sun, Mercury, or Venus is a day before and a day after the exact aspect. A transit of Mars is in effect for about two days coming and going; Jupiter and Saturn lasts for a week or more; and Uranus, Neptune, and Pluto can be two weeks.

Although the Key Dates are the days when a particular alignment is exact, some people are so ready for an event that they'll act on a transit a day or two before. And some of us are so entrenched in the status quo or unwilling to change that it may take a day or two for the effect to manifest. Give yourself an extra day around each Key Date to utilize the energy, maximize the potential, and feel the impact of the event. If you find astrological events consistently unfold in your life earlier or later than predicted, adjust the dates accordingly.

Our goal is to help you understand what is operating within you, below the surface, rather than simply to tell you what's going to happen. This is where you have control so that, to a large degree, what happens is up to you. We describe which buttons are being pushed so that you can see your own patterns and have greater power to change them if you want. Every astrological event has a potential for gain or loss. Fat, juicy, easy ones can make us lazy, while tough ones can temper the will and make us stronger. It usually takes time and hindsight to measure the true value of an experience.

THE PLANETS, THE HOUSES, AND ASPECTS

THE PLANETS

The planets are the basic building blocks of astrology. As our ancestors observed the cycles of these wandering stars, they attributed characteristics to them. Each of these richly symbolic archetypes represents a particular spectrum of meaning. Their intimate relationship to the Greek and Roman myths helps us tell stories about them that are still relevant to our lives today. No matter what your sun sign is, every planet impacts your life according to its symbolism and its placement.

THE SUN

Rules Leo
Keywords: *Consciousness, Will, Vitality*

The Sun is our home star, the glowing filament in the center of our local system, and is associated with the sign Leo. Our ancestors equated it with God, for it is the source of energy and is what animates us. In fact, we base our entire calendar system on the Earth's relationship to the Sun. It represents the core of individual identity and consciousness. The masculine Sun has dignity, courage, and willpower. We feel the Sun's role as our main purpose in life; it fuels our furnace to fulfill our mission. We recognize its brightness in anyone who has a "sunny" personality. It is charismatic, creative, and generous of heart. But it can also be proud, have too much pride, and turn arrogant or self-centered. When the Sun is shining, we can see the world around us; it gives us a world of "things" that we can name and describe. It could be said that the Sun symbolizes objective reality.

THE MOON

Rules Cancer
Keywords: *Subconscious, Emotions, Habits*

We've all seen how the Moon goes through its phases, reflecting the light of the Sun, and have felt the power of the Full Moon. Lunations are important astrological markers. The Moon changes signs every two and a half days and reflects the mood of the public in general. Although our year calendar is based upon the Sun, each month (comes from "moon"—*moonth*) closely approximates the cycle of the Moon. The Moon is closer to Earth than anything else in the heavens. Astrologically, it represents how we reflect the world around us through our feelings. The Moon symbolizes emotions, instincts, habits, and routine. It describes how we nurture others and need to be cared for ourselves. The feminine power of the Moon is also connected with the fertility cycle of women. Because it is the source of security and familial intimacy, our Moon sign is where we feel at home. The Moon is associated with the sign Cancer and with concerns about our home and family.

 MERCURY

Rules Gemini and Virgo
Keywords: *Communication, Thoughts, Transportation*

Mercury, the Heavenly Messenger, races around the Sun four times each year. Its nearly ninety-day cycle corresponds with the seasons of the calendar. Mercury, our intellectual antenna, is the planet of perception, communication, rational thought, mobility, and commerce. It is the mental traveler, able to move effortlessly through the realms of thought and imagination. Mercury organizes language, allows us to grasp ideas, enables us to analyze and integrate data, and assists us in all forms of communication. Cars, bicycles, telephones, delivery services, paperwork, and the mind itself are all manifestations of quicksilver Mercury, the fastest of the true planets. However, Mercury also has a trickster side and can cleverly con us into believing something that just isn't true. Mercury is associated with curious Gemini in its information-gathering mode, and with discerning Virgo when it is analytically sorting through the data.

VENUS

Rules Taurus and Libra
Keywords: *Desire, Love, Money, Values*

Venus is the goddess of love, our relationship antenna, associated with the spectrum of how we experience what is beautiful and pleasurable to us. With Venus, we attach desire to our perceptions. On one end, Venus can indicate romantic and sensual love. On the other end, Venus is about money and all things of value—financial and emotional. This manifests as our attraction to art, music, and even good food. Every beautiful flower and every act of love contains the essence of sweet Venus. We look to Venus to describe what we like—an important key to understanding partnerships, particularly personal ones. To a certain extent, our chemistry with other people is affected by Venus. Although Venus is traditionally associated with femininity, both women and men are impacted by its rhythms. A morning star, Venus rules Taurus and is associated with the simple and sensual side of physical reality. As an evening star, it rules Libra, where it represents the more intellectual side of love and harmony.

MARS

Rules Aries, co-rules Scorpio
Keywords: *Action, Physical Energy, Drive*

Mars, the god of war, is the planet of action, physical energy, initiative, and aggression. It is the first planet beyond Earth's orbit, and its role is to take what we have and extend it to the outer world. Mars represents the masculine force of individuality that helps define the ego and our sense of unique identity. It represents how we move forward in life and propels us toward new experiences and into the future. Mars drives us to assert ourselves in healthy ways, but the angry red planet can also be impatient and insensitive, engendering violence and destruction. When insecure, it turns offensive and can attack others. Mars can also express erotic passion, the male counterpart of the female Venus; together they are the cosmic lovers. As the pioneering risk taker, Mars rules fiery Aries. As a volcanic force of power, it is the traditional ruler of Scorpio.

JUPITER

Rules Sagittarius, co-rules Pisces

Keywords: *Expansion, Growth, Optimism*

Jupiter is the largest of the true planets. It represents expansion, growth, and optimism. It was called the Greater Benefic by ancient astrologers due to its association with good fortune. Today, modern astrologers understand that too much of a good thing is not necessarily beneficial. Jupiter rules the excesses of life; undoubtedly, it's the planet of bigger, better, and more. Wherever there's too much, you're apt to find Jupiter. Often called the lucky planet, Jupiter symbolizes where opportunity knocks. Yet it is still up to us to open the door and walk through. Jupiterian people are jovial, but this gassy giant is also associated with humor, philosophy, enthusiasm, and enterprise. In its adventurous mode, Jupiter rules globetrotting Sagittarius, but as the planet of religion and belief systems, it has a traditional connection to Pisces.

♄ SATURN

Rules Capricorn, co-rules Aquarius

Keywords: *Contraction, Maturity, Responsibility*

Saturn is the outermost planet visible to the naked eye, and as such represented the end of the road for our sky-watching ancestors. In premodern times, Saturn was the limit of our human awareness; beyond it were only the fixed stars. Now, even with our telescopic capability to peer farther into the vastness of space and time, Saturn still symbolizes the limits of perception. It is about structure, order, necessity, commitment, and hard-earned accomplishments. It's the stabilizing voice of reality and governs rules, regulations, discipline, and patience. Saturn is Father Time, and represents the ultimate judgment that you get what you deserve. But Saturn isn't only stern or rigid; it is also the teacher and the wise old sage. When we embrace Saturn's discipline, we mature and learn from our experiences. As the serious taskmaster, Saturn is the ruler of ambitious Capricorn. As the co-ruler of Aquarius, Saturn reminds us that rigid rules may need to be broken in order to express our individuality.

CHIRON

(Does not rule a sign)

Keywords: *Healing, Pain, Subversion*

Chiron is the mythological Wounded Healer, and although not a true planet in the traditional sense, it has become a useful tool for modern astrologers. Chiron is a relative newcomer to the planetary lineup and was discovered in 1977 between the orbits of Saturn and Uranus. It describes where we can turn our wounds into wisdom to assist others. It is associated with the story of the wounded Fisher King, who, in medieval tales about the Holy Grail, fished (for souls) in order to salve his incurable suffering. Chiron not only symbolizes where and how we hurt, but also how our words and actions can soothe the pain of others. It doesn't, however, always play by the rules and can work against the status quo. Its rhythms can stir up old memories of emotional discomfort that can lead to increased understanding, vulnerability, and the transformation of heartache and grief into the gifts of love and forgiveness.

 URANUS

Rules Aquarius

Keywords: *Awakening, Unpredictable, Inventive*

Uranus is the first planet discovered with technology (the telescope). Its discovery broke through the limitations imposed by our five senses. It symbolizes innovation, originality, revolution, and delighting in unexpected surprises. Uranus operates suddenly, often to release tensions, no matter how hidden. Its action is like lightning—instantaneous and exciting, upsetting and exhilarating. Uranus provokes and instigates change; its restless and rebellious energy hungers for freedom. Its high frequency and electrical nature stimulate the nervous system. This highly original planet abhors the status quo and is known to turn normal things upside down and inside out. As the patron planet of the strange and unusual, it is the ruler of eccentric Aquarius.

NEPTUNE

Rules Pisces

Keywords: *Imagination, Intuition, Spirituality*

Neptune is god of the seas, from which all life arises and is eventually returned. Imaginative Neptune lures us into the foggy mists where reality becomes so hazy that we can lose our way. It is the planet of dreams, illusions, and spirituality. It dissolves boundaries and barriers, leading us into higher awareness, compassion, confusion, or escapism. Grasping the meaning of Neptune is like trying to hold water in our hands. No matter how hard we try, it slips through our fingers—for Neptune is ultimately elusive and unknowable. It rules all things related to fantasy and delusion. A highly spiritual energy, the magic of Neptune encourages artistic vision, intuitive insight, compassion, and the tendency to idealize. Neptune governs the mystic's urge to merge with the divine and is associated with the spiritual sign Pisces.

PLUTO

Rules Scorpio

Keywords: *Passion, Intensity, Regeneration*

Pluto, lord of the underworld, is the planet of death, rebirth, and transformation. As the most distant of the planets, Pluto moves us inexorably toward a deeper understanding of life's cycles. Under Pluto's influence, it often seems as though the apparently solid ground has disintegrated, forcing us to morph in ways we cannot intellectually understand. Pluto is the mythological phoenix, a magical bird that rises from the ashes of its own destruction by fire. It contains the shadow parts of ourselves that we would prefer to keep hidden, but healing and empowerment come from facing the unfathomable darkness and turning it into light. Manipulation and control are often issues with Pluto. A healthy relationship with Pluto adds psychological understanding and clarity about our motivations. As the ruler of magnetic Scorpio, it is associated with power and emotional intensity.

NODES OF THE MOON

(Do not rule a sign)
Keywords: *Karma, Soul, Past Lives*

The Nodes of the Moon are opposing points where the Moon's orbit around the Earth intersects the Earth's orbit around the Sun. Although not real planets, these powerful points have an astrological influence in that they describe the ways we connect with others. They are useful in understanding the challenges and opportunities we face in our soul's journey through its lifetime here on Earth. For many astrologers, the Lunar Nodes are symbolic of past lives and future existences. The South Node, at one end of the nodal axis, represents the past—the unconscious patterns of our ancestral heritage or those brought into this life from previous incarnations. These are often talents that can easily be overused and become a no-growth path of least resistance. At the other end, the North Node represents the future—a new direction for growth, development, and integration.

THE HOUSES

Every astrology chart is divided into twelve houses, each ruling different areas of life and colored by a different sign. Just as planets move through the zodiac signs, they also move through the houses in an individual chart. The twelve houses have a correspondence to the twelve signs, but in an individualized chart, the signs in each house will vary based on the sign on the cusp of the 1st House, called a rising sign or ascendant. The rising sign is determined by the exact time of your birth. We use solar houses, which place the sun sign as your 1st House, or rising sign.

1ST HOUSE

Corresponding Sign: Aries
Keywords: *Self, Appearance, Personality*

A primary point of self-identification: When planets move through this sector, the emphasis is on your individuality and surface appearances. It is often associated with how we interact with others when we first meet them. Planets here tend to take on great importance and become more integrated into your personality.

2ND HOUSE

Corresponding Sign: Taurus
Keywords: *Possessions, Values, Self-Worth*
Associated with values, resources, income, and self-esteem: When planets move through the 2nd House, they can modify your attitudes about money and earning. This is a concrete and practical area of the chart, and although it is linked to possessions, the 2nd House typically does not include things you cannot easily move, such as real estate or what you share with someone else.

3RD HOUSE

Corresponding Sign: Gemini
Keywords: *Communication, Siblings, Short Trips*
Relates to how you gather information from your immediate environment: It's associated with the day-to-day comings and goings of your life. **Siblings** can be found here, for this is where we first learn to build intimacy when we're young. Planets moving through this house can affect the pace and quality of your day and how you communicate with those around you.

4TH HOUSE

Corresponding Sign: Cancer
Keywords: *Home, Family, Roots*
Associated with the earliest imprints of childhood, your family roots, and how you're connected to your own feelings: This is your emotional foundation and describes what you need to feel at home. This is where you are nurtured, so when planets travel through this sector, they stir up issues of security and safety. As the deepest place in your chart, it is sometimes only you who knows about it.

5TH HOUSE

Corresponding Sign: Leo
Keywords: *Love, Romance, Children, Play*
Associated with fun, but also represents self-expression, creativity, love affairs, and children: The 5th House is about the discovery of self through play, and includes sports, games, and gambling. When planets move through your 5th House, they can excite you to take risks and connect with the innocence of your inner child.

6TH HOUSE

Corresponding Sign: Virgo
Keywords: *Work, Health, Daily Routines*
Related to service and working conditions: Like the 3rd House, it describes your daily life, but the consistency of it rather than the noisy distractions—it's where you strive for efficiency and effectiveness. Planets here modify your habits, diet, and exercise. Although considered the house of health and hygiene, transits here don't always indicate illness; they can also increase our concern for healthier lifestyles.

7TH HOUSE

Corresponding Sign: Libra
Keywords: *Marriage, Relationships, Business Partners*
Encompasses one-to-one relationships: Its cusp is called the descendant and is the western end of the horizon. It's where and how we meet other people, both personally and professionally. In a larger sense, this is how you project who you are onto others. Planets moving through here can stimulate intimate relationships, but can also increase the intensity of all of your interactions with the outside world.

8TH HOUSE

Corresponding Sign: Scorpio
Keywords: *Intimacy, Transformation, Shared Resources*
A mysterious and powerful place, associated with shared experiences, including the most intimate: Traditionally the house of sex, death, and taxes, it's the place where you gain the deepest levels of relationships, personally and professionally. When planets move through your 8th House, perspectives can intensify, intimacy issues are stimulated, and compelling transformations are undertaken.

9TH HOUSE

Corresponding Sign: Sagittarius
Keywords: *Travel, Higher Education, Philosophy*
Associated with philosophy, religion, higher education of all kinds, and long-distance travel: It's where you seek knowledge and truth—both within and without. Planets moving through this house open portals to inner journeys and outer adventures, stretching your mind in ways that expand your perspectives about the world.

10TH HOUSE

Corresponding Sign: Capricorn
Keywords: *Career, Community, Ambition*
The most elevated sector of your chart; its cusp is called the midheaven: This is the career house, opposite to the home-based 4th House. When planets move through your 10th House, they activate your ambition, drive you to achieve professional excellence, and push you up the ladder of success. This is where your public reputation is important and hard work is acknowledged.

11TH HOUSE

Corresponding Sign: Aquarius
Keywords: *Friends, Groups, Associations, Social Ideals*
Traditionally called the house of friends, hopes, and wishes: It's where you go to be with like-minded people. The 11th House draws you out of your individual career aspirations and into the ideals of humanity. Planets traveling here can activate dreams of the future, so spending time with friends is a natural theme.

12TH HOUSE

Corresponding Sign: Pisces
Keywords: *Imagination, Spirituality, Secret Activities*
Complex, representing the ending of one cycle and the beginning of the next: It is connected with mysteries and places outside ordinary reality. When planets move through this house, they stimulate your deepest subconscious feelings and activate fantasies. It's a private space that can seem like a prison or a sanctuary.

ASPECTS

As the planets move through the sky in their various cycles, they form ever-changing angles with one another. Certain angles create significant geometric shapes. For example, when two planets are 90 degrees apart, they conform to a square. A sextile, or 60 degrees of separation, conforms to a six-pointed star. Planets create aspects to one another when they are at these special angles. All aspects are divisions of the 360-degree circle. Aspects explain how the individual symbolism of a pair of planets combines into an energetic pattern.

CONJUNCTION

0 degrees ★ **Keywords:** *Compression, Blending, Focus*
A conjunction is a blending of the separate planetary energies involved. When two planets conjoin, your job is to integrate the different influences—which in some cases is easier than others. For example, a conjunction of the Moon and Venus is likely to be a smooth blending of energy because of the similarity of the planets. But a conjunction between the Moon and Uranus is likely to be challenging because the Moon needs security, while Uranus prefers risk.

SEMISQUARE AND SESQUISQUARE

45 and 135 degrees ★ **Keywords:** *Annoyance, Mild Resistance*
Semisquares and sesquisquares are minor aspects that act like milder squares. They're one-eighth and three-eighths of a circle, respectively. Like the other hard aspects (conjunctions, oppositions, and squares) they can create dynamic situations that require immediate attention and resolution. Although they are not usually as severe as the other hard aspects, they remind us that healthy stress is important for the process of growth.

SEXTILE

60 degrees ★ **Keywords:** *Supportive, Intelligent, Activating*
Sextiles are supportive and intelligent, combining complementary signs—fire and air, earth and water. There's an even energetic distribution between the planets involved. Sextiles often indicate opportunities based on our willingness to take action in smart ways. Like trines, sextiles are considered easy: The good fortune they offer can pass unless you consciously take an active interest in making something positive happen.

QUINTILE

72 and 144 degrees ★ **Keywords:** *Creativity, Metaphysics, Magic*
Quintiles are powerful nontraditional aspects based on dividing the zodiac circle into five, resulting in a five-pointed star. Related to ancient goddess-based religious traditions, quintiles activate the imagination, intuition, and latent artistic talents. They're clever, intelligent, and even brilliant as they stimulate humor to relieve repressed tensions.

SQUARE

90 degrees ★ **Keywords:** *Resistance, Stress, Dynamic Conflict*
A square is an aspect of resistance, signifying energies at odds. Traditionally, they were considered negative, but their dynamic instability demands attention, so they're often catalysts for change. When differences in two planetary perspectives are integrated, squares can build enduring structures. Harnessing a square's power by managing contradictions creates opportunities for personal growth.

TRINE

120 degrees ★ **Keywords:** *Harmony, Free-Flowing, Ease*
A trine is the most harmonious of aspects because it connects signs of the same element. In the past, trines were considered positive, but modern astrologers realize they are so easy that they can create a rut that is difficult to break out of. When two planets are one-third of a circle apart, they won't necessarily stimulate change, but they can often help build on the status quo. With trines, you must stay alert, for complacency can weaken your chances for success.

QUINCUNX

150 degrees ★ **Keywords:** *Irritation, Adjustment*
A quincunx is almost like a nonaspect, for the two planets involved have a difficult time staying aware of each other. As such, this aspect often acts as an irritant, requiring that you make constant adjustments without actually resolving the under-lying problem. This is a challenging aspect because it can be more annoying than a full-fledged crisis. Quincunxes are a bit like oil and water—the planets are not in direct conflict, but they have difficulty mixing with each another.

OPPOSITION

180 degrees ★ **Keywords:** *Tension, Awareness, Balance*
When two planets are in opposition, they are like two forces pulling at either end of a rope. The tension is irresolvable, unless you are willing to hold both divergent perspectives without suppressing one or the other. More often than not, we favor one side of the opposition over the other and, in doing so, project the unexpressed side onto others or situations. For this reason, oppositions usually manifest as relationship issues.

ASTROLOGY
WORLD REPORT 2009

Astrology works for individuals, groups, and even humanity as a whole. You will have your own story in 2009, but it unfolds among nearly seven billion other tales of human experience. We are each unique, yet our lives touch one another; our destinies are woven together by weather and war, by economy, science, music, politics, religion, and all the other threads of life on this planet. We make personal choices every day, yet there are great events beyond the control of anyone. When a town is flooded, it affects everyone, yet particular astrology patterns will describe the specific response of each person. Our existence is both an individual and collective experience.

We are living at a time when the tools of self-awareness fill bookshelves, Web sites, and broadcasts, and we benefit greatly from them. Yet despite all this wisdom, conflicts among groups cause enormous suffering every day. Understanding personal issues is a powerful means for increasing happiness, but knowledge of our collective issues is equally important for our safety, sanity, and well-being. This astrological look at the major trends and planetary patterns for 2009 provides a framework for understanding the potentials and challenges we face together, so that we can advance with tolerance and respect as a community and fulfill our potentials as individuals.

The astrological events used for this forecast are the transits of the outer planets, Chiron and the Moon's Nodes, as well as the retrograde cycles of Mercury and eclipses of the Sun and the Moon.

MAJOR PLANETARY EVENTS

JUPITER IN AQUARIUS: COLLECTIVE CONSCIOUSNESS

January 5, 2009–January 17, 2010

Expansive Jupiter enters inventive and idealistic Aquarius, opening our minds to unexpected possibilities and futuristic visions for reorganizing society. Philosophical, religious, and political boundaries are crossed as new combinations of beliefs evolve, replacing outmoded ideologies. The rigid rules governing the institutional structures begin to crack, shaking government, business, and educational organizations. The importance of teamwork and cooperation increases as generous Jupiter in group-oriented Aquarius challenges existing hierarchies and dysfunctional authorities. Growing awareness of the interconnectedness of all living creatures favors a holistic view of reality in which environmental issues and unequal distribution of resources can be addressed more effectively. Strict divisions among nations and among social classes start to fade with a revival of humanistic values. The rise of corporate power may have peaked with Jupiter in ambitious Capricorn last year; society is now turning toward a more equitable relationship between business and labor, profit and sustainability, and personal needs versus collective ones.

Jupiter and Aquarius are both associated with mental activity, making this a rich time for breakthroughs in brain research. Practices for developing the mind become popular as baby boomers strive to stay sharp and recent discoveries spur innovative approaches to education. Technology should advance rapidly, especially if it involves networks—an area associated with Aquarius. Yet there is a shadow side to all this intellectual firepower, for both Jupiter and Aquarius have the potential

to "know it all." Combining their energies offers brilliance, but also the possibility for arrogance in which theory overrules reality. Seemingly perfect concepts may leave little room for exceptions that mar their conceptual beauty. The rigidity of intellectual correctness can be cold, uncaring, and blind to its own flaws. The desire to have all the answers is a driving force for human exploration—even as it can engender hubris and an assumption of infallibility that both negate discussion or compromise. Fortunately, such tendencies are tempered this year by Jupiter's conjunctions with Neptune and Chiron.

Neptune is the planet of compassion and spirituality, representing the boundless field of feeling that lies beyond the limits of the mind. Chiron is the Wounded Healer, a reminder of the value of vulnerability in salving the pain of mortality. Jupiter conjuncts Neptune on May 27, July 10, and December 21 and joins Chiron on May 23, July 22, and December 21. The close tracking of these three planets throughout the year softens any tendency toward intellectual self-importance with profound touches of faith and humility. Absolute certainty is undermined by the unexplainable mysteries of Neptune, which make it impossible to articulate ultimate truth. Chiron reveals a human side that casts doubt on even the strongest thinkers. Ideally, the presence of these planets can enrich scholarly advances with emotions that warm theories with an understanding of their impact on individual lives. The super-conjunction of Jupiter, Neptune, and Chiron creates a rare mix of awareness on all levels that can go a long way toward opening individual and collective consciousness. We may begin to see ourselves in a new light with greater understanding of our potential and purpose. Still, the downside of Neptune is that we can believe our own illusions. There's a whiff of fanaticism in the air that can turn the possibility of awakening into a deeper delusional sleep. The desire to know everything can disable the sentry of skepticism that keeps extremism in check. Whenever ideas are driven with excessive righteousness, judgment, and intolerance, it's a signal that what we're thinking or hearing is tainted. Turn down the volume and listen for quiet spaces of acceptance to be sure that what's being offered is as rich in kindness as in concept.

SATURN IN VIRGO: LEAVE NO STONE UNTURNED

September 2, 2007–October 29, 2009

Saturn, the planet of boundaries and limitations, takes twenty-nine years to orbit the Sun and pass through all twelve signs of the zodiac. It demands serious responsibility, reveals the work needed to overcome obstacles, and teaches us how to structure our lives. Saturn thrives on patience and commitment, rewarding well-planned and persistent effort while punishing sloppiness and procrastination with disappointment, delay, and even failure.

Saturn's passage through methodical Virgo is a time to perfect skills, cut waste, and develop healthier habits. Saturn and Virgo are both pragmatic, which makes them an excellent pair for improving the quality of material life. Organizational upgrades and maintenance projects increase efficiency for individuals and groups. Education and training grow more valuable due to increasing demand for highly specialized skills. Carelessness is more costly when minor errors escalate into major problems. Networks break down easily, requiring closer attention than usual. Bodies can be more susceptible to illnesses caused by impure food or water, making this an ideal period to improve our diets. Environmental issues are emphasized as we approach a critical point in the relationship between humanity and planet Earth. Fortunately, Saturn in exacting Virgo is excellent for cleaning up unhealthy toxins produced by old technologies and in leading the way to build new ecologically friendly systems for the future.

Virgo, the sign of the worker, puts labor issues and employee rights in the spotlight. This could mark a major turning point for unions, which might see their rate of decline accelerate—or could find new issues and alliances that restore their lost influence on political life. The globalization of the workforce has already changed the way companies do business, and we can expect this trend to continue, placing additional strains on the economy. And as corporations continue to grow beyond national boundaries, fear of internationalization fuels the ongoing debate about discrimination against foreign workers. But Virgo is less interested in unrestrained consumerism than in acquiring useful things. This opens the door to a new era of relatively modest consumption and shifts the economy away from purchases of plusher cars, bigger homes, and more disposable goods. Do-it-yourself classes and products, personalized services, pets, and outdoor activities will continue to boom.

The stability of Saturn in Virgo is shaken by a series of oppositions with rebellious Uranus that began last November and return this year on February 5 and September 15, culminating on July 26, 2010. This face-off between the planets of order and chaos can manifest as political and social revolution, breakdowns of systems and services, or upheaval of the Earth itself. On a personal level, it represents a time to break free from routine to explore and invent new ways to manage our lives.

Saturn in Virgo highlights flaws—even the little ones—and makes it too easy to be critical of ourselves and others. Yet its true purpose is to solve problems, not simply complain about them. Recognizing our weaknesses can sometimes be a source of despair, but the functional combination of Saturn's commitment and Virgo's analytical skills gives hope that effective change is well within our grasp. Small steps in a positive direction can slowly build up to a tidal wave of improvement wherever you place your attention this year.

SATURN IN LIBRA: TESTING RELATIONSHIPS

October 29, 2009–October 5, 2012

Saturn's shift into peace-loving Libra marks a new chapter in all kinds of relationships. Cooperation and civility allow diplomacy to flourish as reason replaces force. The need to weigh both sides of any argument can slow down personal and public dialogue, yet it's worth the price to build bridges over seemingly impassable chasms. Saturn is "exalted" in Libra according to astrological tradition, suggesting a highly positive link between the planet's principle of integrity and Libra's sense of fair play. The negative side of Saturn, though, is its potential for rigidity, which can  manifest now as a stubborn unwillingness to listen. Resistance to opposing points of view is simply a test of their worth: Only with careful consideration can they be properly evaluated. Responsible individuals and leaders recognize the importance of treating others as equals and with respect as a foundation for any healthy relationship.

Saturn in Libra marks a time of significant legal changes when the scales of justice are recalibrated. The famous *Brown v. Board of Education* case that was critical to reversing segregation in the United States was launched in 1951 with Saturn in Libra. Challenges to contract and marriage laws, the US Fairness Doctrine, and international treaties governing war and peace can be expected.

URANUS IN PISCES: BREAK ON THROUGH TO THE OTHER SIDE

March 3, 2003–May 27, 2010

Uranus takes eighty-four years to orbit the Sun, spending about seven years in each sign. This longer transit's influence tends to be less obvious in daily life than that of the faster-moving Saturn and Jupiter. Nevertheless, its eventual impact can be even greater. This planet of liberation in Pisces, the last sign of the zodiac, is about breaking down the barriers of faith, fantasy, and illusion that subtly shape our lives. The most powerful ones lie just beyond the border of consciousness, yet hold our minds in a universe of assumptions that we almost never question. Uranus's presence in Pisces tears down these invisible walls, awakening us from sweet dreams and nightmares alike.

Pisces is a water sign and Uranus rules electricity, so this combination suggests we may see the development of new technologies that transform water into usable electric power. Because karmic Saturn opposes water-bound Uranus on February 5 and September 15, we can also expect to suddenly encounter new realities concerning water as a natural resource, for both drinking and agriculture. Stories of severe water pollution, unavailable drinking water, or problems with the fishing industry may flood the mainstream media. We have been deluged with watery disasters over recent years, including hurricanes, floods, and tsunamis—and we can expect this unpleasant trend to continue. This is shown not just by Uranus's presence in Neptune's sign Pisces, but also by Neptune's presence in Uranus's sign Aquarius. Such an exchange of ruling planets, called mutual reception, indicates closer connections among the planets and signs involved. Uranus is scientific, the first planet discovered by telescope. Neptune is spiritual, so we can expect continuing debate between academia and religion over ethical issues such as evolution versus intelligent design theory, stem cell research, cloning, and the right to die.

NEPTUNE IN AQUARIUS: SPIRIT INTO SCIENCE

January 28, 1998–April 4, 2011

Aquarius is a sign of intellect, and Neptune is a planet of faith. This paradoxical combination inspires brilliance when operating at its best, but can also make for fuzzy arguments or isolating fantasies. The mix can be disorienting, bringing about possible detachment from a more spiritual path. It's a tricky task to put Neptune's nonmaterial reality into an intellectual form, because it exists beyond the limits of language. However, the idealistic qualities of the planet in socially conscious Aquarius provide an excellent opportunity to apply its highest principles to community affairs. Volunteering for a cause in which you believe serves the needs of others and feeds your soul at the same time. Conjunctions to Neptune from Jupiter—with which it co-rules Pisces—dissolves barriers to direct spiritual experiences. The line between true inspiration and misguided illusion, though, may be difficult to find at times. Feeling drained while serving others can be a signal of misdirected energy. A certain amount of sacrifice for a cause is admirable, but your capacity to help others will be severely reduced if you're exhausted.

As noted earlier with respect to Uranus in Pisces, the mixing of belief and science is both a gift and a curse of Neptune in Aquarius. Doubting the wisdom of organized religion continues to be prominent as intellect replaces blind faith and increasing numbers of people grow disillusioned with overzealous religious leaders. Deception and a willful denial of logic are to be expected. But for the metaphysically oriented, Neptune in Aquarius is likely to continue the popularization of technology as a way to understand our spirituality. The distinction between hardware and software will become less apparent, as will the separation between humans and computers. We may see a wave of biotech innovations that pave the way for microchip implants, fueling a debate about the limits of tampering with or enhancing brain function with artificial intelligence.

On an individual level, Neptune in Aquarius is part of a process that continues to connect feelings and intellect by acknowledging the close relationship between emotions and thoughts. New theories of quantum consciousness will further reveal that the mind is not simply a mechanical system that operates separately from the rest of the body. Neptune activities such as meditation, yoga, and t'ai chi will continue to gain more mainstream popularity to calm jangled nervous systems and to integrate mind, body, and spirit in a peaceful and holistic manner.

PLUTO IN CAPRICORN: RELENTLESS CHANGE

November 26, 2008–March 23, 2023

Pluto takes nearly 250 years to complete one journey around the zodiac, but obser-
vations of its movement quickly reveal its power. Tiny but potent Pluto entered
no-nonsense Capricorn last year, signaling a turn toward major changes in the
architecture of society. Capricorn is associated with established institutions such
as government and business, so transformative Pluto's visit indicates a drawn-out
process that will ultimately alter the most fundamental organizational structures
supporting our culture. Because Capricorn is an earth sign, we can expect growing
urgency in the serious environmental crises facing us. Global warming, for
instance, will likely place unforeseeable pressures on corporations, governments,
and individuals, forcing inevitable upheavals that could radically impact our modern
way of life. The accumulated effects of dumping toxins into the air, water, and soil
will continue to become more evident during Pluto's long transit of this sign.
Obviously, this could overpower all other issues and require a degree of change not
seen since Pluto last transited Capricorn from 1762 to 1778. Democracy, like the
magical Phoenix bird, arose from the destructive American and French Revolutions
that ended monarchy and gave birth to the same individual freedoms we are now
struggling to keep.

The good news is that events of this magnitude do not occur overnight. The cor-
ruption of existing institutions takes time—enough for those capable of adapting to
begin the necessary process of reform. Since Capricorn has to do with rule from
the top, Pluto's transit may well knock down those who pull the levers of power.
Yet regardless of where state, church, education, and industry go, there is constructive work we each can and must do as individuals at this time. Both Pluto and
Capricorn are associated with power, so the application of personal will is a critical issue and can make the difference between utopia and oblivion. Instead of relying on others to maintain and advance civilization, we each have the capacity to
increase our own tangible contribution to the world. Step one is a reexamination of
career ambitions and personal life goals. For some, this could grow out of dissatisfaction or a sense of impotence in life. This is not likely to be the result of a single event or limited to Pluto's transit this year. We're at the beginning of a long
process in which we seek more purposeful lives. Of course, this can feel like an
overwhelming challenge: Meeting our increasing responsibilities can be daunting.
It is best, then, to address small but important issues, where it's possible to see
results more quickly and gain the confidence to continue moving forward. Changes
in diet, exercise patterns, attitude, and behavior, for example, are manageable yet

can ultimately be significant beyond our individual lives. Make a plan and commit to working on it for as long as it takes. Progress may be slow, because it's natural to encounter resistance. Habits don't necessarily surrender easily. But slowly and surely, a sense of mastery will grow with each small step forward. As a result, humanity will become more empowered, allowing us to consciously create the future rather than unconsciously repeating mistakes of the past.

Repetitive Saturn-Pluto alignments can be traced throughout history, revealing social changes that occur when worldviews collide. Saturn-Pluto events include the fall of Rome in 411 AD , Muhammad's establishment of an Islamic state in 628, the Moors' invasion of Spain in 711, the Battle of Hastings in 1066, and the start of World War I in 1914. Saturn and Pluto were opposed at the bombing of the World Trade Towers in New York City on September 11, 2001. These two planets enter into a nine-month square this year on November 15, so we could see a new wave of global unrest as religions clash and nationalistic fervor reaches new heights. Still, the negative potential of this aspect can be ameliorated if we refuse to buy into government-sponsored, media-manufactured fear. Learning to accept different perspectives while seeking common ground can free us from fighting the same old battles that have haunted us for centuries.

CHIRON IN AQUARIUS: THE WOUNDED COMMUNITY

February 21, 2005–April 19, 2010

Chiron, discovered in 1977 between the orbits of Saturn and Uranus, was named after a mythological centaur known for his healing powers. Astrologers studying this new member of our solar system have found it to be a meaningful point that most have added to their charts. Chiron in Aquarius represents wounds in communities and the ideals that bind them together. But its transit through this unorthodox sign can lead to a shift away from traditional group identification to allow new alignments less rooted in old national, regional, or racial differences. Chiron is highlighted by conjunctions from Jupiter on May 23, July 22, and December 7, and its close proximity to Neptune throughout the year. Miracles in medicine can be expected, along with hope that religious zealotry will be softened by compassion.

THE MOON'S NODES

MOON'S NORTH NODE IN AQUARIUS, SOUTH NODE IN LEO: GLOBAL APPROACH

December 15, 2007–August 21, 2009

The North and South Nodes are opposing points—the Dragon's Head and Tail that connect the orbits of the Moon around the Earth and the Earth around the Sun. Habit pulls us toward the South Node, but it is the North Node that points in a direction of growth and integration. The North Node in Aquarius marks a period when we must accept the technologies we have created, even if they seem too futuristic or inhuman. The South Node sign of Leo is concerned with issues of the human heart, which may need to be temporarily set aside to make tough decisions that could impact the survival of the human race.

Nostalgic emotional attachments to the past can place individual needs ahead of the community, but we are required now to bravely face our collective destiny. There is little room for self-centered narcissistic behavior as the intellectually driven Aquarius North Node increases our awareness of the interrelatedness of all humanity. This is an opportunity to move past our personal neuroses and tackle the more significant issues we face together.

MOON'S NORTH NODE IN CAPRICORN, SOUTH NODE IN CANCER: PROFILES IN COURAGE

August 21, 2009–March 3, 2011

The North Node in Capricorn is a time to overcome habits of self-defense and replace them with ambition, concentration, and tenacity. The karmic weakness of the South Node in Cancer is a desire to retreat from the world and seek safety in familiar places. Emotions run strong, as does our instinct is to cling to what we know, staying close to the shores of comfort and security. The cutting edge or growth point of the North Node in strategic Capricorn promises accomplishment, recognition, and respect for those willing to work hard to achieve it. Stepping out from Cancer's emotional shell and using discipline, intention, and a competitive edge to achieve worldly goals brings spiritual as well as material rewards.

MERCURY RETROGRADES

All true planets appear to move retrograde from time to time, because we view them from the moving platform of Earth. The most significant retrograde periods are those of Mercury, the communication planet. Occurring three or four times a year for roughly three weeks at a time, these are periods when difficulties with details, travel, information flow, and technical matters are likely.

Although Mercury's retrograde phase has received a fair amount of bad press, it isn't necessarily a negative cycle. Because personal and commercial inter-actions are emphasized, you can actually accomplish more than usual, especially if you stay focused on what needs to be done, rather than initiating new projects. Still, you may feel as if you're treading water—or worse yet, carried backward in an undertow of unfinished business. Worry less about making progress than about the quality of your work. Pay extra attention to all your communication exchanges. Avoiding misunderstandings and omissions is the ideal way to preemptively deal with unnecessary complications. Retrograde Mercury is best used to tie up loose ends as you review, redo, reconsider, and, in general, revisit the past.

This year, the three retrogrades are in intellectual air signs (Aquarius, Gemini, and Libra), which can be very useful for analysis and remedial studies that help you reevaluate what you already know so you can take your learning to the next level. Mercury has a natural affinity for the air signs, so you are empowered by your mental prowess during these times. However smart you are, don't be so enamored with the workings of your mind that you forget about the practical aspects of your body and the emotional needs of your heart.

JANUARY 11–FEBRUARY 1 IN AQUARIUS: GENIUS AT WORK

Mercury is technically proficient in progressive Aquarius, and its retrograde period can reveal your dependency on home appliances, computers, and gadgets—especially when they stop working. Don't wait until it's too late to back up your data, because electronic equipment is particularly vulnerable to the antics of the Cosmic Trickster. Fortunately, extra doses of intelligence and insight are available when Mercury joins wise Jupiter on January 18. The union of these planets of lower and higher mind in the brilliant sign of Aquarius brings together data (Mercury) and principles (Jupiter) in a new picture of how the world works. Too much information, however, complicates matters, while sticking to essential details reveals patterns to set the lightbulbs popping in your head. Higher levels of understanding make it possible to articulate new visions for humanity and express complex ideas in understandable terms.

MAY 6–MAY 30 IN GEMINI: DELUGE OF DATA

Mercury has barely had time to adjust to its home sign of Gemini, the data collector, when it challenges you by turning around and heading back to the simpler territory of practical Taurus. The assumption that more information is always better than less could be tested now as you face an increasing stream of e-mail, phone calls, and news. You may want to escape the noise so you can review what you already know, reconsider your previous plans, and reevaluate recent decisions. You are challenged these days to determine which information is most useful and which can be discarded. Naturally, Mercury will be up to its old tricks as well—plaguing you with lost keys and cell phones, missed connections, and other miscommunications—so don't lose sight of the details.

The messenger planet slips back into earthy Taurus on May 13, remaining in this resource-measuring sign until June 13, a good period in which to put financial affairs in order.

SEPTEMBER 7–SEPTEMBER 29 IN LIBRA: RELATIONSHIP RECALIBRATION

This Mercury retrograde is likely to impact your social life, for Libra is the sign of partnership. You might be overly dependent on someone, only to seriously reconsider his or her role in your life. This is a contemplative and possibly intense period, for Mercury runs into shadowy Pluto on September 17 and then reenters critical Virgo, heading toward a conjunction with taskmaster Saturn on September 22. Expect slowdowns caused by system failure or minor errors that need maintenance or repairs. Expert skills can be developed and complex tasks completed with sufficient patience and concentration.

DECEMBER 26–JANUARY 15, 2010, IN CAPRICORN: SHARE YOUR IDEAS

Retrograde Mercury in traditional Capricorn can upset order in organizations. The chain of command is likely to be broken, and the limits of authority tested. Yet this can also be a positive time for restructuring a group or reevaluating professional priorities and ambitions.

ECLIPSES

Solar and Lunar Eclipses are special New and Full Moons that indicate meaningful changes for individuals and groups. They are powerful markers of events with influences that can appear up to three months in advance and last up to six months afterward. Eclipses occur when the New or Full Moon is conjunct one of the Moon's Nodes. Solar Eclipses occur at the New Moon and are visible in unique paths, but not everywhere that the Sun appears in the sky. Locations where the eclipse is visible are more strongly influenced by it. Lunar Eclipses occur during Full Moons and are visible wherever the Moon can be seen.

JANUARY 26, SOLAR ECLIPSE IN AQUARIUS: SOCIETY OF THE FUTURE

Eclipses are usually about endings, but this one has plenty of propulsion to drive forward new ideas and organizations. Expansive Jupiter is conjunct the eclipse to seed minds with vision far into the future. Loving Venus is joined with Uranus, Aquarius's inventive ruling planet, revealing fresh forms for relationships and unconventional aesthetics. Stern Saturn's opposition to this unconventional pair could stifle expression, but a constructive trine from productive Mars in Capricorn helps overcome any resistance. Almost the entire visible path of this eclipse passes harmlessly over water, except for a swath passing through Indonesia and close to the Philippines, making these the likeliest candidates for social or environmental upheaval.

FEBRUARY 9, LUNAR ECLIPSE IN LEO: COSMIC COMMUNITY

A Lunar Eclipse in dramatic Leo cuts egos down to size, turning brilliant stars into black holes and overinflated winners into losers. The appearance of loss, however, may be obscured by nebulous Neptune's conjunction with the Sun and opposition to the Moon, allowing illusion and deception to cover up failures. The upside of this event is an awakening to the connectedness of all living things. Spiritual Neptune in collectivist Aquarius reveals identity beyond personal ego, opening individuals and groups to communities of soul and service. Let pride dissolve in waters of compassion while moving from fields of competition to webs of cooperation. Philosophical Jupiter's close conjunction with the integrative Lunar North Node promises wisdom, while energetic Mars can turn ideas into action. Chiron the Wounded Healer stands by the Sun and Neptune, and opposite the Moon, to temper intellect with vulnerability that softens hearts and opens minds.

JULY 7, LUNAR ECLIPSE IN CAPRICORN: REALIGNING RESPONSIBILITIES

This Lunar Eclipse in Capricorn chips away at emotional defenses, revealing gentler ways to manage daily life. The overly ambitious and excessively disciplined may be diverted from their well-defined paths to address personal issues. The usual insecurities associated with an eclipse in hardworking Capricorn are

lessened by a supportive trine from Saturn. This provides a safety rail of relative stability through this wobbly time. Examine the rules you've created for yourself and consider dropping those that no longer serve your needs. Reducing extraneous obligations can help you focus on the tasks and goals most vital for you right now.

JULY 21, SOLAR ECLIPSE IN CANCER: CUTTING THE CORD

This Solar Eclipse in the last degree of nostalgic Cancer can produce a flood of memories, pulling your attention back to the past. Yet this is no time to linger over photo albums, souvenirs, and thoughts of love found and lost. Say good-bye to self-protective habits that inhibit growth and block fulfillment. Independent Uranus forms a supportive trine to the eclipse, suddenly making it easier to cut loose what's no longer needed. Nurturing the future, rather than the past, is the gift of this significant event. The eclipse is visible in central China and India, making these countries prime candidates for dramatic change.

AUGUST 5, LUNAR ECLIPSE IN AQUARIUS: THE KID IN YOU

It's rare that Lunar Eclipses arrive two months in a row, making this summer a period of major transformation. This one in Aquarius challenges us to come down from ivory towers and act on innovative ideas. The Sun in bold Leo opposite the Moon indicates the need for courage and a willingness to take risks. Fortunately,

assertive Mars in multitalented Gemini shows a variety of paths that can lead to success. Quick fixes and last-minute adjustments are easier with a friendly attitude more interested in enjoying the game than in the final score. When heads are made heavy by theory or competition, it's time for the child's heart to appear to bring playfulness to the party.

DECEMBER 31, LUNAR ECLIPSE IN CANCER: TOUGH CHOICES

This Lunar Eclipse in the Moon's own sign of Cancer can stir deep waters within families and close friendships. Powerful Pluto opposes the Moon while stern Saturn squares it, creating tightness and pressure that can be frightening. It's tempting to duck confrontation or avoid any serious change, yet refusing to act only reduces your power. You may have hard choices to make on the cusp of the New Year, yet they demand focus and clear intention—powerful allies for redefining life. Sweet Venus in traditional Capricorn is between Pluto and the Sun, and opposite the Moon, tempting you to do anything to maintain appearances. Still, the prizes of fulfillment go to those bold enough to face outer reality and inner desire without flinching.

THE BOTTOM LINE

This is a year of high hopes and hard work. The close tracking of Jupiter, Neptune, and Chiron is a spiritual chorus of inspiration and imagination. Even the toughest circumstances cannot block out the light pouring in to show a better way for tomorrow. This planetary union in group-conscious Aquarius reveals more and more layers of the nets that connect us as well as the patterns within our individual stories. The meaning of life may not be readily explained, but we can understand it intuitively this year. Such heightened awareness signals humanity's readiness for the next stage of our evolution.

Profound collective change rarely happens overnight. Even cataclysmic events are only stages in a longer chain of circumstances. The key to maximizing the rich opportunities of 2009 is countering higher consciousness with earthly competence. Saturn, the shaper of reality, is in practical Virgo for most of the year. The need to handle details skillfully contrasts sharply with the philosophical buoyancy of the Aquarius super-conjunction. For some, it means that excessive attention to mundane matters blocks the mind from the illumination pouring in from above. For others, failure to take care of material business produces visions that evaporate in the fog of illusion and in hopes abandoned by inaction.

Ideally, we will find the threads that connect the conceptual and the real, turning spiritual values into daily practice, and transforming dreams of a better tomorrow into a more functionally effective today. Developing skills, taking care of our bodies, and protecting the Earth give form to our highest aspirations. A consistent commitment to sanity, health, and self-improvement may seem small on a daily basis, yet it can weave a web of clarity and competence that empowers our highest hopes.

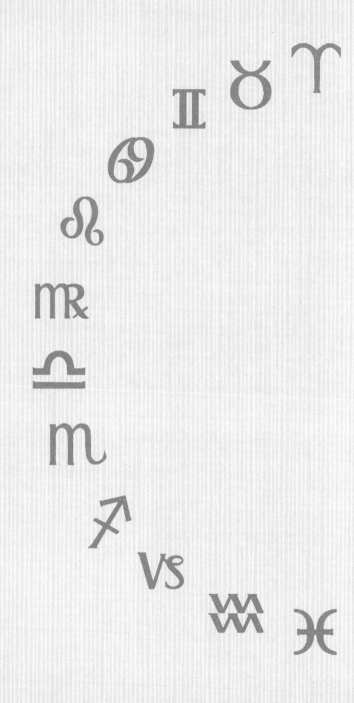

PART 2

AUGUST-DECEMBER

2008 OVERVIEW

2009 ASTROLOGICAL

FORECASTS

ARIES

MARCH 21–APRIL 19

ARIES

2008 SUMMARY

Developing competence increases confidence and is the best way to get out of a work-related rut. Give yourself a little time to get up to speed this year. Although you love surprises and thrive on spontaneity, the challenge ahead of you is to practice self-discipline and pace yourself wisely. Ignoring problems won't make them disappear, but using the friction they produce to intensify your feelings until you put yourself on a new path is sure to be rewarded.

AUGUST—*meet others halfway*

Plan several moves ahead, like a good chess player, so that you can quickly adjust your reactions according to the changing circumstances.

SEPTEMBER—*define your goals*

Focus on what you are trying to accomplish rather than on your shortcomings to best overcome any self-doubt and ultimately reach your objective.

OCTOBER—*all or nothing*

An attitude of guarded optimism helps you sustain the necessary excitement to motivate yourself while working within the limitations of those around you.

NOVEMBER—*shape your future*

A conscious connection between purpose and possibility makes it easy for you to find and follow your star.

DECEMBER—*going out with a bang*

Concentrate on one task at a time to avoid the potential for overextension. Invest your energy in building your confidence rather than tearing others down.

2008 CALENDAR

AUGUST

FRIDAY 1 ★ Demonstrating your good character is important

WEDNESDAY 6 ★ Turn out of control energy into creativity through the 9th

SATURDAY 16 ★ **SUPER NOVA DAYS** Aim your passion with precision

SATURDAY 23 ★ Keep it real! Ask for help with heavy burdens through the 24th

SATURDAY 30 ★ Take it easy and escape the pressure of reality

SEPTEMBER

SUNDAY 7 ★ Tame your aggression when push comes to shove through the 8th

THURSDAY 11 ★ Slow down and enjoy your charmed life through the 12th

TUESDAY 16 ★ Support comes to you from an unexpected source

SUNDAY 21 ★ **SUPER NOVA DAY** Cooperation is key through the 24th

OCTOBER

SUNDAY 5 ★ Consider a new plan through the 6th

FRIDAY 10 ★ Your desire for freedom may cause you to jump the gun

TUESDAY 14 ★ You feel an awakening awareness in relationships

FRIDAY 24 ★ Chill out! Back off in small disputes through the 26th

MONDAY 27 ★ **SUPER NOVA DAYS** Your efforts produce positive results

NOVEMBER

MONDAY 3 ★ Stay skeptical to know if you're being played

WEDNESDAY 12 ★ Alter your alliances and renegotiate through the 13th

SUNDAY 16 ★ If you believe in something strongly, walk your talk

FRIDAY 21 ★ **SUPER NOVA DAYS** There's no holding you back through the 24th

THURSDAY 27 ★ Through tomorrow, consider your audience before unleashing your words

DECEMBER

FRIDAY 5 ★ Take charge of your life! Self-direction is key

THURSDAY 11 ★ Be cautious with risky business until after the 12th

MONDAY 15 ★ Follow the rules and trust your intuition through the 16th

SUNDAY 21 ★ Lighten your load by dropping distractions through the 22nd

SATURDAY 27 ★ **SUPER NOVA DAYS** Your sensitivity is heightened through the 28th

ARIES OVERVIEW

This is an especially active year for you socially, yet you also come face-to-face with pressing responsibilities at work and inevitable changes at home. With optimistic Jupiter now in your 11th House of Friends, Hopes, and Wishes, **your eyes shift away from your career commitments toward the distant horizon as you imagine your life around the next bend.** You will be spending more time with your buddies and co-workers, for your friends will eagerly listen to you spin out your dreams of the future and encourage you to realize them, whether or not these are practical. But Jupiter isn't the only planet now moving through your futuristic 11th House: Chiron the Wounded Healer and Neptune the Dreamer are long-term visitors to this area of your life as well, and now with Jupiter's presence, subtle visions that you've been glimpsing for years begin to take on greater significance. In fact, when Jupiter aligns with Chiron on May 23, July 22, and December 7, you are tempted to avoid painful situations and even perhaps deny unpleasant feelings. When Jupiter joins Neptune on May 27, July 10, and December 21, it becomes even more challenging to discern what is real, for following your intuition seems to be a great idea and pursuing your dreams is more compelling than ever. Although the issues may become more pronounced around these specific dates, **you struggle to pull threads of truth from your most elusive fantasies throughout the year**.

Expansive Jupiter harmonized with restrictive Saturn through 2007 and 2008, balancing the opportunities and the reality of your life, which allowed you to create a foundation for progress. Now Jupiter forms creative biquintiles with Saturn that are exact on March 1, September 13, and January 11, 2010. **You must reach completely outside the box, past your apparent limitations, to find the tools that will allow you to sustain growth and realize your fullest potential.** Jupiter also forms an irritating quincunx with serious Saturn that is exact on March 22, August 19, and February 5, 2010. It's crucial to keep both the encouragement of Jupiter and the sobering reminders of Saturn in perspective, for you are tempted to put one or the other into a blind spot. This can impede your progress in the long term.

You are at the beginning of a long-lasting change symbolized by last year's entry of transformative Pluto into ambitious Capricorn, where it remains until 2023, bringing ongoing intensity to your 10th House of Public Status. Hardworking Saturn moves slowly toward a dynamic square with power-house Pluto on November 15, continuing through much of 2010. This forces you to **narrow your focus onto those projects that have the longest-lasting value**. You will need to eliminate activities that no longer fit into your life purpose or needlessly tax your schedule and waste valuable resources. You must use your power for the good of all, because your plans can backfire if you attempt to selfishly corral Pluto for personal gain.

IN THE MOOD FOR LOVE

You may be tempted to fall back into old relationship patterns while the South Node of the Moon is in your 5th House of Love and Romance, through July 26. Additionally, sensual Venus extends her stay in your sign due to a retrograde phase on March 6–April 17. During this time, you may reignite a flame with an old lover or turn up the heat on a current relationship. Venus enters impetuous Aries on February 22, slips back into compassionate Pisces from April 11 through April 24, and then remains in your sign until June 6, increasing your chances of finding love. Your key planet, Mars, intensifies your drive for pleasure as he moves through your sign on April 22–May 31. On October 16, Mars reenergizes playful Leo and your 5th House of Love, where he remains through the end of the year.

GRADUAL CHANGE

Taskmaster Saturn in perfectionist Virgo remains in your 6th House of Work through October 29, demanding that you attend to details both on the job and at home. Meanwhile, Saturn opposes erratic Uranus on February 5 and September 15 in a long-term cycle that began November 4, 2008, and lasts through the summer of 2010. Unexpected disruptions at work can be upsetting, yet they also point out key areas of dissatisfaction. You may feel even more restless than usual and constrained by the direction of your current career path. Make changes to increase your freedom, but don't turn your world upside down just because you are bored.

SLOW DOWN FOR CURVES

Financial gains come not by leaps and bounds this year, but rather through incremental advances that grow slowly and steadily. You must pay close attention to your work and get the job done as efficiently as possible if you want to make more money. There are, however, a few challenges along the way. Venus rules your 2nd House of Income, so her retrograde on March 6–April 17 can present financial problems if an opportunity produces less compensation than expected. Consolidate an old debt or reconsider a current investment strategy on May 7–30, when Mercury is retrograde in your 2nd House. The New Moon Eclipse on July 21 has Venus tensely squaring Saturn, indicating a possible shortfall of cash during the summer if you don't manage your resources carefully.

 SELF-IMPROVEMENT

Quicksilver Mercury rules your 6th House of Health and Habits, so its movements point to clues about your physical condition. Each of Mercury's retrogrades this year begins in a thoughtful air sign and then backs up into a practical earth sign, indicating that even after you know what's healthy, you still must turn it into actual practice. These three retrograde periods—from January 11 to February 1, May 7 to May 30, and September 6 to September 29—represent windows of opportunity for you to take constructive action that enhances your physical well-being. Additionally, with hardworking Saturn moving through your 6th House until October 29, any health challenges will clearly show you where you need to make changes.

 CHALLENGING DECISIONS

Two eclipses in your 4th House of Home and Family this year prompt unexpected changes that can free you from preexisting challenges. The first, a New Moon Eclipse on July 21, suggests that you must take responsibility for your role within the family and cut back on wasteful expenditures if you are to meet your obligations. The Full Moon Eclipse on December 31 places demands on you at work, pulling your energies away from home and making it difficult to manage your affairs on both fronts. Mars's movement through your 4th House on August 25–October 16 can stir up lots of activity and may be a good time to initiate home improvement projects.

YOUR DISCOVERY CHANNEL

Boundless Jupiter governs your 9th House of Travel and Higher Education, so you often have grandiose plans that can be difficult to bring to fruition. Your ruling planet, Mars, joins Jupiter on February 17, indicating a fortunate time to take a trip or begin a course of study. Mars's tense square to Jupiter on July 6 increases your exuberance. You can have a wonderful time wherever you go, but could be tempted into foolish risk taking—pay attention or you'll find yourself in a precarious situation. Mars's harmonious trine to Jupiter on August 13 is a perfect time for a getaway, especially if it involves being outdoors or doing something physical. You can combine fun with learning if you are pushing beyond your regular boundaries into something you've never done before.

COMPASSIONATE WARRIOR

Your spiritual path may not be a straight one this year, nor is it easy for you to see where it leads. With Uranus finishing up a seven-year stay in your 12th House of Imagination, it's time for you to bring your previous studies to completion and put what you've learned about yourself into practice. Your patience wears thin and you may want immediate results, especially around February 5 and September 15, but it's useless to push too hard. Meanwhile, Jupiter's recurring conjunctions with magical Neptune on May 27, July 10, and December 21 can lead to a deeper understanding of your place in the cosmos.

RICK & JEFF'S TIP FOR THE YEAR:

Independence Without Revolution
You may feel as if time is running out—convinced you'll lose your chance if you don't make a significant move this year. Although you're sorely tempted to give in to your natural impulsive tendencies, it's not advisable to react emotionally without thinking about the consequences. Even if you need change, don't just introduce chaos into your life to stir things up. Remember, it's not about being distracted by excitement; it's about systematically removing the barriers between you and your happiness.

JANUARY

JOB WELL DONE

Although your eyes are on the future, your feet are planted firmly on the ground this month as you place extra emphasis on meeting your obligations. Sometimes you Rams jump into a job quickly, only to lose steam before you finish it. Still, with your ruling planet, Mars, in ambitious Capricorn—energizing your 10th House of Career all month—you have more stamina than usual to complete long-term projects. This is supercharged by the Capricorn Sun until **January 19**, and atypically you aren't interested in avoiding resistance, but rather in exerting steady pressure to overcome it. Your endurance is particularly strong when taskmaster Saturn is harmoniously trined by the Sun on **January 11** and by Mars on **January 24**. You may receive glimpses of what's around the next corner when intellectual Mercury enters futuristic Aquarius on **January 1**. Still, it may take longer to reach your goals, for Mercury turns retrograde on **January 11** and returns to pragmatic Capricorn on **January 21**. Impatience now will only bring you trouble, so control your impulses and concentrate your attention on specific objectives instead of scattering your energy all over the map.

The sensitive Cancer Full Moon on **January 10** falls in your 4th House of Home and Family, reminding you that all work and no relaxation can take a toll. Fortunately, this Full Moon is harmoniously aspected to conservative Saturn and unorthodox Uranus; you can enjoy a well-balanced weekend if you alternate quiet time with exciting activities. The intelligent Aquarius New Moon Eclipse on **January 26** is conjunct opportunistic Jupiter—a harbinger of good fortune, if you can let go of outmoded patterns that have tied you to the past.

> **KEEP IN MIND THIS MONTH**
>
> *Don't worry if you aren't having as much fun as you want. Your hard work now will allow you more time to enjoy yourself next month.*

KEY DATES

JANUARY 3–5 ★ *weekend retreat*

Withdrawing from the social scene this weekend can bring healing, for the reflective Moon is in your sign, pulling your moods first one way and then another. Yet you are not inclined to hide your feelings when sensual Venus enters dreamy Pisces on **January 3**, then harmonizes with passionate Pluto on **January 4**. One way of dealing with your current emotional intensity is by removing extraneous sources of stimulation. Buoyant Jupiter moves on **January 5** into unconventional Aquarius, where it remains for the rest of the year. Additionally, the Moon enters stable Taurus while impetuous Mars kicks up his heels with surprising Uranus, provoking you to initiate activities that get your adrenaline flowing once again.

JANUARY 10-11 ★ *tongue-tied*
You may be anxious to relieve the stress that has built up during the week. The emotional Cancer Full Moon on **January 10** emphasizes the differences between your thoughts and your needs. You have been waiting to express your desires, yet it's difficult to put them into words when communicator Mercury goes retrograde on **January 11**, turning your thoughts inward. Fortunately, your current tendency to play it safe is rewarded, because the Sun trines cautious Saturn the same day. Don't worry about missing a party; you have more important things to do and can relax later.

SUPER NOVA DAYS
JANUARY 21-24 ★ *risky business*
Although retrograde Mercury backs into traditional Capricorn on **January 21**, you are not willing to wait to take action. In fact, you may feel like a firecracker ready to explode. Your excitement mounts on **January 22** when the lovers, Venus and Mars, hook up with electric Uranus, encouraging you to take a risk if the potential for pleasure exists. But just because it's easy doesn't mean it's a good idea. Be careful about making an impulsive emotional disclosure before considering the consequences. Don't invest now without diligent research. Whether it's money or love, you may have regrets when Venus and Mars bump into austere Saturn on **January 24**. Luckily, with a little extra effort on your part, things will all work out.

JANUARY 26-27 ★ *struck by lightning*
The Solar Eclipse in emotionally detached Aquarius on **January 26** can provide the break in energy you need to wake you from your current disillusionment. With expansive Jupiter activating exhilarating Uranus, you are ready to turn the corner and try again, even if your previous efforts did not come to fruition. Talkative Mercury's conjunction with aggressive Mars on **January 27** can make your words even more forceful, so speak softly and respect alternative points of view.

FEBRUARY

The weather may be freezing, but you're sure everything is coming up roses. Rigidity softens and communication flows as mental Mercury ends its twenty-one-day retrograde phase on **February 1**—though it may take a few days before you notice the changes. Sweet Venus brings beauty into your life as she enters creative Aries on **February 2** for a longer-than-usual stay in your sign thanks to her biannual retrograde. Except for a brief return to Pisces in mid-April, the love planet will be in close contact with you, remaining in Aries all the way through **June 6**. This extraordinary period gives you time to indulge yourself and explore new ways to bring more pleasure into your life. Your key planet, Mars enters, airy Aquarius on **February 4**, and will stay in your 11th House of Friends and Wishes until **March 19**—relieving you of unwanted responsibilities and encouraging you to break away from restrictive situations, especially related to your career.

The pressure of the daily grind may become unbearable or the boredom just too much when erratic Uranus opposes hardworking Saturn on **February 5**—the second of five such oppositions in a long-term pattern that began on **November 4, 2008**, and will last through **July 2010**. This may not be the right time to push for change, for if you're too forceful, you could upset the apple cart instead of simply redirecting it. You might make progress toward your dreams, yet you'll find it challenging to put your gains into perspective by the end of the month: Mars creates tense aspects with powerful Pluto and austere Saturn on **February 27–28**.

> **KEEP IN MIND THIS MONTH**
>
> *The temptation to increase your sense of independence must be tempered with fulfilling your responsibilities and delivering on your commitments.*

KEY DATES
FEBRUARY 5 ★ *no way but up*
You'll find it difficult to avoid sudden change as the Saturn-Uranus opposition brings irrepressible desires up from the depths of your imagination into your awareness. Meanwhile, innocent Venus dynamically squares dark Pluto in an emotional struggle for survival. You might feel overwhelmed with despair and believe that your intense needs cannot be satisfied. Avoid acting from desperation, for you

may be on the edge of a real breakthrough. Although it might seem otherwise, this is not an all-or-nothing situation. Let yourself feel the extremes without being attached to the outcome.

FEBRUARY 9–12 ★ *transform fear*

The dramatic Leo Full Moon Eclipse in your 5th House of Romance on **February 9** opposes imaginative Neptune and wounded Chiron, destabilizing your love life and provoking you to overreact from a place of fear. But you have an opportunity to heal an old emotional scar if you understand the difference between what happened in the past and what's occurring now. You can experience a deepening of love by being true to your heart while remaining open to change. This will, however, take concentrated focus as impulsive Mars moves toward stressful aspects with the already tense Saturn-Uranus opposition through **February 12**. Things can get out of hand rather quickly if you act rashly.

SUPER NOVA DAYS
FEBRUARY 16–18 ★ *lucky in love*

Exuberance is the keyword as your ruling planet, Mars, joins confident Jupiter on **February 17**. This alignment occurs every other year, marking a high point in your energy cycle. But too much of a good thing can be problematic, so don't let unbridled optimism sever you from reality. Still, good fortune will likely rule the roost as hot Venus in Aries adds sensual support to the Mars-Jupiter conjunction that sextiles Jupiter on **February 16** and Mars on **February 18**. The Sun shifts into diffusive Pisces on **February 18**, challenging you to make your enthusiasm last longer. Don't worry about what happens next; just enjoy it while you can.

FEBRUARY 24 ★ *attitude is everything*

The compassionate Pisces New Moon can signal a need to readjust your goals and soften your grip on the steering wheel of life. Fortunately, this isn't necessarily difficult now as intellectual Mercury conjuncts jolly Jupiter in quirky Aquarius, blessing you with irrepressible hope for a bright future. Even if you don't have a specific plan, you know that everything will work out for the best. Just remember that overconfidence can easily lead to arrogance, possibly stirring up opposition from those who would be better allies than enemies.

MARCH

A TIME TO REMEMBER

An action-packed month kicks off as your key planet, Mars, in eccentric Aquarius activates talkative Mercury on **March 1**, nostalgic Chiron on **March 5**, and idealistic Neptune on **March 8**. Your desire for friendship deepens, yet your vulnerability also exposes those moments when you fall short of true intimacy or miss the mark in romance. Problems may be highlighted as attractive Venus—in self-directed Aries throughout the entire month—retrogrades on **March 6–April 17**. You may feel the confusing effects more strongly than everyone around you. It looks like love is just beyond your reach, yet Venus's six-week backtrack can slowly reveal opportunities for pleasure you might otherwise have missed. You might take a detour down Memory Lane as an old flame flickers or as habitual emotional patterns resurface within a current relationship. In any event, there is work to do: Clarify your needs and adjust how you relate to others to improve the overall quality of your interactions.

You are more sensitive these days, with the Sun in imaginative Pisces, joined by cerebral Mercury on **March 8** and Mars on **March 14**. Allowing your compassion for both others and yourself to grow is a part of your current spiritual practice. An analytical Virgo Full Moon on **March 10** activates the long-term Saturn-Uranus opposition, rekindling emotional stress in a work situation. Although expressing your individuality is crucial, don't overplay your hand. The independent Aries New Moon on **March 26** reaffirms your need to be true to your own inner values, as its conjunction with retrograde Venus pulls you closer to your desires, whether or not you are satisfied with your current lot in life.

KEEP IN MIND THIS MONTH

Instead of pushing away experiences that don't match your expectations, remain open to the pleasure of the present moment.

KEY DATES

MARCH 5–6 ★ *smoke and mirrors*

An overpowering cluster of four planets in know-it-all Aquarius may amp the energy so high that you want to head for the hills. Communicator Mercury joins spiritual Neptune on **March 5**, softening the boundary between truth and fantasy. Your aggressive behavior can elicit resistance, and your impatience only exacerbates the situation as assertive Mars conjuncts distressed Chiron. You might have all the information you need, but your emotional IQ lags behind your intellect as loving Venus begin her forty-two-day retrograde on **March 6**. Avoid forming conclusions during this time: Things are not as they appear.

SUPER NOVA DAYS
MARCH 8-12 ★ *great escape*
You may lose confidence as Mars joins nebulous Neptune on **March 8**, the same day that Mercury slips into fuzzy Pisces. You become less certain about your destination but more insistent about getting there as the Sun makes its annual opposition to hardworking Saturn. Fortunately, the discriminating Virgo Full Moon on **March 10** in your 6th House of Work can help you meet your responsibilities and then move on. Optimism replaces despair as sweet Venus sextiles opulent Jupiter on **March 11**, setting the stage for a much-needed breakthrough when the Sun joins volatile Uranus on **March 12**.

MARCH 18-23 ★ *high-wire act*
Intuitive Mercury runs into authoritative Saturn on **March 18** as someone rains on your parade by demanding that you validate your opinions with irrefutable facts. Before you can even make it back to the drawing board, Mercury aligns with electric Uranus on **March 22**, lighting up your mind with one brilliant thought after another. The Sun's entry into fiery Aries on **March 20** marks the Vernal Equinox—a time for you to consciously begin anew. Although a Sun-Pluto square on **March 23** indicates struggle ahead as you take care of your innermost needs, a long-term quincunx between permissive Jupiter and restrictive Saturn on **March 22** suggests that balance may be elusive. It's surely best to take life one step at a time now, even while you keep an eye on the distant horizon.

MARCH 26-28 ★ *cuts like a knife*
The combative Aries New Moon on **March 26** can help you clear the air of whatever continues to hold you back, but you may have to fight for everything you gain. Although fast-talking Mercury in impetuous Aries crosses swords with dark Pluto on **March 27**, you are up for the challenge and are ready for whatever comes next. Be as forceful as necessary now, for your clarity of purpose is strong as the Sun and Mercury align with Venus through **March 28**.

APRIL

IN THE HALL OF MIRRORS

It's hard for you to tell this month whether you're coming or going or just having a déjà vu experience. The culprit is retrograde Venus: She releases strong desires when she squares Pluto on **April 3**, backtracks into wishful Pisces on **April 11**, turns direct on **April 17**, reenters your sign on **April 24**, and then pushes toward repeating her dynamic square with Pluto, which will be exact on **May 2**. At times, you feel like you are relearning all the emotional lessons you once knew. It's a delicate balance between retreating into memories and fantasies, on the one hand, and simultaneously conquering new territory on the other. But your ruling planet, Mars, is in illusory Pisces until **April 22**, so it could be quite a challenge to muster up the energy you need to follow through on your ideas.

The gracious Libra Full Moon on **April 9** offers an opportunity to peer directly into the mirror of relationship to see a clear picture of who you truly are. Remember, however, that Jupiter's influence on this Full Moon may encourage you to focus on the positive aspects rather than seeing where you need to improve. There is nothing wrong with this tactic, for the power of positive thinking can have uplifting effects—as long as you don't deny difficult issues you may need to face. A practical Taurus New Moon on **April 24** gives you enough common sense to realize that you cannot sustain the breakneck speed for long. Additionally, this New Moon is trining potent Pluto, empowering you with another helping of much-needed stamina. Still, complexity returns as aggressive Mars crosses swords in a duel for survival with Pluto on **April 26**, ending the month with the same intensity that opened it.

> **KEEP IN MIND THIS MONTH**
>
> *Don't measure your progress by external standards—you may be sorely disappointed. Instead, focus on your inner experiences, where you'll discover real meaning.*

KEY DATES

APRIL 3–5 ★ *can't get no satisfaction*

Retrograde Venus squares unforgiving Pluto on **April 3**, demanding that you process the rich emotional material buried in your subconscious. Agile Mercury's supportive sextile to buoyant Jupiter on **April 4** enables you to talk about your feelings with greater ease. But Pluto's retrograde turn adds intensity to an already volatile situation. Frustration reaches the boiling point yet may generate no change when aggressive Mars opposes constrictive Saturn. Your best intentions can be thwarted as the Sun quincunxes Saturn on **April 5**. Patience isn't your usual style, but you won't make anything better now by using force.

APRIL 9-11 ★ *sharing secrets*
You cannot contain your emotions around the intense Scorpio Full Moon on **April 9**, so go ahead and express them—you'll feel better. The smooth Sun-Jupiter sextile on **April 10** puts your vision into motion. Then communicator Mercury harmonizes with passionate Pluto on **April 11**, making it easier to talk about even the most private issues. What began as an insurmountable power struggle last week can now be handled with finesse.

SUPER NOVA DAYS
APRIL 15-17 ★ *ride the current*
Your excitement is irrepressible as warrior Mars joins surprising Uranus on **April 15**, presenting you with the chance to vent your pent-up energy and to manufacture enough adrenaline to feel fully alive. Problems arise, however, if circumstances prevent you from acting on your feelings. You may be courting an accident by suppressing your emotions—anger can unconsciously manifest physically if you are careless. Fortunately, a harmonious trine between authoritative Saturn and mentally unflappable Mercury in Taurus on **April 17** gives your thoughts more significance and helps you express them in a clear and matter-of-fact manner.

APRIL 19-24 ★ *make it last*
The Sun leaves your sign and enters the slower world of Taurus on **April 19**, just a few days prior to the New Moon on **April 24**. But Mars storms his way into brash Aries on **April 22**, followed by Venus on **April 24**. This is a powerhouse of a time for you. It will be challenging to maintain an even pace when your world seems ready to break into a gallop.

APRIL 25-26 ★ *love thine enemy*
Contradictions abound as mental Mercury, still in sensible Taurus, squares fanciful Neptune on **April 25**. Meanwhile, assertive Mars dukes it out with potent Pluto in a fight to the finish, exact on **April 26**. Unfortunately, there won't be any winners unless you can work out your differences constructively. The key to success is overcoming your fear and approaching the struggle from a place of love.

MAY

GIVE LOVE A CHANCE

You are surely feeling your oats this month as your ruling planet, Mars, marches his way through your sign, boosting your physical energy level. Additionally, romantic Venus is in Aries throughout the month, increasing your pleasure potential by stimulating your senses to experience each moment as fully as possible. Nevertheless, the month begins as precariously as April ended, with Venus dynamically squaring intense Pluto on **May 2**, dredging hidden fears out of the shadows and into the light of day. You may believe that you should act on your emotions, yet a domineering person might attempt to control you if you do.

Your intensity may scare others away now, because sharp-tongued Mercury in Gemini gains power as it slows down and turns retrograde on **May 7**, returning to determined Taurus on **May 13**. Your words carry extra weight this month, especially when you revisit practical issues that you thought were already resolved. Mercury remains in trickster mode through **May 30**, so keep an eye on all the details. Loose ends can unravel even the best of your plans. The magnetic Scorpio Full Moon on **May 9** can show you just how complicated things are when the simplest task turns into a messy can of worms. Common sense and patience can help you find your way back to the heart of love, but the ultimate solution and happiness may be farther off than you like. The Sun's entry into verbose Gemini on **May 20** and the subsequent Gemini New Moon on **May 24** mark an ideal time to prioritize your goals and to create a clever plan to reach them.

> **KEEP IN MIND THIS MONTH**
>
> *Instead of aiming too high and then feeling discouraged by failure, set realistic expectations that you can meet without throwing your life out of balance.*

KEY DATES

MAY 5–7 ★ *strategic review*

The Sun slides into a reassuring trine with stabilizing Saturn on **May 5**, enabling you to smooth over the rough edges at work and find practical solutions to any emotional turmoil. If you've been thinking about making improvements to your diet or stepping up your exercise program, now is the time. Although you may be ready to take giant steps forward, mental Mercury has other ideas and can stir up a backwash of resistance as it turns retrograde on **May 7**. Remember, the trickster planet's twenty-three-day retrograde phase can frustrate your efforts unless you admit that you aren't as ready to advance as you think. Instead of heightening your stress level by forging ahead, take time to rework your plans and create a more solid base for your future.

MAY 11–12 ★ *count to ten*

You still might struggle to find the elusive balance between unproductive aggression and less productive acquiescence as just-do-it Mars—overactive in your sign now—forms an irritating quincunx with nay-saying Saturn on **May 11**. Communication is the key, with retrograde Mercury stressing feisty Mars on **May 12**. Your impulses are not to be trusted, for they can lead you astray. Calmly think about the potential ramifications of your words before you just blurt out inflammatory accusations. Don't be so stubborn that you turn down a sensible compromise.

MAY 16–20 ★ *fantasy island*

You find yourself drifting in uncharted waters **May 16–20** when both the Sun and retrograde Mercury form squares with abundant Jupiter and dreamy Neptune, widening the gulf between your ideals and the practical world in which you must exist. Nevertheless, open your mind to imagining new goals, even if your actions are currently constrained.

SUPER NOVA DAYS
MAY 24–27 ★ *dream a little dream*

The curious Gemini New Moon on **May 24** forms a tense quincunx with potent Pluto, bringing up issues of insecurity and a lack of confidence. You receive extraordinary strength from energetic Mars as he supportively sextiles Chiron, Jupiter, and Neptune on **May 26**. Pay special attention to your dreams when adventurous Jupiter joins visionary Neptune on **May 27** in the first of three conjunctions—the next occurrences are on **July 10** and **December 21**—that can open your mind far and wide. The danger is in believing that all dreams can come true. Respect the practical limitations of your life, and you can avoid the disappointment that occurs when you chase the pot of gold at the end of one rainbow after another.

JUNE

FOLLOW YOUR DREAMS

You Rams are attracted to action, yet these past months may have been overwhelming with so much emphasis on creative expression and achieving deeper personal satisfaction. Now that the storm has passed, it's time to get down to serious work, rebuild what has been damaged, and solidify the positive changes that have occurred. On **May 31**, self-directed Mars entered earthy Taurus—where he'll remain until **July 11**, slowing you down while giving you unprecedented determination to complete what you've started. Don't worry, the fire of enthusiasm has not died; it's just time to conserve your energy so you aren't exhausted as you step over the finish line. On **June 6** Venus, too, moves into sensual Taurus, where she lingers for the balance of the month. Your desire for simplicity entices you to get back to basics. Although life may not move quickly these days, it is plodding pleasantly forward. Be patient; thoughtful Mercury—still in sensible Taurus until **June 13**—has recently come out of its retrograde phase and will soon be pulling your thoughts into exciting new intellectual territory.

On a deeper note, your dreams are larger than life as boundless Jupiter, visionary Neptune, and healing Chiron remain in a tight triple conjunction throughout the month. But an adventurous Sagittarius Full Moon on **June 7** is constrained by a difficult square with authoritative Saturn, revealing the holes in your current plans. Fortunately, Venus's trine to Pluto ameliorates some of the negativity, showing you the treasures that will be yours if you're willing to delve into your emotions. The Sun enters Cancer on **June 21**, followed by the nurturing Cancer New Moon on **June 22**, reminding you that taking care of your needs is crucial if you hope to support others.

> **KEEP IN MIND THIS MONTH**
>
> *Instead of attempting giant steps toward your goals, settle in to a comfortable pace that you can sustain without depleting your energy.*

KEY DATES
JUNE 2–5 ★ *persistence wins*
Venus harmonizes with the Jupiter-Neptune-Chiron super-conjunction on **June 2**, tinting your fantasies with a rosy glow. On the other hand, the Sun's harsh square to restrictive Saturn on **June 5** can throw up roadblocks that thwart your best intentions. Fortunately, assertive Mars's powerful trine with intense Pluto on **June 3** gives you extra stamina and deepens your physical reserves. There's no time for feeling sorry for yourself—you have plenty of work to do.

JUNE 9–12 ★ *think different*

Mental Mercury's dynamic square on **June 9–10** to the grand conjunction of Jupiter, Neptune, and Chiron has you fretting over your plans if the goals are too unrealistic. But a magical quintile from courageous Mars on **June 11–12** suggests that you can find a new way to solve this old dilemma. You cannot reach your destination unless you're willing to creatively transform the ground rules and approach the problem from an entirely new perspective.

JUNE 14–17 ★ *velvet revolution*

Sweet Venus, right behind Mars, colors your fantasies as she quintiles the Jupiter, Neptune, and Chiron super-conjunction on **June 14–15**. You are more comfortable with the transformation that began over the past few days. The Sun's dynamic square with anything-goes Uranus on **June 17** can mess with communications and twist your process in a totally surprising way. Still, the Sun's trine to the super-conjunction on **June 16–17** assures a positive outcome, as long as you can balance your overly rebellious attitude with a willingness to cooperate with others.

SUPER NOVA DAYS
JUNE 21–22 ★ *angst feeds creativity*

The Summer Solstice on **June 21** and the protective Cancer New Moon on **June 22** are turning points that shift your attention inward. The New Moon opposes passionate Pluto, so the battle between your thoughts and your feelings might be quite strong. The cosmic lovers, Venus and Mars, have traveled the skies in close proximity for the past few weeks. They reach an exact conjunction on **June 21**, indicating great potential for spontaneity, creativity, and romance. Their tense semisquare to the Sun, however, suggests that nerves may be on edge as you try to incorporate your desires into your long-range plans. Fortunately, Venus and Mars harmoniously trine stabilizing Saturn on **June 22**, indicating that self-restraint and common sense will prevail.

JUNE 26 ★ *constructive criticism*

There are no easy answers to complex relationship issues when logical Mercury squares strict Saturn on **June 26**, once again confronting you with the flaws in your thinking. Instead of being discouraged, use this time positively to communicate your needs while listening carefully to the response you receive.

JULY

SURREAL LIFE

Problems surface at the beginning of the month that seem to require your immediate attention, yet it may take several attempts to find your way through the current maze of social issues as your individual will clashes with the needs of others. Overcoming past disappointments by replacing old dreams with new ones is an ongoing theme while joyful Jupiter, idealistic Neptune, and wounded Chiron continue to travel together in your 11th House of Friend and Wishes. Contradictory messages come your way as cautious Mercury swims into emotional Cancer on **July 3**, remaining there until **July 17**. During this phase, you will be more inclined to keep your thoughts to yourself until you truly know how you feel. Yet sweet Venus enters flirtatious Gemini on **July 5** and remains in this easily amused sign for the rest of the month; your desires may pull you all over the place. It's crucial to ground yourself by maintaining the consistency of your daily routine.

The enterprising Capricorn Full Moon Eclipse on **July 7** encourages hard work. However enthusiastic you may be at this time, though, your long-term vision can be unclear as giant Jupiter perfects its conjunction with blurry Neptune on **July 10**. This first of three such alignments impacts the rest of the year, producing dreamy visions of the future that are difficult to manifest. The moody Cancer New Moon Eclipse on **July 21** can temporarily increase your discontent, making you aware of insufficient resources to satisfy your current needs. Scaling back your expectations and delaying big expenditures will help you get through this tight period.

> **KEEP IN MIND THIS MONTH**
>
> *Your dreams loom large enough to distract you from the real work at hand. Nevertheless, don't suppress your imagination even as you work to fulfill your current obligations.*

KEY DATES

JULY 1 ★ *sweet temptation*

Venus squares the Jupiter-Neptune-Chiron super-conjunction as Mercury trines it on **July 1**, highlighting irresolvable differences between your head and your heart. Something doesn't feel right, because it's hard to distinguish the boundaries as you pursue romantic or financial goals.

SUPER NOVA DAYS
JULY 5-7 ★ *surprise ending*
Your key planet, Mars, complicates issues as he squares the imaginative Jupiter-Neptune-Chiron conjunction **July 5–6**. You are distracted with unrealizable fantasies that divert energy from your main purpose. Stress climaxes on **July 7** at the ambitious Capricorn Full Moon Eclipse. Its trine to diligent Saturn, however, allows you to receive credit for your hard work. A crisis may arise as you realize that you've gone too far, too fast, and need to tie up loose ends before moving on. A supportive sextile from assertive Mars to quirky Uranus adds originality and surprise to your plan's execution.

JULY 11-13 ★ *razor's edge*
Mars enters restless Gemini on **July 11**, increasing your curiosity about nearly everything and diverting your focus. The Moon enters Aries on **July 13** while Mercury conjoins the Sun, sharpening your sense of purpose, clarifying your goals, and empowering you to express them. Mars, though, creates an irritating quincunx with dominating Pluto that can provoke a showdown over trivial matters. Stick to core issues to avoid stirring up unnecessary conflict.

JULY 16-18 ★ *risky conversation*
Talking about a difficult issue can get you what you want on **July 16–18**, when Mercury and the Sun trine out-of-the-box Uranus. Express your needs honestly, but remember to consider other people's feelings. It's easy now to become so concerned with yourself that you forget you're not the only one involved, especially with mental Mercury moving into dramatic Leo on **July 17**.

JULY 21-22 ★ *the sun will come out tomorrow*
Valuable Venus dynamically squares austere Saturn during the Solar Eclipse on **July 21**, causing you to wonder if all your effort is really worth it. Fortunately, you can ride the increasing light of the Moon toward enjoyment once the Sun moves into proud Leo on **July 22**. Your spirits will improve as the relentless Leo Sun warms your heart and pushes you into creativity.

JULY 26-28 ★ *unconventional fun*
Starting on **July 26** beautiful Venus trines Jupiter, Neptune, and Chiron, paving the way for smooth sailing, heightened pleasure, and enjoyable company. In contrast, however, Venus's square to Uranus on **July 28** increases tension along with excitement as you push the boundaries of expression to the extreme.

AUGUST

SUMMERTIME BLUES

Although this month brings pleasure, it also presents challenges. A difficult quin-cunx between optimistic Jupiter and realistic Saturn that began on **March 22** comes to its second culmination on **August 19**. This background note sets a tone for the month that may pull you off center when you cannot find the balance point between too much and not enough with respect to both work and play. An inventive Aquarius Full Moon Eclipse on **August 5** can unveil a path through the darkness while giving you the drive to solve a current personal or professional relationship problem. Solutions may be temporary, however, as frustrations build over the days ahead. Your energies may be somewhat scattered now with Mars in flighty Gemini. As he moves toward an uncomfortable square with constrictive Saturn on **August 10**, your drive and enthusiasm seem to run into insurmountable walls.

The playful Leo New Moon on **August 20** gives you a quick chance to catch your breath as you deal with the larger issues of restoring balance to your life. Then nor-mally forceful Mars hesitantly steps into sensitive Cancer on **August 25**, where he remains through **October 16**, taking another layer of edginess off your feelings. Nevertheless, a series of squares and oppositions among Mercury, Mars, and Pluto on **August 25–26** forewarns that your challenges aren't over. Avoid arguments over insignificant differences while staying alert to potential power struggles. Instead of trying to control everything, accept that there may be many ways to reach the same destination. Allowing others personal freedom may prevent an unnecessary escalation of wounded feelings. Protecting your territory may not be as urgent as it seems.

> **KEEP IN MIND THIS MONTH**
>
> *Instead of seeking ultimate solutions, focus your energy on making the present moment work as best you can for everyone involved.*

KEY DATES

AUGUST 1–3 ★ *resistance is not futile*
A tense opposition from innocent Venus to experienced Pluto on **August 1** evokes unexpressed passions, presenting a deeper and darker side of love. Perhaps someone is trying to control you and you are unwilling to yield. Fortunately, Mercury gains power as it moves into analytical Virgo on **August 2**, reaching a har-monious trine with Pluto on **August 3**. This gives you the words to describe those feelings that are usually not easy to talk about.

AUGUST 10–14 ★ *a cautionary tale*

You cannot just charge ahead right now as you Rams often do, for cold Saturn squares red-hot Mars on **August 10** to issue a reality check. It's best to slow down and take the bitter medicine if necessary so you can learn an important lesson along the way. Fortunately, Mars's harmonious trine to buoyant Jupiter on **August 13** corresponds with your waxing optimism. Your enthusiasm might grow so great that nothing can stand in your way; however, the Sun's annual opposition to Jupiter on **August 14** indicates where you may have overestimated your capability or underestimated the amount of work needed to accomplish your tasks.

SUPER NOVA DAYS

AUGUST 15–18 ★ *running down a dream*

Fiery Mars's trine to Chiron the Healer on **August 15** helps you balance your previously inflated expectations with your ability to deliver. But you may be confused by the Sun's opposition to imaginative Neptune on **August 17**, the same day that analytical Mercury joins authoritative Saturn. Your imagination is fed by the dreamy Mars-Neptune trine, but you are able to keep one foot on the ground—not because you want to, but because you know you must. Depending upon your willingness to respond to change, a dynamic square between aggressive Mars and surprising Uranus on **August 18** can either show you a viable escape route from a current problem or unexpectedly turn your world upside down.

AUGUST 20–23 ★ *organized chaos*

The lively Leo New Moon on **August 20** pushes you into a new cycle of creativity, but a high-strung Mercury-Uranus opposition on **August 21** makes it difficult for you to settle down. Venus's trine to unconventional Uranus on **August 22** suggests that you can discover ways to enjoy yourself even if this creates anxiety. Thankfully, the Sun's entry into earthy Virgo on the same day and its harmonious trine to Pluto on **August 23** present you with a logical point of view that can help you smooth your ruffled feathers and motivate you to make efficient changes during the week ahead.

SEPTEMBER

CH-CH-CH-CHANGES

This transitional month can tell you a lot about the effectiveness of your work so far this year while also revealing your options for the next few months. Hardworking Saturn opposes anything-can-happen Uranus on **September 15**, pushing you close to your breaking point. It's a long-term cycle that began last November and finalizes next summer, forcing you to revisit a frustrating situation that you may have faced at its previous occurrence in early February. Perhaps you're in a rut and find your responsibilities and commitments holding you back from making the changes you desire. You may wish to act now, but some things aren't very clear as Saturn forms an annoying quincunx with foggy Neptune on **September 12**, making it difficult to distinguish your fantasies from what's really happening. On the other hand, when opportunistic Jupiter forms a creative biquintile with Saturn on **September 13**, you have the chance to turn a difficult situation into a most fortunate one. Overall, this confluence of planetary activity sets the stage for a month that you will likely remember for a long time to come.

The boundless Pisces Full Moon falling in your 12th House of Spirituality on **September 4** may take the wind out of your sails as it fills your waking life with dreams that have little to do with your real-world obligations. Completing required tasks with efficiency, however, can free up personal time for imagination and faith to broaden your vision of the future. The discriminating Virgo New Moon on **September 18** falls in your 6th House of Daily Routines and conjuncts stern Saturn, making this an excellent time to successfully quit an undesirable habit, start a new exercise regimen, or be more conscious of your diet.

> **KEEP IN MIND THIS MONTH**
>
> *Although you might feel you're at the end of your rope, there is plenty of time to manifest the grand changes you seek.*

KEY DATES

SEPTEMBER 3–6 ★ *crossed signals*

Picky Mercury's dynamic square with energetic Mars on **September 3** can cause communication difficulties through the dreamy Pisces Full Moon on **September 4**. Your psychic intuition is high, yet you can quickly jump to a wrong conclusion. Misunderstandings might provoke angry words if you're unable to hold your temper, as Mercury slows down and turns retrograde on **September 6**. The twenty-three-day period when the messenger planet steps backward can wreak havoc on relationships unless you speak carefully and avoid incorrect assumptions.

SEPTEMBER 9–11 ★ *hold your tongue*

Action-hero Mars creates a sesquisquare with nebulous Neptune on **September 9**, increasing your hesitancy about acting on your feelings. You are likely now to keep a controversial topic to yourself for fear of offending someone you like. But buoyant Jupiter receives both a dramatic kiss from sweet Venus and an irritating wake-up call from the Sun on **September 11**. Ready as you are to take a risk for love or fun, you may have to do some quick backtracking if you overstep any social boundaries.

SUPER NOVA DAYS
SEPTEMBER 15–18 ★ *concrete breakthrough*

The culmination of restrictive Saturn's opposition to breakthrough Uranus on **September 15** can trigger a powerful release of tension, especially if you've been under too much pressure at work. But a magical quintile from forceful Mars to Saturn spurs you to apply what you already know in an entirely new way that can bring an original solution to a previously unsolvable problem. Additionally, loving Venus opposes spiritual Neptune, activating your imagination so you aren't as restrained by reality. Be careful; although this can attract magic and beauty, you may be seeing your world through rose-colored glasses. A series of tense aspects on **September 17** can quickly shake you awake from your fantasies and bring you back down to earth just in time for the practical Virgo New Moon on **September 18**.

SEPTEMBER 22–23 ★ *shock and awe*

The Sun's entry into reflective Libra on **September 22** marks the Autumnal Equinox—a time when you are more likely to see yourself in the mirror of relationships rather than viewing other people simply as extensions of yourself. The Sun squares off with powerful Pluto on **September 23**, evoking possible power struggles within a personal or business partnership. Yet mental Mercury's tense opposition to high-strung Uranus can escalate a quick exchange of disagreeable words into a more uncontrollable exchange. Additionally, feisty Mars's quincunx to judgmental Jupiter might make it difficult to back down once words have been spoken or actions taken.

OCTOBER

LOOK BOTH WAYS

As an Aries, you are usually more concerned with self-expression than with how your actions affect others. This month, however, with planets in relationship-oriented Libra—the Sun until **October 23**, Mercury on **October 9–28**, and Venus joining the pack **October 14**—you focus on everyone but you. The dilemma you face is a familiar one: How do you stay true to yourself while being supportive of other people's desires? The movement of these planets through Libra offers you some much-needed balance as you learn more about successful cooperation. It's crucial that you focus on establishing social harmony, for slow-moving Saturn enters Libra on **October 29**—where it stays until **October 5, 2012**—setting a long-term theme for the next few years. You are required to seriously reevaluate your relationship to the world as you see yourself reflected in the reactions of others. Although such ambitious concerns may be a bit beyond your current thinking, identity issues are now activated that you will be processing for a longtime.

The impetuous Aries Full Moon on **October 4** in your 1st House of Self reinforces your need for independence, while the Sun in your 7th House of Others forces you to take someone else's perspective into consideration. The New Moon in artistic Libra on **October 18** is trine imaginative Neptune, tempting you to repaint the hard, cold facts of reality with the dreamy magic of your fantasies. Although this can be great for personal expression, it may not be as useful for practical planning. A difficult quincunx between assertive Mars and immovable Pluto adds complexity to this otherwise spiritual day. Don't fall prey to fear—yours or anyone else's.

KEEP IN MIND THIS MONTH

You can learn a lot about yourself once you accept that there are at least two ways to look at every situation.

KEY DATES

SUPER NOVA DAY

OCTOBER 4 ★ *quick thinking*

The enterprising Aries Full Moon brings forth a flood of original ideas. Mars harmonizes with rebellious Uranus and communicative Mercury, activating your ability to clearly express your unorthodox thinking. But Mars is also quincunx to fuzzy Neptune, suggesting that you don't know what's best for you in the long term. Still, with analytical Mercury opposing Uranus, talking about what you want is the way to go, even if resolution doesn't come easily.

OCTOBER 8-10 ★ *all over the map*

Mercury in critical Virgo joins authoritative Saturn on **October 8**, making it tough to talk about the same things that were so easy to discuss only a few days ago. Fortunately, sweet Venus opposes erratic Uranus on **October 9**, giving you the impetus to break through any restraints and freely express your desires. Emotions intensify when Mercury crosses swords with potent Pluto on **October 10**. Differences of perspective can escalate into a war of words. Fortunately, the Sun's harmonious trine to Jupiter suggests a positive outcome, enabling everyone to feel some sense of resolution.

OCTOBER 12-13 ★ *real love*

Venus and Mars, the cosmic lovers, tag-team restrictive Saturn on **October 12-13** while warm Venus bumps into Saturn, possibly throwing the cold water of realism on a romantic interest. But Mars's sextile to both Saturn and Venus can indicate the beginning of a meaningful, and enduring relationship—if it has a healthy foundation.

OCTOBER 15-16 ★ *don't back down*

Sweet Venus dynamically squares volatile Pluto on **October 15**, stimulating suppressed feelings and motivating you to demand more of life. Alternatively, a powerful person may require so much from you that you consider walking away from it all. Your key planet, Mars, gains strength as he enters dramatic Leo on **October 16**, encouraging a bold response, firing up your creativity, and turning on your love lights.

OCTOBER 23-24 ★ *only the shadow knows*

The Suns enters magnetic Scorpio and your 8th House of Intimacy and Transformation on **October 23**, deepening your awareness of life's mysteries. Normally, you are more concerned with results than causes, but as the Sun connects with dark Pluto on **October 24**, you grow fascinated with uncovering the hidden truth.

OCTOBER 29 ★ *delicate negotiations*

The Sun-Mars square on **October 29** suggests a day when tempers can flare, but fighting for what you want will not get you any closer to your goal. Instead of engaging in conflict, try to understand the other person's point of view, for Saturn's entry into Libra the Scales today can be a compelling reminder of the usefulness of compromise.

NOVEMBER

INTO THE DEEP

This can be quite an explosive month, yet it also offers the potential for breaking through stubborn resistance—both others' and your own. The interpersonal landscape has shifted now that Saturn the Tester is in your 7th House of Partnerships, forcing you to take relationships much more seriously. Strict Saturn is square omnipotent Pluto throughout the month, underscoring a very tough decision that you must face. This aspect is exact on **November 15** and will repeat on **January 31, 2010**, and **August 21, 2010**, testing you in ways that can be especially demanding, for you are made aware of your limitations without necessarily knowing how to change them. On the positive side, this aspect can supply you with an amazing reservoir of strength, empowering you to overcome even the most difficult obstacles. Still, don't push so hard in your haste to reach your goals that others perceive you as ruthless or selfish.

The stable Taurus Full Moon in your 2nd House of Personal Resources on **November 2** offers a fine antidote for the complexities that arise now with difficult aspects from Mercury, Venus, and Mars to unsettling Uranus. Although you would prefer peace and quiet, you probably won't be able to relax with so much action in your life. The intense Scorpio New Moon on **November 16**—just one day after the hard-core Saturn-Pluto square—trines Uranus and squares Neptune, giving you the information you need to make the best decision. Don't worry if your current choices don't make sense yet; if your course of action feels right, you needn't rationally justify what you are doing to anyone.

> **KEEP IN MIND THIS MONTH**
>
> *Giving up unnecessary luxuries is just one way to conserve resources. Stretching your money while also carefully planning your time can make the difference between failure and success.*

KEY DATES

NOVEMBER 1–2 ★ *shelter from the storm*

Interactive Mercury in secretive Scorpio tensely squares Mars in proud Leo on **November 1**, increasing the potential for verbal sparring, even if there's no substantial basis for disagreement. You are more argumentative than usual, so don't say anything that can be construed as overly aggressive unless you're willing to deal with the consequences. Fortunately, the easygoing Taurus Full Moon on **November 2** is supported by a sweet trine between loving Venus and spiritual Neptune. If the tension of everyday life becomes overwhelming, take some time to remember the higher truths and divine delights that can bring you solace in the midst of a storm.

NOVEMBER 5–8 ★ *strong convictions*

The Sun's conjunction with intelligent Mercury on **November 5** aligns your will and your words, so make use of your increased ability to speak with a sense of purpose. It may be challenging, however, to stay on track, for Mercury and the Sun form tense semisquares with both Saturn and Pluto on **November 6–8**, intensifying a deeper struggle that will continue to build throughout the rest of the year.

SUPER NOVA DAYS
NOVEMBER 14–16 ★ *gut instinct*

You can act with great originality on **November 14** thanks to the Sun's harmonizing trine to innovative Uranus. But the Sun's square to nebulous Neptune on **November 15** can confuse you on the same day that ambitious Saturn squares skeptical Pluto. These energies lead up to an emotional Scorpio New Moon on **November 16** that makes it difficult to trust your judgments unless they are supported by an intuitive hunch.

NOVEMBER 19–23 ★ *relax the rules*

Problems with children may surface when Venus squares Mars on **November 19** in your 5th House of Fun and Games. Unfortunately, it's hard to be nonjudgmental when Venus semisquares Saturn and Pluto on **November 21**, so attempts to overly control kids or to suppress your own inner child can prove tricky. Fortunately, the Sun's entry into philosophical Sagittarius on **November 21** can put you in a friendlier frame of mind. Venus squares excessive Jupiter on **November 23**, enticing you to set your responsibilities aside and indulge your senses. This may be a great time for pleasure, but be careful—it's possible to overdo almost anything.

NOVEMBER 25–26 ★ *overactive imagination*

Your plans for a feast may suddenly swell out of control when Venus trines surprising Uranus on **November 25**. The celebrations will likely work out well with help from a Mercury-Mars trine on **November 26**. A Venus-Neptune square on the same day, however, suggests that you could set yourself up for disappointment by letting your fantasies overrule reality.

DECEMBER

HOLDING PATTERN

Look for a flurry of activity this month—yet you may feel you're heading nowhere fast as events fly by, leaving you in the same place you started. The primary culprit for this apparent lack of forward movement is your key planet, Mars. Although Mars doesn't actually turn retrograde until **December 20**, his motion is virtually frozen in the sky throughout December, locking you in a holding pattern as if you're awaiting further instructions from the control tower. Fortunately, Mars is in Aries-friendly Leo, so it's quite likely that you will be content, as long as you can stay in the present moment. By recognizing that delays may serve a necessary purpose, you can alleviate potential frustration while putting your life in order to make the most of the exciting changes next year. Mars is suspended in a semi-square to restraining Saturn and a sesquisquare to potent Pluto, so it's a smart idea to buckle down and do the work that's expected of you while acknowledging authority and respecting that which you cannot change.

The restless Gemini Full Moon on **December 2** falls in your 3rd House of Communication to speed up the pace of your life: Expect an inbox crammed with noisy e-mail and a phone ringing off the hook. The inspirational Sagittarius New Moon on **December 16** widens your mental horizons so you can visualize your future in a way that is unconventional and exciting, especially because this lunation squares surprising Uranus. An emotional Cancer Full Moon Eclipse on **December 31** provokes mixed feelings as you attempt to balance your need for security with your ambitious plans for the year ahead.

> **KEEP IN MIND THIS MONTH**
>
> *Pay attention to what you can learn from delays or setbacks, rather than trying to prematurely force decisions or push along a process that needs more time to mature.*

KEY DATES
DECEMBER 1–2 ★ *wanderlust*
Venus's entry on **December 1** into fellow fire sign Sagittarius—where she stays until **December 25**—has an uplifting effect on your life, offering the possibility of new friendships or even joyous love. The airy Gemini Full Moon on **December 2** fans the flames of your desire for adventure, with or without someone to share it. Even if very real obstacles stand in your path, don't forget that your positive attitude can turn the tide in your favor.

DECEMBER 7-10 ★ *stretch yourself*

Opportunistic Jupiter joins healing Chiron on **December 7**, filling your vision of the future with idealistic goals, but intelligent Mercury's hard aspects to tough guys Pluto and Saturn could place your dreams just out of reach. Fortunately, an energetic Sun-Mars trine on **December 10** suggests that success will arise from your current creative activities, especially when you focus on the big picture rather than specific details.

DECEMBER 17-21 ★ *the eye of the storm*

A harmonizing trine from sweet Venus to assertive Mars on **December 17** alleviates romantic pressures and enables you to find joy in each moment without striving for more. But the love planet's square to Uranus on **December 19** can raise your anxiety level, making you aware of what you want rather than what you have. This is normally a time to express yourself in unorthodox ways, but Mars's retrograde beginning on **December 20** suggests that things may take longer to gel then you wish. Even so, the Winter Solstice on **December 21** can be a magical time for self-reflection as Venus forms a supportive sextile with the conjunction between joyful Jupiter and dreamy Neptune. Don't let worry or conflict from mental Mercury's irritating quincunx to Mars prevent you from making the most of this moment.

DECEMBER 24-26 ★ *end-of-year review*

The Sun's conjunction with Pluto and its square with Saturn on **December 24-25** reveal a more serious side to the holiday season. Mercury turns retrograde on **December 26**, reemphasizing the frustrating stall in the forward progression of your life. Don't waste precious energy by talking about your problems now; instead, review the shortcomings of your current strategy and patiently work toward improvement.

DECEMBER 28-31 ★ *heart on the line*

Venus joins Pluto and squares Saturn on **December 28-29**, deepening your feelings and urging you to express what you might normally keep to yourself. But you cannot hide anything now, for the needy Cancer Full Moon Eclipse on **December 31** pushes you right to the edge, provoking you to disclose your deepest secrets to gain the confidence of someone you love.

TAURUS

APRIL 20–MAY 20

TAURUS

2008 SUMMARY

It's a year of slow and steady progress that can set the stage for a long time to come. Keep working hard and you should be able to enjoy the fruits of your labor throughout 2008. Give yourself enough time to indulge your senses, but remember that your real struggle this year is no longer about stabilizing your world. With the mundane aspects of your life in working order, it's vital that you don't unconsciously slip into a rut of predictable routines.

AUGUST—*let go of the past*

Stress arrives in successive waves this month, so it's a good idea to relax when you have the opportunity.

SEPTEMBER—*narrow your focus*

You have the chance to manifest your wildest dreams. Graciously accept what is offered without pushing your luck and asking for more.

OCTOBER—*take your time*

You have more time than you think to free yourself from a challenging situation.

NOVEMBER—*caterpillar into butterfly*

Don't rest on your past actions. Creating a simple plan that gets you back to the basics can vastly improve your business and personal relationships.

DECEMBER—*power and pleasure*

Your drive for fame, fortune, or fun can get out of hand unless you practice restraint. Remember, short-term victories won't necessarily assure long-term success.

2008 CALENDAR

AUGUST

TUESDAY 5 ★ Intensity creates results

WEDNESDAY 13 ★ **SUPER NOVA DAYS** Love turns lemons into lemonade

THURSDAY 21 ★ Make positive changes

FRIDAY 29 ★ Rediscover harmony by establishing balance

SEPTEMBER

WEDNESDAY 3 ★ Balance your cautious attitude with an open mind

TUESDAY 9 ★ Save your strength for long-term goals

MONDAY 15 ★ **SUPER NOVA DAYS** Fuel your dreams with reality

MONDAY 22 ★ Journey into your fears is fruitful through the 24th

OCTOBER

SUNDAY 5 ★ Big ideas require hard work through the 7th

FRIDAY 10 ★ You're off the beaten path. Stay open to surprises through the 11th

TUESDAY 14 ★ Aim high! The pleasure is in the journey ahead through the 18th

TUESDAY 28 ★ **SUPER NOVA DAYS** Make intimacy count through the 31st

NOVEMBER

MONDAY 3 ★ **SUPER NOVA DAYS** Be careful of impulsive actions

MONDAY 10 ★ Be true to yourself

SUNDAY 16 ★ Think realistically and success will materialize

THURSDAY 27 ★ Return to common sense and take life seriously through the 29th

DECEMBER

MONDAY 1 ★ Indulge yourself when old investments or efforts pay off

SUNDAY 7 ★ Today is a good day to experiment

WEDNESDAY 10 ★ **SUPER NOVA DAYS** Changes help avoid blowups

SUNDAY 21 ★ Ride your ambition through the 23rd, but stay mindful of others

SATURDAY 27 ★ Look at your assumptions with a beginner's mind

TAURUS OVERVIEW

The stark contrast between your dreams of a more fulfilling future and the demands of daily life can pull you back and forth between hope and surrender this year. Optimistic Jupiter in your 10th House of Career expands your professional horizons with promises of greater responsibility and recognition. **An open-minded attitude is essential to reach these heights, because you're forced out of your comfort zone to encounter new and unconventional ways of doing business.** Jupiter's conjunctions with spiritual Neptune on May 27, July 10, and December 21 reveal creative ways to express your highest ideals through your job. Still, the balloon of hope can float so high that it seems always beyond your grasp. Think of this vision as a model meant to motivate you, rather than a fixed target you must reach to succeed. **You may have to step back from the concrete Taurus sense of reality** that expects tangible results to recognize that simply aspiring to greatness is a significant achievement.

A Solar Eclipse in socially conscious Aquarius activating your 10th House on January 26 is enriched by a conjunction with Jupiter while Venus, your ruling planet, is joined with inventive Uranus. **You may experience a sudden awakening to a totally new professional path.** Yet a Lunar Eclipse in Leo on February 9 opposing nebulous Neptune could trick you into believing in a fantasy that might never come true. Imagine, dream, and hope—but gather and absorb information, analyzing it before committing yourself to radical change. Venus turns retrograde in your secretive 12th House on March 6, giving you a chance to review key relationship issues before the love planet turns direct on April 17. Another Lunar Eclipse in your 10th House on August 5 is supported by a harmonious trine from busy Mars in Gemini, enabling you to take steps in a new direction without abandoning the safety and security of what you've already built.

Saturn, the planet of contraction and limits, is in your 6th House of Employment until October 29, anchoring your aspirations with discipline—or burying them under the weight of petty details and mundane tasks. **It's essential that you operate with greater efficiency on the job and in routine matters to gain enough time to advance your larger interests.** If you match your high hopes with training and dedication, you might even catch that elusive balloon. Hardworking Saturn, though, began a series of tense oppositions with Uranus, the planet of surprise and independence, last November that will repeat on February 5, September 15, and through the summer of 2010. The stress between Saturn sticking to business in practical Virgo and rebellious Uranus in Pisces's yearning for freedom may provoke a desire to give up your ambitions and run away from it all. These aspects are reminders that **you will need breaks from the pressure to perform at a peak level**. Forcing yourself to plod along without taking time off can lead to a breakdown—quitting a job, abandoning your goals, or creating a conflict over control that ends your project.

THOU SHALT PLAY

You can expect a mature, realistic, and responsible approach to love with serious Saturn in your 5th House of Romance through late October. You will benefit by making a concerted effort to enhance your image, but that doesn't come from hard work alone. Having fun gives you a glow that makes you instantly more attractive. Taking time to play is essential for creating space in your heart to give and receive the pleasure you desire. Joy is part of your job now and needs to be on your schedule. Commit to activities that help you feel young, enthusiastic, and expressive. These traits are necessities, not luxuries, if love is to blossom in your life. The downside of Saturn in this part of your chart can be feelings of isolation or emotional fatigue that tempt you to give up on love. Happily, spontaneous Uranus's oppositions to Saturn on February 5 and September 15 should break you out of any funk. Venus's retrograde period of March 6–April 17 is a critical time to reexamine core patterns in matters of love, partnership, and self-worth. Her passage through the haze of your 12th House of Secrets can stir up feelings that you've kept hidden even from yourself. Discovering these needs can challenge you to approach intimacy in new and different ways.

OPPORTUNITY KNOCKS

Generous Jupiter in your 10th House of Status can earn you a higher profile professionally this year. Flexible thinking and being a good team player are keys to taking advantage of this planetary opportunity. No matter how right you believe you are, remain open to alternative views for harmony with colleagues, clients, and even the general public. Success now comes from exploring uncharted waters and permitting inventiveness and intuition to guide you as much as common sense. Jupiter's conjunctions with dreamy Neptune on May 27, July 10, and December 21 might you to Fantasyland, so be careful about the commitments you make. You will be uplifted by your idealism yet so carried away by it that you lose sight of the basic principles that have brought you this far.

NO-SPECULATION ZONE

Over the long term, your finances look reasonably solid. Still, with Jupiter, the ruler of your 8th House of Shared Resources, conjuncting spacey Neptune three times this year, you should avoid speculative investments and unsecured loans. Financially astute Venus, your key planet, is retrograde March 6–April 17, hampering your usually sharp sense of value. Steer clear of large financial commitments during this period. Mercury, the ruler of your 2nd House of Resources, is retrograde May 6–June 30, demanding cautious money management to eliminate any questionable purchases and errors in paperwork.

GENTLE STRETCH

Venus is the planetary ruler of both Taurus and your 6th House of Health and Habits, making her retrograde period of March 6–April 17 one of your most physically vulnerable times of the year. Retreat from the world to rest, recuperate, and focus on your own needs rather than draining yourself with too much work and play. Energetic Mars is in Taurus from May 31 through July 11—a time when you have more energy to burn and increased stamina. A lack of exercise can leave you irritated, but overexertion is counterproductive. Establish a regular pattern of movement that gently stretches your muscles and increases your endurance rather than trying to do too much, too fast.

REASONABLE EXPANSION

You're likely to see big movement at home this summer as two Sun-Moon conjunctions touch the domestic section of your chart. A Solar Eclipse on July 21 forms an expressive trine with innovative Uranus, bringing fresh ideas that make renovation, relocation, or family issues easy to handle. The Leo New Moon on August 20 opposes optimistic Jupiter and fanciful Neptune, dramatizing emotions and stirring your dreams of a grander living place. Fortunately, agile Mars in Gemini's supportive trine to these giant planets guides you to intelligently maneuver through crises and enhance your environment without going overboard.

PLAY IT SAFE

Transformative Pluto's long-term transit of your 9th House of Travel opens you to life-changing journeys this year. A tense Jupiter-Pluto semisquare on March 27 and edgy Mars-Pluto opposition on August 26 could complicate trips, however, so be extra cautious if you are planning to be on the road. Back away from stressful situations that could escalate if you add fuel to the fire. Education, whether formal or not, works best this year when you favor practice over theory. Abstract ideas without direct application can be fascinating, but are not the optimal use of your mental and physical resources.

DEEP DIVING

Psychic activity and spiritual awareness churn into high gear on March 8 when Mars, the ruler of your 12th House of Soul Consciousness, joins otherworldly Neptune. The fiery Aries New Moon in this house on March 26 is in a heated square with intense Pluto, which could help you release deep fears and desires. Bringing them to the surface is healthy if you don't allow them to overpower you. Seek support or step back from the emotional edge if you feel unsafe. Mars sextiles the spiritually rich Jupiter-Neptune conjunction on May 26, opening your heart and soul to inspiring ideas and exhilarating experiences.

RICK & JEFF'S TIP FOR THE YEAR:
When You Win, We All Win

Elevated aspirations, self-discipline, and hard work are your major allies this year. Instead of battling to maintain your present position in life, you might as well aim as high as you can. It won't take much more effort to achieve greatness, so why not go for the biggest prizes you can imagine? A bit of idealism is the secret sauce that can turn your personal desires into reality. Recognizing the connection between your own ambitions and benefits to humanity as a whole turns your individual success into a collective gain. With this picture vividly in mind, you can attract the kind of friendly support that makes even the toughest tasks manageable and pleasant.

JANUARY

PROFESSIONAL REDIRECTION

Expansive Jupiter moves into your 10th House of Career on **January 5**, opening your mind to a broader vision of your professional future. An inspiring idea can nudge you to seek a higher purpose in your present job or expose you to a fresh concept that could lead you into a totally new field. The illuminating Full Moon in sensitive Cancer on **January 10** casts its light on your 3rd House of Information, where facts and feelings mix to intensify conversations and deepen your curiosity. Yet insecurities can trigger arguments where trust has been eroded by uncertainty. Backing off from your habitual emotional reactions can reveal the true source of your behavior and make different choices possible. Communicative Mercury turns retrograde on **January 11**, which can complicate matters at work through the end of the month. Crossed signals, lost data, and equipment failure may be more common, so double-check details to reduce confusion and lost time.

The Sun's entry into intelligent Aquarius and your 10th House on **January 19** can raise your public profile and enhance your leadership status. Adjusting to new responsibilities could be a challenge, especially if you insist on doing everything the old way. Learning new methods isn't easy with Mercury retrograde, but take the time to retrain yourself for more efficiency later on. The Aquarius New Moon Eclipse on **January 26** could turn your work life upside down. Insatiable Jupiter contacts the on-going opposition between restrictive Saturn and independent Uranus on **January 27–30**, which is unlikely to put you in the mood to compromise. The desire to do your own thing could cause conflict with an authority figure. Just have an alternative route to take if you burn any bridges.

> **KEEP IN MIND THIS MONTH**
>
> *Pressuring yourself to act quickly will only push you farther off track. Patience is a slower but surer way to regain control of your life.*

KEY DATES

JANUARY 3-4 ★ *pleasure hunt*

Your ruling planet, Venus, enters spiritual Pisces on **January 3**, softening your heart and touching your soul. Making magic with friends can wash away your worries in a sea of temporary pleasure and delight. Lose yourself in the company of caring pals who ask little of you but are willing to offer so much. A savvy sextile between Venus and potent Pluto on **January 4** gives you the power of gentle persuasion to motivate others in subtle ways. Connections deepen with an easy flow of feelings that draws you closer as you discover hidden treasures and talents in yourself and those around you.

JANUARY 9–11 ★ *ingenious applications*

On **January 9**, the creative power of the Sun aligns favorably with inventive Uranus on its way to a harmonious trine with responsible Saturn on **January 11**. The solar link between these opposing planets gathers up original ideas and flashes of intuition, blending them into a new workable form to start making them real. Mental Mercury's retrograde turn on the **11th**, though, slows down this process of capturing lightning in a bottle. You may have to experiment with a variety of approaches before finding the right formula.

JANUARY 17–18 ★ *all over the map*

Brainy Mercury skids into a 45-degree semisquare with eccentric Uranus on **January 17**, stirring up your nervous system and prompting strange conversations. The intellectual intensity of this high-frequency hookup grows even stronger when gigantic Jupiter brings a wave of information by joining the messenger planet on **January 18**. This union in unconventional Aquarius is enough to overwhelm anyone, especially during Mercury's quirky retrograde period. *Brilliant but erratic* describes the mental landscape as awesome insights mix with totally unrealistic ideas. You're swamped with speculations about future possibilities—just remember that your perception of down-to-earth events could be sketchy now. Stay loose to keep from getting uptight about others' craziness or even your own unusual thoughts.

SUPER NOVA DAYS
JANUARY 22–24 ★ *relationship management*

Vivacious Venus joins electric Uranus on **January 22**, bringing surprises to your style, taste, and relationships. You're restless enough to fire up conflict with an authority figure, so be ready to take bold action if you push issues to the limit. Serious negotiations with a partner or close friend are likely on **January 24**, when Venus opposes strict Saturn. Any tendencies to feel undervalued or hopeless are balanced by assertive Mars receiving supportive aspects from both Venus and Saturn. You'll handle complicated personal business with courage and maturity, reducing conflict and restoring your trust and confidence both in yourself and in those closest to you.

FEBRUARY

A GROWING SENSE OF COMMUNITY

Expect your long-term plans to crystallize when intellectual Mercury turns direct in your 9th House of Big Ideas on **February 1**. This provides a healthy balance between current needs and future possibilities that makes it safe to explore uncharted waters. Structuring Saturn's opposition to eccentric Uranus on **February 5** is the cornerstone of this unconventional month. This is the second in a series that began late last year and doesn't finish until **July 2010**. Still, patterns set now can determine whether you put yourself in a defensive position by digging in your heels and resisting change or find the will to take bold steps to create more freedom in your life. Connecting with friends or groups that motivate you to explore new experiences is an excellent way to move in a positive direction. Active Mars enters Uranus's home sign, Aquarius, on **February 4**, underscoring the importance of stepping out of your comfort zone. His passage through your 10th House of Career signals a need to try different methods if you want to advance professionally.

The Full Moon in lively Leo on **February 9** is a Lunar Eclipse in your 4th House of Home and Family. Emotional excess can trigger drama out of proportion with reality. Imaginative Neptune's opposition to the Full Moon makes it difficult to separate fact from fiction, but it also represents the presence of compassion that can heal all wounds. The spiritual Pisces New Moon on **February 24** warms you with the company of caring friends and inspires you with group activities that build a sense of community. Cultivating common cause with like-minded individuals multiplies your power, enabling you to affect your environment in ways you cannot achieve on your own.

> **KEEP IN MIND THIS MONTH**
>
> *Pushing the limits of your potential can feel awkward at first. That doesn't mean it's the wrong thing to do.*

KEY DATES

FEBRUARY 2 ★ *safety dance*

Your ruling planet, Venus, enters fiery Aries, which tends to bring out your impulsive side—but it's in your 12th House of Escapism, where your decision making may not be at its best. Careless pursuit of pleasure can cost you more than you expect, yet your need for spontaneous fun is very real. Find ways to express this playful side of your personality without risk to yourself, your bank account, or an important relationship.

FEBRUARY 4-5 ★ *negotiating your worth*

Mars's entry into Aquarius on **February 4** sparks an electric power intensified by the Saturn-Uranus opposition on **February 5**—yet both may be cloaked by the dark clouds of personal issues. Venus creates a tense semisquare with the Sun the same day that both planets form challenging aspects to potent Pluto, which can undermine trust and self-worth. Getting what you want from others can be difficult—or the price may be more than you are willing to pay. Either way, it's healthier to discuss your differences than to suffer in silence.

FEBRUARY 11-12 ★ *performance pressure*

Aggressive Mars clashes with Saturn on **February 11** and Uranus the next day, which can put you under great stress. Prioritize your responsibilities, since meeting all of them right now may not be possible. A fuzzy Sun-Neptune conjunction on **February 12** can represent misdirection, where an authority figure leads you astray or you take on a new role without proper preparation. Avoid putting additional tasks on your schedule until you are certain that your current ones are under control.

SUPER NOVA DAYS
FEBRUARY 16-18 ★ *personality plus*

A juicy Venus-Jupiter sextile on **February 16** launches a festival of fast-and-furious fun and productivity. This generous and ego-enhancing aspect is followed by an enterprising conjunction between initiating Mars and visionary Jupiter on **February 17** that brings inventiveness and energy to the workplace. Attractive Venus forms a sweet sextile with Mars on **February 18**, highlighting your social skills and creative abilities. This happy hookup between the lover planets makes it easy to mix work and play; you may seem to be flirting even when you're not. Charm is indeed a powerful force in your personal and professional life, but use it carefully to avoid confusion. The Sun's entry into idealistic Pisces the same day adds another layer of fantasy that potentially blurs boundaries.

FEBRUARY 24-25 ★ *fireside chats*

A brilliant conjunction between Mercury and Jupiter on **February 24** sparks bright ideas and scintillating conversations. Chatty Mercury's favorable sextile with loving Venus on **February 25** helps you turn routine tasks into pleasurable ones and difficult discussions into a caring and constructive exchanges of ideas.

MARCH

RELATIONSHIPS REDUX

You revisit old relationship, financial, and self-worth issues this month, for your ruling planet, Venus, turns retrograde on **March 6** and will continue her reversal until **April 17**. The cycle begins in the forward-leaning sign of Aries, indicating that looking back to the past will probably bring you a fresh perspective on where to go next to find love, pleasure, and approval. Don't defend old positions that no longer suit your current needs. Changing your mind is a sign of intelligence rather than weakness. The discerning Virgo Full Moon on **March 10** falls in your 5th House of Love and Play, which usually opens the door to pleasure. This time, though, stern Saturn conjuncts the Moon while unpredictable Uranus conjuncts the Sun, bringing the long-term opposition of these outer planets into the foreground. Restraint and rebellion battle for control as you find yourself holding back your feelings and then allowing them to explode. Emotional extremes are possible, especially with friends and lovers, so let the dust settle instead of making hasty decisions or shocking ultimatums.

The Sun's entry into enterprising Aries on **March 20** marks the Vernal Equinox, a seasonal shift that illuminates your spiritual 12th House. Retreating from the world—for a month or a minute—offers you a healthy balance, reducing the stress of daily life. The freshness of the Aries New Moon on **March 26** is tainted by a tense square from Pluto. The challenging presence of this transformational planet can evoke power struggles that are more about learning to let go than gaining control. Pluto's riches come from eliminating what's no longer needed so you can clear a space for New Moon seeds to take root and grow.

> **KEEP IN MIND THIS MONTH**
>
> *The most important work you do this month is inner and private. Give yourself enough time alone to do it well.*

KEY DATES

SUPER NOVA DAYS

MARCH 6-8 ★ *unchecked idealism*

Protect yourself during these tender times as Venus's retrograde turn on **March 6** is followed by a vulnerable Mars-Neptune conjunction on **March 8** in your 10th House of Career and Public Life. You can exhaust yourself trying to complete impossible tasks. Ask for help if the burden is too great, rather than pushing ahead without the support you need. The Sun's opposition to rigid

Saturn and Mercury's entry into visionary Pisces increase your sense of obligation without the benefit of a practical point of view. Still, it's fine to aim high as long as you keep your feet on the ground.

MARCH 14 ★ *fork in the road*

Relationships can take a rocky turn when sweet Venus forms a cranky semisquare with assertive Mars just before the warrior planet enters passive Pisces. An unsettled mood that shifts between aggression and surrender is complicated by the Moon's passage through your 7th House of Partnerships. Dealing intelligently with strong feelings, though, can be the catalyst that either strengthens a current connection or shows you that it has reached its limit.

MARCH 18-19 ★ *finely tuned machine*

Expect serious conversations with talkative Mercury opposite disciplined Saturn on **March 18**. Colleagues may be demanding and friends less than friendly as you feel pressed to solve problems on your own. Fortunately, a potent Mars-Pluto sextile on **March 19** helps you eliminate distractions and operate at a very high level of efficiency to cut a big task down to an easily manageable size.

MARCH 22 ★ *a glimpse of tomorrow*

Wild ideas and intellectual impulsiveness prove exciting, but not necessarily practical. A mentally charged conjunction of Mercury and Uranus cranks up originality while tense aspects from the Sun to expansive Jupiter and Venus to boundless Neptune replace reality with grand dreams and fantasies. A slippery quincunx between hopeful Jupiter and doubting Saturn reflects the difficulty of making big plans stick. Theorizing and speculating, however, widen the landscape of future possibilities, even if you're not ready to manifest them now.

MARCH 27-28 ★ *sweet persuasion*

You see your beliefs challenged on **March 27** with an uncomfortable semisquare between Jupiter in idealistic Aquarius and Pluto in skeptical Capricorn. It's best not to get bogged down in philosophical, political, or religious debates, since emotions are much stronger than reason. Mercury squares Pluto and semisquares Jupiter to intensify your desire to prove your point. Pressure only increases resistance though, so seek a more diplomatic way to influence others. Happily, gracious Venus forms conjunctions to the Sun on **March 27** and to Mercury on **March 28**. Pay attention when she shows you how to avoid conflict by applying charm, not force, to convey your message.

APRIL

PLEASURE PRINCIPLE

Intense feelings complicate the first weekend of the month as expressive Venus in Aries squares potent Pluto on **April 3**, one day before the tiny, distant planet turns retrograde. A fierce face-off between go-for-it Mars and no-go Saturn on **April 4** ratchets up tension. The slightest delay or alteration in plans can trigger fears out of proportion with the situation. You may in fact be sensing deeper issues about trust, safety, and intimacy that are better expressed dramatically than shoved back into the closet of denial. Mental Mercury's entry into dependable Taurus on **April 9** supports objective thinking and clear communication that adds authority to anything you say. The Libra Full Moon on the same day falls in your 6th House of Work and Service, highlighting imbalances that are undermining business relationships. However, optimistic Jupiter's happy trine to the Full Moon should bring you enough recognition, or hope for professional advancement, to keep you from feeling undervalued.

The Sun enters sensual Taurus on **April 19** to begin your season of birthday celebration. The sweet self-indulgence of your sign is worthy of a monthlong party for the senses. Yet solar pride and courage bring out your confident side, so put down the Ben & Jerry's to impress others with your boldness and creativity. The Taurus New Moon on **April 24** brings newfound awareness of your untapped inner resources. A dynamic trine from deep-diving Pluto to this Sun-Moon conjunction balances any Taurus tendency toward laziness with a desire to make the most of yourself. Travel, training, and education are ways to transform potential talents into practical tools for personal and professional growth.

> **KEEP IN MIND THIS MONTH**
>
> *Follow your heart's desire and you can find diamonds of ability in yourself that simply need time and attention to fully develop.*

KEY DATES

APRIL 3-4 ★ *at the crossroads*

The rising emotions of romantic Venus stressed by demanding Pluto reveal deep layers of dissatisfaction on **April 3**. However, learning what doesn't work in your life can be a powerful first step toward meaningful change. Pluto's retrograde turn and the unrelenting Mars-Saturn opposition on **April 4** mark the end of one road and the beginning of another. Fortunately, an inventive sextile between fast-moving Mercury and philosophical Jupiter gives you the clarity to speak the truth without anger or guilt.

APRIL 9-11 ★ *realistic nostalgia*

Thoughts turn serious as Mercury enters your sign and makes a challenging sesquisquare with Saturn on **April 9**. Expect difficulty with details and a need to explain yourself slowly to be understood. Your mood brightens with a generous Sun-Jupiter sextile on **April 10**, pulling you out of the shadows and into the spotlight. Venus backpedals into sensitive Pisces on **April 11** to reawaken old romantic dreams and reconnect you with friends and groups who inspired you in the past.

APRIL 15-17 ★ *take a deep breath*

A shocking Mars-Uranus conjunction in your 11th House of Friends and Associates on **April 15** stirs rebellion in the ranks and spawns surprises. Trying to put a lid back on the situation will only build up even more steam, possibly leading to a major explosion. Overcome your instinct to stifle change and allow as much movement as you can stand. Venus turns direct on **April 17** while strained by a semi-square from Mercury. Hypersensitivity can make innocent comments feel like major criticism, so it's wise to step back before responding.

SUPER NOVA DAYS
APRIL 21-24 ★ *burning love*

Magnetic Venus meets passionate Mars in the last degree of psychic Pisces on **April 21**, and game playing becomes almost unavoidable. Flirting and teasing are too delicious to stop unless you invest this energy in a creative project instead. Mars rams into bold Aries on **April 22**, turning the heat up another notch before finally boiling over when Venus returns to the fire sign on **April 24**. You bubble with intensity during this sizzling time, swinging from extreme attraction to total rejection. Stay in the moment to keep things from getting out of hand. Consider this a free zone in which you have the right to explore without having to justify your behavior.

APRIL 26 ★ *damage control*

Playtime is over as a deadly serious Mars-Pluto square sets the cost of carelessness too high. Put away distracting thoughts and focus on taking care of the essential business at hand. There is some vital cleaning up for you to do, and it can't wait until tomorrow.

MAY

LOOKING BACK ONE MORE TIME

Mercury—keeper of messages and master of details—turns retrograde on **May 7** in your 2nd House of Resources, which can lead to some backtracking on monetary matters. Avoid signing important papers or making significant financial investments until this Trickster turns direct on **May 30**. The passionate Scorpio Full Moon on **May 9** turns up the heat in your 7th House of Partnerships. A pushy square from strident Jupiter can overburden you at work or exaggerate philosophical differences with your other half. However, supportive aspects from solid Saturn and unorthodox Uranus add stability and originality, bringing a breath of fresh of air and broadening the horizons of relationships.

On **May 13**, retrograde Mercury returns to Taurus, where it will stay until **June 13**. Its second visit to your sign gives you a chance to review recent decisions from a new perspective. Yet your fixed Taurus nature could lead you to simply dig in your heels and resist the new and strange. Notice whether you're reacting out of habit or standing up for a principle that's worth defending. Saturn turns direct on **May 16**, typically a good time to put plans into action. It's probably best to wait until skillful Mercury also goes direct next month, though, before making any serious commitment. The restless Gemini New Moon on **May 24** is a lively lunation that opens your mind to alternative sources of income and underdeveloped talents. Acquiring education to elevate your earning potential is a wise investment. Purging Pluto's crunchy quincunx to this multifaceted Sun-Moon conjunction is a reminder to focus on one subject at a time.

> **KEEP IN MIND THIS MONTH**
>
> *A flexible mind reduces friction and opens the door to possibilities that are easy to miss if you're stubborn.*

KEY DATES

MAY 2 ★ *insatiable hunger*

A heart-wrenching Venus-Pluto square can drive you to the depths of your feelings. Disappointment may spew out dramatically, but connecting to your core desires also helps you reach a new level of intimacy. Letting go of someone or something you want is difficult, but well worth it if it leads you to the closeness you crave.

MAY 11–12 ★ *spunky speech*

Feisty Mars tangles with Saturn in an awkward quincunx on **May 11** and a scrappy semisquare with Mercury on **May 12**. The warrior planet wants to rush ahead in impulsive Aries, yet the constraints of his passage through your 12th House of Endings may test your patience. Argumentative individuals give you easy targets for your frustration—but unless you enjoy fighting, it's probably a waste of time. Speak clearly and simply to reduce complications, and avoid roundabout conversations that lead you nowhere you want to go.

MAY 14-15 ★ *pleasure without limits*

Vivacious Venus puts you in a spending mood with a semisquare to extravagant Jupiter on **May 14**. Dreams of luxury and romance may cause you to overestimate the value of someone or something. Venus forms the same unstable aspect with idealistic Neptune on **May 15** to continue this impractical theme. Still, a greater vision of love, creativity, and pleasure can lift your spirits and stir your imagination. Fantasies of a more rewarding future motivate you to work harder for a bigger payoff down the road.

SUPER NOVA DAYS
MAY 20-23 ★ *idealism and achievement*

Venus runs into a bruising quincunx with Saturn on **May 20** that can put the brakes on fun as you are blocked by overly conservative authority figures. Happily, the Sun's entry into lighthearted Gemini and Mercury's optimistic square with Jupiter provide distraction that quickly overcomes disappointment. Intellectual Mercury's savvy sextile with innovative Uranus on **May 21** reveals shortcut solutions to unresolved issues that are brilliant in their simplicity. Self-conscious Venus in Aries makes a tough semisquare with the Sun on **May 22** that can exaggerate your insecurities, but could also provide a more objective view of your assets. Wise and generous Jupiter joins Chiron in your 10th House of Career on **May 23**, blessing you with a way to combine idealism and material success.

MAY 31 ★ *yours for the taking*

Macho Mars enters your sign to fire you up with energy and enthusiasm for the next six weeks. Use this power to advance your interests rather than wasting it in a defensive mode. This is your time to take the lead—but don't forget that practicality and patience will produce tangible results.

JUNE

SWEET TALK

This month bursts with special sweetness as lovely Venus, your ruling planet, enters sensual Taurus on **June 6**. Her annual visit to your sign enhances your capacity for pleasure and casts you in a more attractive light. Take the time to enjoy the delights available to you now. The Full Moon in outgoing Sagittarius on **June 7** falls in your 8th House of Intimacy, which can encourage boldness in your personal life. Stern Saturn, however, forms a tense square to this Sun-Moon opposition, penalizing risky behavior. Stretching your boundaries and speaking the truth are powerful ways to widen the road to love, but carefully choose the time and place for your revelations so that others feel safe enough to truly hear what you have to say. On **June 13**, chatty Mercury zips into its airy home sign of Gemini, where it starts spilling fresh ideas into your 2nd House of Money and Resources. New insights for earning money arise easily but require focus and long-term commitment to turn concept into reality.

Giant Jupiter stops its forward motion and turns retrograde on **June 15**, beginning four months of backpedaling in your 10th House of Career. This doesn't have to block professional advancement, but tells you to assimilate any gains and new duties slowly before you forge ahead. Handling what you already have on your plate is the best way to make a positive impression. The Sun enters Cancer in your 3rd House of Communication on **June 21**, marking the Summer Solstice and warming you up for more personal conversations that draw you closer to others. The protective Cancer New Moon on **June 22** opposes transformational Pluto, stirring deep feelings that could alter your long-range plans.

> **KEEP IN MIND THIS MONTH**
>
> *Putting pleasure first is not self-indulgent now; it's the best way to nourish yourself and raise your abilities to their highest potential.*

KEY DATES

JUNE 2 ★ *touched by angels*

Beautiful Venus brings a bit of heaven down to earth with her harmonious sextiles to the close conjunction of Jupiter, Neptune, and Chiron. The high ideals of this three-planet cluster come alive with spontaneous intuitive insights, instant spiritual connections, inspired art, and the gift of immediate gratification. You sense that everything you want and need is already present, bringing joy to even the most ordinary tasks and elevating your routine to rapture.

SUPER NOVA DAYS
JUNE 6-8 ★ *testing relationships*
Venus's entry into Taurus should begin a period of ease and grace, but strict Saturn has some tests for you to pass before letting you climb aboard the gravy train. This hard-nosed planet forms a challenging sesquisquare to Venus on **June 6**, indicating self-doubt and delays before pleasure is served. Its purpose is to help you define your worth and be clear about what you expect from others. The Full Moon on **June 7** is square Saturn, continuing the demand for clarity in relationships. Venus's square to the Moon's Nodes also reflects a need to alter the ways you connect with others if you are not being true to yourself. A potent trine between Venus and regenerative Pluto on **June 8**, however, helps you cut past superficial issues and get to the heart of the matter, offering satisfaction that may have seemed out of reach before.

JUNE 16-17 ★ *shifting terrain*
Surprises and secrets may shake your confidence in others with an erratic Mars-Uranus semisquare and a grumpy Mercury-Pluto quincunx on **June 16**. The expressive Sun's creative trines with Neptune and Jupiter on **June 17** provide inspiration for happier days. Patience may be lacking, though, as the Sun squares and Venus semisquares volatile Uranus, bringing personal issues to a boil. Avoid impulsive actions unless they provide brilliant solutions or real breakthroughs that excite you with a newfound sense of freedom.

JUNE 21-23 ★ *push and pull*
Romantic Venus conjoins with passionate Mars on **June 21** while also forming a stressful semisquare with the Sun. You can expect a playful and seductive mood, although your insecurity can make anything less than total acceptance feel like rejection. Fortunately, a stabilizing trine between Venus and Saturn on **June 22** helps you create balance and reason to counter emotional extremes. A constructive Mars-Saturn trine the same day exhibits your competence, reliability, and leadership potential. Yet crunchy sesquisquares from Venus and Mars to dark Pluto on **June 23** can evoke jealousy and undermine trust. Seek an opportunity for a private heart-to-heart conversation to work through differences before they get out of hand.

JULY

EXPLORATION AND EXPERIMENTATION

Eclipses often mark unexpected changes, but the two this month appear to be well mannered and easily managed. A **July 7** Lunar Eclipse in businesslike Capricorn and your 9th House of Big Ideas could put a crimp on plans for travel or education. However, solid Saturn forms a stabilizing trine to the Moon, giving you a handle on the situation, even if you're in unfamiliar territory. Then a Solar Eclipse in sensitive Cancer on **July 21** touches your 3rd House of Information. This would normally scramble messages or complicate details, but innovative Uranus forms a trine to the Sun-Moon conjunction, spurring intuitive answers to resolve problems in unexpected ways. Discussing delicate personal matters may prove less difficult than you anticipate, freeing you to be more emotionally honest and vulnerable.

Intellectual Mercury's shift into watery Cancer on **July 3** adds feeling to every thought and conversation, yet Venus and Mars move into airy Gemini on **July 5 and July 11** to favor playfulness and flexibility. While you may display a more flirtatious attitude, you're probably not as carefree as you seem. Mentally, you are mindful to stay within safe boundaries even as you taste different experiences and explore novel styles of expression, opening you to new people and pleasures. Joyful Jupiter joins compassionate Neptune on **July 10** and healing Chiron on **July 22** to reinvigorate imagination and faith in the second of a series of conjunctions that began in late May and finishes in December. Their union in idealistic Aquarius expands your professional horizons with a sense of higher purpose, motivating you to make a more meaningful contribution to society.

> **KEEP IN MIND THIS MONTH**
>
> *Experimenting with different ways to work, play, and love is not a sign of uncertainty, but one of self-confidence and trust.*

KEY DATES

SUPER NOVA DAYS
JULY 1–2 ★ *in the lap of luxury*
Venus makes a stressful square with imaginative Neptune on **July 1** that clouds your judgment. Avoid self-sacrifice for love, and beware careless purchases that don't offer a fair return on your investment. Mercury's trines to Jupiter and Neptune make for inspiring conversation, but a sudden communication breakdown is possible as erratic Uranus also squares the

messenger planet. The square on **July 2** between pleasure-loving Venus and abundant Jupiter can lead you to indulge or overestimate yourself. Luckily, an insightful Venus-Uranus sextile gives wiser paths to pleasure.

JULY 6-7 ★ *chasing rainbows*
Avoid overcommitting yourself right now, especially at work. With assertive Mars squaring squishy Neptune and extravagant Jupiter on **July 6**, chasing illusions or stretching yourself too far can undermine your credibility. Venus's quincunx with Pluto the same day reminds you to be selective in your personal and professional choices. You can't satisfy everyone at the same time, so make your priorities clear. The strategic Capricorn Full Moon Eclipse on **July 7** helps you let go of old ambitions that don't correspond with your current needs, while a Mars-Uranus sextile can connect you with a clever colleague to produce original work.

JULY 14-16 ★ *verbal dodgeball*
A clunky quincunx between Mars and Pluto on **July 14** brings unfinished business to the surface in less-than-gracious ways. Whether you are the target or want to vent your own feelings, it takes a cool head to keep emotions from veering off course and becoming destructive. Mercury and Jupiter also form a quincunx on **July 15**, fomenting exaggeration that complicates communication. Happily, common sense arrives on **July 16** with the Moon in Taurus and a brilliant Mercury-Uranus trine to spark your intuition. Still, Mercury's tense semisquare to Venus suggests that personal opinions tend to touch soft spots, so be gentle when sending and sterner when receiving.

JULY 21-22 ★ *the price of love*
A tough Venus-Saturn square on **July 21** tests both your relationships and your self-worth, but you will gain much more than you lose if it forces you to be more specific about your desires and values. The Sun's entry into expressive Leo and conjunction with the karmic Lunar South Node on **July 22** may provoke a family drama, yet events also arouse your inner child and warm your heart with playfulness.

JULY 27-28 ★ *boundless joy*
Venus trines lucky Jupiter on **July 27** and Neptune on **July 28**, expanding feelings of hope and faith and enriching relationship and financial prospects. However, a square from Venus to Uranus on the **28th** requires flexibility if you are to adapt to rapidly changing conditions and turn an unexpected problem to a source of pleasure.

AUGUST

OPEN YOUR HEART

Venus entered protective Cancer on **July 31** and opposes passionate Pluto on **August 1** to get the month off to an emotionally charged start. Fortunately, mental Mercury enters its earthy home sign, Virgo, on **August 2** to balance strong feelings with rational thinking. This combination is ideal for discussing delicate issues, especially about love and money. The Full Moon in futuristic Aquarius on **August 5** is a Lunar Eclipse falling in your 10th House of Career, placing the relationship between home and work on the front burner. If your public responsibilities leave little time for a personal life, you're likely to feel the stress now. Mars, the action planet in adaptable Gemini, is trine the Full Moon, however, suggesting alternative methods to meet your obligations that help you avoid a crisis.

You're hard-pressed to resist overexpansion when Mars trines Jupiter on **August 13** and the Sun opposes Jupiter on **August 14**. Such enthusiasm is admirable, but the sense of enterprise and adventure you feel works best when you apply it slowly over time, rather than all at once. Binge shopping, eating, exercising, and romance can be fun but are likely to leave you dissatisfied in the end. The New Moon in generous Leo on **August 20** lights up your 4th House of Home and Family to bring joy, drama, and creative impulses to your household. Its oppositions to expansive Jupiter, compassionate Chiron, and imaginative Neptune enrich your personal life with greater spiritual awareness and inspire your professional life with a more fulfilling sense of purpose. Muscular Mars supports this Sun-Moon conjunction with an energetic sextile to turn great ideas into positive action.

> **KEEP IN MIND THIS MONTH**
>
> *Brightening up your home and enhancing your family life inspire and motivate you to also act more creatively outside the house.*

KEY DATES

AUGUST 1–2 ★ *attitude adjustment*

An opposition from self-conscious Venus to inscrutable Pluto on **August 1** exposes flaws in relationships and uncertainty in yourself. Talking with a supportive person helps you express your concerns without fear of criticism. Once you expose your feelings, it's time to move on and turn worry into action. Mercury's entry into your 5th House of Romance and Self-Expression on **August 2** is excellent for this purpose. Clear thinking reveals a road map to repairing a broken heart or the means to demonstrate your creative abilities with skillful precision.

AUGUST 9–10 ★ *tender and tough*

Venus's sesquisquare to Neptune on **August 9** draws you into tasting a world of fantasy much sweeter than reality can provide. Take inspiration from a magical vision of love, beauty, and delight, but hold on tight to your heart or wallet to avoid an expensive misadventure. Sobering Saturn squares Mars on **August 10**, throwing up barriers of restraint and responsibility that put an end to your illusions. However, if a dream is worthy, this is the day to find the focus and commitment to start working toward its realization.

AUGUST 17–19 ★ *rebel without a cause*

A Mercury-Saturn conjunction on **August 17** demands that you pay attention to details, but a fuzzy Sun-Neptune opposition can leave you focusing on the wrong issue. Don't confuse effort with efficiency when a wobbly Mercury-Jupiter quincunx casts bread crumbs on a false trail. Intuition may work better than facts, as a Mars-Neptune trine guides you accurately if you follow your instincts. Electric Uranus throws off sparks with a square to Mars and quincunx to the Sun on **August 18**, provoking a sudden outburst of anger or an urge to rebel. Free yourself to try new techniques and explore unconventional methods. Venus forms a constructive sextile with mature Saturn and a shaky quincunx with Jupiter on **August 19** that contrasts steady values and common sense with a tendency toward excess.

SUPER NOVA DAYS
AUGUST 26–28 ★ *decision time*

Venus conjuncts the karmic Lunar South Node before roaring into rowdy Leo on **August 26**, creating a perfect storm for relationship drama when unfinished business from the past clashes with your need for affection and recognition right now. A powerful Mars-Pluto opposition increases the potential for conflict due to unwillingness to compromise. Yet if you can stick to the core issue, you have the strength to overcome almost any obstacle. The key question is whether to hold on to someone or something that no longer satisfies you. A Venus-Pluto quincunx on **August 27** increases pressure but finally, on **August 28**, Mercury comes to the rescue, providing much-needed perspective and the ability to discuss delicate matters with intelligence and grace.

SEPTEMBER

Advancing your romantic and creative abilities is on the agenda this month with planets lighting up your 5th House of Self-Expression. The courageous Sun's presence through **September 22** is ideal for taking calculated risks that reveal both your feelings and your talent. Your key planet, Venus, enters this house on **September 20** to further encourage your playful side and refine your capacity to attract others with charm and grace. The emotional Pisces Full Moon in your social 11th House on **September 4** contrasts responsibilities to friends and groups with your own personal interests, but could also inspire you to participate in an humanitarian or political cause. Communicative Mercury turns retrograde in your 6th House of Work and Service on **September 7** and will remain in reverse until **September 29**. Complications on the job require more concentration and time at work, but revising your exercise and diet will ensure good health.

Strict Saturn makes its third opposition to independent Uranus on **September 15**, upping the tension between your need for control and the rebellious behavior of others. The fussy Virgo New Moon on **September 18** can make your desire for order even stronger, yet its conjunction with Saturn and opposition to Uranus demand compromise. Any attempt to dominate will spur strong reactions; respect everyone's free will to maintain harmony. The Sun's entry into fair-minded Libra on **September 22** marks the Autumnal Equinox, enabling you to overcome extreme positions and reach the common ground where you can work well with others. Still, the Sun's square with intense Pluto and Mercury's high-frequency opposition to Uranus on **September 23** could put reason on the sidelines as buried feelings explode in strong words and rash actions.

> **KEEP IN MIND THIS MONTH**
>
> *Progress, rather than perfection, should be your measure of success, for even baby steps will advance your interests.*

KEY DATES

SEPTEMBER 2–4 ★ *sweet anticipation*

Your confidence dips when Venus forms a semisquare with stifling Saturn on **September 2**. You can overcome a feeling of being underappreciated with some discipline and patience that will earn you respect. A tight Mercury-Mars square on **September 3** triggers fast thinking and snappy comments that can rile sensitive co-workers. With an itchy Venus-Uranus semisquare on **September 4**, avoid a rush to judgment; a more open-minded approach may take you to unexpected delights.

SEPTEMBER 11–12 ★ *the road of excess*

An expansive Venus-Jupiter opposition on **September 11** can put you in the mood to love excessively and spend lavishly. Enjoy some self-indulgence, but don't completely lose touch with reality. An irritating semisquare between retrograde Mercury and Venus on **September 12** awakens unfinished relationship issues. Reviewing the past is helpful as long as it provides a healthy perspective that keeps you from repeating the same old story.

SUPER NOVA DAYS
SEPTEMBER 15–17 ★ *rider on the storm*

The deep divide between duty and freedom revealed by a Saturn-Uranus opposition on **September 15** comes at a very sensitive time, with Venus opposite Neptune. This idealistic but vulnerable connection makes for tender feelings better suited to romance and spirituality than confrontation. You may want to run away from the harsh realities of the present, and certainly can benefit from some time to relax. However, a failure to address serious issues now may prove costly later. An unsettled Venus-Uranus quincunx on **September 16** feeds frustration and can give you even more reason to flee. Yet if you are willing to let go of fixed expectations and rigid values, you might discover unexpected pleasure or a surprising solution. **September 17** looks like a day of extremes with the Sun opposing Uranus and joining Saturn. A menacing Mercury-Pluto square can undermine trust and trigger power struggles, but the messenger planet then backs into logical Virgo, bringing you the tools to untangle a knotty situation.

SEPTEMBER 20–21 ★ *constant gardener*

Venus enters earthy Virgo on **September 20**, helping you create a garden of joy. You can make beauty bloom like flowers in the desert and bring happiness to those nearby. Venus also forms a productive trine with resourceful Pluto, which empowers you to transform awkward moments into pleasant ones and extract what you need under almost any conditions. This harmonious aspect deepens relationships with controlled passion that produces lasting delight. Connections with others may be less smooth on **September 21** when aggressive Mars rubs against Venus in an irritating semisquare. However, the forces of Eros are rising to turn an ordinary day into a sassy and sensual time.

OCTOBER

ON-THE-JOB TRAINING

The process of redefining your professional life begins this month as successful Jupiter goes direct in your 10th House of Career on **October 12.**This vocational emphasis is reinforced when disciplined Saturn enters your 6th House of Work and Service on **October 29**. Jupiter expands your vision and increases opportunities for greater recognition and more fulfilling responsibilities. Saturn suggests that additional training may be required to achieve these potentials. Several planets in relationship-oriented air signs underscore your ability to work with others as a critical element to reaching your goals. The impatient Aries Full Moon on **October 4**, however, stirs hidden desires—perhaps even an urge to run away from it all. This is a reminder of how important it is to take breaks from the stresses of daily life. A relaxing hobby, physical activity, or spiritual pursuit with no connection to your job is a not a waste of time, but an essential factor in maintaining good health and productivity.

Domestic challenges are possible when assertive Mars enters brash Leo and your 4th House of Home and Family on **October 16**, followed by a testy quincunx with Pluto on **October 18**. You can turn dramatic emotions in a constructive direction by clearing out unneeded objects and outdated attitudes that stand in the way of making your living space more reflective of your highest values. The gracious Libra New Moon, also on **October 18**, forms a forgiving trine with sympathetic Neptune, helping you release past grievances and become more open to cooperative alliances on the job. Your feelings of insecurity, or those of your co-workers, can be significantly reduced if you step back and take a strategic approach rather than allowing your immediate impulses to rule.

> ### KEEP IN MIND THIS MONTH
>
> *Your support and loyalty to others build a reserve of goodwill that is well worth the sacrifice of your time.*

KEY DATES

OCTOBER 4 ★ *reckless fun*

Electric Uranus is giving you an itch for excitement with its opposition to mental Mercury and trine to active Mars. Fast thinking and unconventional experiences can bring thrills you don't usually seek. But measure the costs, because your values may be skewed by an overly optimistic Venus-Jupiter quincunx and your physical judgment blurred with Mars forming the same unstable angle with illusory Neptune.

OCTOBER 8-9 ★ *watch your step*

A strict Mercury-Saturn conjunction on **October 8** is excellent for making a clear statement as long as it's all fact and no fluff. If you are uncertain about specific details, hold your tongue until you find the right answer. Sensible Venus in Virgo drops the usual social and financial rules on **October 9** with her opposition to shocking Uranus and a quincunx with dreamy Neptune. New sources of delight can spice up your life, yet restlessness can shake a relationship or lead to a questionable purchase.

SUPER NOVA DAYS
OCTOBER 13-15 ★ *rise to the challenge*

A restraining conjunction between Venus and Saturn on **October 13** can put you in a serious mood. The purpose, though, is not to eliminate pleasure but to make you clarify what you want and what you're willing to do to get it. Don't complain if you feel undervalued; instead, commit to developing your talents to their full potential. Venus enters artful Libra and your 6th House of Skills on **October 14**, bringing grace to the workplace, along with ideas for polishing your creative gifts. However, a square between Venus and intense Pluto on **October 15** challenges you to dig deeply within yourself to find what you need. Relationship resentment is possible, but it's only a problem if you refuse to make any changes.

OCTOBER 23-24 ★ *relationship repair*

The Sun enters passionate Scorpio on **October 23** and sextiles intense Pluto on the **24th**. The healthy alignment of this powerful pair deepens relationships, helping you deal with touchy subjects more effectively to regain trust and restore self-confidence.

OCTOBER 28-29 ★ *play nice*

Be sociable on **October 28** as talkative Mercury enters into your 7th House of Relationships while Venus forms a sweet trine with upbeat Jupiter. Make time for a little midweek partying or a shopping spree with friends to celebrate. On the other hand, a tense Sun-Mars square on **October 29** can incite conflict with a controlling person. Avoid locking down in a battle of wills that can wear you out. Use the pressure you feel to push yourself ahead instead of trying to push someone else out of the way.

NOVEMBER

FRESH PERSPECTIVES

The Full Moon in stubborn Taurus on **November 2** is square assertive Mars, stirring up relationship conflicts and perhaps even anger with yourself. Channel the powerful energy you feel in a positive direction with healthy physical activity or by starting a new project. Balancing force with finesse will help keep the peace and allow you to sustain a long-term effort by avoiding obstacles instead of battling them. Idealistic Neptune's direct turn in your 10th House of Career on **November 4** awakens dreams of more inspiring work that could turn an ordinary job into a meaningful contribution to society. Your ruling planet, Venus, enters emotionally deep Scorpio and your 7th House of Partnerships on **November 7**, which is bound to intensify relationships. The stakes in the game of love are getting higher as your desire for more may upset a current companion or attract the ardor of a new one.

On **November 15**, planetary heavyweights Saturn and Pluto make the first of three stressful squares that agitate the work-related houses in your chart. Difficulty with authorities on the job or increased pressure with reduced rewards may force you to consider a major change by the time this pattern finishes next August. The New Moon in magnetic Scorpio on **November 16** increases your drive to deepen your connections with others. A creative trine with unusual Uranus reveals surprising ways to bring excitement to your relationships, but a stressful square to imprecise Neptune could lead you to disappointment if fantasy overcomes common sense. The Sun's entry into adventurous Sagittarius and your 8th House of Intimacy on **November 21** encourages risk taking and generosity; these can be the keys toward empowering your emotional and financial alliances.

> **KEEP IN MIND THIS MONTH**
>
> *Letting go of what you already have may not be easy, but it frees you to receive even more in return.*

KEY DATES

NOVEMBER 2–3 ★ *a wild ride*

Intellectual Mercury, sociable Venus, and assertive Mars all form tense aspects with eccentric Uranus on **November 2**. Brilliant ideas and spontaneous fun are positive potentials, yet require faith and a good deal of flexibility. If you insist on resisting change, expect an unsettled day of less-than-pleasant surprises. Happily, a Venus-Neptune trine reveals potential for confidence in people and things that you don't fully understand. Venus squares the Moon's Nodes on **November 3**, which can make you more sensitive to how people react to you. If you're not receiving the love or respect you believe you deserve, think carefully before making an issue of it.

SUPER NOVA DAYS
NOVEMBER 7-9 ★ *your heart's desire*

Venus's entry into Scorpio on **November 7** offers richness in relationships, but may require some complex negotiations. A Mercury-Pluto semisquare takes conversations below the surface to address underlying issues that you might prefer to avoid. It's healthier to engage your concerns than to deny them. The Sun in your 7th House of Partnerships forms tense semisquares with Saturn and Pluto on **November 8** that may attract jealousy, delay gratification, and cause you to measure your moves very carefully. Information overflow from a Mercury-Jupiter square engenders exaggeration: Cut what you hear in half for a more accurate assessment. Lovely Venus sextiles regenerative Pluto on **November 9**, bringing you to the heart of love and value. Your radar for connecting with the essence of yourself and others accurately guides you to obtain what you desire at the best possible price.

NOVEMBER 19-21 ★ *long-term commitment*

Venus bounces from a square to Mars on **November 19** to semisquares with Saturn and Pluto on **November 21** that first excite you, incite you, and then slow you down. Venus-Mars leads to sparring that can be erotic when it's playful or destructive when it's not. The love planet's hard angles to Saturn and Pluto may stir resentment, mistrust, and doubt. Yet reason brings clarity and the resolve needed to define limits and set clear goals that can be achieved with patience and dedication.

NOVEMBER 25-26 ★ *nothing to prove*

A creative Venus-Uranus trine on **November 25** opens your taste buds to new and different experiences that could unlock a sticky relationship or financial situation. Allow your imagination free rein, since unconventional thinking spurs possibilities ordinary logic would never find. A Venus-Neptune square on **November 26** increases your sensitivity to others' opinions. If you are feeling vulnerable, avoid trying to prove yourself; take shelter in spirituality, romance, and fantasy instead.

DECEMBER

GROWING PAINS

Three lunations (New and Full Moons), three planets changing direction, and two outer planet conjunctions create a very busy month. Revolutionary Uranus turns forward on **December 1** in your 11th House of Groups, sparking original approaches to teamwork. Venus enters Sagittarius and your 8th House of Intimacy the same day to provoke a more adventurous spirit in emotional and financial matters. The Full Moon in mutable Gemini on **December 2** tickles your 2nd House of Income, stimulating new ideas about making money, while a helpful trine from practical Saturn provides patience and a manageable plan. Hopeful Jupiter joins wounded Chiron on **December 7**, enriching painful experiences with meaning that can hasten healing. The enthusiastic Sagittarius New Moon on **December 16** is supported by sextiles from Jupiter, Neptune, and Chiron to empower your dreams and fulfill your material and spiritual needs.

Macho Mars turns retrograde in your 4th House of Roots on **December 20**, perhaps forcing you to step back and deal with unfinished business at home before advancing professionally. Generosity and faith bless your holiday season when Jupiter joins spiritual Neptune on the Winter Solstice, **December 21**. Venus enters your 9th House of Travel and Higher Education on **December 25**, gifting you with a desire to expand your horizons. However, chatty Mercury turns retrograde on **December 26**, retracing its steps in this house so you can reevaluate your beliefs and reconsider educational or travel-related plans. A Lunar Eclipse in moody Cancer on **December 31** ends the year on a somber note as Saturn squares and Venus and Pluto oppose the Full Moon. Emotionally intense conversations can feel threatening, but facing the truth is hard work that rewards you with greater trust and respect.

> **KEEP IN MIND THIS MONTH**
>
> *Taken with care and thought—not fear—a step backward can be more courageous than blindly forging ahead.*

KEY DATES

DECEMBER 4–5 ★ *stay in control*

A smart sextile between value-based Venus and thrifty Saturn on **December 4** helps you make wise shopping decisions. Your good sense shines through in relationships, too, allowing you to maintain a clear and solid presence in an emotionally charged situation. On **December 5**, Mercury enters pragmatic Capricorn and impulsive Mars is slowed by a semisquare to Saturn, thwarting spontaneity; avoid

changing plans at the last minute. Organizing your time carefully, however, produces desirable results.

DECEMBER 9 ★ *surprising answers*

You can work your way out of tricky situations as your planet, Venus, forms clever
quintiles with Jupiter and Chiron. If you are stressed by a conflict between professional obligations and personal needs, this creative 72-degree alignment reveals
unconventional solutions.

DECEMBER 17 ★ *friendly frolic*

A sassy Venus-Mars trine puts you in the mood to play and could attract someone
special to share the fun. Creative activities, games, and flirting come easily to you
now; even when you mean well, however, you could hit a sore spot with a highly
sensitive person. The issues feel totally real to this individual, so respect his or her
reactions without becoming defensive about what you've said or done.

SUPER NOVA DAYS
DECEMBER 19–21 ★ *make it happen*

An excitable Venus-Uranus square on **December 19** brings more surprises
than stability. Quick changes in tastes and opinions may rattle your sense of
safety, especially in relationships. Yet if you can keep an open mind, discovering new sources of delight makes any inconvenience worth the price. Venus
forms supportive sextiles to buoyant Jupiter late on **December 20** and to
Neptune early on **December 21**—fortunate alignments that lift your spirits
and carry you through any emotional storm. Jupiter and Neptune's precise
conjunction, along with the Sun's entry into ambitious Capricorn, make this a
rare occasion when your highest ideals and aspirations are matched with the
will and the plan to make them real.

DECEMBER 28–29 ★ *take a stand*

The air thickens with deep feelings as Venus joins Pluto and sesquisquares Mars
on **December 28**. Resentment, mistrust, and jealousy are possible, yet discomfort
can force you to expose your fears and clarify your desires. Venus's square to
karmic Saturn on **December 29** is a time to draw a line in the sand regarding relationships and self-worth issues. Be prepared to simply say no or to state your
position without equivocation. Respect is more important than approval now, so
stand up for what you know is right.

GEMINI

MAY 21–JUNE 20

GEMINI

2008 SUMMARY

Rebuilding and realigning emotionally are your key issues this year. Regardless of the limits of the people closest to you or the barriers you encounter professionally, you have the capacity to turn the course of your life in a more fulfilling direction. Being clear about your goals in a partnership is essential, since anything less than a well-defined purpose can limit the benefits you collect. The magic of metaphysical meaning is all around you—in every cloud, tree, bird, and child.

AUGUST— *shifting perspectives*

Pressuring others is more likely to push them away than pull them over to your side. Maintaining your cool is actually much more appealing and persuasive.

SEPTEMBER—*strategic planning*

Aim high but move slowly. The farther you want to go, the more cautious you need to be at this point in your journey.

OCTOBER—*professional pressure*

Don't isolate yourself when you're feeling down. People will support you, or at least listen, when you share your feelings.

NOVEMBER—*adventures in relationships*

Overselling yourself could harm your credibility. Temper your excitement now with a more controlled way of communicating your strengths.

DECEMBER—*transformational holidays*

Take full responsibility for your feelings to avoid turning frustrations into arguments that could undermine the support you need from others.

2008 CALENDAR

AUGUST

WEDNESDAY 6 ★ Nerves are taut today, but don't stress

SATURDAY 9 ★ Mercury brings focus that sharpens your mind through the 10th

FRIDAY 15 ★ **SUPER NOVA DAYS** Overcome old obstacles now

THURSDAY 21 ★ Mellow out when responsibilities increase through the 23rd

WEDNESDAY 27 ★ Improve your image and invite romance through the 30th

SEPTEMBER

SUNDAY 7 ★ **SUPER NOVA DAYS** Excesses can be exhilarating through the 9th

SUNDAY 14 ★ A surprising turn of events can shift duties through the 15th

FRIDAY 19 ★ Relationships swing between extremes through the 24th

SUNDAY 28 ★ Encourage a spirit of playfulness now

OCTOBER

MONDAY 6 ★ More isn't always better! A little goes a long way.

MONDAY 13 ★ **SUPER NOVA DAYS** Lines blur between flirting and fighting through the 15th

TUESDAY 21 ★ Put your attention where your passion is through the 22nd

SATURDAY 25 ★ An inner struggle leads you in a positive direction

NOVEMBER

TUESDAY 4 ★ Deep thinking can save you

WEDNESDAY 12 ★ Partnership pressures intensify through the 13th

SUNDAY 16 ★ **SUPER NOVA DAYS** You're sharp as a tack through the 17th

SUNDAY 23 ★ Apply fiery intensity to a worthy cause

THURSDAY 27 ★ Your opinions can be too hot to handle now

DECEMBER

FRIDAY 5 ★ You may experience twists and turns through the 7th

WEDNESDAY 10 ★ **SUPER NOVA DAYS** Explosive words can force changes through the 12th

MONDAY 15 ★ Discipline and smart thinking help

WEDNESDAY 24 ★ Earn trust through straight talk through the 26th

GEMINI OVERVIEW

One of your talents, Gemini, is your ability to stay in the present moment—so much so that you can fall short when it comes to planning your future. This year, however, philosophical Jupiter is in your 9th House of Travel and Higher Education, opening your mind to so many more possibilities. The idea of returning to school to expand your intellectual horizons or of purchasing tickets to a faraway place is appealing; you dream of heading off on the journey of a lifetime, mental or geographic. Either way, you won't be able to make the most of this transit without plenty of forethought, so **get used to the idea of scheduling ahead more often**. As Jupiter moves through futuristic Aquarius in your 9th House, it joins the Moon's North Node, Chiron the Wounded Healer, and Neptune the Dreamer. When Jupiter joins the karmic North Node on February 11, networking opportunities may bring you people who can assist you on your adventures. When lucky Jupiter reaches Chiron and Neptune on May 23–27, July 10–22, and December 7–21, you may be closer to fulfilling your dreams than ever before. Unfortunately, you may reach out and grab one only to have it slip through your fingers.

The key to turning your fantasies into reality this year may be in the challenging dance that optimistic Jupiter does with realistic Saturn. Saturn the Taskmaster is in your 4th House of Security until October 29, and its ongoing irritating quincunx to Jupiter suggests that **you may need to work hard at developing an inner stability unshaken by outer events**. It's particularly difficult to balance your family responsibilities around March 22 and August 19; how you handle the stress at these times can be crucial when you get closer to your goals. Additionally, Saturn's quincunx with dreamy Neptune on September 12 suggests a need to find a balance between what you must do (Saturn) and your unrestrained dreams (Neptune). Saturn, which entered analytical Virgo and your personal 4th House in September 2007, moves into artistic Libra and your 5th House of Love on October 29, beginning a two-year period in which you'll need to pay more attention to your creative process to stabilize your life.

Professional rigidity shatters under the irrepressible forces of change around February 5 and September 15—part of an ongoing opposition between authoritative Saturn and rebellious Uranus that began on November 4, 2008, and continues through July 26, 2010. Uranus is nearing the end of its seven-year visit to your 10th House of Career, where it has likely brought surprising changes along with a bit of instability. Now, with serious Saturn in direct opposition to it, responsibilities to your family may prevent you from taking risks that could potentially give you more freedom at work. The frustration may be severe at times, and it's important to acknowledge when you feel stuck. **Work toward incremental changes to avoid experiencing the destabilizing side of erratic Uranus as it suddenly releases pent-up tensions.**

 ### FRIENDSHIP FIRST

The distinction between friends and lovers may be tested early this year, for sweet Venus in impulsive Aries spends most of February, March, April, and May in your 11th House of Groups and Friends. Threats to your emotional well-being can provoke powerful interactions with others during these months, creating crucial relationship turning points when Venus squares intense Pluto on February 5, April 5, and May 2. Romance may come more easily as Venus moves through your sign on July 6–August 1, but her opposition to Pluto on August 2—as with her squares earlier in the year—can once again bring up difficult issues. Serious Saturn enters Libra and your 5th House of Romance on October 30, where it remains for a couple of years. Settling down into practical and enduring relationships will become top priority.

 ### IMAGINE THE POSSIBILITIES

Little will discourage you in your quest for success this year, even when you're facing challenging issues, but it's hard to tell where your idealistic optimism fades into outright denial. Fill in your dreams with as many details as possible when Jupiter and Neptune hook up on May 27, July 10, and December 21. Positive thinking is useful, but avoiding the truth can set the stage for difficult setbacks around March 22–27 and August 19. You may feel the frustration most strongly when Saturn opposes Uranus in your professional 10th House on February 5 and September 19. All in all, this is a transitional year professionally, and it may be well into 2010 before you fully understand where the current changes are taking you.

UNEVEN PROGRESSION

This year's lunar eclipses tell a story of change, for your 2nd House of Money is ruled by the Moon. The dramatic Leo Full Moon Eclipse on February 9 falls in your 3rd House of Communication. Its quincunx to Uranus suggests that you may receive unexpected information, suddenly changing your financial picture. The intelligent Aquarius Full Moon Eclipse on August 5 in your 9th House of Higher Education indicates the need for on-the-job training to increase your earning power. The security-conscious Cancer Full Moon Eclipse on December 31 activates your financial 2nd House. Its opposition to valuable Venus in your 8th House of Shared Resources suggests that changes in a business relationship can positively impact your bank account.

STICK TO YOUR PLAN

Set physical goals early in the year when Mars, the ruler of your 6th House of Health, joins confident Jupiter on February 17, healing Chiron on March 5, and spiritual Neptune on March 8. Visualize your body in a happy and healthy state, for what you imagine now can manifest if you're willing to work for what you want. Your efforts may be blocked when Mars opposes stern Saturn and joins surprising Uranus on April 15. Don't accept self-imposed limitations, though: You can push beyond them with relentless insistence. Pluto, the co-ruler of your 6th House, squares Saturn on November 15, possibly requiring you to demonstrate your resilience by overcoming a minor problem. Take special care of yourself or you might face exhaustion as tensions build toward the end of the year.

NO SUDDEN MOVES

You must rise to the challenge of your family obligations this year. Yet this may feel so overwhelming that you want to cut the ties that bind and escape—particularly around February 5 and September 15, when Saturn opposes shocking Uranus. Although you may be sorely tempted to take drastic action, slow and methodical change will have a more lasting impact than an impulsive break for freedom. Mental Mercury, the ruler of your 4th House, moves through this house August 2–25, then retrogrades back there September 17–October 9. It's particularly overwhelming to deal with all the contradictory information at this time. Wait until the middle of October before making final decisions.

DREAMS OF EXOTIC LANDS

The co-rulers of your 9th House of Travel and Higher Education, responsible Saturn and unpredictable Uranus, are locked in a long-lasting opposition, anchoring you to the home front with commitments that must be kept. But unexpected travel—possibly for work—is likely. Meanwhile, a rare super-conjunction of Jupiter, Chiron, and Neptune in your 9th House has you dreaming about going places that you have never been and learning things you never knew. Although this is ideal for taking a journey in the real world or in your mind, you may have to wait until you've fulfilled your responsibilities before you can go.

UNLIMITED POTENTIAL

No matter how tied you are to your daily routine, this is a year in which your fantasies are larger than life and can seep through the barrier that normally keeps them from overtaking reality. Although this can be confusing, it also offers great potential for your personal development and spiritual growth. Still, you will need tools to help you manage the intensity of your visions. It would be a serious mistake to ignore the metaphysical magic that is being down-loaded into your consciousness just because it doesn't make sense or compli-cates your life. Open your mind while keeping your feet on the ground by prac-ticing yoga, martial arts, or dance.

RICK & JEFF'S TIP FOR THE YEAR:
Find Your Center

New ideas are so appealing to you now that you may forget about the basics, such as eating, sleeping, and working. Still, it's essential to main-tain continuity in the practical side of living. Your greatest challenge this year may be finding balance—a way to feel the excitement without turning everything upside down and back-ward. Even if you are restless and need to make significant changes, don't lose sight of what you currently possess as you blindly rush off to find what you want next. Remember, you needn't cross the river to find water.

JANUARY

SLOW HAND

The year starts on a promising note with intelligent Mercury entering progressive Aquarius on **January 1**, followed by abundant Jupiter on **January 5**. This emphasizes your 9th House of Journeys, which is perfect as you envision the unpainted canvas of possibilities during the year ahead. Valuable Venus enters compassionate Pisces and your 10th House of Career on **January 3**, attracting support for your professional endeavors, especially when she sextiles Pluto on **January 4** and conjuncts surprising Uranus on **January 22**. Life becomes more complicated, however, when the sensitive Cancer Full Moon on **January 10** in your 2nd House of Self-Worth can leave you wondering if you'll be able to deliver on all your promises. Your impatience is exacerbated as your key planet, Mercury, turns retrograde on **January 11**, backing into serious Capricorn on **January 21** and resuming its forward direction on **February 2**. Your recent optimism may sour as you're required to revisit the basic assumptions on which you built your plans. Your willingness to go back and review previous work can make this month enormously productive, but if you rush ahead with your old strategy, you may confront one maddening obstacle after another.

The quirky Aquarius New Moon on **January 26** is a Solar Eclipse in your expansive 9th House that conjuncts Jupiter. Pressured to grow, you may not be able to contain your desire for change. You can feel the excitement as Jupiter activates unrestrained Uranus on **January 27**, but even though the long-term opposition from restrictive Saturn to Uranus isn't exact until **February 5**, it's close enough to prevent you from taking unnecessary risks.

> ### KEEP IN MIND THIS MONTH
>
> *Although you may be enthusiastic about your future, it remains just out of reach. Slowing down now will help you get it right later.*

KEY DATES

JANUARY 5 ★ *blue skies*

Horizons broaden and your confidence grows as buoyant Jupiter enters unconventional Aquarius in your 9th House of Future Vision, where it remains for the entire year. Additionally, Mercury and Mars agitate Uranus, freeing you from tired old ways of looking at your life. Although no action is required at this time, don't be afraid to imagine what you can do in a limitless universe.

JANUARY 10–11 ★ *planning for the future*
The emotional Cancer Full Moon on **January 10** opposes the responsible Capricorn Sun in your 8th House of Shared Resources, stirring up issues with a partner. The source of a problem may be technical in nature, a simple misunderstanding, or a small miscalculation—for Mercury turns retrograde on **January 11**. Thankfully, the Sun's stabilizing trine to ambitious Saturn offers necessary support. Backing up your computer files, cleaning your home, and tying up miscellaneous loose ends increase your overall efficiency in the days ahead. Seek a manageable balance between getting what you want right away and patiently working toward your long-term goals.

JANUARY 18–20 ★ *minimalist approach*
Mercury's retrograde continues to annoy you, but when it joins confident Jupiter on **January 18**, relief finally arrives. Discouragement dissipates, and once again you are able to see where you're going. The Sun's entry into Aquarius on **January 19** and its conjunction with Mercury on **January 20** reemphasize the need for intelligent planning. Don't talk until you know exactly what you will say—and don't say too much. The additional information will only dilute your important message.

JANUARY 22–24 ★ *intention into action*
A powerful friend or co-worker arrives with surprising news or offers of assistance as energetic Mars harmonizes with Saturn and Uranus. But attractive Venus joins erratic Uranus on **January 22**, tempting you to be overly impulsive. Follow through on your commitments or Venus's opposition to austere Saturn on **January 24** will leave you with regrets.

SUPER NOVA DAYS
JANUARY 26–30 ★ *stay just a little bit longer*
A cathartic Aquarius New Moon Eclipse on **January 26** can open your mind as the lightning of awareness illuminates your thinking. What you see is most likely pleasant, for Mercury—nearing the end of its retrograde cycle—is receiving an encouraging kiss from lovely Venus. But the messenger planet also receives a boost from Mars on **January 27**, the same day that giant Jupiter tensely semi-squares erratic Uranus. You have waited long enough; it feels as if it's now or never. Even so, it's wise to hang on to the status quo a few more days until Jupiter passes its tense connection with restrictive Saturn on **January 30**. Once you're around this bend, you can confidently take the next step.

FEBRUARY

THE TEMPTATION OF CHANGE

Although Mercury turns direct on **February 1**, indicating a productive month of putting your previous plans into action, it may still take a few days until the Winged Messenger gathers enough speed to make you feel you're truly back in flight. But the big news of the month is responsible Saturn's opposition to erratic Uranus on **February 5**—a slow-moving aspect that began on **November 4, 2008**, and lasts through **July 2010**. You should take your responsibilities to home and family seriously, but things may be somewhat unstable in your career, requiring you to emphasize your professional rather than your private life. You may be more restless than usual and want to make something big happen. But this Saturn-Uranus aspect is more significant than its effect on the current moment alone. Start making changes now without totally disrupting your life; put another way, be sure to fulfill your current obligations as you work toward independence.

On **February 4**, assertive Mars enters unorthodox Aquarius, where he remains until **March 14**, motivating you to try new methods—even if you must do the same old thing. As Mars moves through Aquarius, he catches up with jubilant Jupiter on **February 17**. This dynamic duo of force and enthusiasm can infuse you with optimism and energy to back up your big ideas. The danger here, however, is that you can all too easily overcommit your time, resources, or heart to something or someone. With Venus's cooperative sextile to the Mars-Jupiter conjunction on **February 16–18**, your charisma is strong and your charm can be disarming. Just stay aware of your powerful impact on others, so you don't set anyone up for disappointment.

> **KEEP IN MIND THIS MONTH**
>
> *It's time to transform your past experiences into a practical plan that allows you to respond compassionately to the needs of others while also taking care of yourself.*

KEY DATES

FEBRUARY 5 ★ *wait it out*

It's a struggle to get your ideas heard as innocent Venus tensely squares shadowy Pluto, symbolizing a clash between your core values and your current experience. You may feel threatened and fight to regain control. Additionally, the Sun forms semisquares with both Venus and Pluto, possibly placing you right in the middle of someone else's conflict. This emotional intensity feeds into the larger Saturn-Uranus opposition, provoking risky behavior as you reach for something or someone beyond your current grasp. Yet no matter how urgent it seems, patience, not impetuous behavior, will be rewarded.

FEBRUARY 9–12 ★ *nothing to fear but fear itself*

The dramatic Leo Full Moon Eclipse on **February 9** exacerbates your discomfort with your present circumstances, but things may not be as difficult as they seem. Every little disappointment and annoyance looms large and your emotional reactions can be swift, especially as the eclipsed Full Moon forms an irritating quincunx with electric Uranus. The Sun's conjunctions with wounded Chiron on **February 9** and nebulous Neptune on **February 12** highlight the difficulties, challenging you to trust the silver lining within the dark clouds. This is indeed a turning point. Actions taken now can have positive long-term ramifications—if they originate from awareness and love.

FEBRUARY 14 ★ *all together now*

Quicksilver Mercury, now moving full speed ahead, on **February 14** reenters high-strung Aquarius, where it was on **January 1–11**. The messenger planet journeys through humanitarian Aquarius until **March 8**, making this a time to focus on the global thinking you must engage in if you are to reach your altruistic goals.

FEBRUARY 21–24 ★ *say it with feeling*

Mercury's alignments with the Moon's North Node on **February 21** and Jupiter on **February 24** enable you to talk openly about your path ahead, unencumbered by negativity and the details that you can fill in later. The psychic Pisces New Moon on **February 24** falls in your 10th House of Career, initiating a new cycle of professional growth. Your ability to understand how others feel now augments your communication skills to make you more popular at work.

FEBRUARY 27–28 ★ *your own worst enemy*

Fiery Mars forms a tense semisquare with potent Pluto on **February 27**, followed by an irritating quincunx with Saturn on **February 28**, placing serious obstacles in your path. Someone might be threatened by your show of confidence. You needn't retreat: A bit of humility can ameliorate a tense situation. Additionally, Mercury's semisquare to Pluto can put a strain on communication, making it difficult for you to be heard. Don't let a sharp edge of defensiveness get in your way.

MARCH

HASTE MAKES WASTE

Keeping mild annoyances in perspective is crucial as this month begins with your key planet, Mercury, joining aggressive Mars on **March 1**. Its presence in your 9th House of Higher Truth motivates you to express what's on your mind, even if it riles up someone else. Venus is retrograde **March 6–April 17** in your 11th House of Goals—a perfect opportunity to reexamine your core values and move your life into closer alignment with your desires. Investments in financial matters or in a relationship may take time to pay off, and your willingness to wait will be well compensated.

The analytical Virgo Full Moon on **March 10** reminds you that you cannot ignore your obligations as it conjuncts responsible Saturn, but its opposition to unconventional Uranus suggests that you can gain independence while still doing what's expected of you. The emphasis on your spiritual growth becomes more important when Mars enters compassionate Pisces on **March 14**—remaining in your professional 10th House until **April 22**—indicating a significant connection between your inner work and your outer path during this time. The Sun's entry into pioneering Aries on **March 20** marks the Spring Equinox and can be just the boost you need to overcome whatever obstacles are in your path. You receive another jolt of energy as your key planet, Mercury, enters feisty Aries on **March 25**, followed by an Aries New Moon on **March 26**. You may be eager to begin a new venture, but your desire to do it with others can be problematic—resistance can delay your progress.

> **KEEP IN MIND THIS MONTH**
>
> *It's challenging to maintain spiritual integrity while also meeting your obligations. Instead of seeing your life as choices between black and white, try living in shades of gray.*

KEY DATES

MARCH 5–6 ★ *surrealistic pillow*

You are likely to believe your fantasies when thoughtful Mercury conjuncts imaginative Neptune on **March 5** in your 9th House of Faraway Places. You are less interested now in the facts than in the possibilities of your dreams. Be careful, for it's easy to lose perspective. The horizon may appear much closer than it actually is, and you may be left somewhat unsatisfied as loving Venus turns retrograde on **March 6** in your 11th House of Dreams and Wishes. Give yourself as much time as you need to get what you want.

SUPER NOVA DAYS

MARCH 8–12 ★ *no escape*

It's difficult to see where you are going, for self-directed Mars joins fuzzy Neptune on **March 8**, the same day that Mercury enters dreamy Pisces. But the Sun's annual opposition to sober Saturn—normally an unforgiving reality check—may be exactly what you need to keep you grounded. Mercury's supportive sextile to passionate Pluto and the practical Virgo Full Moon on **March 10** can catalyze deep feelings, yet sweet Venus's sextile to positive Jupiter on **March 11** transforms a difficult encounter into one that's quite rewarding. The Sun's conjunction with electric Uranus on **March 12** lights up your inner world as clarity returns in a flash. Your willingness to communicate with kindness makes the difference between an unpleasant confrontation and a most delightful experience.

MARCH 18–20 ★ *strike while the iron is hot*

Mercury's tense opposition from your 10th House of Career to stern Saturn in your 4th House of Home and Family on **March 18** can widen the gulf between domestic demands and your idealistic concepts. Even as you meet resistance to your efforts, Mars's supportive sextile to potent Pluto on **March 19**, coupled with the Sun's entry into Mars's sign Aries on **March 20**, can spur you past procrastination into action.

MARCH 22–23 ★ *off balance*

Mental Mercury joins high-strung Uranus on **March 22** to unleash a firestorm of wild ideas, yet it may be nearly impossible to make practical use of them. Only extraordinary effort can balance your life as expansive Jupiter quincunxes contractive Saturn in a slow-moving dance, shifting your center of gravity. Instead of becoming frustrated with your inability to get it right once and for all, cut yourself some slack and simply do the best you can without too much self-judgment. Nevertheless, the Sun's dynamic square to Pluto on **March 23** elicits a strong response, especially if your efforts are being thwarted. Taking a stand can be healthy, but don't invest too much energy in seeking a final resolution yet.

APRIL

DON'T BACK DOWN

This is quite a social month—beginning with the Sun, Mercury, and Venus all in your 11th House of Friends and Associates—yet you must also face dark feelings to overcome discouragement. Loving Venus is retrograde until **April 17**, delaying pleasure and asking you—sometimes not so nicely—to reexamine your heart instead of attempting to maintain an untenable position. You may be convinced that someone is exerting unnecessary control, or even manipulating you, to increase his or her powerful hold. Full Moons often increase emotional tension, but the peaceful Libra Full Moon on **April 9** could actually bring some relief as Mercury enters practical Taurus in your 12th House of Endings, where it stays until **April 30**. Think about letting go of bad habits, outmoded ways of communicating, and anything that has run its course.

Sweet Venus follows Mars into trailblazing Aries on **April 24**, the same day as a sensual Taurus New Moon in your 12th House of Soul Consciousness. This lunation trines Pluto, Lord of the Underworld, giving you a deeper understanding of the mysteries of the universe. Pluto remains active throughout the rest of the month, with Mars tensely squaring it on **April 26** and Venus edging closer to this square through **May 2**. Similar power struggles from earlier in the month may return in a different form now. If you pay close attention to your feelings and work toward manifesting love, your emotional interactions will be less severe this time and can bear intensely juicy fruit. But if you have neglected your heart, it will be quite difficult to avoid this unpleasant wake-up call.

> **KEEP IN MIND THIS MONTH**
>
> *Your personal relationships will become more rewarding if you're willing to plummet to the depths of your own emotions when faced with difficult issues.*

KEY DATES

SUPER NOVA DAYS
APRIL 2–4 ★ *keep your cool*
Interactive Mercury is quite gregarious now in bold Aries, yet its annoying quincunx to authoritative Saturn on **April 2** suggests that someone in your group may be raining on your parade. Then Venus's square to passionate Pluto on **April 3** substantially raises the emotional stakes, requiring you to fight for your survival. Meanwhile, assertive Mars reaches his biennial opposition

to Saturn on **April 4**, erecting blockades where there should be open road. Don't aim your anger at the wrong target—a temper tantrum will only make matters worse. Fortunately, Jupiter's sextile to Mercury allows you to discuss the problems intelligently on the way toward resolution.

APRIL 9–11 ★ *spontaneous affection*
Benevolent Jupiter is sweetly aspected by the creative Libra Full Moon on **April 9** in your 5th House of Love, opening your mind to the possibility of a new romance or to the hope of rekindling an old one. Your sharpened clarity and ability to find exactly the right way to express yourself combine to give your words more emotional impact on **April 11**, when talkative Mercury harmonizes with passionate Pluto.

APRIL 15 ★ *surprise attack*
It's easy to slip into your fantasies as the Sun aligns with imaginative Neptune on **April 15**, but an electric conjunction between red-hot Mars and erratic Uranus suggests that you may not be in control on the job. Buried tensions come to the surface, whether or not you are a willing participant. This conjunction occurs in your 10th House of Career, suggesting that preemptive action may be better than waiting for something to happen at work.

APRIL 19–22 ★ *calm before the storm*
Create a spiritual retreat for yourself as the Sun enters indulgent Taurus and your 12th House of Inner Peace on **April 19** before the high-spirited Venus-Mars conjunction on **April 21** fires you back into the social scene. Energetic Mars blasts his way into enthusiastic Aries and your progressive 11th House on **April 22**, the same day that a Mercury-Jupiter square scatters your thoughts all over the globe. Containing your energy now is a challenge; you're ready for just about anything.

APRIL 30 ★ *mental high jinks*
Your key planet, Mercury, whizzes into your restless sign on **April 30**, turning up the volume on your thoughts and increasing your need to communicate. Quicksilver Mercury remains in your 1st House of Personality until **May 13**, so be aware that your words may be moving faster than others can follow. It's great to be clever, but don't let your wit lead you off course and get in the way of more serious interactions.

MAY

SPIRITUAL REAWAKENING

Your social calendar is overcrowded this month as Venus and Mars, the cosmic lovers, continue to move through your 11th House of Friends. And yet your need for solitude grows and motivates you to retreat from too much organized activity, no matter how much pleasure others may bring. Your key planet, Mercury—which has entered your own sign, making you even more talkative than usual—turns retrograde on **May 7** and remains in apparent backward motion until **May 30**. The entire month is subdued by Mercury's lack of forward motion. Reenergize your soul by revisiting your past, redoing any incomplete projects, and reconsidering your overall direction in life.

The emotionally intense Scorpio Full Moon on **May 9** falls in your 6th House of Health, emphasizing the connection between mind and body. This Full Moon reveals where your issues of self-esteem can manifest as external obstacles with energetic Mars moving toward an irritating quincunx with restrictive Saturn, exact on **May 11**. You have a chance now to work with your own process to eliminate these self-imposed limits. The restless Gemini New Moon on **May 24** is quincunx passionate Pluto, making it difficult for you to assess how much effort to apply toward getting what you want. On the one hand, you are ready to avoid a power struggle and move on; on the other, you're tempted to dig in your heels and fight for your cause, whether or not it's sufficiently important. Luckily, Mars is sextile to a superconjunction of Jupiter, Chiron, and Neptune that culminates on **May 27**, firing you up with an infectious faith that strengthens your spiritual convictions.

> **KEEP IN MIND THIS MONTH**
>
> *Even if you feel like a hamster running around on a wheel, you can still make great spiritual progress—so don't judge yourself by material success alone.*

KEY DATES
MAY 2-5 ★ *night moves*
Pleasant Venus—quite excitable now that she's back in rowdy Aries until **June 6**—crosses paths with domineering Pluto on **May 2**, raising primal fears about possible abandonment or stimulating dark passions that may be difficult to express. Even if you normally avoid the shadows, you are attracted to the magic they hide. Although you may be afraid that your feelings will overwhelm you, your desire for a deeper experience lures you into the back alleys of your subconscious mind. Your enthusiasm

will likely bring you through this difficult time as fiery Mars is activated by confident Jupiter on **May 4**. The Sun's harmonious trine to stable Saturn on **May 5** can help settle your edgy emotions while you focus on more practical matters.

MAY 13–17 ★ *realistic dreamer*
You are more introspective, serious, and less chatty on **May 13** when retrograde Mercury backs into stoic Taurus in your 12th House of Privacy, where it remains for the balance of the month. You are less concerned now with demonstrating your cleverness than with delving into the mysteries of your own imagination. But the sensible Taurus Sun's dynamic square with overbearing Jupiter and cooperative sextile with innovative Uranus on **May 16** goad you into action. Additionally, the Sun squares Chiron the Healer and Neptune the Dreamer on **May 16–17**, showing you the difference between your dreams and your real obligations. Walking in both worlds teaches you much about yourself.

MAY 20 ★ *with a grain of salt*
The Sun returns to airy Gemini for a month—a time when you express your natural adaptability much more easily. Your key planet, Mercury, forms a dynamic square with grandiose Jupiter, empowering you with extraordinary confidence, even if it isn't justified by reality. You believe that your opinions are correct and that your power of persuasion is great. This may be true; however, your tendency now to overestimate your ability or to underestimate the size of a job can create headaches for you later on.

SUPER NOVA DAYS
MAY 23–27 ★ *vision quest*
You are interested in walking a more enlightened path these days as boundless Jupiter makes its first of three conjunctions with healing Chiron on **May 23** and with visionary Neptune on **May 27**. This is a great time to go on a pilgrimage, retreat to a magical destination, or attend a conference where you can experientially explore alternative healing that involves mind, body, and spirit. Your dreams are close enough to touch, yet the patterns established now will develop throughout the year.

JUNE

STRESS MANAGEMENT

Your key planet, Mercury, is traveling direct again this month, freeing you to explore new ideas and to engage intellectually with the present rather than continuing to review your past. But the Winged Messenger only completed its retrograde period on **May 30**, so expect several days to pass before you notice positive changes in your thinking processes and conversations with others. Mercury reenters clever Gemini on **June 13**, remaining in your 1st House of Physicality until **July 3**. You tend to be anxious and excited this month, especially with the Sun also in restless Gemini until the Summer Solstice on **June 21**—when it swims into emotional Cancer. Stressful situations create worries that manifest somatically now, making it crucial to eat well, get exercise, and process emotions instead of denying them. Thankfully, you receive lots of support, starting with soothing sextiles from sweet Venus to the still-active triple conjunction of Chiron, Neptune, and Jupiter on **June 2** that can ease your troubled heart and mind.

The adventurous Sagittarius Full Moon on **June 7** opposes your Sun and falls in your 7th House of Partnerships. Look for unrealized relationship potential instead of wasting time and energy on ineffective self-criticism. Fortunately, this Full Moon is assisted by romantic Venus, now resolute in practical Taurus and harmoniously trining potent Pluto. Instead of avoiding intense emotional interactions, dive deeply into the passionate pool of love. The normally defensive Cancer New Moon on **June 22** is opposite Pluto, strengthening your resolve as you face a powerful opponent or a situation that requires you to deliver the goods— and you do, whether or not you consciously realize how much you have to give.

KEEP IN MIND THIS MONTH

Problems are really your best opportunities to improve, so don't surrender. Focus your energy toward the future rather than fretting about the present moment.

KEY DATES

JUNE 2–5 ★ *no guts, no glory*

Beautiful Venus creates harmonious aspects on **June 2**, stimulating romantic fantasies. Fortunately, energetic Mars in Taurus forms a steady trine with passionate Pluto on **June 3**, deepening your energy reserves and gracing you with sufficient stamina to pursue your desires. You have more follow-through than usual as you pursue extraordinary people and intense experiences. The Sun's dynamic square with repressive Saturn on **June 5**, however, can block or slow your progress. You don't have the luxury of allowing yourself to get discouraged; there is work to do, and now is the time to do it.

JUNE 9–10 ★ *intuitive genius*
Mental Mercury in your 12th House of Privacy forms a cooperative sextile to electric Uranus on **June 9** that floods you with heightened awareness, yet its dynamic square with Jupiter and Neptune on **June 9–10** makes it difficult to separate fact from fantasy. Be careful, for the communication planet is also known as the Trickster, teasing you to reveal more than you intend.

SUPER NOVA DAYS
JUNE 15–17 ★ *in for the long haul*
You may find yourself totally annoyed with the delays in your life as quicksilver Mercury forms an irritating quincunx with dark Pluto on **June 15**, the same day that giant Jupiter begins its retrograde period. Mercury finally steps into brand-new territory on **June 16**, moving past the point of its retrograde last month, while energetic Mars activates shocking Uranus. You are leaning over the edge of an exciting conceptual shift, and the Sun's harmonious trines to Chiron, Neptune, and Jupiter brilliantly illuminate the best part of your dreams. Even if you're ready to jump, though, remember that the Sun's square to Uranus on **June 17** can tempt you with immediate distractions when you should stay focused on long-term goals.

JUNE 21–22 ★ *change in the weather*
The Summer Solstice on **June 21**, followed by the cautious Cancer New Moon opposite Pluto on **June 22**, are turning points as the hectic pace of recent days begins to quiet down. Even as graceful Venus conjuncts fiery Mars—a creative and expressive alignment—they simultaneously harmonize with austere Saturn, restraining your reactions to the events of these days.

JUNE 26 ★ *no free lunch*
Mercury's square to mature Saturn on **June 26** is a reminder that your fast wit and charm are no substitutes for a solid plan, impeccable integrity, and common sense. If you have a run-in with authority now, there is likely a deeper issue behind the surface tensions. Understanding real differences may be more important at this time than glossing over the problem with a quick, but temporary, solution.

JULY

CURIOUSER AND CURIOUSER

Communicator Mercury's faster speed creates a brisk pace in your daily life, yet underneath the noise your dreams feel more real than ever. Although the cosmic Messenger's visit to moody Cancer on **July 3–17** is short-lived, you can experience a wide gamut of emotions at a rapid clip. Speedy Mercury is still racing forward with your thoughts as it moves through outgoing Leo and into your 3rd House of Immediate Environment on **July 17–August 2**. You are even more clever and witty, yet your challenge is to follow any single thought to its conclusion. Allow an idea to come to fruition before impatiently moving on to the next one. Your mental hyperactivity is amplified when attractive Venus enters restless Gemini on **July 5**, followed by go-getter Mars on **July 11**. Your interest is piqued by many things now; your curiosity is heightened and you are all too ready to head off into another direction with the slightest provocation.

The serious Capricorn Full Moon Eclipse on **July 7** falls in your 8th House of Deep Sharing. Because eclipses often turn things around, you may realize that, in your haste to experience what's next, you missed the depth and intensity of what's right in front of your nose. Charming Venus in your 1st House of Personality works in your favor, but runs into unforgiving Saturn on **July 21**, the same day that a hypersensitive Cancer New Moon Eclipse falls in your 2nd House of Self-Worth. Even if you're feeling good about yourself, something may happen that brings up insecurity. Fortunately, the Sun enters proud Leo on **July 22**, helping you reestablish your confidence and encouraging you to move forward.

> **KEEP IN MIND THIS MONTH**
>
> *Your dreams loom so large that you want to share them with everyone, but it's smarter to limit who you include in your closest circle of confidants.*

KEY DATES

JULY 1–2 ★ *impossible dream*

Mercury's clever trine to the triple conjunction of Chiron, Neptune, and Jupiter on **July 1** opens a direct line into your imagination, while Venus's dynamic square to these three planets can heighten your desires and tempt you with the exquisite perfection of unreachable dreams. Take a chance, but be aware that the Sun's tense semisquare to this super-conjunction on **July 2** may leave you dissatisfied if your expectations are too high.

SUPER NOVA DAYS

JULY 6-8 ★ *strategic maneuvers*

Your enthusiasm is on the rise when energetic Mars dynamically squares imaginative Neptune and generous Jupiter on **July 6**. You can visualize your goals within your mind's eye, but don't know exactly how to attain them. Mars's cooperative sextile with brilliant Uranus on **July 7** drives you into action, even if you're still uncertain about your direction. The ambitious Capricorn Full Moon Eclipse on the same day delivers a shot of Saturn's realism, slowing you down but possibly leading you to buried treasure. If you rush through this chance too quickly, Mercury's high-stress aspects on **July 8** can lay bare your mental tap dancing as you try to reclaim a missed opportunity.

JULY 10 ★ *somewhere over the rainbow*

The spiritual giants Jupiter and Neptune reach exact conjunction on **July 10**—the second of three such conjunctions that activate your dreams throughout the year. A deep wave of hope illuminates irrepressible optimism despite current disappointments. Even if you cannot talk about your faith, it is still a guiding light for you during this time.

JULY 13-16 ★ *all tied up*

Mars's irritating quincunx to relentless Pluto and clever Mercury's conjunction to the Sun on **July 13** give you clarity without the ability to put your ideas into action. Your gestures may seem shallow compared with your intent. Mercury's quincunx to Chiron, Jupiter, and Neptune on **July 15** further muddles your words as you try to explain yourself, but its trine to Uranus on **July 16** heralds the breakthrough that you've been seeking.

JULY 26-28 ★ *generosity of spirit*

Gracious Venus forms a sweet trine with the Jupiter-Chiron-Neptune super-conjunction on **July 26-28**, opening the door of opportunity to a pleasurable adventure. But Venus's tense square to surprising Uranus on **July 28** indicates an unexpected twist. Being flexible allows you to accept the gift that is offered.

JULY 30-31 ★ *friendly advice*

Mercury's opposition to the super-conjunction in Aquarius can symbolize an important discussion with a friend who can help you clarify how best to reach your elusive dreams. Although this conversation can open your eyes, remember that there's a lot more to do before you can rest.

AUGUST

KEEPING THE PEACE

The pace of your life slows as your key planet, Mercury, readies to turn retrograde next month. You are more critical now as your intellectual filters discern what's most useful and instruct you to ignore the rest while the Winged Messenger moves through new territory in practical Virgo, its other home sign, in your 4th House of Roots on **August 2–25**. This is very different from your normal style of collecting all the information you can, categorizing it, and tucking it away in case you need it later. Spunky Mars remains in your sign until **August 25**, bestowing you with more get-up-and-go than usual. Be careful that you don't needlessly scatter your energy in too many directions.

The Aquarius Full Moon Eclipse on **August 5** in your 9th House of Future Vision—the third and final eclipse in a series that began last month—can evoke sudden glimpses of an ideal destination that feels very far away. This eclipse reemphasizes the ongoing conjunction of Jupiter, Chiron, and Neptune in intellectual Aquarius that continues to offer you spiritual enlightenment, even though pressing personal matters may prevent you from allowing yourself to pursue your dreams. It's tough to find a balancing point as unavoidable domestic responsibilities frustrate your ability to follow through on big ideas, especially when expansive Jupiter forms an irritating quincunx to contractive Saturn on **August 19**. The dramatic Leo New Moon on **August 20** in your 3rd House of Information adds anxiety to this unsettling time as Venus and Mercury form multiple quincunxes to the Aquarian lineup, amplifying the already imbalanced energy. Pushing harder now only frustrates you, so relax; there isn't anything you need to do.

> **KEEP IN MIND THIS MONTH**
>
> *Self-restraint may be a challenge when your restlessness provokes rash behavior, but there's too much at stake to prematurely risk what you have for castles in the air.*

KEY DATES

AUGUST 1–3 ★ *survival of the deepest*

Sweet Venus confronts hell-raiser Pluto on **August 1** as you come to terms with deep desires that may not be pretty. Passions arouse jealousy, and fears of abandonment raise the stakes in an intimate relationship. Don't withdraw from the intensity even if it makes you uneasy, for communicator Mercury in your 4th House of Security connects with intense Pluto on **August 3**, indicating a satisfying outcome to a difficult interaction as long as you stay focused on the core issue.

AUGUST 10-13 ★ *no rest for the weary*

A tough square between red-hot Mars and cold, calculating Saturn on **August 10** can present obstacles that are temporary reminders of what you must do to achieve lasting results. Mars in your 1st House of Physicality squares sobering Saturn, raising health issues if you've been careless or wasteful with your energy. Happily, Mars harmonizes with extroverted Jupiter on **August 13**, giving you the courage to recognize your limitations and the motivation to overcome them.

AUGUST 14-18 ★ *elusive solution*

The Sun in your 3rd House of Siblings opposes Jupiter, Chiron, and Neptune on **August 14-17**, creating disagreements over your long-term goals. Mars's psychic trine to imaginative Neptune on **August 17** and square to unorthodox Uranus on **August 18** suggest that intuition, not logic, will bring new perspectives to a current problem. Paradoxically, your powers of discrimination are strongest when Mercury reaches conjunction with realistic Saturn on **August 17**, yet its quincunx to buoyant Jupiter makes it difficult to express yourself. There are no final answers now, so just roll with the changes as best you can.

SUPER NOVA DAYS
AUGUST 19-22 ★ *out of whack*

The Jupiter-Saturn quincunx on **August 19** reactivates concerns about the general direction of your life that first surfaced around **March 22**. You feel off kilter, and the demonstrative Leo New Moon on **August 20** encourages you to do something about it. Tensions at work add to your current imbalance as Mercury opposes erratic Uranus in your 10th House of Career on **August 21**. Flexibility improves your chances of being sweetly surprised when Venus happily trines exciting Uranus on **August 22**.

AUGUST 25-26 ★ *artful dodger*

Even if you need to defend your emotional position, managing anger can be crucial to your happiness. You are quite diplomatic now with talkative Mercury entering gracious Libra on **August 25**, yet its simultaneous squares to both ends of a powerful Mars-Pluto opposition on **August 25-26** can expose a difference of opinion that could escalate into a full-blown power struggle. Consciously work to alleviate the hostilities before they go too far.

SEPTEMBER

This is not an easy month for you, yet a variety of stressful circumstances can provide you with fuel for a major change. Applying extra effort where it's needed will allow you to look back at this month with pride, knowing that you accomplished something important. The proverbial tug-of-war between your past (Saturn) and your future (Uranus) began last November and continues through next summer—yet now stands at a turning point that can profoundly change the direction of your life. This ongoing theme for the year originates from Saturn the Tester in your 4th House of Home and Family opposing radical Uranus in your 10th House of Public Status on **September 15**. Additionally, with your key planet, Mercury, moving retrograde **September 6–29**, the conflicts you currently face may feel like déjà vu, but rest assured this is not an endless return to Groundhog Day. Rather, it's an opportunity to consciously turn the tide and respond to familiar pressures in a radically new manner that can positively affect your personal life and your career.

The abstract theme of responsibility versus independence—emphasized by the current Saturn-Uranus opposition—is brought down to a very personal and immediate level by the intuitive Pisces Full Moon on **September 4**. Your dissatisfaction may be greatest at work, for this lunation falls in your 10th House of Career. The perfectionist Virgo New Moon on **September 18** is closely aligned with the Saturn-Uranus opposition, adding great urgency to the decisions you must make. Seek ways to acknowledge your current obligations without letting go of your dreams for change.

> **KEEP IN MIND THIS MONTH**
>
> *Although it may feel as if you have too much on your plate, managing current circumstances as efficiently as possible can assure smoother sailing ahead.*

KEY DATES

SEPTEMBER 1-4 ★ *step outside yourself*

Mental Mercury and physical Mars form tense sesquisquares with visionary Jupiter on **September 1–2**, presenting you with enticing new ideas about your future. Getting there, however, isn't so easy. Thoughtful Mercury in your 5th House of Love is locked in a slow-motion square with assertive Mars in your 2nd House of Self-Worth on **September 3**, setting your drive for security against your desire for pleasure. You are lured away from personal issues by the Pisces Full Moon in your public 10th House on **September 4**. Nevertheless, talking about your fears can help you overcome your inability to initiate action.

SEPTEMBER 12 ★ *dream journal*
Stable foundations are beginning to dissolve, and it's hard to know where to stand. Realistic Saturn's annoying quincunx to nebulous Neptune can add confusion to your life, opening your mind to fantastic scenarios of the future that, unfortunately, may be unrealistic. Still, you must claim these dreams as the guiding lights for the positive changes you're now making.

SUPER NOVA DAYS
SEPTEMBER 17–18 ★ *honest to a fault*
Retrograde Mercury dynamically squares exacting Pluto on **September 17** before backing into critical Virgo. You must tell the truth, even if your disclosure disturbs the status quo. Meanwhile, the Sun's annual opposition to surprising Uranus and its conjunction with somber Saturn set the stage for an all-too-delicate house of cards to come tumbling down. This leads into the logical Virgo New Moon on **September 18**, which offers closure and forces you around the bend into your next phase.

SEPTEMBER 22–23 ★ *prioritize your efforts*
Mercury joins Saturn on **September 22**, giving you another reality check on the same day that the Sun enters Libra to mark the Autumnal Equinox. It's time to begin internalizing recent changes and reestablishing balance wherever you can. The Sun's dynamic square to dark Pluto, combined with Mercury's opposition to wild Uranus on **September 23**, remind you that you cannot let down your guard, especially if someone is fighting the changes you're making. Mars's irritating quincunx to boundless Jupiter makes it difficult to ascertain the effectiveness of your actions. Overcompensating by attempting too much can be counterproductive; it's wiser now to do less but with greater focus.

SEPTEMBER 29 ★ *thanks for the memories*
A month of intense reevaluation and reflection comes to a close today as Mercury turns direct. Tie up as many loose ends as possible, for the Winged Messenger pushes forward over the days and weeks ahead, requiring you to move on without the luxury of revisiting familiar places.

OCTOBER

TAKING FUN SERIOUSLY

If you felt pushed to your limits last month, you now have time to catch your breath, integrate the recent changes, and reestablish a manageable pace of life. Your key planet, Mercury, is again moving direct, which frees you to entertain new ideas and learn fresh ways to interact with others. But first the communication must move through the waning Saturn-Uranus opposition, offering you another chance to put last month's successes and failures into a healthy perspective. Mercury opposes erratic Uranus on **October 4**, possibly shocking you with a wild card in the form of someone who behaves outrageously to provoke a swift and critical response from you. Mercury catches up to authoritative Saturn on **October 8**, testing the validity of your logic while infusing you with the strength of your convictions.

The enthusiastic Aries Full Moon on **October 4** falls in your 11th House of Dreams and Wishes, increasing your desire to find like-minded people with whom you can share your fantastic dreams. The lovely Libra New Moon on **October 18** can be a magical time as long as you don't try to micromanage others, while the Sun's entry into intense Scorpio and your 6th House of Self-Improvement on **October 23** brings your attention back to the details of your own affairs. Saturn steps over the threshold into Libra and leans its weight on your 5th House of Romance and Self-Expression on **October 29**, a powerful shift that will take a couple of years to play out in its entirety. The reawakening of your inner child is not just a flash in the pan; you must summon extra effort to integrate your creative and playful side with your outer adult world.

> **KEEP IN MIND THIS MONTH**
>
> *You are ready for some fun and games, so don't let an obligation get in the way of your enjoyment. You deserve the rest and relaxation.*

KEY DATES

OCTOBER 4 ★ *twists and turns*

Clever Mercury comes into extreme focus on **October 4**, placing an intellectual spin on the otherwise spontaneous Aries Full Moon. You are able to express your desires, for Mercury cooperatively sextiles assertive Mars, yet its irritating quincunx to foggy Neptune and tense opposition to odd Uranus suggest that this day will not unfold according to your expectations. Mars's crunchy quincunx to Neptune and auspicious trine to Uranus reassert the surprising nature of this Full Moon. Don't assume that you know where your actions will lead; stay open to all possibilities to make the most of this exciting day.

SUPER NOVA DAYS
OCTOBER 8-13 ★ *paying the price*

Mental Mercury meets restrictive Saturn on **October 8**, but beautiful Venus's electric opposition to Uranus on **October 9** suggests that you won't be crying over spilled milk. Instead, you may be gleefully turning things upside down for the thrill of it. You are ready for a weekend of fun as a joyful Sun-Jupiter trine positively impacts your 5th House of Play on **October 10**. Still, there is a deeper side to your thinking with Mercury running into dark Pluto the same day. Ultimately, you can have a great time getting a little crazy, but Venus's conjunction with Saturn on **October 13** may remind you that you cannot arbitrarily escape from reality. You are restrained by the rules of the game and the commitments you've made.

OCTOBER 14-16 ★ *sweet masquerade*

Venus gains strength as she waltzes into her home sign of graceful Libra and your 5th House of Self-Expression on **October 14**, only to dance a complicated tango with domineering Pluto on **October 15**. Your senses are heightened, though the line between pleasure and pain may be quite thin. The show continues as assertive Mars enters dramatic Leo on **October 16**, further encouraging you to strut your stuff. But others may not totally understand you now, for Neptune casts a spell that enables you to be many things to different people. You may be irresistible, but be careful not to intentionally mislead anyone.

OCTOBER 28 ★ *get physical*

Sweet Venus trines lucky Jupiter on **October 28**, one of the most fortunate aspects possible, activating your playful 5th House along with your adventurous 9th House, but this isn't all fun and games. Mercury enters relentless Scorpio and your 6th House of Health and Work, focusing your thoughts on specific tasks you must address to maintain your well-being. Additionally, a Sun-Mars square floods your system with adrenaline, possibly sparking unnecessary conflicts about something trivial. Redirect anger into healthy competitive sports or vigorous exercise.

NOVEMBER

CONSCIOUS CUTBACKS

Something big has changed, yet it might be difficult to put your finger on exactly what. The culprit is Saturn the Taskmaster, which has just moved into indecisive Libra in your 5th House of Romance, Children, and Creativity—where it stays until **October 5, 2012.** Although its long-term presence can make you more serious about expressing your creativity, improving your love life, and stabilizing relationships with your children or parents, it can be rather rocky at first. Restrictive Saturn squares evolutionary Pluto on **November 15,** yet you will likely feel the effects of this powerhouse duo throughout the month. Your best intentions can run into obstacles that seem to thwart your development and stand in the way of your happiness. But this is no time for denial or quick fixes. You can't cleverly dance your way around what's in your path, for this transit lasts through **August 21, 2010.** Although you may worry whether you can withstand the slow but intense pressure to change, have faith that you are up to the task. Instead of fighting the inevitable, examine the limitations on your freedom of expression and determine how to get by on less. Reducing excess and waste can minimize the struggles ahead.

> **KEEP IN MIND THIS MONTH**
>
> *Your fearful resistance to the process of transformation can make life more challenging. When you lovingly embrace the changes, the caterpillar is freed to become the butterfly.*

Although the underlying theme created by the Saturn-Pluto square is a sobering one, you can also have your share of fun this month. The sensual Taurus Full Moon on **November 2** falls in your 12th House of Fantasy, revving up your dreams of escape. A magnetic Scorpio New Moon on **November 16**—just one day after the Saturn-Pluto square—is a new beginning and can empower you to change your daily routine to create more freedom at work.

KEY DATES

NOVEMBER 1-2 ★ *realistic romantic*

Sarcastic Mercury dynamically squares energetic Mars in your 3rd House of Siblings on **November 1,** suggesting the possibility of a family squabble. Demands at work can add tension at home when Mercury and Mars both sesquisquare rebellious Uranus in your 10th House of Career on **November 2.** The Taurus Full Moon in your 12th House of Spirituality gives you a dose of much-needed common sense, while Venus creates a delicious trine to dreamy Neptune on the same day. Your feet may be on the ground, but your heart sees love through rose-colored glasses now.

SUPER NOVA DAYS
NOVEMBER 8–11 ★ *giant leap of faith*
Tension-producing squares from the spiritual trio of Jupiter, Chiron, and
Neptune supercharge intelligent Mercury in your 6th House of Self-
Improvement beginning on **November 8**, stimulating your hopes for a happier
and healthier life. You can see a more perfect version of yourself in your
mind's eye, but may worry that you'll fall short of your vision. Fortunately, a
Sun-Jupiter square on **November 10** and Mercury's sympathetic trine to brilliant Uranus on **November 11** can be powerful catalysts that elicit a dynamic
change in your thinking, enabling you to break through the status quo and
propelling you to make a much-needed change.

NOVEMBER 19 ★ *seek common ground*
Intense feelings aren't always easy for you to manage, especially when they're at
odds with your actions. Seductive Venus in Scorpio dynamically squares hot Mars
in selfish Leo, testing your patience with someone close to you. Venus and Mars,
the cosmic lovers, are not happy with each other right now, and yet this is often a
time when conflict can fuel the heat of passion. Instead of arguing about your differences, be flexible enough to find your way back to a place of pleasure.

NOVEMBER 25–26 ★ *blurred lines of reality*
You are ready for something different when romantic Venus trines unique Uranus
on **November 25**. Talkative Mercury in your 7th House of Partnerships trines
assertive Mars on **November 26**, urging you to say what you want. Be careful,
though, for Venus is also squaring murky Neptune. You may discover that you've
been misled by your own fantasies.

NOVEMBER 29–30 ★ *count to ten first*
Mars sesquisquares militant Pluto on **November 29**, daring you to face resistance
head-on. Additionally, Mercury's anxious square to erratic Uranus on **November 30**
can force you to talk before you think about the consequences. Take a few deep
breaths and consider the effects of your words before speaking them aloud.

DECEMBER

IMMEASURABLE PROGRESS

Much of December is defined by boundless Jupiter, wounded Chiron, and spiritual Neptune, as these three spiritually oriented planets coalesce in a slow-motion dance that has lasted throughout the year. Jupiter joins Chiron on **December 7** in your 9th House of Higher Thought and Faraway Places, offering you rare glimpses of the pot of gold at the end of the rainbow. Your quest for healing may take you on a metaphysical journey, combined with travel in the real world. Jupiter's conjunction with mystical Neptune on **December 21**, also the Winter Solstice, is the crowning glory of this year and can greatly enhance your understanding of your place in the world and the path ahead.

The month begins with growing anticipation as the restless Gemini Full Moon in your 1st House of Self on **December 2** brings your most personal feelings to the surface while the friendly Sagittarius New Moon on **December 16** falls in your 7th House of Others. Its sextile to the Jupiter-Chiron-Neptune super-conjunction can herald the arrival of a significant mentor or healer. The New Moon's square to unpredictable Uranus in your 10th House of Status suggests a sudden shift in your role at work or within your community. You may feel blocked by your lack of accomplishment because of physical Mars's retrograde turn on **December 20** and mental Mercury's backward turn on **December 26**. This is just an illusion; you are simply being given an opportunity to put your life in order before both planets turn direct next year. The Cancer Full Moon Eclipse on **December 31** is a final exclamation point to a year of extremes that can rouse you to reveal the truth in a relationship.

> **KEEP IN MIND THIS MONTH**
>
> *You cannot judge yourself by what you accomplish publicly; even the most profound inner work won't show results right away.*

KEY DATES

DECEMBER 4–5 ★ *just friends for now*

Serious Saturn receives a sweet kiss from Venus on **December 4**, giving you the ability to act maturely in love. Saturn in your 5th House of Self-Expression, however, can take the edge off the excitement, while a semisquare from Mars on **December 5** adds an element of discouragement—especially if your romantic overtures are not being reciprocated. Still, smart Mercury's entry into ambitious Capricorn helps you weigh the long-term consequences of your present actions.

DECEMBER 7 ★ *glass half full, not half empty*

Mercury joins transformative Pluto and squares restrictive Saturn on **December 7**, reenergizing the long-lasting Saturn-Pluto square that has you tipping the balance of power in a current relationship or questioning the price you're willing to pay for security in love. Broad-minded Jupiter joins healer Chiron, encouraging you to look at the potential of what you currently have, rather than becoming pessimistic about what's missing. Meanwhile, the Sun's metaphysical quintile to Saturn makes room for magic—as long as you're willing to apply the spiritual tools that you've gathered to your current situation.

DECEMBER 20–21 ★ *spiritual muse*

Self-directed Mars turns retrograde on **December 20**, convincing you that what you want will remain—at least for now—just beyond your reach. The third and final conjunction between prophetic Jupiter and spiritual Neptune combines with the Sun's entry into traditional Capricorn on **December 21** to offer hopeful dreams as you look toward the New Year. This Winter Solstice is sweetened by a lovely Venus-Neptune sextile, sugarcoating your dreams and adding a twinkle to your eye.

SUPER NOVA DAYS

DECEMBER 24–26 ★ *all in due time*

Loving Venus enters conservative Capricorn on **December 25**—yet another indicator that you are willing to wait for what you want. The Sun's conjunction with Pluto and square to Saturn on **December 24–25** reemphasize your commitment to engage in your emotional process, even if you don't know where it will lead. Mercury turns retrograde in your transformational 8th House on **December 26**, requiring you to go back over issues you thought were already handled. Accept the slower speed at which events unfold, rather than frustrating yourself by trying to force the universe to stick to your preferred schedule.

DECEMBER 28–31 ★ *love beyond fear*

On **December 28–29**, Venus in your 8th House of Intimacy joins Pluto and squares Saturn, intensifying your emotional reactions. Reevaluate what you want if others aren't willing to meet you halfway. The possessive Cancer Full Moon in your 2nd House of Values on **December 31** can also expose fears about changing dynamics within a relationship. Letting go of irrational insecurities can help solidify what is truly yours.

CANCER

JUNE 21–JULY 22

CANCER

2008 SUMMARY

Relationships open your life and widen your horizons this year, but some opportunities won't prove quite as amazing as they seem at first glance—exercising caution and using common sense could be your best weapons against disappointment. Pluto has tentatively moved into Capricorn—also in your 7th House—signifying that you are taking the first small steps toward a much larger transformation that will take years to fully unfold.

AUGUST— *a marathon of change*

Fear of change might upset you, but retreating will not be helpful. Flexibility in the face of adversity will always be your greatest ally.

SEPTEMBER—*balancing act*

Unexpected events may require immediate attention, but don't change your overall direction—the distractions will fade, allowing you to continue on your way.

OCTOBER—*closer to success*

You are preparing to step into something new, but must decide what to leave behind so you can pursue the opportunities ahead.

NOVEMBER—*at the edge of a new world*

Maintain your daily routines as best you can. It makes sense to fulfill your current responsibilities, even if you are seeking to radically change the direction of your life.

DECEMBER—*be true to yourself*

Be prepared to take a stand for what is in your heart if sharing your dreams arouses any resistance in others.

2008 CALENDAR

AUGUST

FRIDAY 1 ★ Confidence can bring healthy abundance

TUESDAY 5 ★ Powerful and passionate forces are at work through the 6th

WEDNESDAY 13 ★ **SUPER NOVA DAYS** Trust your logic and judgment

SATURDAY 23 ★ Keep an open mind during emotional swings

FRIDAY 29 ★ Release the past now. It's time to move forward

SEPTEMBER

SUNDAY 7 ★ Keep your eye on the prize through the 9th

MONDAY 15 ★ **SUPER NOVA DAYS** Follow your instincts through the 19th

SATURDAY 20 ★ Keep the personal separate from the professional through the 22nd

SUNDAY 28 ★ Blend fantasy with reality through the 29th

OCTOBER

THURSDAY 2 ★ Grin and bear it, or express anger kindly through the 4th

FRIDAY 10 ★ **SUPER NOVA DAYS** Tell the truth and accept the consequences through the 15th

WEDNESDAY 22 ★ A joyful flow of energy encourages spontaneity

TUESDAY 28 ★ Life is on a track to happiness through the 31st

NOVEMBER

MONDAY 3 ★ **SUPER NOVA DAYS** Tensions increase and something must give by the 4th

WEDNESDAY 12 ★ An unexpected opportunity turns night into day through the 13th

FRIDAY 21 ★ Receive just compensation for past work through the 23rd

THURSDAY 27 ★ Take baby steps through the 29th

DECEMBER

MONDAY 1 ★ Treat yourself today, but try to stay within your budget

FRIDAY 5 ★ You want to stay silent, but express your hurt anyway

FRIDAY 12 ★ **SUPER NOVA DAY** Deep emotions are not easily communicated

SUNDAY 21 ★ Embrace inevitable metamorphosis now

SATURDAY 27 ★ Show your vulnerability and risk rejection

CANCER OVERVIEW

Yomething you are attracted to visions of a more inspiring life that strongly contrasts with the seemingly endless demands put on you every day. The gap between the two may be disconcerting, but the message is one of hope rather than despair. Optimistic Jupiter floats through idealistic Aquarius in your 8th House of Intimacy and Transformation, where it joins spiritual Neptune on May 27, July 10, and December 21. **It is time to forgive others and let go of past disappointments in relationships.** The goal isn't to let someone else off the hook but to untangle yourself from old patterns that keep you turning in circles. Detaching from your history is necessary to fulfill your potential. It may feel disorienting to jettison doubt and toss bad memories away, so allow yourself to wander a bit until you familiarize yourself with new emotional territory.

Eclipses are especially important to you since they always involve your ruling planet, the Moon. They are passages—keyholes in time where a sudden insight or change of circumstances can propel you in a new direction in the weeks leading up to or following the event. Of the five eclipses occurring this year, two of them this summer are bound to hit home. A Capricorn Lunar Eclipse on July 7 falls in your 7th House of Partnerships, sending a message about how you connect with others. Saturn's harmonious trine to the Moon suggests that **emotional clarity and discipline can lead to a well-reasoned shift in relationship patterns**. A Solar Eclipse in your sign on July 21 helps you flush away habits that have been holding you back. Revolutionary Uranus's creative trine to this Sun-Moon conjunction makes change easier than you expect.

Stern Saturn spends most of the year in your 3rd House of Immediate Environment, where the details of daily life require your close attention. Tying up your thoughts with a million and one little tasks may keep you so buried in work and worry that you miss the clouds of opportunity floating by. **It's essential to separate yourself from the clutter of your daily routine to catch your breath and open your mind to other possibilities.** Moments for meditation, quiet walks, or silent time alone turn down the endless drone of responsibilities and show you glimpses of a more fulfilling life. Even if this seems unrealistic, however, it can point you in a positive direction; even falling short of your ideal can elevate your spirits. **Draw a clear line between work and play** instead of allowing your days and nights to blend into a murky mix where inspiration is lost. Dutiful Saturn's oppositions with rebellious Uranus on February 5 and September 15 are moments when you may be pushed to your limit and feel like running away from everyone and everything. You are unlikely to do that, of course, but rather than repressing the urge for change, consider these aspects a reminder of the need to break your routine.

HIGHER PURPOSE

Hopeful Jupiter in unconventional Aquarius occupies your 8th House of Deep Sharing to transform the nature of your relationships. Your boundaries may be stretched by unusual individuals or novel approaches to intimacy. Let your mind lead your heart—it takes imagination to absorb all the gifts that partnership can bring you this year. Common ideals and spiritual interests can bring you to a higher level of understanding with a mate by reinforcing your connection with a higher purpose. Jupiter's conjunctions with Neptune on May 27, July 10, and December 21 offer moments of sublime delight, romantic fantasy, and blind faith, allowing you to overlook down-to-earth matters necessary to sustain a long-term partnership. The Lunar Eclipse in practical Capricorn on July 7 in your 7th House of Others will, however, temporarily bring you back to reality. Love is a wonderful thing, but you need plans and commitment to assure its longevity. If you're single, this event marks a period when a clear sense of purpose, self-respect, and a willingness to talk frankly about your needs enables you to come out of your shell and pursue your desires more directly.

CONTROLLED GROWTH

Assimilate growth slowly this year, for boundless Jupiter in theoretical Aquarius is countered by Saturn in Virgo's need to master technical details. Executing your work skillfully, demonstrating a high level of competence, and communicating effectively can turn a short-term opportunity into a long-term position. Venus, the planet of beauty and sociability, shifts into reverse gear in your 10th House of Career on March 6 and will remain retrograde until April 17. You may need to reevaluate on-the-job relationships, reconnect with professional contacts, and cut expenses to maintain your current status. Reuniting with old colleagues can be helpful, especially if you're looking for different employment or trying to stir up new business. Mars, the ruler of your 10th House, makes a stubborn square from earthy Taurus to visionary Jupiter and Neptune on July 6 that can stretch you thin with overcommitment or excess responsibility. Temper expansive tendencies with a more realistic view of your limitations.

SENSIBLE SPENDING

A Leo Lunar Eclipse on February 9 falls in your 2nd House of Resources, which could put some pressure on your finances. Returning an expensive item or cutting back on your elaborate lifestyle might not be your first choice, but it's better than borrowing money and increasing debt. That perfect whatever that you can't live without just might be more than you really can live with. Generous Jupiter and imaginative Neptune in your 8th House of Shared Resources reveal potential profitability via investments and partners this year. Idealism backed by careful research is a winning combination, but speculation based on a hunch or unsupported feelings could be costly.

ALTERNATIVE HEALING

Jupiter, the ruler of your 6th House of Health, is sensitized by three conjunctions with fuzzy Neptune, which can make diagnoses more difficult. However, you're also likely to be more responsive to subtle forms of healing such as homeopathy, visualization, and gentle massage. The Solar Eclipse on the last degree of your sign on July 21 could spawn symptoms related to previous illnesses. Fortunately, liberating Uranus's creative trine to the eclipse allows you to rapidly adjust your responses and send any pesky pain on its way. The message is that your willingness to change is a critical asset in maintaining your physical well-being.

AVOID DENIAL

Harmony on the home front may be your goal, but going back in time to address unfinished emotional business is a challenge worth facing this year. The retrograde turn of loving Venus, the ruler of your 4th House of Family, stirs deep waters between March 6 and April 17. Your feelings can fluctuate between a desire for flight and an urge to fight, yet there is no single way to navigate the complex emotions that are emerging. Trust that every stance you take can be useful as long as you keep working at solving the problem rather than trying to repress it.

UNEXPECTED JOURNEYS

Unpredictable Uranus in your 9th House of Travel and Higher Education is opposed by repressive Saturn on February 5 and September 15, throwing obstacles in your path for a week or so coming and going. If you're on the road, leave time in your schedule for unplanned delays and detours. Course work could be interrupted as well, or you might feel a sudden urge to quit your studies. Pursuing an unconventional educational path or traveling freely without an itinerary are two ways to make good use of these unusual alignments.

SELF-REFLECTION

Curious Mercury is the ruler of your 12th House of Spirituality and represents the open connection you have with other dimensions and altered states of reality. Its retrograde periods offer different access points to these nonmaterial domains. Other people may be your guides from January 11 through February 1 with Mercury backpedaling through your 7th House of Partners and 8th House of Shared Resources. The messenger planet shifts into reverse in your 12th House on May 6, opening an especially rich three-week period of otherworldly experiences. Mercury's retrograde in your 4th House of Home and Family on September 6–29 triggers memories to deepen soul connections, while its retrograde on December 26 starts another cycle of introspection in your 7th House of Relationships.

RICK & JEFF'S TIP FOR THE YEAR:
Learn to Grow by Letting Go

Memory is a gift and a curse. It is the source of identity—the constant stream of experience that connects the days and years of your life. Yet it can also be a burden when the presence of the past inhibits your ability to live fully in the present and to evolve in the future. Jupiter, astrology's traditional "Greater Benefic," blesses you with an abundance of awareness and opportunity when you step out of what you knew before and open yourself to what there is to be learned right now. Truth cuts across all beliefs and expectations; let go of your outmoded illusions so you can replace them with a richer reality.

JANUARY

EMOTIONAL EXPLORATION

A fresh wind hits the sails of your relationships on **January 5** when buoyant Jupiter enters airy Aquarius and sets up shop for a year in your 8th House of Intimacy. Exposure to different people and unique ways to dig deeper can stretch your ideas about sharing while encouraging experimentation. Every Full Moon raises emotional tides, but the one on **January 10** is in your sign, making it even more dramatic and heartfelt. You may find your insecurities exaggerated when you interpret small slights as major insults. Fortunately, inventive Uranus forms a brilliant trine to the Full Moon from your 9th House of Higher Truth, enlightening you with an original perspective or an unexpected opportunity to break free from old habits and attitudes. If crisis arises, stay cool and step out of character to find a surprising new way to respond that can quickly turn things in a favorable direction.

Communicative Mercury turns retrograde in your 8th House of Shared Resources on **January 11**, which could require backtracking in agreements you've made with others. Renegotiating financial or personal deals may seem more complicated than necessary, but patiently untangling any knots of misunderstanding will be well worth the effort. The New Moon in intellectual Aquarius on **January 26** is a Solar Eclipse that can undermine faith in a person you trust. Zealous Jupiter's close proximity indicates that his or her big promises may fall short of the mark.

The point, though, is for you to discover your own truth rather than relying on the judgment of others. Jupiter forms tense aspects to the ongoing Saturn-Uranus opposition on **January 27 and 30**, which can provoke rapid expansion and contraction. Temper your initial excitement with a bit of caution to avoid extreme reactions.

> **KEEP IN MIND THIS MONTH**
>
> *No matter how familiar a situation may seem, there are always new ways to react to it.*

KEY DATES

JANUARY 3–4 ★ *magical journey*

Sweet Venus swims into imaginative Pisces and your 9th House of Faraway Places on **January 3**, inspiring you to dream about a romantic getaway. Whether you're able to leave town with a desirable companion or not, adding something exotic into your life is especially rewarding now. Spiritual, artistic, or musical events, especially of a foreign nature, can lift you above your ordinary surroundings and make you feel like an angel. Venus forms a constructive sextile with adept Pluto on **January 4**, which is ideal for handling delicate relationship matters with a gentle determination.

SUPER NOVA DAYS
JANUARY 9-11 ★ *expression sets you free*
The Sun in your 7th House of Partnerships forms a favorable sextile with unconventional Uranus on **January 9**, supplying a newfound sense of freedom that can release you from limits imposed by others. The Full Moon in your sign on **January 10** persuades you to show your feelings. Even if you're overly emotional, it's better to express yourself than to remain silent now. Although trickster Mercury's backward turn on **January 11** tends to tangle up messages and create more confusion, it's still vital to address complicated issues. Have enough patience to explain yourself repeatedly and listen carefully to others. The understanding you eventually reach will certainly be worth the effort. The Sun forms a stabilizing trine with rock-solid Saturn, bringing maturity and discipline to strengthen alliances and earn you respect.

JANUARY 17-18 ★ *fast learner*
Someone may unexpectedly back out of an agreement on **January 17** when retrograde Mercury forms a skittish semisquare with erratic Uranus. Clingy emotions are a means to compensate for uncertain thoughts, so you may be tempted to hold on even when it's clear that conditions have radically changed. No matter how you feel, it's sometimes better to let go and start all over than to stick to a plan whose time has passed. Good news is more likely on **January 18** as Mercury joins positive Jupiter. Your capacity to understand new concepts about intimacy is enhanced by a skillful teacher.

JANUARY 24-25 ★ *realistic optimism*
The Sun and Jupiter join in your 8th House of Deep Sharing on **January 24**, encouraging you to take more chances with people. Wise Saturn gets a boost thanks to an energetic trine from dynamic Mars, increasing your efficiency and providing a sense of safety and competence under any circumstances. Sociable Venus opposes Saturn to reveal doubt, but then aligns favorably with Mars to overcome insecurity through action. The Sun shifts from a rebellious semisquare with Uranus on the **24th** to a somber sesquisquare with Saturn on **January 25** that is bound to bring you back down to earth.

FEBRUARY

OPEN YOUR MIND

Chatty Mercury turns direct in your 7th House of Partnerships on **February 1**, allowing information to flow more easily in the days and weeks ahead. Expressing your expectations of others in concrete terms puts relationships on a more solid foundation. Vivacious Venus enters fiery Aries and your 10th House of Career on **February 2**, stirring excitement on the job with a new creative project or an attractive colleague. Impulse drives you to set aside caution and say yes to a project without considering the weight of responsibility you may be accepting. A willingness to jump into unexplored territory will enhance your professional status as long as you follow through on the commitments you make. The Full Moon in gutsy Leo on **February 9** is a Lunar Eclipse that falls in your 2nd House of Resources. Managing your time, money, or energy can be challenging as nebulous Neptune's opposition lures you to chase a dream without regard to its cost. Nurture your vision with a practical perspective to turn it into reality.

Clever Mercury returns to inventive Aquarius and your 8th House of Intimacy and Transformation on **February 14**. Complex conversations can be tiring, tempting you to retreat to more familiar patterns of perception. Yet doors may open in your professional and personal life when you're willing to let go of comfortable assumptions and look at your interactions from different angles. The New Moon in sensitive Pisces on **February 24** rains drops of inspiration in your 9th House of Big Ideas. They water visions of spiritual awakening through religious practice, travel, or education that may seem out of reach, but could be well worth pursuing.

> **KEEP IN MIND THIS MONTH**
>
> *An idea doesn't have to feel right to be right—your thinking can be more advanced than your emotions now.*

KEY DATES
FEBRUARY 5 ★ *to thine own self be true*
On **February 5**, strict Saturn and rebellious Uranus form the second of five powerful oppositions that come and go until **July 2010**. Tension can rise as the struggle to meet your day-to-day obligations is countered by unexpected events or uncooperative individuals. Striving to stay on schedule ups your stress levels when what you really need is a break. Take mental mini-vacations to put your mind somewhere else, even if only for a few minutes a day. The Sun, Venus, and Pluto hook up in hard aspects that can attract bullies and undermine self-confidence. Look

deeply within to discover your true desires, stand firm for what you want, and resist the pressure to cave in to someone else's demands.

FEBRUARY 11–12 ★ *creative conflict*
Confrontation is possible as assertive Mars forms hard aspects to the ongoing Saturn-Uranus opposition. His sesquisquare to Saturn on **February 11** represents unwanted restraint, while a semisquare to Uranus on **February 12** stirs feelings of rebellion. Positively, this is a time to discover radical solutions for stubborn problems by turning anger into constructive action. A spacey Sun-Neptune conjunction on **February 12** could bring a cloud of confusion that facilitates denial, making it more difficult to channel frustration effectively. Still, the idealism and imagination of this pair offer forgiveness and faith.

SUPER NOVA DAYS
FEBRUARY 16–17 ★ *relationship adventure*
Your open-minded attitude attracts interesting individuals and supportive allies where you least expect them. Mars joins the Moon's North Node in unconventional Aquarius on **February 16**. This connection in your 8th House of Deep Sharing is strengthened by a sweet sextile between loving Venus and adventurous Jupiter. Delight in the company of unusual people and pleasure in new activities arise when you can let go of preconceived ideas and let yourself be surprised. Mars joins outgoing Jupiter on **February 17** to put rocket fuel in the tank of relationships, taking you to places you've never gone before. Your enthusiasm convinces others to surpass their own limits, infusing more passion into any partnership.

FEBRUARY 27–28 ★ *minefield*
The air thickens and the pace of progress slows with normally mobile Mars caught up in tense aspects with Pluto and Saturn. His semisquare with ponderous Pluto on **February 27** can make a small disagreement feel like a major war. Avoid dramatizing differences unless you want to force a confrontation now. Mars makes an irritating quincunx with Saturn on **February 28** that may throw you off schedule. Mercury's semisquare with Pluto deepens your thoughts, but adds an edge to conversations that provoke strong reactions. Focus and choose your words carefully for maximum effect and minimum fuss.

MARCH

STARTING OVER

Venus turns retrograde in your 10th House of Public Responsibility on **March 6**, allowing you to review recent battles for approval, especially on the job. Has it been worthwhile to push yourself so hard? If you have been uncertain in relationships or slow in developing new skills, this is a chance to catch your breath, and in some cases start over. Consider your own desires before surrendering yourself to the needs of others as Venus, the planet of self-worth, moves through bold Aries. The practical Virgo Full Moon on **March 10** reinforces the tension of the ongoing opposition between dutiful Saturn and rebellious Uranus. Fortunately, its presence in your 3rd House of Information helps you analyze your emotions and communicate with calm efficiency. The spiritual Pisces Sun shines in your 9th House of Higher Truth until **March 20**, adding faith to the mix, opening a perspective wide enough to blend Saturn's competence and commitment with Uranus's hunger for freedom. Your emotional intelligence may be especially valuable in helping others navigate these choppy waters.

Lucky Jupiter forms hard aspects with Saturn and Pluto on **March 22 and 27** that can make it hard for sore losers to completely let go. Know-it-all Jupiter in your 8th House of Deep Sharing can represent partners who have a choke hold on the truth and won't allow any opposing points of view. But it's also possible that the need to be right hooks you so deeply, you become obsessed that others see things your way. Philosophical struggles and disagreements about long-range plans will be revisited in **mid-August**, with final adjustments in place by Jupiter's last quincunx to Saturn in early **February 2010**.

> **KEEP IN MIND THIS MONTH**
>
> *Changing the way you work can seem like a step backward now, but it will almost certainly help you achieve quicker results later.*

KEY DATES

MARCH 5–8 ★ *the fuzzy zone*

Mental Mercury joins dissolving Neptune on **March 5**, a pair that's strong on imagination and weak on details. Facts fade as feelings fuse with thinking, inspiring vision but provoking misunderstanding. Vulnerability runs rampant with approval-seeking Venus teetering at her turning point on **March 6**, so try not to take what you hear too personally. Mars conjuncts Neptune on **March 8**, enabling you to soften your anger, put spirituality into action, or waste energy chasing illusions.

Mercury's entry into psychic Pisces tones up your intuition while a tough Sun-Saturn opposition pushes you against a wall of reality. Strong intentions are best expressed with flexibility.

SUPER NOVA DAYS
MARCH 10–11 ★ *clear the decks*
The volatile Virgo Full Moon on **March 10** may rock your boat emotionally but should sweep away cobwebs of confusion. Strong feelings push you past lingering uncertainty and put issues on the table, where you can see them more clearly. Frank communication gets a boost from an intelligent sextile between rational Mercury and passionate Pluto, helping you uncover patterns of thought and behavior that are ripe for change. A joyous Venus-Jupiter sextile on **March 11** may bring rewards and recognition for previous work or provide generous support from a friend or colleague.

MARCH 20 ★ *professional propulsion*
The Sun enters the initiating fire sign of Aries and your 10th House of Career, igniting new interests and challenges, marking the Spring Equinox and the start of a new astrological year. A battle with an authority figure is one way to express your internal conflict between preservation and pushing forward. Don't be distracted by problems with others, though, because the real issue is about what you choose to do for yourself. If you're happy where you are, you can advance your career more quickly. But if you're bored or blocked, this can motivate you to start looking elsewhere for fulfillment.

MARCH 26–30 ★ *make your move*
The New Moon in enterprising Aries on **March 26** scatters seeds of stimulation in your 10th House of Public Responsibility. You may be itching to take on big projects, hungry for attention, or fed up with your boss. Mercury and Venus join the Sun and Moon through **March 30**, taming the flames of passion with reason and sensitivity. Don't talk yourself out of taking a chance if your other options are to shut down emotionally or strike out in anger. Penetrating Pluto's tense square to the New Moon increases your desire for change, which only makes movement feel more dangerous. Fortunately, you don't need to plot every step to reach your goal. When action aligns with intention, you'll be guided in the right direction.

APRIL

TAKE THE LEAD

Dark Pluto turns retrograde in your 7th House of Partnerships on **April 4**, beginning a long process of digging through unresolved relationship issues. Don't shy away from looking at the unpleasant parts of yourself and others: The power for positive change lies in facing them. Fortunately, an uplifting perspective on personal alliances is presented by the Full Moon in cooperative Libra on **April 9**. This opposition to the Sun in independent Aries normally can shake your tree by rousing feelings of insecurity. But supportive trines from the spiritual trio of Jupiter, Neptune, and Chiron in Aquarius put any struggle you encounter between inner needs and external obligations into a wider perspective. Rather than feeling pulled apart, recognize how your personal and public sides are connected in a meaningful whole. If you can't see this on your own, intelligent individuals are there to show you the way.

Sociable Venus in your 10th House of Status shifts out of her retrograde phase on **April 17**, helping the wheels of romance turn more easily and, perhaps, lighting a fire of hope in your professional life. The creative Sun enters stable Taurus in your 11th House of Groups on **April 19**, providing you with a surer sense of yourself among friends and colleagues. Taking a leadership position is easy for you now if you believe in the cause. The New Moon in sensible Taurus on **April 24** is square the Moon's Nodes, calling for more finesse in relating to other people's feelings. However, powerful Pluto forms a constructive trine to this Sun-Moon conjunction to intensify Taurus's often laid-back energy. This enables you to tap into your deepest desires and apply them with passion and control, overcoming obstacles and producing tangible results.

> **KEEP IN MIND THIS MONTH**
>
> *Once you're fully engaged in a project, you will discover additional resources that weren't obvious when you began the process.*

KEY DATES

APRIL 3–4 ★ *eyes on the road*

Sweet Venus backs into a tense square with tough Pluto on **April 3**, possibly undercutting your confidence in a partner. Don't give in to manipulation or coercion—it sets a pattern for abuse. Take criticism at work with professionalism, since learning from any mistakes or misunderstanding will increase your value. A smart Mercury-Jupiter sextile on **April 4** sharpens your mind and attracts chatty people.

Be careful of charming distractions, though, as a stone-cold Mars-Saturn opposition leaves little room for mistakes. Get an early start if you're traveling: Haste can lead to problems, while a patient approach can produce powerful results.

APRIL 9–11 ★ *relaxed realism*
Mental Mercury enters Taurus on **April 9**, bringing ideas down to earth. Its sesquisquare to stern Saturn reflects pessimism rather than realism, however, so be careful not to let doubt stop you in your tracks. The Libra Full Moon reminds you that there are at least two sides to every story. This could make it harder for you to take a stand, yet its purpose is to show you how to graciously balance yourself between opposing forces. Friendly Jupiter sextiles the Sun on **April 10**, providing gifts of encouragement and insight from generous people. A discerning Mercury-Pluto trine on **April 11** makes deep conversation possible as Venus retrogrades into sensitive Pisces, adding compassion to the mix for greater intimacy.

APRIL 15–17 ★ *revolutionary thoughts*
An electric Mars-Uranus conjunction on **April 15** can provoke shocking comments when you can no longer keep opinions to yourself. This may initiate an argument, but could also provide you with the push you need to make a radical move. Further education, travel, and battling for a cause that excites you are excellent ways to apply this impulse. An imaginative Sun-Neptune sextile, however, shows a gentler way to make your point that doesn't drive others away. Mercury brings reason with a trine to Saturn on **April 17** that helps contain vulnerable feelings associated with Venus changing direction.

SUPER NOVA DAYS
APRIL 21–24 ★ *work becomes play*
A spicy Venus-Mars conjunction on **April 21** enhances creativity and brings fun to the workplace. Mars then moves into fiery Aries on **April 22**, followed by Venus on **April 24**. These personal planets illuminate your 10th House of Career with enthusiasm and charisma. New activities and professional relationships add excitement in your current position or make it clear that it's time to move on to greener pastures. Romance on the job is possible, so curb flirtatious behavior unless you're ready to take it beyond work. Intelligence shines with Mercury connecting to global Jupiter on the **22nd** and brilliant Uranus on the **24th**, but you may need to do some editing to make your ideas usable.

MAY

SPIRIT QUEST

Mercury, the communication planet, turns retrograde on **May 7**, mixing up messages, data, and details before shifting back into forward gear on **May 30**. Most of the retrograde activates your 11th House of Groups, suggesting that you seek clarity by cleaning up unfinished business with friends and colleagues. Conversely, structuring Saturn going direct on **May 16** helps you reap the rewards of hard work and study while also supporting more substantial conversations with partners. Although finalizing matters is unlikely before Mercury is direct at the end of the month, the maturity of Saturn in your 3rd House of Information lays down a foundation of objective analysis and honesty to strengthen alliances. The Sun enters interactive Gemini and your 12th House of Spirituality on **May 20**, commencing a phase of meaningful connection with other dimensions. Make time for quiet contemplation, metaphysical research, and communion with nature to allow the lessons of the universe to sink in.

Faithful Jupiter begins a series of conjunctions with Chiron the Wounded Healer and mystical Neptune on **May 23 and 27**, reinforcing your relationship with the divine. Words alone cannot describe the awareness that occurs when you drop judgment and open your heart. These waves of higher consciousness return in July and December and can transform a crisis into a transcendental experience. The curious Gemini New Moon on **May 24** shines light into your 12th House in the form of intuitive guidance or magical support. Its crunchy quincunx with curmudgeonly Pluto in your 7th House of Partnerships may confront you with a skeptical response. However, you have nothing to prove to others when you find the ultimate truth within yourself.

> **KEEP IN MIND THIS MONTH**
>
> *The insights you are receiving are more powerful when you don't dilute the messages by trying to explain or justify them to anyone else.*

KEY DATES

MAY 4–5 ★ *more or less*

Leaping before looking can stress you out at work as a hyperactive Mars-Jupiter semisquare pushes you past your limits on **May 4**. Fortunately, the Sun aligns with responsible Saturn in a constructive trine on **May 5** that helps you to pull back and manage your time and energy more efficiently.

MAY 9 ★ *love magnet*

The Scorpio Full Moon falls in your 5th House of Romance, boosting passion, creativity, and your ability to attract attention and keep it. The sensual Scorpio Moon gives you subtle gifts of seduction for personal fulfillment or professional gain. Your instincts make it easy for you to touch others where they are most receptive; you can provoke strong responses with little obvious effort. A harmonious trine from quirky Uranus adds new elements to your game so that you can engage others intensely without evoking jealousy or resentment.

MAY 16-17 ★ *fantasy trumps fact*

Overextending yourself to friends, or believing their outrageous promises, can be a big issue with an exaggerating Sun-Jupiter square on **May 16**. A Sun-Uranus sextile offers unexpected gifts of excitement and inspiration, yet a pal or co-worker can wear you out as the Sun also squares vulnerable Chiron. This trend continues on **May 17** with a Sun-Neptune square that favors illusion over reality. Blissful moments are possible, but are best appreciated with plenty of free time and no expectations of productivity.

SUPER NOVA DAYS
MAY 20-21 ★ *it's all in your head*

Mercury squares dreamy Neptune on **May 20**, increasing the likelihood of more retrograde confusion. When you feel certain about a fact, it's quite possible that you're wrong—so triple-check your sources before forcing the issue. An edgy Venus-Saturn quincunx makes it difficult to satisfy critics, bosses, or even yourself. If you aren't getting the approval you desire, wait for a better day to seek it. The Sun's entry into chatty Gemini and Mercury's unstable square with excessive Jupiter provide an overload of information, making this a day when, perhaps, less is more. Your mind sharpens noticeably on **May 21** with a Mercury-Uranus sextile that speeds through conflicting data and allows you to cleverly find exactly what you need.

MAY 26-27 ★ *accurate impulses*

Assertive Mars pushing through your 10th House of Career aligns nicely with Chiron and Jupiter on **May 26** and Neptune on **May 27**. Putting intuition into action is easy, so trust your instincts, even if your methods are unconventional. Take the initiative and others will join in with their energy and experience. Enthusiasm rises and brilliant strategies are launched as you inspire others with a gentle touch.

JUNE

Venus enters her earthy home sign of Taurus on **June 6** to awaken the senses and increase your potential for delight. Her passage through your 11th House of Teamwork heightens the pleasure that comes from working well with friends and colleagues. The expansive Sagittarius Full Moon on **June 7** helps you realize how overstretched you feel. Demanding Saturn's tense square to this Sun-Moon opposition, though, reminds you to reduce your commitments and simplify your life to maintain good health and vitality. Job stress in the following days could force you into a decision that leads to a change of responsibilities. Mercury revisits mentally active Gemini and your spiritual 12th House on **June 13**, where it turned retrograde a month ago. Glimpses of inspiration you had back then return in fuller form, enabling you to articulate your dreams more clearly. Everyone, it seems, has an idea about what you should do with your life, but don't be in a hurry to make a move just yet.

Philosophical Jupiter turns retrograde in your 8th House of Shared Resources on **June 15**, initiating four months of reflection and revision about your most important relationships. Joint projects can misfire or veer off track if you stick too rigidly to a plan; you and a partner must make on-the-fly adjustments to keep pace with unexpected changes. The Sun enters your sign on **June 21**, marking the Summer Solstice and a new year of personal growth. However, the New Moon in cautious Cancer on **June 22** can put you through an emotional grinder and force you to eliminate extraneous activities or individuals keeping you from concentrating on what you value most.

> **KEEP IN MIND THIS MONTH**
>
> *You see many more possibilities than you can possibly act upon. Feel free to observe them without choosing until the moment is ripe.*

KEY DATES

JUNE 4–5 ★ *concentrated force*

A trine between active Mars and potent Pluto on **June 4** can help you get more out of relationships by focusing on what's essential right now and letting go of the rest. Greater efficiency in working partnerships is likely, and your power to motivate others increases. Eliminating obstacles to focus on core issues makes the Sun-Saturn square on **June 5** easier to handle. This demanding aspect can represent additional responsibilities that slow your progress. But if you are well organized, it's an opportunity to earn respect from someone difficult to please.

JUNE 9-10 ★ *mind expansion*
Communication is usually reliably simple with Mercury in sure-footed Taurus, but right now information overwhelms and faulty facts can damage your credibility. A clever Mercury-Uranus sextile on **June 9** spurs bright ideas, yet the messenger planet's difficult square with nebulous Neptune follows with a cloud of confusion. Speak precisely and listen carefully to clarify the difference between solid statements and wild speculations. Mercury's square to Jupiter on **June 10** enhances your ability to sell your beliefs yet warns against exaggeration or buying into grandiose claims made by others.

JUNE 16-17 ★ *the gift of chaos*
An intense period begins on **June 16** with a Mercury-Pluto quincunx that can undermine trust with rumors, innuendo, and incomplete information, as well as an explosive Mars-Uranus semisquare that lacks the patience to dig deeply for answers. Act with a bit of restraint, though, and you can uncover shortcuts for reaching your goals in record time. The Sun's sweet trine with forgiving Neptune on **June 17** offers compassion and idealism for patching up differences. Then, however, a square between the Sun and Uranus can flare into rebellious reactions that put the end to peace. Fortunately, an opportunity-rich Sun-Jupiter trine shows that channeling your desire for change brings originality to the workplace and raises your professional profile.

SUPER NOVA DAYS
JUNE 21-23 ★ *upping the ante*
The Sun's entry into defensive Cancer on **June 21** is no sleepy affair, with tense semisquares from Venus and Mars. The line between fighting and flirting is easily blurred when these planets of love and war challenge the Sun. Their union in your 9th House of Higher Truth turns you on to guides, gurus, and teachers who appear to have entertaining answers to life's biggest questions. Venus and Mars create constructive trines with serious Saturn on **June 22** to anchor your playful plans in reality. Budding confidence, though, may be shaken on **June 23** when the Sun, Venus, and Mars form tough aspects with hungry Pluto, tossing you out of your comfort zone in search of deeper rewards.

JULY

RELEASING THE PAST

Mental Mercury starts the month off powerfully by entering your sign on **July 3** and opposing fatalistic Pluto on **July 4**. Your mind grows super-sensitive and strives to give voice to your feelings. Conversations tend to be more intimate, and Pluto's presence can reveal delicate issues. Hiding and blaming are two tactics that won't advance your interests, yet sharing a secret with someone you trust can lift a burden and release emotional energy for more productive use. A Lunar Eclipse in karmic Capricorn on **July 7** sweeps across your 7th House of Partnerships to bring unsettled relationship issues to a peak. Control may be a concern in your personal and professional connections, so devise a new arrangement if the present one isn't working to your satisfaction. Responsible Saturn's harmonious trine to the Moon helps you put your thoughts in order, enabling you to recognize when an outmoded alliance has reached its limits and where a viable one needs to go next.

Retrograde Jupiter conjuncts otherworldly Neptune on **July 10** and Chiron on **July 22**, turning your thoughts toward spiritual matters. Imagination and faith can guide you through choppy waters, but may also blind you to the shortcomings of others. Compassion is a precious gift to share as long as it's not a way to deny the realities of a relationship. A Solar Eclipse in the last degree of Cancer on **July 21** is a time to review your life and recommit to what works, while allowing yourself to let go of what doesn't. Inventive Uranus's trine to the eclipse facilitates movement in surprising ways that make fundamental changes easier than you might expect.

> **KEEP IN MIND THIS MONTH**
>
> *When in doubt, throw it out. Instead of preserving what was, it's time to become a creator of what will be.*

KEY DATES

SUPER NOVA DAYS
JULY 1–2 ★ *love interrupted*

A dreamy Venus-Neptune square on **July 1** awakens romantic feelings, but your thoughts are so busy that it's tricky to settle in and enjoy the sweetness. Mercury trines Neptune, Chiron, and Jupiter, inspiring optimism and creative thinking, while a late-night square to shocking Uranus can suddenly turn your head in a different direction. Venus squares Jupiter on **July 2**, tempting you to overpay for something or overestimate someone, while her sextile to Uranus makes you fast enough on your feet to turn a potential loss into a gain.

JULY 6-7 ★ *organized risk*
Mars in practical Taurus loses self-restraint on **July 6** as squares to diffusive Neptune and overconfident Jupiter tempt you to pursue your dreams. A Venus-Pluto quincunx leaves you feeling underappreciated and encourages reckless behavior. Stretch your limits, but within the bounds of common sense. The strategic Capricorn Lunar Eclipse on **July 7** can show you how to make a bold move with sufficient planning to assure its success.

JULY 13-14 ★ *on the sly*
Chatty Mercury joins the Sun on **July 13**, aligning your intellect and life purpose to help you understand and express yourself more clearly. With the uncomfortable quincunx between Mars and Pluto on **July 14**, you feel like you're in a battle you can't win. Don't take on the challenge directly; working quietly and cleverly behind the scenes can help you settle matters with a minimum of conflict.

JULY 21-22 ★ *reinvent yourself*
A tough-love Venus-Saturn square on **July 21** requires you to be clear about your needs if you aren't getting what you want from others. The Solar Eclipse in self-protective Cancer suggests that you may have come to the end of the road, even if you aren't ready to quit a job or a relationship quite yet. Then on **July 22**, the Sun enters expressive Leo and your 2nd House of Resources; add a healing Jupiter-Chiron conjunction and you can transform wounded feelings, power your way to more money, and increase your overall sense of self-worth.

JULY 27-28 ★ *love without limits*
A sense of joy and delight grows within you when loving Venus aligns in harmonious trines with Jupiter and Chiron on **July 27** and Neptune on **July 28**. Faith blends with pleasure as a buoyant attitude lifts your spirits from the limitations of daily life and opens your heart to the boundless spaces of possibility. You can see far beyond your present circumstances, recognizing enchanting opportunities that comfort you with hope. A challenging square from eccentric Uranus to Venus on **July 28** could interrupt your reverie—a temporary break in an otherwise beautiful picture.

AUGUST

BRING BACK THAT LOVING FEELING

Relationships move to the foreground this month: Venus, the planet of love, entered watery Cancer on **July 31** and opposes potent Pluto on **August 1**. Your desires can be very strong if you aren't pushed back into the defensive by a manipulative individual. Dig deeply within yourself to be sure that you're pursuing what you truly want and aren't overlooking any resources you might use to achieve your goals. The intelligent Aquarius Lunar Eclipse in your 8th House of Intimacy on **August 5** uncovers a whole new world of possibility in partnerships. Energetic Mars's supportive trine from diverse Gemini reveals a variety of approaches to alter the course of an important personal or professional alliance.

Jupiter and Saturn make the second of three crunchy quincunxes on **August 19** in a series that began on **March 22** and ends on **February 5, 2010**. This slippery relationship between the planet of expansion in inventive Aquarius and the planet of contraction in practical Virgo can send a big project off the rails unless you handle the details carefully. Before you commit to someone else's brilliant plan, make sure its foundation is solid—otherwise you might wind up cleaning someone else's mess. The New Moon in creative Leo on **August 20** falls in your 2nd House of Finances to help you cook up money-making ideas. Oppositions from Jupiter, Chiron, and Neptune, though, can drain your resources if you rely on blind faith or fantasy to fund your dreams. Active Mars entering security-conscious Cancer on **August 25** can bring you back into focus and provoke sufficient passion to fight for your own interests. It's better to take the initiative or even go solo now than to follow another's lead.

> **KEEP IN MIND THIS MONTH**
>
> *Pleasing yourself first prevents you from falling for someone else's fantasy and sets you up to take more control of your life.*

KEY DATES

AUGUST 1–3 ★ *crystal clear*

Pluto's opposition to Venus in your sign on **August 1** can feel like a loss of innocence as you face a hard decision about what's worth fighting for and what needs to go. Sharp thinking helps clarify your situation when mental Mercury enters analytical Virgo and your 3rd House of Communication on **August 2**. This gives you the ability to discuss complicated issues from a practical and calm perspective. A beneficial trine between Mercury and Pluto on **August 3** narrows your vision to focus on a key point, enabling you to express yourself with power and precision.

AUGUST 10 ★ *slow going*
Aggressive Mars in your secretive 12th House forms a tense square with demanding Saturn that could leave you feeling overburdened. Slowing down to take on one task at a time will help you regain control. You might not be able to count on the support of others and could even sense that someone is sabotaging your efforts. Recognizing the problem is a good place to start, but it's probably not an ideal day for direct confrontation.

AUGUST 13-14 ★ *lucky you*
The generosity of Jupiter rings loudly and clearly with an energetic trine to Mars on **August 13** and an expansive opposition to the Sun on **August 14**. Receiving help from a friend boosts your spirits and encourages you to act more boldly. Manage growth carefully, though: Going too far, too fast can leave you out on a limb.

SUPER NOVA DAYS
AUGUST 17-19 ★ *sudden change of direction*
Planets are popping in every direction as the Sun sextiles Mars on **August 17** and then opposes fuzzy Neptune in a swing from efficiency to fantasy. Mercury reverses the flow with a serious conjunction to Saturn and then a careless quincunx with jolly Jupiter. Fortunately, a Sun-Mars trine enables you to hold it together if you relax and follow your instincts. Surprises arrive on **August 18** with the Sun and Mars forming hard aspects to unpredictable Uranus. Turning urges to lash out or hide into inventive ways to meet your responsibilities can transform trouble into productivity. Avoid major decisions when Venus wobbles between cautious Saturn and excessive Jupiter on **August 19**.

AUGUST 25-26 ★ *fightin' words*
Mercury enters cerebral Libra and Mars enters moody Cancer on **August 25**, when the two meet in a tense square that can foment anger or argument. Both tangle with volatile Pluto on **August 26** as Venus passes over the Moon's South Node before entering Leo. Dramatic words can have lasting impact, so be prudent while speaking. Push yourself to a higher level of creativity rather than expecting others to speak your language.

SEPTEMBER

FREEDOM NOW . . . OR LATER

You take yourself very seriously this month, yet may feel as if you're pushing a boulder up a steep hill. The communication planet turns retrograde on **September 7** in your 4th House of Roots, returns to your 3rd House of Information on **September 17**, and begins moving forward there on **September 29**. Reviewing family history and making home improvements bring coherence to your inner life. Subjects discussed last month may resurface for further consideration. Keep an open mind and avoid serious commitments during the shifting Mercurial winds—inconsistent thinking can be problematic. Saturn and Neptune form an unstable quincunx on **September 12** that adds uncertainty to what people say. What you hear is probably not what you get, so filter information with the extra caution that's always recommended during Mercury retrogrades. Positively, this aspect allows faith to wash away unnecessary self-doubt or cynicism and bestow more hope that you can make a dream come true. This aspect repeats next spring, which will determine how well you have integrated the ideal with the real.

The tension between duty and your urge for independence is activated on **September 15** when responsible Saturn and erratic Uranus form their third opposition in a series of five such aspects that will continue through **July 26, 2010**. The stress escalates when the Sun enters the picture on **September 17**. A well-placed outburst could lead to a breakthrough in what you see or say. Surprising yourself with a novel idea or observation might be a powerful step toward freedom. The Virgo New Moon on **September 18** adds fuel to the Saturn-Uranus fire. Look carefully before you leap: A well-planned move can produce magic, while an impulsive one could make a mess.

KEEP IN MIND THIS MONTH

Back up your intuition with enough research and detailed analysis that you feel totally confident in any move you make.

KEY DATES

SEPTEMBER 2–4 ★ *in overdrive*

Going too far is a danger with assertive Mars's sesquisquare of Jupiter pushing you toward excess on **September 2**. Your drive to take charge is admirable, but not if it wears you out. A self-doubting Venus-Saturn semisquare can act as a check on this behavior, helping you choose how and where you demonstrate your worth. A Mercury-Mars square on **September 3** adds another degree of impatience and feistiness, yet you'll be more effective with a calm demeanor. On **September 4**, a Venus-Uranus sesquisquare combines with the confusing Pisces Full Moon's presence in your 10th House of Public Responsibility to scramble social plans. Letting go of your expectations can free you from excessive stress.

SEPTEMBER 9–11 ★ *too much of a good thing*
Mars in emotional Cancer forms a squishy sesquisquare with spacey Neptune on **September 9**. You can easily find your energies misdirected; guide them with great sensitivity, however, and you're inspired to act with creativity, compassion, and imagination. The likelihood for overindulgence is strong with a Venus-Jupiter opposition on **September 11**. This aspect spans your 2nd and 8th Houses of Material and Emotional Values, making excessive spending possible, but also opening the gates to a sweet time with a generous person. Still, the Sun's quincunx to Jupiter reinforces the potential for poor judgment driven by baseless optimism. Being hopeful is fine as long as it's balanced with practical thinking.

SUPER NOVA DAYS
SEPTEMBER 17–18 ★ *reaching your limit*
A high-powered Saturn-Uranus opposition is triggered by the Sun on **September 17**, which could provoke conflict with authorities. Retrograde Mercury squares suspicious Pluto before backing into Virgo to undermine trust. Dark thoughts, muttered words, and unresolved fears can lead to a verbal explosion. The intensity continues with the Virgo New Moon on **September 18**, yet open confrontation might not be the best response. Denying your feelings isn't recommended; think carefully before you speak if your communication is meant to build bridges rather than tear them down.

SEPTEMBER 20–23 ★ *complex negotiations*
Relationship problems are more easily resolved when Venus enters analytical Virgo, forming a healing trine with Pluto on **September 20**. You are able to address difficult issues with the power and self-control required to produce the desired outcome. A Venus-Mars semisquare on **September 21** and Mercury-Saturn conjunction on **September 22** indicate that additional adjustments and explanations are needed. The Autumnal Equinox occurs with the Sun's passage into diplomatic Libra, helping you to see another perspective, yet its tense square to Pluto and a nervous Mercury-Uranus opposition on **September 23** reintroduce complications. Taking a totally fresh look at a sticky old problem can be quite liberating.

OCTOBER

SECURITY-CONSCIOUS

New and Full Moons this month shake and stir your chart's security houses. The Full Moon in Aries on **October 4** shoots flames of impulsiveness into your 10th House of Career, perhaps inciting conflict with a boss in the days that follow. Crises may occur if you react fearfully to new tasks for which you feel unprepared. On the other hand, this is a good time to strike out in a fresh direction if you're bored or feeling stifled. Trying to maintain the status quo is your least effective move, so push forward in your current position or seek a new one to catch this wave of opportunity. The Libra New Moon on **October 18** occurs in your 4th House of Home and Family, placing a premium on harmony within your household. Supportive trines from the spiritual trio of Jupiter, Neptune, and Chiron can infuse you with the inner peace and inspiration that make your life magical. Creating more attractive surroundings reflects the grace of inner beauty growing in you now.

Abundant Jupiter turns direct in your 8th House of Intimacy and Shared Resources on **October 12**, slowly opening the coffers of partnership to offer you love, approval, and financial reinforcement. Barriers to getting what you desire are starting to fall, encouraging you to be more direct in expressing your needs and more open to deeper emotional and physical exchanges. The Sun's entry into passionate Scorpio on **October 23** arrives in your 5th House of Romance and Self-Expression to increase your confidence, creativity, and charisma. Saturn enters peace-loving Libra and your 4th House of Roots on **October 29**, challenging you to shore up your foundation by finishing old emotional business during the next two years.

> **KEEP IN MIND THIS MONTH**
>
> *Keeping your cool at home makes it possible for you to turn up the heat in public without burning yourself out.*

KEY DATES

OCTOBER 4 ★ *instinctive actions*

The impatient Aries Full Moon on **October 4** occurs as Mercury aspects efficient Mars, spacey Neptune, and unconventional Uranus, shifting your mind from sharp and snappy to soft and dreamy to brilliantly explosive in the blink of an eye. A Venus-Jupiter quincunx skews values, leading to overindulgence, overpaying, or overestimating someone's worth. Physical Mars in Cancer wobbles through a misleading quincunx to Neptune that can drain your energy, but ends up with a trine to Uranus that allows you to make the right move with a flash of intuitive insight.

SUPER NOVA DAYS
OCTOBER 8-10 ★ *releasing steam*

A Mercury-Saturn conjunction on **October 8** adds a serious note to your thinking. Focus on problems you can fix rather than worrying about those you can't. Patiently attending to immediate issues takes precedence now over long-term concerns. The tone shifts completely on **October 9** with an experimental and socially restless Venus-Uranus opposition. This aspect between the planets of pleasure and originality can shake relationships with a desire for something new and different. An aggressive Mars–South Node conjunction touches old wounds and can arouse anger. Mercury's shift into diplomatic Libra offers hope for compromise, but its tense square with vengeful Pluto on **October 10** may keep stirring the ashes of the past. Happily, a generous Sun-Jupiter trine offers you a philosophical perspective, enabling you to find meaning in the midst of crisis.

OCTOBER 13-15 ★ *tough love*

Lovely Venus enters tough territory with a conjunction to demanding Saturn on **October 13** and a square to withholding Pluto on **October 15**. While a sassy Venus-Mars sextile on **October 13** and the romance planet's entry into Libra on **October 14** promise moments of delight, they are sandwiched between moments of doubt and dissatisfaction. Taking a stand in relationships and developing self-discipline can be hard work, but the long-term rewards of recognition and self-respect are well worth it.

OCTOBER 23-24 ★ *sex appeal*

Your powers of seduction increase as the Sun's entry into steamy Scorpio on **October 23** in your romantic 5th House is followed by its cozy sextile with potent Pluto the next day. Instead of trying to please everyone, direct your charm and creative skills where they will have the greatest impact.

OCTOBER 28-29 ★ *unbridled passion*

Healthy quantities of pleasure are likely on **October 28** when Mercury enters your 5th House of Love and Play while joyful Venus and Jupiter align in an expressive trine. A hot Sun-Mars square on **October 29**, though, narrows the line between fun and fighting, reminding you to be aware of exactly what game you're playing and who you are playing it with.

NOVEMBER

PASSION AND POWER PERSONIFIED

Friends and colleagues push your buttons when an edgy Full Moon in Taurus on **November 2** is spiked by a tense square from aggressive Mars. You may feel competitive whether others are challenging you directly or not. The warrior planet's presence in your 2nd House of Self-Worth is prodding you to get more out of yourself, even if it means risking failure. You could increase your income potential by investing in professional education or buying materials for your own business. Vivacious Venus enters sexy Scorpio and slinks into your 5th House of Love on **November 7**. Desire arises from the depths of your being with subtle power that spurs strong reactions. Revisit old creative interests and forgotten talents that may be ready for resurrection.

Planetary heavyweights Saturn and Pluto are square on **November 15**, a tense aspect that will return on **January 31** and **August 21, 2010**. The tough angle between these dominating forces represents a struggle to maintain a peaceful inner life against relentless pressure imposed by others. Observe carefully to see who and what riles you; recognize when to engage and when to withdraw. Power is in play. Avoiding the subject will likely leave you with less of it, but choosing your battles wisely allows you to relax until you decide that a cause is worth defending. The magnetic Scorpio New Moon on **November 16** squares Jupiter, Neptune, and Chiron, tempting you to pursue a romantic fantasy. However, a brilliant trine from inventive Uranus can pull you back from the brink of folly and reveal a less costly way to achieve your goal.

> **KEEP IN MIND THIS MONTH**
>
> *Attitude is everything now, so use the strong emotions you feel to attract what you desire and repel what you no longer want.*

KEY DATES

NOVEMBER 2 ★ *rapid changes*

Your loyalty to friends and co-workers may be tested as the reliable Taurus Full Moon in your 11th House of Groups opposes the enigmatic Scorpio Sun in your 5th House of Love and Play. Resentment can arise when you overcommit to others and don't set aside time to enjoy yourself. Fortunately, a spiritually motivated Venus-Neptune trine creates enough room to accept differences that would normally undermine trust. Love strong enough to heal the wounds of misunderstanding is now within your reach.

SUPER NOVA DAYS

NOVEMBER 7-10 ⋆ *love in the fast lane*

Venus's entry into inscrutable Scorpio on **November 7** is accompanied by a penetrating Mercury-Pluto semisquare that exposes secrets and touches sore spots. Intense conversation can be an interesting form of seduction. The Sun semisquares Saturn and Pluto on **November 8**, spurring struggles for control and a desire to purge yourself of overly protective behavior. Big promises or spreading yourself too thin can be costly as a Mercury-Jupiter square makes miscalculation likely. A Venus-Pluto sextile on **November 9** urges you to dig deep to get more from what you already have before seeking other sources of pleasure. Nevertheless, on **November 10** an inflationary Sun-Jupiter square makes someone new and different appealing, even when your instincts are warning you not to believe everything you hear.

NOVEMBER 19 ⋆ *laser control*

The Moon is in your 7th House of Partnerships while Venus and Mars hook up in a highly charged square that throws sparks into relationships. Your pride may motivate you to be more direct than ever in expressing your desires or demonstrating your creative power. Still, your passion can intimidate an emotionally restrained individual. Be strong without coming on too strong if you want to win someone's heart. You have plenty of force to make an impression, but using it with discretion will ensure that it produces the outcome you want.

NOVEMBER 23-26 ⋆ *costly adventure*

A delicious but imprudent Venus-Jupiter square on **November 23** increases your appetite for fun at the price of good judgment. Spending too much, expecting more than a person can give, or exposing emotions inappropriately may be awkward to say the least. Fortunately, a solid Sun-Saturn sextile on **November 24** brings your attention back down to earth, where you can regain reason and self-control. Playful spirits return on **November 25**, when a friendly Venus-Uranus trine draws you toward unfamiliar flavors of experience. While a smart Mercury-Mars trine on **November 26** sharpens your intellect and facilitates clever communication, a fuzzy Venus-Neptune square could spur you to abandon common sense in the pursuit of a dream.

DECEMBER

SEEDS OF CHANGE

The Moon, your planetary ruler, is busy this month, stirring your emotions and fomenting change. The first Full Moon is in inquisitive Gemini on **December 2**, pouring the light of awareness into your 12th House of Soul Consciousness, arousing a sense of spiritual connection, and stimulating your intuition. The New Moon in opinionated Sagittarius on **December 16** is likely to trigger changes in your 6th House of Work and Service. Eccentric Uranus's hard square to this Sun-Moon conjunction creates a hectic environment, but might also provide you with the impetus to seek more inspiring employment. You tend to be security-conscious, so temper an impulse to leap if you don't have a reasonably safe place to land. The Lunar Eclipse in your sign on **December 31** is the second Full Moon of the month—popularly known as a "Blue Moon"—a very memorable way to end the year. Stern Saturn squares this Cancer Full Moon while Venus opposes it, challenging you to start reshaping relationships and find ways to fulfill your creative potential.

You find it difficult to move forward financially when normally active Mars turns retrograde in your 2nd House of Resources on **December 20**. However, optimistic Jupiter makes its third and final conjunction to Chiron on **December 7** and Neptune on **December 21**, raising your spirits with the help of positive people. The Sun energizes your 7th House of Relationships as it enters dutiful Capricorn on the Winter Solstice, **December 21**, and you gain even more support for happy holidays when Venus follows on **December 25**. Still, mental Mercury turns retrograde in this house on **December 26**, scrambling messages and skewing schedules for three weeks. Nevertheless, serious conversations about unresolved issues can help untangle knots of misunderstanding if you temper your feelings with logic.

> **KEEP IN MIND THIS MONTH**
>
> *Avoid attachment to moods, which can swing widely in the mixture of anxiety and anticipation that accompanies the holiday season.*

KEY DATES

DECEMBER 1–2 ★ *from heaven to earth*

Innovative Uranus goes direct on **December 1**, increasing the intensity, while friendly Venus enters vibrant Sagittarius to keep the social fires burning. Bringing your joy to the job is an excellent way to ride this wave of enthusiasm. The thoughtful Gemini Full Moon on **December 2** brightens your 12th House of Divinity with a solid trine from Saturn that helps you apply spiritual principles in practical ways.

DECEMBER 5-7 ★ *rigid rules*

A tough Mars-Saturn semisquare on **December 5** sets a stern tone that leaves little margin for error. Mercury's same-day entry into Saturn's home sign—hierarchical Capricorn—reinforces rules and the need to follow them carefully. The communication planet then joins Pluto and squares Saturn on **December 7**, making conversations feel more like commands and lectures. Sticking to facts is essential in this no-nonsense environment, yet there is still a place for kindness: Jupiter's conjunction to compassionate Chiron reveals the healing potential in the midst of this stressful period.

DECEMBER 14-17 ★ *ready to play*

Feelings of restlessness are stirred by a crackling Sun-Uranus square and an adventurous Sun-Jupiter sextile on **December 14**. Excitement may cause you to overlook details in your daily duties or rebel against your responsibilities. Forgiving Neptune slides into a softening sextile with the Sun on **December 15**, stretching the limits of tolerance that help overcome minor differences. A flirtatious Venus-Mars trine on **December 17** mixes work and pleasure, making room for more creativity on the job.

DECEMBER 20-21 ★ *smart shopper*

Manage your resources more carefully when Mars turns retrograde on **December 20**. Yet a Venus-Jupiter sextile makes it hard to dampen your urge to spend money, so look for bargains that fulfill your penchant for purchasing without breaking the bank. Venus sextiles Neptune while Jupiter conjuncts it on **December 21**, adding a sympathetic and spiritual tone even as serious issues continue. The Sun's entry into earthy Capricorn in your 7th House of Partnerships reminds you of limits imposed by another and your need for more security in relationships. A testy Mercury-Mars quincunx requires careful attention to what you say if you hope to avoid friction.

SUPER NOVA DAYS
DECEMBER 24-25 ★ *give peace a chance*

A Sun-Pluto conjunction on **December 24** ratchets up the holiday tension and sensitizes you to power issues—it's hard to trust anyone. The Sun's tense aspects to Saturn and Mars on **December 25** could exacerbate the situation, so maintain as much self-control as possible. The pressure you are feeling is best applied to yourself as you forge a stronger sense of will and purpose in the year ahead.

LEO

JULY 23–AUGUST 22

LEO

2008 SUMMARY

Your primary focus this year is likely to be on practical matters as Jupiter and Saturn, the planetary regulators, are both in realistic earth signs. For the most part, gains accrue when you make a plan and stick to it. Develop your expertise in one area at a time instead of scattering your attention across broad fields of interest. Don't confuse sentiment with commitment, or compassion with a contract.

AUGUST— *letting go to get ahead*

Turning loss into gain when it's time to let go makes it possible to take one step back and leap ten steps ahead.

SEPTEMBER—*sudden changes*

Convert enemies into allies by thinking fast on your feet to catch opportunities that come when you least expect them.

OCTOBER—*transforming your past*

Once you clear your heart of what is no longer needed, you can utilize your precious resources to focus on manifesting your dreams for the future.

NOVEMBER—*solid financial growth*

A clear sense of your long-range goals will guide you well, so don't let petty details get in the way of your big-picture view.

DECEMBER—*holiday madness*

Respond to tension by making big changes in your life instead of uselessly trying to hold on to what you don't even want anymore.

2008 CALENDAR

AUGUST

FRIDAY 1 ★ Change can encourage a wave of creativity

WEDNESDAY 6 ★ Step back from the edge and steer clear of disputes

WEDNESDAY 13 ★ **SUPER NOVA DAYS** Dig hard to find gold through the 17th

FRIDAY 22 ★ Break the rules and enjoy creative possibilities through the 23rd

WEDNESDAY 27 ★ Untapped resources can increase your income through the 30th

SEPTEMBER

WEDNESDAY 3 ★ Look at the objective picture through the 4th

SUNDAY 7 ★ **SUPER NOVA DAYS** Restraint moderates rage through the 8th

FRIDAY 12 ★ Impulse rules through the 14th

SATURDAY 20 ★ Reveal yourself through the 23rd. Remember you're not alone

MONDAY 29 ★ Stick to the basics to avoid complicated communication

OCTOBER

SATURDAY 4 ★ **SUPER NOVA DAYS** Express strong opinions softly through the 6th

SUNDAY 12 ★ A new mind-set gets information flowing through the 15th

SATURDAY 18 ★ It's all about fun today, so don't hold yourself back

TUESDAY 21 ★ Your power grows through the 25th, but avoid conflict

NOVEMBER

MONDAY 3 ★ Social awkwardness and insecurity is possible through tomorrow

MONDAY 10 ★ **SUPER NOVA DAYS** Successfully apply brilliant ideas through the 13th

SUNDAY 16 ★ Clear thinking today turns dreamy by tomorrow

FRIDAY 21 ★ Temper honesty with humor and love through the 23rd

TUESDAY 25 ★ Kill them with kindness through the 26th

DECEMBER

FRIDAY 5 ★ It's showtime! You're ready to hit the stage through the 6th

WEDNESDAY 10 ★ **SUPER NOVA DAYS** Break the rules with awareness

MONDAY 15 ★ Hard work brings precious rewards

SUNDAY 21 ★ Prioritize your tasks to make time for fun

SATURDAY 27 ★ Take time out through the 28th to enjoy the season

LEO OVERVIEW

The tables are turned on you this year with a strong planetary emphasis on your 7th House of Partnerships and Public Life. Spiritual Neptune has been camped out here since 1998 in a very slow-moving cycle that continues to inspire yet also confuse one-to-one relationships, including those based on business, love, or even conflict. **It can be challenging to find true clarity, for it's hard to tell when your perceptions are distorted.** You tend see the world through rose-colored glasses during these years—until 2011, when Neptune enters Pisces. This long-lasting influence can be subtle and perhaps you've grown accustomed to it, yet this year the action in your 7th House becomes even more intense. Chiron the Wounded Healer remains here until next year; the karmic North Node of the Moon entered Aquarius on January 7, 2008, and stays in your 7th House until July 26. Expansive Jupiter joins this coalescence of planetary energy on January 5, lingering through the year, conjoining the North Node, Chiron, and Neptune in a slow-motion dance forward and backward and forward again. Jupiter's arrival can expand your self-awareness, but paradoxically by not paying attention to yourself. Proud Lions can be relentless in the drive for self-enhancement, but now it's your relationships that matter the most as **Jupiter opens your mind, enabling you to learn from others**.

The South Node in Leo until July 26 shows where you're trapped by your own habits. This is yet another indication that it's time to step beyond yourself, past old assumptions and into the future. Undoubtedly, **your life currently includes other people who can impact your direction in ways you never anticipated**. They can salve your pain by enticing you with surefire solutions to whatever ails you when Jupiter conjuncts Chiron on May 23, July 22, and December 7. These same people could make promises to you that they cannot keep when Jupiter joins idealistic Neptune on May 27, July 10, and December 21. Although their intentions may be honorable, their confidence is based on ungrounded hope and blind faith. This can be tricky territory, for the spiritual trio of Jupiter, Chiron, and Neptune can certainly be the stuff dreams are made of—and the dreams can cross over this year to manifest as real events in your life.

Saturn's entry into social Libra and your 3rd House of Communication on October 29 is the beginning of a two-year phase in which you discipline your thinking and **gain greater control over your day-to-day life**. The taskmaster planet's subsequent square to evolutionary Pluto on November 15 initiates a long-term transit that can force you to limit your growth because you don't have the resources or time to do everything. You must make tough decisions and **start eliminating patterns, people, and activities that will not contribute to your development over the coming years**.

LOVE POTION

Although the Jupiter-Chiron-Neptune super-conjunction falls in your 7th House of Partnerships, placing an idealistic and hopeful spin on all your relationships, it is generous Jupiter that rules your 5th House of Love. Accordingly, its conjunctions to Chiron and Neptune in May, July, and December are opportunities to heal old emotional wounds. Forgiving and forgetting are in theory simple concepts whose reality is complicated and sometimes painful, yet someone may come into your life during these periods to help you along. Additionally, the love planet Venus extends her stay in spontaneous Aries for most of February, March, April, and May—activating your 9th House of Adventure. Romance is more than just having a good time; it must also widen your horizons and open your mind to exciting new possibilities beyond your wildest imagination.

INEVITABLE CHANGE

Transformational Pluto, in your 6th House of Work until 2023, encounters disciplined Saturn to produce real change this year. Your resistance to these profound shifts surges when Saturn squares Pluto in November, setting the stage for what will follow throughout 2010. Venus, the ruler of your 10th House of Career, retrogrades from March 6 to April 17, delaying projects and recognition of your work; you may need to be patient until appreciation and compensation arrive. Saturn also impacts your professional status, and its oppositions to eye-opening Uranus on February 5 and September 19 can highlight what you must do to bring your work into closer alignment with your personal values.

LEO

 TREADING WATER

Saturn's presence in your 2nd House of Resources until October 29 indicates that you will need to work hard this year just to stay even. Still, there are signals of surprising shifts in your financial condition, especially when money planet Venus joins unpredictable Uranus on January 22 and opposes austere Saturn on January 24. Her ongoing opposition to erratic Uranus—exact on February 5 and November 15—again suggests sudden changes in income and possibly a windfall if you've applied yourself diligently. Put your money to work intelligently around June 21, when Venus and Mars join in a creative conjunction in practical Taurus while both harmoniously trine stabilizing Saturn. This expressive conjunction is in your 10th House of Status, empowering you to publicly voice your intention to earn more money and then supporting you in doing just that.

 A STITCH IN TIME

Pluto's entry into your 6th House of Health initiates a fourteen-year period when you can completely rebuild your physical body with proper diet and exercise, even if you've recently let things slide. Leaving health unattended, conversely, could open the door to physical problems—though this is not indicated unless you completely ignore any symptoms now. Jupiter's connection with Chiron the Healer in your 7th House of Others on May 23, July 22, and December 7 encourages you to share healthy mind-body practices such as yoga or meditation with a partner. Saturn's square to Pluto on November 15 can grab your attention as a chronic problem resurfaces if you've been neglecting your health.

 HOME IMPROVEMENT

Mars and Pluto are the co-rulers of your 4th House of Home and Family, and their dynamic square on April 26 can stir up control issues in your household. With Pluto moving through your 6th House of Self-Improvement, it's important to continually refocus on making who you are even better. Apply your deep reserve of energy around June 3—when Mars harmoniously trines Pluto—by directing extra effort toward constructive change. Consider remodeling or just switching how you use a particular room in your house. The Sun's entry into private Scorpio in your 4th House on October 23, followed by Mercury on October 28 and Venus on November 7, encourages you to create a cozy home environment that's reflective of your current passions, allowing you take pride in entertaining your closest friends.

ROOM FOR TWO

Jupiter, the planet of journeys, is in your 7th House of Partners this year, suggesting that you won't be traveling alone—or if you do, there could be someone waiting for you at a distant airport. Jupiter's alignment with metaphysical Neptune indicates that you may travel for spiritual reasons such as to a retreat or conference. Impulsive Mars rules your 9th House of Adventure, and his alignments with Jupiter on February 17, May 26, July 6, and August 13 are windows of opportunity for traveling or studying. Mars turns retrograde on December 20; carefully consider the logistics of any holiday excursion or be prepared for your plans to fall apart at the last minute.

LEARNING FROM OTHERS

This is a year when you can learn more from others than you do from yourself as the spiritual trio of Jupiter, Chiron, and Neptune activate your 7th House of Relationships. Remember, however, that Neptune's presence can also gloss over almost any negativity, luring you into accepting a teacher based upon your illusions rather than on what he or she actually has to offer. Be careful, for what you acquire in haste may not be as enduring as those truths you discover patiently over time. Relationships can take on a spiritual flavor, offering you the sweet possibility of sharing your faith with someone you love.

RICK & JEFF'S TIP FOR THE YEAR:
Build from the Ground Up

Saturn's moves through methodical Virgo and your 2nd House of Possessions until October 29. This may create financial stress, yet its real job is to teach you to work hard so you can reestablish fiscal integrity. Saturn is not only about how much money you earn, though: Self-worth is a result of how you value yourself. Accordingly, consider what you bring to each new situation and let others know what they can expect from you. Be smart and you will overcome all your challenges as you gather the resources you need to pay for your big plans.

LEO

JANUARY

RECONSIDERING RELATIONSHIPS

The pileup of planets in progressive Aquarius in your 7th House of Partnerships begins the year with a strong emphasis on your friends, co-workers, spouse, and even professional relationships with accountants, astrologers, attorneys, or doctors. Interactive Mercury enters your 7th House on **January 1**, increasing your desire to discuss ideas and concepts, even if they have no practical value. Your tendency to intellectualize feelings grows stronger when Mercury turns retrograde on **January 11**. Talking about what you want is even easier than usual, but you may need to discuss the same issue a few times before everyone reaches agreement. Mercury backs into careful Capricorn on **January 21**, giving you another chance to review the assumptions on which you're building your relationships. Making corrections now is less painful than waiting until something falls apart weeks down the road. Abundant Jupiter enters your 7th House on **January 5**, where it remains for the rest of the year, bestowing blessings on you through your associations with others.

The contemplative Cancer Full Moon on **January 10** falls in your 12th House of Secrets, temporarily alleviating pressure as you realize that your feelings belong to you and you alone. You can choose what to share when you're ready; nothing requires you to bare your soul unless you're willing. The Aquarius New Moon Eclipse on **January 26** can abruptly shift the prevailing winds when a partner surprises you with a change of feelings. Although you might try to maintain the status quo, it's really not a wise move to attempt to hold on to anything that isn't truly yours.

> **KEEP IN MIND THIS MONTH**
>
> *Relationships are not separate from your identity, your fears, and your hopes; recognize them as mirrors of your soul.*

KEY DATES

JANUARY 5–8 ★ *soften your stance*

Quicksilver Mercury's tense semisquare to revolutionary Uranus on **January 5**, followed by its sesquisquare to stabilizing Saturn on **January 8**, can create disagreements about money with an intimate partner. If you become overly rigid too early in the discussions, you could suddenly reach a stalemate. What happens now can trigger a series of events throughout the month leading up to the Saturn-Uranus opposition on **February 5**, which falls on your resource axis of the 2nd and 8th Houses. Meanwhile, impetuous Mars semisquares confusing Neptune on **January 6**, pulling the rug out from under your feet and leaving you less sure of your position than before. There's no need to act with certainty if you don't feel it.

JANUARY 18 ⋆ *eyes wide open*

Mercury the Messenger backs into broad-minded Jupiter, widening your horizons of thought and opening vistas of unrealized possibilities. This conjunction in your 7th House of Others can be a harbinger of good news. Let someone who enters your life now show you what you've previously missed. Don't be resistant to new ideas, even if you think you know better. Ultimately, what you learn will be beneficial in ways you cannot yet realize.

SUPER NOVA DAYS

JANUARY 22–25 ⋆ *heroic measures*

Mars in your 6th House of Skills comes to the rescue when he forms a cooperative sextile with unorthodox Uranus on **January 22** and a highly efficient trine with hardworking Saturn on **January 24**. You are able to bring order to chaos and effectively manage your time, setting you up to be the hero as you successfully pull off an impossible scheme. Beautiful Venus's conjunction to Uranus—also on **January 22**—dares you to take a chance and to express your passion. Her opposition to Saturn on **January 24** helps you maintain a sense of realism, especially as the Sun's conjunction to cheerful Jupiter encourages you to look at the bright side of life. The Sun adds tension to the unfolding drama on **January 24–25**, replaying a now familiar theme that pits conservation against risk. Ultimately, you must stand in the center of this tug-of-war and hold your position in the midst of change.

JANUARY 27–30 ⋆ *no easy answers*

Reasonable Mercury joins direct Mars on **January 27**, enabling you to talk about your plans in a simple manner that's easy for others to understand. But philosophical Jupiter moves into place to take its turn on center stage on **January 27–30**, offering impractical solutions to an ongoing struggle between innovation (Uranus) and the status quo (Saturn) that will reach its climax **February 4**. It's difficult to form a sensible plan without applying enough creativity to make the most of each side.

FEBRUARY

ON THE EDGE OF CHANGE

February starts with a rush of energy as Mercury the Messenger turns direct **February 1** and beautiful Venus enters capricious Aries in your 11th House of Adventure on **February 2**. The action ratchets up another notch when courageous Mars enters high-strung Aquarius on **February 4**, followed by Mercury on **February 14**. This boosts the intensity of your 7th House of Partners—already crowded with the presence of Jupiter, the Sun, Chiron, and Neptune. Your attention is drawn away from your center and toward others, yet a powerful undertow places a relentless grip on you, preventing you from being washed away by the excitement of so many possibilities. Suppressive Saturn opposes expressive Uranus on **February 5** in a tug-of-war between past limitations and future potential. This slow-moving aspect is a repeat performance that began on **November 4, 2008**, recurs on **September 15**, and continues into next year. Saturn in your 2nd House of Self-Worth encourages thrift, while Uranus in your 8th House of Shared Resources can tempt you to impulsively invest time and money in new projects.

The Lunar Eclipse on **February 9** falls in your 1st House of Personality, activating your desire for a complete makeover. This dramatic Leo Full Moon Eclipse may have you changing your look even as it encourages a more substantial metamorphosis. The Sun's conjunction with compassionate Chiron reminds you that real healing is not about physical appearance, but about your attitude. The Sun enters Pisces and your 8th House of Intimacy on **February 18**, yet it's the intuitive Pisces New Moon on **February 24** that helps you begin to transform your fantasies into real experiences filled with mystery and passion.

> **KEEP IN MIND THIS MONTH**
>
> *Someone might spin a story so well that you'll believe the most fantastic things. Checking all the facts along the way can prevent disappointment later on.*

KEY DATES

SUPER NOVA DAY
FEBRUARY 5 ★ *letting go*
The tension from taskmaster Saturn's opposition to wild Uranus can pull you so close to the limits of your patience that you may do something rash, only to quickly regret it. Venus's dynamic square to passionate Pluto, along with the Sun's semisquare to both Venus and Pluto, can bring hidden motives up to the

surface, setting the stage for an emotional power struggle. Instead of attempting to hold on to something or someone out of fear, seek ways to accept inevitable change. Once you become an agent of transformation instead of a champion of the status quo, the dark clouds can dissipate, revealing lost clarity.

FEBRUARY 11–12 ★ *anger management*
Mars's tense aspects with the Saturn-Uranus opposition on **February 11** can stimulate anger and create problems. Since this opposition is in your resource houses and Mars is in your 7th House of Others, you may need to handle any hostility that arises from your desire to restrain spending. Meanwhile, the Sun's conjunction with spiritual Neptune on **February 12** brings into your life someone who helps you see a greater truth to guide you through this tense period.

FEBRUARY 16–18 ★ *as good as it gets*
Things are looking up when lovely Venus supportively sextiles an over-the-top Mars-Jupiter conjunction on **February 16–18**. Your enthusiasm may be uncontainable if you are attracted to a new person or intriguing idea. On the other hand, it may be another's conviction that now lights a fire under you. Either way, there is no reason to say no. Just remember that given your present zeal, you could take things too far or exhaust yourself by taking on too much at once.

FEBRUARY 24 ★ *inflationary thinking*
Mental Mercury's conjunction with optimistic Jupiter on **February 24**—a day that also features a dreamy Pisces New Moon—can inflate your expectations about a current relationship. Make sure you cover all the details carefully before making any agreements or signing a contract. A beneficial outcome is likely—as long as you can rein in your current tendency toward turning molehills into mountains.

FEBRUARY 27–28 ★ *up against the wall*
Angry Mars provokes erratic behavior while he's in quirky Aquarius, and his semi-square to domineering Pluto on **February 27** can have you fired up and ready for combat—only to find yourself facing an opponent much stronger than yourself. Mars's unsettling quincunx with restraining Saturn on **February 28** makes you realize that you have misjudged the situation and possibly overplayed your hand. Do what you can to alleviate the tension without escalating the conflict.

MARCH

MONEY MATTERS

The pressure for change eases as retrograde Saturn cautiously backs away from its opposition to irrepressible Uranus. Nevertheless, you may not be content with the way things are, because repressive Saturn and expressive Uranus are both active throughout the month. Saturn is opposed by the Sun on **March 8** and by Mercury on **March 18**, presenting you with obstacles and forcing you to adjust your financial plans. The Sun is conjoined by Uranus on **March 12** and by Mercury on **March 22**, upsetting the status quo and revealing innovative solutions to ongoing problems. Your one-on-one interactions become less frequent yet more intense as planets leave your 7th House of Partners to enter your 8th House of Intimacy. The sensitive Pisces Sun in your 8th House is joined by Mercury on **March 8** and by red-hot Mars on **March 14**, but you aren't necessarily comfortable with the increased level of emotional vulnerability this brings. While you may glimpse opportunities for growth, Jupiter's quincunx to conservative Saturn on **March 22** and its semisquare to controlling Pluto on **March 27** make you less willing to take risks for unrealistic rewards.

The practical Virgo Full Moon in your 2nd House of Possessions on **March 10** conjuncts responsible Saturn—requiring you to stabilize your finances, even if it means having less fun for now. The Sun's entry into pioneering Aries on **March 20** marks the Vernal Equinox and reinforces your desire to learn about something that's new and different. Mercury's entry into Aries is followed by the Aries New Moon on **March 26**, kicking you into high gear. Although Venus doesn't turn direct until **April 17**, you're already dreaming and scheming about what you want.

> ### KEEP IN MIND THIS MONTH
>
> *Remembering an old emotional wound allows you to transform a light and easy relationship into one of much deeper significance.*

KEY DATES

SUPER NOVA DAYS
MARCH 5–8 ★ *can't get no satisfaction*

Impetuous Mars in your 7th House of Relationships meets up with Chiron the Wounded Healer on **March 5** and with Neptune the Dreamer on **March 8**, muddling your actions and frustrating your intentions. Others may misinterpret your behavior, even if you mean well. You're in for another change as

attractive Venus begins her retrograde phase on **March 6,** sending you
backward in time. You may hear from an old friend or lover, reevaluate a
recent relationship, or watch a current one stall. The Sun's tense opposition
to austere Saturn on **March 8** is another sign of the resistance you must
overcome. Handling any disappointment may be easier once you realize that
your ultimate satisfaction is not being denied, only delayed.

MARCH 10–12 ★ *sweet and sour*

You want others to take you seriously, especially as the meticulous Virgo Full Moon
conjuncts Saturn on **March 10.** But this Sun-Moon opposition can be unsettling,
because the Sun's conjunction to electric Uranus on **March 12** polarizes a situation
and provokes you to risk too much on a long shot. Your chances of finding personal
satisfaction improve as alluring Venus receives a boost from fearless Jupiter on
March 11, but the odds are not necessarily in your favor. Consider letting this wild
energy settle down before changing course.

MARCH 20–23 ★ *two steps forward, one step back*

The Sun's entry into fiery Aries on **March 20** marks the first day of spring and a
time when your excitement escalates. Intellectual Mercury—a bit lost now in foggy
Pisces—gains temporary clarity as it joins Uranus the Awakener in your 8th House
of Regeneration on **March 22.** You have ideas about upgrading your current personal or financial situation, but you cannot set them into motion while the Jupiter-
Saturn quincunx simultaneously encourages and blocks you. The Sun's square to
potent Pluto on **March 23** charges your system with enough power to reach your
goal, but you could exhaust yourself in the struggle. Knowing where to let go will
actually help you move forward.

MARCH 26–27 ★ *practice tolerance*

The Aries New Moon on **March 26** falls in your 9th House of Future Vision, focusing
your eyes on a very distant horizon. But this rowdy New Moon is dynamically
square passionate Pluto, with mental Mercury stepping into a war of words on
March 27. Generous Jupiter semisquares demanding Pluto, helping you handle a
deep difference of perspective about work, preventing it from escalating into outright conflict. Luckily, an amicable Sun-Venus conjunction sweetens your charm
and your ability to find a workable compromise.

APRIL

EVERYTHING TAKES TIME

Planetary waves rock you back and forth this month, but you can successfully navigate the tumultuous waters. You can also derive pleasure by looking in your rearview mirror to reevaluate your current direction in life. It's hard to know what to do with all your enthusiasm, for although the month begins with three planets in exciting Aries in your expansive 9th House, sweet Venus is retrograde until **April 17**, subduing your high spirits and delaying satisfaction. A story about opposing currents of restraint and expression is best told by energetic Mars swimming through the changeable emotional waters of Pisces until **April 22**. The forcefulness of Mars is rebuked by taskmaster Saturn on **April 4**, requiring you to cool your heels even if you're raring to go. But when Mars joins wired Uranus on **April 15**, fireworks light up the sky. This is no time to be lazy: If you don't do something, the lightning of awareness may strike to show you exactly what needs to happen. Don't delay. Bold preemptive action is better than a timid response later on.

The pleasant Libra Full Moon on **April 9** harmoniously trines buoyant Jupiter in your 7th House of Partners, bringing into your life people who joyously lift your spirits. The Sun enters sensible Taurus and your professional 10th House on **April 19**, emphasizing steady gains at work in the weeks ahead. Yet you can feel the flames of passion burning when Mars enters his energetic home sign of Aries on **April 22**. The solid Taurus New Moon on **April 24** is trine regenerative Pluto in your 6th House of Work, gracing you with the stamina to finish what you start.

> **KEEP IN MIND THIS MONTH**
>
> *It is just as challenging to contain your optimism when you see great potential as it is to keep a positive attitude when everything takes longer than you wish.*

KEY DATES

APRIL 2-4 ★ *you've got a friend*

Clever Mercury in Aries is now in your 9th House of Adventure, forming an exasperating quincunx with somber Saturn on **April 2**. This challenges you to maintain a steady course even if someone's raining on your parade. It's hard to be lighthearted when innocent Venus—also in Aries—squares experienced Pluto on **April 3**, bringing you face-to-face with negative emotions, jealousy, or fear of abandonment. Something needs to change, but aggressive Mars is engaged in a tug-of-war with calculating Saturn until **April 4**, slowing your attempts to overcome obstacles.

Luckily, Mercury's cooperative sextile to lucky Jupiter the same day indicates that someone may arrive with a workable solution if you're willing to talk about what's bothering you.

APRIL 9–11 ★ *take your time*

April 9's diplomatic Libra Full Moon falls into your 3rd House of Communication on the same day that Mercury the Messenger enters practical Taurus in your 10th House of Status. Career-related conversations take longer to reach fruition now, yet their impact can be more enduring. The Sun's sextile to hopeful Jupiter on April 10, along with Mercury's superconductive trine to intense Pluto on April 11, can give you the extra confidence you need to bring up a difficult subject. Venus backs into compassionate Pisces—also on April 11—helping you to soften your position enough that others don't need to protect themselves from your overbearing energy, thus taking the conversation to even deeper levels of sharing.

SUPER NOVA DAYS
APRIL 15–17 ★ *stretch it out*

The explosive Mars-Uranus conjunction on April 15 falls in your 8th House of Intimacy and Transformation, catalyzing unexpressed emotions. Don't ignore your sudden impulses; instead, seek ways to move any stuck energy, but do use a little moderation to make your efforts more constructive. Taking your time and staying engaged in this process through April 17—when Venus turns direct and Mercury harmonizes with mature Saturn—may produce more lasting results from this exciting opportunity.

APRIL 22–26 ★ *distant prize*

The pace quickens as fiery Mars enters speedy Aries on April 22, followed by romantic Venus on April 24—the same day as the New Moon in sensual Taurus. But Mercury's dynamic squares to visionary Jupiter on April 22 and to spiritual Neptune on April 25 make it difficult for you to focus on the mundane aspects of your job without considering where your current path will lead. Don't let impatience get the best of you, for an intense Mars-Pluto square on April 26 can provoke extreme behavior best managed with purpose and self-control.

MAY

A DREAM IS A WISH YOUR HEART MAKES

Enthusiastic as you may be about what's ahead, you're probably still doing a bit of emotional cleanup this month. Sensual Venus is now moving direct again in excitable Aries, revisiting territory she traced during her retrograde last month. The retrograde torch is passed from Venus to mental Mercury as the messenger planet backtracks on **May 7–30**, intensifying communication at work, especially when entering your 10th House of Public Responsibility on **May 13**. Your physical energy remains high this month while Mars blasts through fiery Aries. You may need to adjust plans for financial when Mars quincunxes restrictive Saturn in your 2nd House of Money on **May 11**. Another round of corrections—this time more in style than in deed—are due when Venus quincunxes Saturn on **May 20**.

You tend to go out of your way to give others the benefit of the doubt this month. Your unchecked idealism could unwittingly invite someone to take advantage of your blind optimism as far-reaching Jupiter, wounded Chiron, and illusory Neptune join in a slow coalescence on **May 23–27**. This is the first of three such alignments this year in your 7th House of Relationships, and it's crucial to remember that you are viewing the world through rose-colored glasses. Although you're able to see more potential than usual, it can be a challenge to tell the difference between an unrealistic vision and a solid plan for success. You can't rely on others to help you with your decisions now, for they will likely tell you only what you want to hear. Remain open and trust your own intuition instead of anyone else's rationalizations.

> **KEEP IN MIND THIS MONTH**
>
> *Your overactive imagination can reveal exquisite possibilities everywhere you look. It's up to you, however, to use the best of your dreams to guide you into the future.*

KEY DATES

MAY 2–5 ★ *out of the shadows*

Passionate Venus in forceful Aries helps you express your desires, but her magnetic square with dark Pluto on **May 2** can steer you into an emotionally shady place. Feelings intensify, perhaps reactivating jealousies last stirred on **April 26** when Mars made this same aspect, and it could take a few days to restore your confidence. The Sun's stabilizing trine with authoritative Saturn on **May 5** reassures you of your worth, enabling you to act from inner strength rather than insecurity.

MAY 9 ★ *your own melodrama*

The complex Scorpio Full Moon on **May 9** falls in your 4th House of Foundations, possibly luring you into a family drama involving hidden agendas and unspoken feelings. You may feel as if the rug is being pulled from under your feet as you struggle to stabilize your home base. The simplistic Taurus Sun in your professional 10th House offers a way out of the murky personal waters by concentrating your efforts on obtaining tangible results.

SUPER NOVA DAYS
MAY 16–17 ★ *bend with the breeze*

The stubborn Taurus Sun forms dynamic 90-degree squares with powerhouse Jupiter and compassionate Chiron on **May 16** and with imaginative Neptune on **May 17**, heightening tension with others. You could get discouraged if you've been operating under the illusion that all is well. This is no time to act as if you know it all; your openness to change can turn an impossible situation into the treasure you're hoping to find. Fortunately, the Sun receives support from revolutionary Uranus on **May 16**, urging you to shift your attitude radically.

MAY 20 ★ *midcourse correction*

You are fired up and ready to act on your feelings with heroic Mars, sexy Venus, and the reflective Moon in just-do-it Aries in your 9th House of Big Ideas. But the best of intentions may need serious revision now, because Venus forms an irritating quincunx with austere Saturn. This is not a showstopper, yet your enthusiasm may dwindle. Luckily, the Sun enters dualistic Gemini and your 11th House of Long-Term Goals, helping you see past any current negativity. Additionally, a Mercury-Jupiter square boosts your confidence. Just be careful not to promise more than you can deliver.

MAY 24 ★ *you and your shadow*

The interactive Gemini New Moon in your 11th House of Friends is an indicator of your busy social calendar, but its inconvenient quincunx with extreme Pluto suggests that out-of-control feelings can get in the way of an otherwise lighthearted time. Being aware of what you pay for your desires can keep you from getting hooked by your own emotions.

JUNE

DRESS FOR SUCCESS

Your thoughts may be focused on career issues, but the curious Gemini Sun illuminates your 11th House of Long-Term Goals for most of the month, enticing you with possibilities way beyond your current responsibilities. The emphasis is clearly on your role in the outer world, your career, and your status within your extended family or community with mental Mercury in practical Taurus and your 10th House of Career until **June 13**. Additionally, Mars just arrived in the sign of the Bull on **May 31**, and Venus follows close behind on **June 6**. Mars's connection with powerful Pluto in your 6th House of Work on **June 3**, shadowed by the Sun's dynamic square with constrictive Saturn on **June 5**, together symbolize your strong professional drive, even when you face frustrating obstacles.

The inspirational Sagittarius Full Moon on **June 7** falls in your 5th House of Love and Creativity, encouraging you to move beyond a recent disappointment. You want more from your life now as Venus, moving through materialistic Taurus, hooks up with possessive Pluto. You may be seduced by your unquenchable thirst for pleasure. If you attempt to satisfy this urge with objects or investments, though, you could be left feeling empty unless you also address your deep emotional needs. A series of unexpected twists and turns on **June 16–21** can derail even the best-laid plans, yet a positive attitude, combined with faith in your co-workers and friends, opens a window of opportunity wide enough for you to climb through. You can move ahead without a lot of fanfare as the Sun enters reflective Cancer on the Summer Solstice, **June 21**, followed by a quiet Cancer New Moon on **June 22** in your spiritual 12th House.

> **KEEP IN MIND THIS MONTH**
>
> *Don't let the expectations of others limit you. There are many ways to express your creativity, and it's your job to find the outlet that works best for you.*

KEY DATES

JUNE 3–6 ★ *nose to the grindstone*

Energetic Mars is determined as he trines potent Pluto on **June 3** from your 10th House of Career and Public Life, empowering you to succeed against great odds. You can reach deep into your energy reserves to overcome issues of low self-esteem or lack of resources. Keep a stiff upper lip even as you're being tested by the Sun squaring taskmaster Saturn on **June 5**, followed by Venus on **June 6**. You may have to miss out on some of the fun because of the heavy responsibilities you now carry.

JUNE 9-12 ★ *license to show off*
A few days of communication difficulties can plague you at work when messenger Mercury squares Chiron, Neptune, and Jupiter on **June 9–10**. Yet this can turn out to be a fantastic opportunity for you to exhibit your creative talents as Mars forms a magical quintile with these same three planets on **June 11–12**.

JUNE 13-15 ★ *skillful illusionist*
Quicksilver Mercury enters restless Gemini on **June 13**, picking up the pace of your social life. Unfortunately, you cannot talk your way out of a sticky situation. Still, Venus's quintile to the spiritual Chiron-Neptune-Jupiter super-conjunction on **June 14–15** enables you to pull a rabbit out of the hat and make everyone believe in the magic.

SUPER NOVA DAYS
JUNE 21-22 ★ *drive all night*
The Cosmic Lovers, Venus and Mars, create an expressive conjunction on **June 21**—a propitious sign for romance on the Summer Solstice. These two planets' stabilizing trines to astute Saturn in your 2nd House of Money on **June 22** help you fortify your resources and enhance your ability to make intelligent fiscal decisions. The needy Cancer New Moon on the same day falls in your 12th House of Endings. Its opposition to domineering Pluto adds a sense of urgency as you consider everything you must yet accomplish before the moment passes. Your likelihood of achieving your goals is high, yet you may have underestimated the effort involved.

JUNE 26 ★ *try, try again*
No matter how successful you are, self-criticism can get in your way on **June 26** when analytical Mercury squares pragmatic Saturn. The hard, cold reality of your shortcomings may temporarily dissipate your optimism and your resolve, but this is no time to feel sorry for yourself. You have too much work to do to waste your energy on self-pity. You have been given an opportunity to strengthen your plan and try again. Don't gloss over differences of opinion; instead, communicate with others so you know exactly where your disagreements are, and then work toward a compromise before moving forward again.

JULY

HELP IS ON THE WAY

Although you may receive a great deal of support from others this month, it's tricky to separate the generous promises from what will actually be delivered. If this feels like familiar ground, rest assured that you have been here before—when grandiose Jupiter joined compassionate Chiron and idealistic Neptune on **May 23–27**. Now retrograde Jupiter, in your 7th House of Others, revisits Neptune and Chiron, bringing mentors, teachers, or even a spiritual guru into your life. It may take until the final pass in **December** before you understand how the current good news will ultimately impact your life. Look for shifts in the cosmic weather on **July 3** when mental Mercury swings into emotional Cancer in your 12th House of Dreams, joining the Sun to illuminate your fantasies.

The ambitious Capricorn Full Moon Eclipse on **July 7** trines karmic Saturn in your 2nd House of Self-Worth, suggesting that your extra-hard work will produce the results you desire. But keeping your feet on the ground can be quite challenging when boundless Jupiter joins dreamy Neptune on **July 10**. Analytical Mercury in your spiritual 12th House receives support from austere Saturn on **July 11** to help you hold on to a thread of reality. The self-protective Cancer New Moon Eclipse on **July 21** falls in your introspective 12th House, heralding jovial Jupiter's conjunction with healing Chiron the following day. You may attempt to keep your feelings to yourself, but you probably won't be able to stay out of the spotlight for long. The Sun enters lively Leo on **July 22**, following Mercury's arrival on **July 17**, drawing you out of hiding and onto center stage, poised to enjoy the love and appreciation that shine on you.

> **KEEP IN MIND THIS MONTH**
>
> *Disillusionment can be discouraging, yet seeing things the way they truly are can open the way for a more realistic partnership over the days ahead.*

KEY DATES

JULY 1 ★ *cautious optimism*

July begins on an uplifting yet anxious note as social Mercury in your 11th House of Friends harmoniously trines the Jupiter-Chiron-Neptune super-conjunction on **July 1**. Important information arrives at your doorstep, giving you a new perspective and clearing an exciting path you wish to explore. But Mercury and sensual Venus both create a complex series of aspects, preventing you from being comfortable with the wide-open horizon. Even if everything looks great, something doesn't feel right. Keep your uneasiness in perspective and don't overreact. This is a wonderful opportunity if you can offset your inflated idealism with a bit of sensible caution.

JULY 5-7 ★ *dream globally, act locally*

You are anxious and eager for more social activity when pleasant Venus enters restless Gemini in your 11th House of Friends and Associates on **July 5**. But you may not be ready to take the leap with physical Mars still plodding along in Taurus in your professional 10th House. You grow impatient with yourself—or someone else who doesn't follow through on a promise—when Mars squares the hopeful Jupiter-Chiron-Neptune super-conjunction on **July 5–6**. Nevertheless, it's important to pay careful attention to your daily routine, because the self-disciplined Capricorn Full Moon on **July 7** is a Lunar Eclipse that falls in your 6th House of Health and Work. Your focus on details can help you complete your tasks and even improve your physical well-being.

JULY 16-18 ★ *honest to a fault*

You may grow tired of waiting for the right moment to speak your mind, yet an uneven sense of timing makes it difficult to take advantage of your potential. Even expressive trines from communicator Mercury and the illuminating Sun to any-thing-goes Uranus on **July 16 and July 18** might not be enough to smooth out the wrinkles. In fact, you could take honesty too far. If you do offend someone's social sensibilities by overstepping a boundary, don't get self-righteous. Convey your good intentions, apologize, and then move on.

JULY 26-28 ★ *knock knock knocking on heaven's door*

Your heart opens wide enough to let love enter on **July 26–28**, when romantic Venus aspects the magical trio of Jupiter, Chiron, and Neptune in your 7th House of Relationships. Even if you have responsibilities, make time to relax. Your charm factor is on high, and the sweetness that you feel these days can raise your self-esteem. But don't expect everything to go as you imagine, for Venus also dynamically squares unpredictable Uranus on **July 28**, foreshadowing an unexpected twist to your pleasurable journey.

AUGUST

RELATIONSHIP DILEMMA

It's time for summer play . . . but you also have your share of work to do this month. The Sun remains in your sign until **August 22**, illuminating recent relationship joys and struggles. The harsh realities of your day-to-day life confront your sweet fantasies of secure love as Venus—now sequestered in your 12th House of Inner Peace until **August 26**—opposes domineering Pluto on **August 1**. Your own emotions are raw; you might feel too vulnerable to engage in a confrontation about getting your needs met. Although your passions are aroused, you may choose to withdraw and save the battle for another day. You're more interested in building on what you've already created, and cerebral Mercury's entry into hardworking Virgo and your 2nd House of Personal Resources on **August 2** has you thinking about the practical side of things until it enters indulgent Libra on **August 25**.

The unsettling Aquarius Full Moon Eclipse on **August 5** can offer up a relationship surprise. You have one too many options with hyperactive Mars skating in Gemini through your 11th House of Goals, dispersing your focus. The push-pull theme becomes obvious if you compare the constraining forces of **August 10**—when hot Mars squares cold Saturn—with the potentially explosive energy of **August 18**, when he squares erratic Uranus. Suppressing your need for independence will not work, but be careful aboutoverreacting or you'll upset the status quo. You may feel your resistance to change as you experience alternating waves of optimism and pessimism, culminating in an uncomfortable Jupiter-Saturn quincunx on **August 19**, followed by an expressive Leo New Moon on **August 20**.

> ### KEEP IN MIND THIS MONTH
>
> *Instead of making a big decision followed by sweeping changes, maintain your balance with a series of smaller adjustments throughout the month.*

KEY DATES

AUGUST 3–5 ★ *bend in the road*

Mental Mercury's hookup with powerful Pluto on **August 3** adds precision to your words, allowing you to express what was elusive a couple of days ago. The Moon's entry into thoughtful Aquarius and your 7th House of Relationships on **August 4**, and the Full Moon Eclipse on **August 5**, create a replay of the relationship issues you've been facing since May. You could be hopeful about where the current shift in dynamics will lead even if you're still unsure how this will all play out.

SUPER NOVA DAYS
AUGUST 10-17 ★ *push me, pull you*

Mars's frustrating square to restrictive Saturn on **August 10**, followed by his easy trine to buoyant Jupiter on **August 13**, can become a drama as you try to balance excessive restriction with overindulgence. It's difficult to know what to do next as you're pulled in two directions—into your own center of certainty or toward the possibilities brought into your life by someone else—but it seems impossible to choose one over the other. The Sun's opposition to Jupiter, Chiron, and Neptune on **August 14-17** places you directly in the middle of this tug-of-war. Fortunately, harmonious aspects from Mars keep your spirits up, preventing you from getting stuck in your current melodrama. You may believe that any move is better than none, yet a serious Mercury-Saturn conjunction on **August 17** requires you to think before you act or you'll end up wasting valuable time and energy.

AUGUST 20-23 ★ *back to business*

There are no simple answers to life's questions now—yet just knowing this can alleviate pressure. The bold Leo New Moon on **August 20** may be the turning point you need. Many previously unrelated events reach a confluence as separate strands of reality are woven together to change the course of your life. Events have conspired to throw you off course, and although the distractions may have been exciting at times, you haven't progressed toward your goals as much as you intended. You are ready to get back to work when the Sun enters practical Virgo on **August 22** and trines relentless Pluto on **August 23**.

AUGUST 26 ★ *compromise is key*

Mars's entry into manipulative Cancer and your 12th House of Privacy pulls your energy inward, so avoid passive-aggressive behavior while responding to someone who tries to control you. The warrior planet's opposition to unyielding Pluto can turn into a protracted conflict, but keep in mind that there may be no winner unless you're flexible enough to seek common ground.

LEO

SEPTEMBER

Tensions at the beginning of the month can set the tone for relationship struggles; fortunately, you can learn a great deal about yourself and those around you in the process. Much of your time is spent reevaluating your recent interactions with others, sifting through the positive and the negative, and considering what changes you must make. Excessive Jupiter, emotionally wounded Chiron, and elusive Neptune, still traveling in a pack, are retrograde all month in your 7th House of Partnerships. Mercury's retrograde phase on **September 6–29** is a perfect opportunity to do this kind of relationship review and analysis, allowing you to be more discerning as it backs into organized Virgo in your 2nd House of Values on **September 17**.

A series of oppositions to the planets in your 7th House help you gain perspective on issues of the heart as loving Venus crosses Jupiter on **September 11**, Chiron on **September 14**, and Neptune on **September 15**. But the most significant aspect of the month is also on **September 15**, when reluctant Saturn opposes progressive Uranus in a series that began on **November 4, 2008**, and doesn't end until **July 26, 2010**. This wake-up call crosses your resource-oriented 2nd and 8th Houses, reminding you to pay close attention to what you own, what you earn, and what you want. You may feel a great sense of urgency to break out of the rut into which you have fallen, take immediate action to alleviate boredom, and multiply your resources. Keep in mind, however, that you're still in the middle of a long-term process. Don't expect amazing epiphanies to suddenly liberate you or a magical transporter beam to instantaneously take you to a galaxy far, far away.

> **KEEP IN MIND THIS MONTH**
>
> *Financial issues can reflect your sense of self-worth. Taking steps to improve your self-esteem might also be an effective way to increase your income.*

KEY DATES

SEPTEMBER 1–4 ★ *spinning your wheels*

It's difficult to balance your own needs with someone else's, especially if you two aren't talking about the real issues. Yet you might find it hard to get traction in any serious discussion as mental Mercury in socially oriented Libra and assertive Mars in tenacious Cancer both form tense sesquisquares with excessive Jupiter in your 7th House of Partners on **September 1–2**. Your actions are at odds with your thoughts, and the Mars-Mercury square on **September 3** can add more impatience to aggravate your current dissatisfaction. Your emotions swell with the compassionate Pisces Full Moon on **September 4**, though it's hard to discern the extent to which you should trust your own feelings.

SEPTEMBER 11–12 ★ *insatiable appetites*

Desire can get out of hand when opulent Jupiter meets up with vivacious Venus in dramatic Leo on **September 11**. This opposition activates your relationship houses, encouraging you to overindulge your senses in search of pleasure. Jupiter is further illuminated by a crunchy quincunx from the Sun, a difficult aspect that can push your common sense beyond the boundaries of reason. Don't reach too far or you could lose your balance. This is uncharted territory, and your perceptions may not be accurate when a slow-moving quincunx between realistic Saturn and delusional Neptune reaches fruition on **September 12**.

SUPER NOVA DAYS
SEPTEMBER 15–18 ★ *catalyst for change*

Someone can turn the tables on you by unexpectedly changing the rules of the game on **September 17** when the Sun makes its yearly opposition with surprising Uranus. This isn't a light and easy time; you have suddenly come to the end of the road and don't know what's next. The efficient Virgo New Moon on **September 18** reactivates the Saturn-Uranus opposition that was exact on **September 15**, giving you a chance to handle large issues that set sensible caution against reckless abandon. The New Moon is also conjunct thoughtful Mercury in your 2nd House of Self-Worth, so pay special attention to those things you value most—both tangible and intangible. Don't wait to put your plan into action, especially if you're trying to increase your income or improve your technical skills.

SEPTEMBER 20–22 ★ *time management*

Careful communication is your order of business as information processor Mercury in discriminating Virgo conjuncts the Sun on **September 20** and authoritative Saturn on **September 22**. The Sun's entry into friendly Libra and your 3rd House of Communication on **September 22** is the Autumnal Equinox, increasing the day-to-day pace of your life and initiating a period when you have so much to do that you may forget about taking time to enjoy yourself.

OCTOBER

ENDINGS AND BEGINNINGS

You are coming to the end of a circuitous journey that began in **September 2007,** when Saturn the Tester entered Virgo and your 2nd House of Self-Worth. Although this may have brought financial adversity, hopefully you were able to stabilize your material world and in the process clarify what is most important to you. If money is still tight, this month may prove to be a transition that lightens your worries. Saturn enters cooperative Libra and your 3rd House of Communication on **October 29,** a moment that can be a significant turning point as your hard work finally begins to pay off. This isn't an overnight success, but the first step in a process that will build momentum over the days and weeks ahead.

The fiery Aries Full Moon on **October 4** shows you the big picture and forces you to think about what you may be hiding. Assertive Mars's entry into demonstrative Leo on **October 16** enables you to take suppressed feelings and push them out into the open. Mars remains in exhibitionist Leo for the rest of the year as he slows down to turn retrograde on **December 20.** This extended visit by Mars gives you plenty of time to accomplish your goals, so rather than rushing in and doing sloppy work, take your time and get it right. Your imagination is vividly active, especially with respect to romance, when the lovely Libra New Moon on **October 18** aligns favorably with dreamy Neptune in your 7th House of Relationships. Remember that you are looking at others through a fantasy filter now, so be cautious about making commitments based upon your current experience.

> **KEEP IN MIND THIS MONTH**
>
> *Don't drop the ball when it comes to financial issues, even if you get super-busy. Take care of your current obligations while also planning for the future.*

KEY DATES

OCTOBER 4 ★ *packed and ready to go*

The rambunctious Aries Full Moon on **October 4** falls in your 9th House of Higher Thought and Faraway Places. It's challenging to stay focused on the present when you can see so many options for what lies ahead. Mars's harmonious hookup to futuristic Uranus can clear a path to larger-than-life goals, including the chance to enroll in an advanced course of study or perhaps to go on an adventure someplace exotic. But be careful, because Mercury's opposition to Uranus the same day can flood your mind with original thoughts that may not be practical enough to turn into something real.

SUPER NOVA DAYS
OCTOBER 8-10 ★ *up for the challenge*
You are restrained by your caution one moment and tempted to take a risk the next. Mental Mercury's conjunction with sobering Saturn on **October 8** can stop you in your tracks when you encounter the hard, cold truth. With attractive Venus's opposition to unconventional Uranus on **October 9**, though, you may forget all your reasons to stay put as you're swept up in a thrilling swirl of emotions. Still, even if your confidence is high, there are still very real obstacles for you to handle. When messenger Mercury squares immovable Pluto on **October 10**, you may come up against such a wall. Denial won't work at this time, so isolate the problem and discuss what can be done to make it work for everyone involved.

OCTOBER 12-15 ★ *delayed gratification*
Powerhouse Jupiter turns direct on **October 12**, the same day that active Mars cooperatively sextiles wise Saturn. This combination allows you to be more organized than usual, and able to execute a well-constructed plan. But success is not immediately forthcoming, for sweet Venus's conjunction with strict Saturn on **October 13** can delay the rewards that are rightfully yours. Venus's entry into tactful Libra on **October 14** can help you to accept current circumstances, though her tough square to Pluto on **October 15** will certainly intensify the day.

OCTOBER 28-29 ★ *delicate navigation*
Although it may take awhile for you to adjust to the easier pace of life foretold by Saturn's entry into harmonizing Libra on **October 29**, the mishmash of planetary good news and bad news on **October 28** will likely impact you in a more immediate fashion. Mercury's entry into passionate Scorpio and an aggressive Sun-Mars square agitate your emotions and incite impulsive behavior. But a lovely Venus-Jupiter trine offers delicious pleasures and encourages generosity. Your best bet is to find a path between these extremes.

NOVEMBER

EXTREME MAKEOVER

You are beginning a long-term process by establishing healthy patterns in your everyday life that will sustain you for years to come. You can hear different footsteps coming down the planetary path now that Saturn the Taskmaster has entered your 3rd House of Immediate Environment. Personal success can be the result of working very hard to overcome limitations. Saturn forms a slow-moving square with Pluto the Terminator throughout this month, forcing you to eliminate destructive behavior and excessive consumption of resources. Although the square between persistent Saturn and transformative Pluto is exact on **November 15,** you will most likely feel the relentless pressure to change for the rest of the year.

The first few days of the month can be confusing as the sensual Taurus Full Moon pulls you back to your center while lovely Venus forms a relaxed trine with wistful Neptune on **November 2,** highlighting your world with the bright colors of your imagination. You believe that anything you want can be yours, only to face the challenge of putting your fantasies into language that others can understand. This metamorphosis does not come easily, and you may be quite unwilling to relinquish control; however, the powerful Saturn-Pluto square is unforgiving and will take from you whatever is necessary to make room for the positive changes ahead. Be smart by preemptively cutting waste, focusing your attention on what's most important, and voluntarily giving up your attachment to things that don't help your transformative process. If you're living a life aligned with your true purpose, this transit can guide you to the next level. But if you've lost your way, you may struggle now to regain your direction.

> **KEEP IN MIND THIS MONTH**
>
> *The resistances you face are challenging your resolve, so don't hesitate to respond. Hard work can make a significant difference in which direction your life goes.*

KEY DATES

NOVEMBER 2–5 ★ *say what you mean; mean what you say*

On **November 2,** a practical Taurus Full Moon in your public 10th House brings your fantasies down to earth, prodding you toward simple yet determined behavior. A little extra caution can help you balance the erratic Mars-Uranus connection the same day. Make use of your sharper-than-normal perceptions as the Sun conjuncts Mercury on **November 5,** boosting your communication skills and enabling you to make your point clearly.

NOVEMBER 6-8 ★ *hidden agenda*

Your life grows more complex on **November 6–8**, when a series of tough aspects increase stress and tension in your daily life. Personal matters are complicated as Venus enters secretive Scorpio in your 4th House of Security on **November 7**, making you less likely to reveal your feelings as you try to keep up appearances. It's easy for you to go overboard or overstate your case when intelligent Mercury squares overconfident Jupiter on **November 8**.

NOVEMBER 10-11 ★ *a brilliant save*

The personal dynamics at home can make you feel uncomfortable if hurtful words poke at old insecurities. Intelligent Mercury's square to wounded Chiron on **November 10** makes it hard to keep a painful memory in perspective, while the Sun's square to boundless Jupiter can turn molehills into mountains. Loss of perspective can get in the way of effective communication until the Mercury-Uranus trine on **November 11** provides a surprising solution to your problem.

SUPER NOVA DAYS
NOVEMBER 14-16 ★ *stress and release*

Paradoxically, the heavy Saturn-Pluto square on **November 15** is offset by a brilliant Sun-Uranus trine on **November 14**, showing you infinite possibilities everywhere you look. But there's no immediate path to reach the great potential you see in front of you. Your direction may be clouded by a lack of good judgment as the Sun squares confusing Neptune, yet your thoughts are freed from the constraints of reality as Mercury enters inspirational Sagittarius, also on **November 15**. The passionate Scorpio New Moon on **November 16** confirms this shift and marks the start of your adventure.

NOVEMBER 21-26 ★ *beyond the horizon*

The Sun's entry into fiery Sagittarius and your 5th House of Self-Expression on **November 21** clears the air, lifts your spirits, and provokes acts of spontaneity. But you need to exercise self-restraint, for sensual Venus is in an indulgent phase as she squares excessive Jupiter on **November 23**, then compassionate Chiron on **November 24**, and dreamy Neptune on **November 26**. Additionally, her superconductive trine to outrageous Uranus on **November 25** awakens suppressed desires and emboldens your behavior. You could astonish yourself and others with your appetite for pleasure unless you set limits and stick to them.

DECEMBER

If last month put you through the wringer, this one brings you out the other side. Not only can you see what may be around the next bend, but you also gain clarity about your recent challenges. You know that hard choices still need to be made, but understanding that these important decisions will take time can give you a reprieve for the holiday season. The third and final conjunction among boundless Jupiter, healing Chiron, and imaginative Neptune in your 7th House of Relationships can put an ethereal touch on the otherwise mundane activities of the month. The current gathering of these three spiritual planets can replay issues that were prominent in your life around **May 23–27** and **July 10–22**. Jupiter's conjunction with Chiron on **December 7** could offer hope and happiness—and although positive effects are likely, so is disappointment if your expectations are unrealistic. Jupiter's conjunction with Neptune on **December 21** is indicative of your current attraction to the subtle yet powerful experiences that transcend the three-dimensional world. Relationships, too, can seem infused with magic. Yet as glamorous as someone may appear, you must stay aware of where reality ends and your fantasies begin.

The playful Gemini Full Moon on **December 2** falls in your 11th House of Groups and Friends, raising the social bar and filling your calendar with fun yet distracting activities. The fun-loving Sagittarius New Moon on **December 16** falls in your 5th House of Love and Creativity, urging you to jump into the holiday spirit. You may choose to end the year on a retreat instead of going to a party, though, as the self-protective Cancer Full Moon Eclipse on **December 31** falls in your 12th House of Spirituality.

KEEP IN MIND THIS MONTH

Be on the lookout for opportunities that come to you through people who engage your imagination, and through experiences that put you in closer touch with your dreams.

KEY DATES

DECEMBER 5–10 ★ *the virtue of patience*

Expect frustrations over these days as household chores and work projects interfere with elusive pleasure. Much to your chagrin, even your most secure plans can fall apart when go-getter Mars, in showy Leo in your 1st House of Self throughout the entire month, now runs into a tense semisquare with strict Saturn on **December 5**—possibly appearing to you as a nay-saying authority figure. Circumstances continue to curb your enthusiasm when quicksilver Mercury is temporarily restrained by Saturn on **December 7**. Unfortunately, you may not be able to use your charisma to overcome the current negativity. Perseverance, however, is your smartest strategy, for the Sun's smooth hookup with Mars on **December 10** allows you to break through the resistance and happily move on.

SUPER NOVA DAYS
DECEMBER 16–20 ★ *time is on your side*
The adventurous Sagittarius Full Moon on **December 16** puts you in a party mood that is further enhanced by a sweet trine between the cosmic lovers, Venus and Mars, on **December 17**. Although you're lighthearted, you can become discouraged if you're trying to accomplish a specific goal prior to the end of the year, for self-directed Mars—moving uncharacteristically slowly all month—turns retrograde on **December 20**. You may feel as if you've come so very close to your destination, only to see the finish line recede into the distance. This is, however, no time to give up. Instead, accept that success could take longer while being thankful that you have the time necessary to polish your act before you take center stage.

DECEMBER 21 ★ *guided by spirit*
Your current commitment to excellence and success becomes more practical when the Sun steps into ambitious Capricorn on **December 21**. This Winter Solstice can be a powerful time to internalize your energies and seek inner stillness, even if you have social or professional obligations to honor. Reflection is further encouraged by the spiritual Jupiter-Neptune conjunction. Involve a partner or teacher, if you can, as you ponder the wonders of life. Unhappily, you may be busier than you wish when communicator Mercury forms a vexing quincunx with retrograde Mars, challenging you to find calm amid all the noisy distractions.

DECEMBER 24–26 ★ *long winter's nap*
Intensity builds as the Sun joins shadowy Pluto on **December 24**—and you become even more introspective when Venus enters serious Capricorn on **December 25**. Mercury's retrograde turn on **December 26** is yet one more sign of your contemplative mood as you approach the final days of the year.

VIRGO

AUGUST 23–SEPTEMBER 22

VIRGO

2008 SUMMARY

This is a karmic year for you as Saturn, the gatekeeper of reality, moves steadily through your sign, testing the integrity of the foundations upon which you continue to build your life. Its time to refocus your best intentions and take care of the serious business at hand, instead of waiting for a better time. The good news is that you are blessed with continued support all year as optimistic Jupiter counteracts the realism of somber Saturn.

AUGUST—*winds of fate*

Your stress level is high, so it's crucial to look beyond differences of opinion. Otherwise, unexpected conflicts might turn even the smallest disagreements into major meltdowns.

SEPTEMBER—*consolidate your gains*

Instead of worrying about how you can fix everything all at once, reevaluate your life and develop a strategy to preserve what's already working.

OCTOBER—*you are what you think*

Instead of being sure that what you know is enough, remain open to receiving new information that can change your mind, however unexpected and unconventional the source.

NOVEMBER—*eyes on the distant future*

It's difficult to gauge the relative importance of specific events now, so treat each one—no matter how insignificant it seems—as a life-changing moment.

DECEMBER—*stress management*

Allowing for imperfection in yourself and others doesn't mean you have to sacrifice your high standards. Maintain a healthy perspective and positive results will follow.

2008 CALENDAR

AUGUST

FRIDAY 1 ★A leap of faith has profound results through tomorrow

TUESDAY 5 ★Postpone decisions until your head clears, after the 6th

SUNDAY 10 ★**SUPER NOVA DAYS** You can't turn back from recent choices

SATURDAY 23 ★Mental fireworks are exciting, but pursue only the best ideas

WEDNESDAY 27 ★A change of perspective requires diplomacy through the 28th

SEPTEMBER

WEDNESDAY 3 ★Deliver more than promised for results

SUNDAY 7 ★The antidote to temptation is realism through the 9th

FRIDAY 12 ★**SUPER NOVA DAYS** Newfound freedom elates through the 15th

SATURDAY 20 ★Reassess your resources through the 24th

SUNDAY 28 ★Let go of logic and indulge your imagination through the 29th

OCTOBER

SATURDAY 4 ★Find balance, or else overindulge through the 6th

FRIDAY 10 ★A new perspective reduces conflict through the 11th

TUESDAY 14 ★**SUPER NOVA DAYS** Let go of self-criticism through the 15th

SATURDAY 18 ★Set habits aside and accept unexpected adventure and love

THURSDAY 30 ★Flexibility is key in tense relationships through the 31st

NOVEMBER

MONDAY 3 ★Face the music! Stress won't disappear without effort through the 4th

MONDAY 10 ★**SUPER NOVA DAYS** Overcome your fears through the 13th

SUNDAY 16 ★The sky's the limit if you embrace unconventional thoughts

SUNDAY 23 ★Leave daily reality and partake in theoretical discussions

FRIDAY 28 ★You find a sensible path to unique desires through the 29th

DECEMBER

MONDAY 1 ★Make time for fun even if there's work to finish

WEDNESDAY 10 ★**SUPER NOVA DAYS** Clear the air through the 12th and move on

MONDAY 15 ★A positive attitude and sincere effort will bring relief

SUNDAY 21 ★Shine a light on your fears through the 22nd

SATURDAY 27 ★Set your goals for next year and resolve to succeed

VIRGO OVERVIEW

The patterns you establish and the choices you make this year will
have an enduring impact on your life. Saturn, the planet of form and
structure, remains in efficient Virgo until October 29—returning for a
brief encore in 2010 before taking up a two-year residence in Libra. The presence of this crystallizing planet in your sign represents constraint, but it's not
designed to bind you to your present circumstances. Its purpose is instead to
help you recognize the relationship between your current limits and your
future potential. While it can be discouraging to face the hard, cold reality of
situations that have not lived up to your expectations, seeing exactly where you
stand is a powerful position from which to make positive change. Saturn helps
you define your goals, solidify plans, and apply the discipline and commitment
required to make them work. **Don't allow self-doubt to deter you from reaching for the stars; you need only advance one careful step at a time to succeed.**

Unconventional individuals and impulsive partners bring surprises when revolutionary Uranus in emotional Pisces opposes Saturn on February 5 and
September 15. This is part of a long series of destabilizing aspects between
the planets of change and resistance that began late last year and ends next
summer. Overcome a tendency to try to maintain the status quo, especially in
relationships, because rigidity will only increase tension, perhaps leading to an
explosion. **The unusual ideas you are facing can be just what you need to
break down your barriers to a happier and more exciting life.** Feed your
growing ambitions from a spring of innovation that reveals new ways to solve
old problems. Balance stern Saturn's need for control with shocking Uranus's
promise of discovery by maintaining flexibility in the face of the unexpected.

Expansive Jupiter in inventive Aquarius highlights your 6th House of Health,
Work, and Daily Routines this year, broadening your perspective in these
important areas. However, a Solar Eclipse on January 26 and a Lunar Eclipse
on August 5 in Aquarius fall in the 6th House, indicating that you need to let go
of some old ways before filling up on new ones. You're generally careful about
making alterations in your life, but the natural effusiveness of Jupiter is
increased by its conjunctions to idealistic Neptune on May 27, July 10, and
December 21. Their union could float you on clouds of hope that overcome
your practical nature, leaving you with inspiration but no ground in which to

nurture its growth. You might find yourself swinging between extremes of optimism and despair—clearly not the best way to go. Don't allow cynicism to darken the essence of your ideals or dissuade you from aspiring to the highest levels of delight. **Temper your hopes with just a smidge of realism to ensure that they don't disappear in a puff of smoke** but become a long-lasting template for a more fulfilling future.

YOU'RE NUMBER ONE

Make yourself the top priority in relationships this year: Responsible Saturn in your 1st House of Self through October 29 puts the focus on your needs, desires, and well-being. Rather than making service to others the keystone of partnerships, pull back to a place of greater self-interest; this will give you the time, energy, and inclination to maximize your own strengths. Loving Venus goes retrograde in your 8th House of Intimacy on March 6 and turns direct in your 7th House of Partnerships on April 17—a period to reevaluate and, perhaps, alter your expectations of relationship and your commitments to others. If you're not satisfied with what you have, renegotiations are appropriate. A Capricorn Lunar Eclipse in your 5th House of Romance on July 7 is another potential turning point in matters of the heart, showing you that a current plan isn't working or that the burdens of responsibility you're carrying are too heavy. Don't be afraid to change course if you aren't headed in the right direction.

ON THE CUTTING EDGE

Trying different tasks at work or developing a brand-new set of skills can bring magic to your job this year. A superconjunction in Aquarius with visionary Jupiter, imaginative Neptune, and healing Chiron occurs in your 6th House of Employment, combining high tech, community service, and idealism on the job. Putting yourself on the cutting edge in your field will be more fun and fulfilling than playing it safe by sticking to what you already know. The retrograde periods of Mercury, ruler of your 10th House of Career, are times when minor complications and miscommunications can turn into major problems. Use these four critical periods—starting on January 11, May 6, September 6, and December 26—to backtrack and complete unfinished tasks, rebuild professional relationships, and tighten up your schedule to increase your efficiency.

CAREFUL REASSESSMENT

Investments, loans, and shared finances are due for a significant review this year when money-conscious Venus turns retrograde on March 6. The planetary ruler of your 2nd House of Income will travel backward in your 8th House of Joint Holdings until April 17. Backing out of existing deals to cut your losses or delaying new investments is wiser than forging ahead during this period. Enthusiastic Jupiter joins entrepreneurial Mars on February 17, stirring interest in a business opportunity. Yet Venus's pending retrograde and Mars's conjunction with illusory Neptune on March 8 turn yellow caution flags into red stoplights. Additionally, pay careful attention to the fine print when dealing with financial matters September 6–19, when messenger Mercury travels retrograde in your 2nd House of Money.

 ## LET'S GET METAPHYSICAL

You tend to know more about diet and health than most people, yet your interests in these areas could be even stronger this year. Serious Saturn in your 1st House of Physicality instructs you to change habits to increase your level of fitness. However, oppositions to this otherwise stable planet from eccentric Uranus on February 5 and September 15 may produce sudden swings in your energy level. Exploring unconventional ways to attain optimal performance and vitality become especially appealing with "hungry to learn" Jupiter in your 6th House of Health. Its ongoing conjunctions with mystical Neptune and Chiron entice you to explore more subtle forms of healing.

 ## PEACE AND UNDERSTANDING

Wisdom, faith, and inspiration enter your household this year, enlarging your perspective on family matters. Joyous Jupiter, the ruler of your 4th House of Home and Family, sails through progressive Aquarius in the company of Chiron and Neptune, allowing you to view your domestic situation in a more global manner. It's easier to let go of old grievances and negative patterns as hope is fueled by a vision of potentials—especially around May 23–27 and throughout December, when Jupiter, Chiron, and Neptune conjoin. Modernizing your living space or moving to a place with less restrictive values is possible now.

MARK YOUR CALENDAR

An Aquarius Lunar Eclipse on January 26 may trigger frustration on the road or an unexpected turn in academic matters. Venus, the ruler of your 9th House of Travel and Higher Education, is joined with erratic Uranus and opposed by Saturn during this important event. Stern Saturn forms a demanding square with Venus during the Cancer Solar Eclipse of July 21, which can also signal delays. Being flexible at these times helps you find alternative routes that allow you to reach your destination with less stress. Travel for pleasure when Venus opposes Jupiter on September 11. Schedule an important business trip around October 13 when Venus and Saturn connect in your sign while receiving organizational help from assertive Mars.

FINDING SPIRIT IN MATTER

Spirituality comes down to earth as part of your daily existence this year, illuminating the meaning of life through ordinary events. The metaphysically rich trio of Jupiter, Neptune, and Chiron transit your 6th House of Work and Service, elevating the significance of routine events and infusing you with hope and a sense of purpose on the job. The magic can strike you even while doing mundane chores, showing that you don't require an external authority or a special teacher to learn the most important lessons. A Leo Lunar Eclipse in your 12th House of Soul Consciousness on February 9 is charged up by electric Uranus, producing an epiphany that helps you let go of unnecessary psychological baggage.

RICK & JEFF'S TIP FOR THE YEAR:
Stumbling to Success

The ongoing push-pull dynamic between your attraction to the new and your unwillingness to let go of the past is your theme this year. It may not be easy to find graceful ways to shift between these contrasting urges. Allow yourself to stumble awkwardly, if that's what it takes, rather than waiting for the perfect moment to change gears. Periods of transition and exploration of new territory are times when substance is more important than style. Permit yourself to be a beginner who makes mistakes in the process of learning, rather than having to be a pro who must master every move.

JANUARY

BACKING INTO THE FUTURE

Your ability to adapt to fluctuating conditions is tested this month as Mercury, your ruling planet, takes your mind on a wild journey. It starts on **January 1** when the Messenger enters quirky, airy Aquarius in your 6th House of Work and Service. Alterations of routine can unravel your well-crafted ways of managing daily life. Unpredictable events or new procedures at your place of employment can threaten efficient systems that you understand thoroughly. Opportunistic Jupiter's entry into Aquarius on **January 5** reinforces a trend of experimentation that requires you to upgrade your skills and adjust your habits. You can't fight progress, even if you're certain that it's really a step backward. Help arrives on **January 10** with a tenacious Cancer Full Moon in your 11th House of Groups that forms harmonious aspects to inventive Uranus and stable Saturn, revealing a safe path between the future and the past.

Mercury turns retrograde on **January 11**, beginning its three-week period of backtracking that so often messes with communication, travel, and technology. Be as patient as you can—this is a better time to reorganize and complete unfinished tasks than to start new projects. The progressive Aquarius New Moon on **January 26** is a Solar Eclipse conjoined by Jupiter that's likely to dramatize issues at work. Differences of opinion can grow into major battles—or you may simply be so bored or stressed that you're itching for change. Jupiter forms tense aspects to the slow-moving Saturn-Uranus opposition on **January 27–29** that emphasize the conflict between playing it safe and breaking free. It's a good time to broaden your perspective, but not yet the moment to act.

> **KEEP IN MIND THIS MONTH**
>
> *You might not be able to keep all your ducks in a row, so lower your standards a little to keep your blood pressure down.*

KEY DATES

JANUARY 3-4 ★ *the power of love*

Kind Venus enters your 7th House of Partnerships on **January 3**, attracting compassionate individuals who don't require you to be perfect. Allow yourself the pleasure of sharing time with someone who has no ambition other than to enjoy you as you are. Venus aligns in an easygoing sextile with potent Pluto on **January 4**, enabling you to repair wounds and take a relationship to a deeper level.

JANUARY 11 ★ *constructive self-reflection*

Mercury turns retrograde, complicating life with miscommunications for the next three weeks that could have you heading one way while a colleague is going off in another direction. Double-check conversations with teammates to avoid errors that waste time and undermine trust. Reexamining your own methods can indicate where inefficiency slows you down or limits the quality of your work. A positive trine between the creative Sun and concrete Saturn gives you a solid center of self-awareness, allowing you to develop practical plans to achieve your long-range goals.

JANUARY 18–21 ★ *hold your tongue*

Your mind stretches with bright ideas as Mercury joins broad-minded Jupiter on **January 18**. Absorbing so much information takes time, so don't expect to understand everything immediately. Your tendency to overexplain can add confusion when brevity would let you make your point. The Sun enters futuristic Aquarius on **January 19** and is conjoined by retrograde Mercury on **January 20**. Heightened mental activity can stress your nervous system, especially if you feel pressured to justify yourself. You may connect with critical information about yourself, but remember that you don't have to share it with others. Your need for privacy and verbal restraint is reinforced when Mercury backs into pragmatic Capricorn on **January 21**.

SUPER NOVA DAYS
JANUARY 22–24 ★ *pleasant surprises*

Excitement stirs on **January 22**, when sociable Venus connects with experimental Uranus. Sudden shifts of mood can take you quickly from moments of delight to detachment and back again. Happily, active Mars aligns favorably with Uranus, giving you the agility to keep pace with these rapid changes. In fact, you should enjoy exploring new experiences that lighten your heart and open your eyes to different forms of fun. The planets fire in diverse directions on **January 24**, starting with a joyous aspect of hope and optimism between the Sun and jolly Jupiter. Mars is supported by responsible Saturn and sweet Venus to combine productivity with pleasure. However, Saturn also casts a shadow of self-doubt that can deflate delight with feelings of insecurity. Its goal, though, is not to stifle happiness, but to blend it with enough clarity and accountability to keep things real.

FEBRUARY

TESTING THE WATERS

Data, details, and communication slowly get back on track as your key planet, Mercury, shifts into forward gear on **February 1**. Its direct turn in your 6th House of Health, Work, and Daily Routines begins a settling-in period as you get more comfortable with new systems that you may have had difficulty grasping during the previous three weeks. Reliability in relationships of all kinds can be threatened by a powerful opposition between safe Saturn and unpredictable Uranus on **February 5**. This is the second in a series of five face-offs from your 1st House of Self to your 7th House of Others that's liable to keep partnerships on edge. You can reduce the pressure, however, if you focus on yourself and relax your expectations of a mate, colleague, or friend. New forms of alliances can emerge that give others more space to be themselves without the threat of a breakdown or breakup.

On **February 9**, a dramatic Leo Full Moon may spur you to let go of dreams that don't match your current reality. This Lunar Eclipse falls in your 12th House of Endings, reminding you that you don't have to hold on to every fantasy or try to be a hero for causes you've outgrown. Withdrawing from an exhausting struggle is not a surrender to outside forces, but a victory for your own well-being. Relationships return to the foreground when the Sun enters Pisces and your 7th House of Partnerships for a monthlong stay on **February 18**. The sensitive Pisces New Moon on **February 24** attracts charismatic individuals who encourage you to express your feelings more openly, which is bound to warm individual relationships and enhance your intuitive connection with others.

> **KEEP IN MIND THIS MONTH**
>
> *No degree of preparation can keep surprises away. Adapting to the unexpected is much more effective than trying to suppress it.*

KEY DATES

FEBRUARY 1–2 ★ *sugar and spice*

The pace of life picks up with Mercury's forward turn on **February 1**, followed by Venus's entry into fiery Aries on **February 2**. The love planet in your 8th House of Deep Sharing sparks impulses that could shake up an intimate relationship. A sudden attraction or urge for new forms of fun with a current partner puts you in a risk-taking mood. Don't be shy about initiating change when you sense the need for more excitement.

SUPER NOVA DAYS

FEBRUARY 4-5 ★ *steep learning curve*

Assertive Mars pops into conceptual Aquarius and your 6th House of Work on **February 4**, perhaps increasing tension on the job. New tasks or procedures require a period of adjustment, so don't expect a smooth transition immediately. The Saturn-Uranus opposition on **February 5** can tempt you to do something extreme, but there are brilliant solutions available that can produce change without disruption. You may feel underappreciated or manipulated as Venus, the Sun, and Pluto form difficult aspects with one another. Buried resentment may surface and undermine trust. If you focus on one issue at a time, however, you will discover resources to repair the damage.

FEBRUARY 13-14 ★ *mind games*

Optimistic Jupiter joins with the karmic North Node of the Moon on **February 13**, attracting a wise teacher or helping you tap into your experience to guide others. Mental Mercury returns to intellectual Aquarius on **February 14**, adding a quirky twist to Valentine's Day. Talking is good, but if ideas become too abstract, the spirit of love can be lost.

FEBRUARY 17-18 ★ *with a little help from your friends*

A high-powered conjunction between active Mars and Jupiter on **February 17** can light your passion for a project. If you want to make it work in the long run, though, don't overreach right now. Assistance can come from an unexpected source on **February 18** with a sweet Venus-Mars sextile and the Sun's entry into your 7th House of Partnerships. There may be some complicated details to sort out when Mercury's tense sesquisquare to Saturn slows communication. Patient explanations provide clarity to overcome obstacles.

FEBRUARY 24-25 ★ *too much information*

Expect a wave of data and fresh ideas as fact-filled Mercury joins visionary Jupiter on **February 24**. You can make the strongest impact by tempering your enthusiasm enough to keep your feet solidly on the ground. Streams of data from others may leave you dizzy unless they slow down long enough to show you how it all can be applied. A harmonious hookup between charming Venus and chatty Mercury on **February 25** serves up sweet conversations and boosts your self-esteem.

MARCH

Prepare to revisit relationship issues this month as Venus, the planet of love, turns retrograde in your 8th House of Intimacy on **March 6**. Reevaluating emotional and financial connections can stir up problems, but it's better to take the initiative than to sit back and react to what others do. The Full Moon in analytical Virgo in your 1st House of Self on **March 10** clearly puts the ball in your court. Stern Saturn's conjunction to the Moon shows the importance of discipline and self-control, especially in opposition to a potentially wild Sun-Uranus conjunction in your 7th House of Others. Even the most dependable allies may behave erratically and upset your plans. When you maintain personal authority, however, you're able to capture the sparks people ignite and use them to light a fire of inspiration for yourself. Assertive Mars entering vulnerable Pisces in your 7th House on **March 14** continues pushing buttons in relationships; be gentle if you'd like to turn conflict into the coziness that strengthens unions.

The Sun's entry into restless Aries on **March 20** marks the first day of spring and adds fire to your 8th House of Deep Sharing. Dramatic personal exchanges may threaten peace and harmony, but increase the likelihood of passion. Mental Mercury joins the scene on **March 25**, sharpening exchanges with quick comments and bright new ideas. Temper the tendency to tease, criticize, or respond to negative comments by others unless you're looking for a way out. The reckless Aries New Moon on **March 26** continues to flirt with the boundaries of partnerships. A hard square from compelling Pluto to this Sun-Moon conjunction could force a decision to make a definitive change, saving an alliance or finally ending it.

> **KEEP IN MIND THIS MONTH**
>
> *There is no safety in standing still. Taking action, even if it seems risky, is the best way to keep your life on track.*

KEY DATES

MARCH 1 ★ *sparring match*

Chatty Mercury is sideswiped by a slippery quincunx from Saturn early in the day, frustrating communication or unraveling plans. Later, however, Mercury catches up with hyperactive Mars to provoke fast talk and aggressive conversation. Enjoy the mental stimulation of a healthy debate or difference of opinion, but back off if the need to be right threatens to overrule love and kindness.

MARCH 8–10 ★ *avoid assumptions*

An idealistic but impractical Mars-Neptune conjunction on **March 8** can turn an act of charity into an exhausting experience. Measure your expenditures of time and energy carefully to avoid wasting too much of either. Mercury enters compassionate Pisces and your 7th House of Partners, bringing sweet but misleading conversations. Don't assume that someone understands you because you share an emotional connection. An opposition between the Sun and rigid Saturn requires precision and a well-defined purpose to avoid irritation. A stressful semisquare from delicate Venus to Mercury tempts you to avoid speaking frankly and thus spare someone's feelings. Fortunately, a selective sextile between Mercury and Pluto on **March 10** will help you and find the right words to untangle any recent knots created by miscommunication.

MARCH 18 ★ *busy signal*

Mercury's opposition to stifling Saturn can block or slow communication. If you aren't getting your message across, restate your point as clearly as you possibly can. If that doesn't work, don't despair, but wait for a better day to tell your story.

MARCH 22–23 ★ *shocking insights*

A conjunction between Mercury and Uranus early on **March 22** tightens up your nervous system and attracts unconventional ideas. Conversations can suddenly end or head off in strange directions. Keep an open mind, though, and a fresh perspective could give you a brilliant breakthrough. Expansion is awkward as Jupiter is challenged by Saturn and the Sun, preventing you from executing your big plans. An unrealistic Venus-Neptune semisquare may blur your financial or emotional judgment. You could have a moment or two of bliss, but a tough square between the Sun and purging Pluto on **March 23** is meant to help you cut through superfluous dreams and get you to the bottom line.

MARCH 27–28 ★ *soften your approach*

Your bright ideas are hard to sell when speedy Mercury in Aries is snagged by challenging aspects from over-the-top Jupiter and hard-to-please Pluto on **March 27**. Calm your emotions to express your ideas with controlled passion, and you may be able to win over a demanding audience. Communication should be much easier on **March 28** when Mercury joins accommodating Venus, putting others in a more receptive mood.

APRIL

INVEST IN YOURSELF

Standing up for yourself is essential on **April 4** as assertive Mars in your 7th House of Others opposes Saturn in your 1st House of Self. Set clear boundaries with those who are unwilling to be cooperative, and state your expectations precisely. You are establishing a pattern in relationships that will work best when you know exactly what you want and aren't afraid to express it. The Full Moon in cooperative Libra on **April 9** falls in your 2nd House of Personal Resources, giving opportunities to increase your income and enhance your self-worth. A supportive trine to the Moon from generous Jupiter suggests that upgrading your work skills could lead to a raise. Clever Mercury's entry into earthy Taurus, also on **April 9**, grounds your thinking in practical terms and tempts you with the rewards of travel and additional education.

Romantic Venus stops her retrograde movement and shifts into direct motion on **April 17**. This may not produce an immediate impact on your love life, but it does initiate a process of moving forward in matters of the heart that may have recently been on hold. Consider renegotiating the terms of a personal or professional relationship if you're not happy. The Sun enters determined Taurus and your 9th House of Travel and Higher Education on **April 19**, a positive signal for widening your mental and physical horizons. Using the common sense of Taurus should help you find the most economical ways to explore your options. The practical Taurus New Moon on **April 24** is favored by a creative trine from regenerative Pluto. This potent heavenly body might help you resurrect an abandoned project and emboldens you to promote your beliefs with passion and power.

> **KEEP IN MIND THIS MONTH**
>
> *Your distant goals can become attainable when they are rooted in realism, nourished with careful planning, and approached with patience.*

KEY DATES

APRIL 2-4 ★ *high-wire act*

Information may not flow easily on **April 2**, when verbal Mercury forms an awkward quincunx with grumpy Saturn. Avoid spending too much time on details that you can address later. A tense square between supersensitive Venus and "tough as nails" Pluto on **April 3** makes minor comments feel like major criticism. Instead of taking offense, investigate deeply into what is being expressed. Tension remains on **April 4** with a stressful Mars-Saturn opposition that leaves little room for mistakes or ambiguity. However, a smart sextile between Mercury and Jupiter provides a perspective that helps you make quick adjustments to correct your course or skillfully explain your behavior.

APRIL 9-11 ★ *communication complexity*
Expect a serious turn of mind on **April 9**, when your planet Mercury enters steady Taurus and forms a demanding sesquisquare with "straight shooting" Saturn. Stick to facts and avoid locking down in a protracted debate where stubbornness overrides common sense. An optimistic Sun-Jupiter sextile on **April 10** generates a more relaxed atmosphere in which you are not held accountable for every little thing you say or do. Deep thinking and powerful conversations flow naturally with a harmonious trine between Mercury and Pluto on **April 11**, making it possible to discuss delicate issues without wounding anyone.

APRIL 13-15 ★ *spontaneous combustion*
Mercury aspects impatient Mars and eccentric Uranus on **April 13-14**, spurring weird conversations, verbal explosions, or brilliant breakthroughs. Mars and Uranus join on **April 15**, fomenting a rebellion in your 7th House of Partnerships that can shake up existing relationships or find you recklessly leaping into the arms of someone new. Experiment and have some fun when you feel safe enough to play.

APRIL 22 ★ *itching for action*
Assertive Mars enters feisty Aries and is ready to rumble. A volatile square between Mercury and Jupiter leaves you prone to overstatement and can trigger an explosive difference of opinion. You hunger for adventure in your personal life or a chance to try something new in business. Don't stop these feelings; act on them with caution and sensitivity to turn a restless impulse into a lasting reward.

APRIL 24-26 ★ *twisted logic*
Loving Venus returns to hot Aries and your 8th House of Intimacy on **April 24**, stoking your desires. If you're being pushed by someone else, however, don't make any quick decisions. Mercury's supportive sextile with electric Uranus suggests mental sharpness, yet its square with squishy Neptune on **April 25** can be a source of confusion. Mars forms a forceful square with Pluto on **April 26** that adds potency to everything you do, but makes it harder to change course if you go in the wrong direction.

MAY

Communication issues, especially in business matters, are key concerns this month with Mercury turning retrograde in your 10th House of Status on **May 7**. The speedy Messenger slipped into chatty Gemini on the last day of April, but its usual fast thinking and talking in the sign of the Twins are slowed by this backward turn. It's essential to avoid spreading yourself so thin with projects that you leave loose ends. Even your notorious attention to detail can waiver until Mercury rights its course and turns direct on **May 30**. The activities of outer planets are also critical this month as optimistic Jupiter joins compassionate Chiron on **May 23** and idealistic Neptune on **May 27** in your 6th House—the first in a series of super-conjunctions of this spiritually oriented trinity that recurs in **July** and **December**. This represents a wave of rising awareness of how you apply your energies in your daily life, opening the door to better health, opportunities to advance your skills, and more happiness on the job.

Complex personal issues may come to light on **May 9**, with the Full Moon in piercing Scorpio exposing secrets in your 3rd House of Communication. Intimate conversations can reveal uncomfortable facts as excessive Jupiter squares the Moon, but a higher level of emotional honesty is a worthwhile risk when you're seeking the truth. The New Moon in versatile Gemini on **May 24** plants so many seeds of possibility in your 10th House of Career, you may be overwhelmed with choices. Purging Pluto's cleansing quincunx to this Sun-Moon conjunction demands that you make your priorities clear and eliminate any inessential activities standing in the way of reaching your most compelling professional goals.

> **KEEP IN MIND THIS MONTH**
>
> *You don't have to be great at everything to be successful. Concentrate your efforts on the most vital tasks, even if you must temporarily ignore other obligations.*

KEY DATES

MAY 5 ★ *management material*

The creative power of the Sun in resource-rich Taurus in your 9th House of Big Ideas aligns with concrete Saturn in your 1st House of Physicality, paving the way to turning your future hopes into your present reality. Impress others now with your mature, competent, and trustworthy approach.

MAY 12-13 ★ *starting over*
Backpedaling Mercury forms an edgy semisquare with anxious Mars on **May 12**, increasing stress and inciting arguments. Breathe slowly and deeply to gain clarity. Although your perceptions are sharp, remaining calm is key to being constructively creative instead of reacting in negative ways. Mercury returns to Taurus on **May 13**, which can prompt stubborn thinking. Familiar ideas are appealing, even if they are outmoded. When you return to basics, make sure that it's more about finding a solid foundation on which to stand than retreating from current reality.

SUPER NOVA DAYS
MAY 16-18 ★ *fearless flier*
The Sun passes from a tense square with overconfident Jupiter to an integrating sextile with unorthodox Uranus on **May 16**, opening you to risky experiences that take you to the edge while also revealing new ways to find your way back to safety. Experimenting with unfamiliar activities is less dangerous than it seems, so push yourself a bit beyond your comfort zone. Stable Saturn turns direct in your sign, adding ballast to keep you grounded. However, feelings of vulnerability are possible on **May 17** with a dreamy Sun-Neptune square and a sensitive Mercury-Venus semisquare, undermining security and self-confidence. Retrograde Mercury joins the Sun on **May 18**, a great day for introspection to help you uncover a core issue, even if you aren't yet ready to explain it to others.

MAY 20-21 ★ *connect the dots*
Ideas pop when the Sun enters airy Gemini and Mercury squares Jupiter on **May 20**. Maintain your credibility by avoiding information overload and exaggeration. Mercury's smart sextile with Uranus on **May 21** brings unexpected insights that enable you to link individuals and synthesize data from diverse sources.

MAY 30-31 ★ *get off your soapbox*
Communication begins to flow easily—allowing you to be a more convincing spokesperson for your beliefs—when Mercury turns forward in your 9th House of Truth, Travel, and Higher Education on **May 30**. Dynamic Mars pushes into the 9th House on **May 31**, increasing your desire to state your case, perhaps even to the point of argument. Be especially cautious as the warrior planet makes a sticky sesquisquare with stern Saturn that can entrench you in a long-term dispute. Focus on the facts to avoid endless debate.

JUNE

UNEASY TEAMWORK

Managing your emotions is critical with the Full Moon in outgoing Sagittarius on **June 7**. The usual enthusiasm of this sign is constrained by a hard square from strict Saturn in Virgo as the demands of work and family can extend you to your limits. Setting boundaries may be exactly what you need. If you are overstretched with responsibilities, redefine your priorities and direct your resources appropriately. The Sun's presence in multifaceted Gemini in your 10th House of Career until **June 21** provides distractions that can scatter your forces. Your key planet, Mercury, enters Gemini on **June 13**, however, which can open your eyes to alternative ways to handle your job and also facilitate communication and connections that enhance your career. Visionary Jupiter turns retrograde in your 6th House of Work and Service on **June 15**, suggesting the value of retraining and refining your skills.

The Sun enters caring Cancer on **June 21**, marking the Summer Solstice in your 11th House of Groups and initiating a more dynamic period of teamwork and reliance on others. The importance of your relationships with pals and colleagues is underscored by the New Moon in gentle Cancer on **June 22**, which reveals challenges ahead. Potent Pluto's close opposition to the New Moon is associated with power struggles and, perhaps, a loss of trust with an associate. Aggressive Mars forms an edgy sesquisquare with Pluto on **June 23** to add more fire to an already tense situation. Fundamental differences regarding group goals and the best methods to achieve them may force you to back off from a project. It's better to recognize where your efforts won't be adequately rewarded than to spin your wheels with frustration.

> **KEEP IN MIND THIS MONTH**
>
> *Putting others first can work for a while, but will wear you out if you continue to ignore your own needs to serve theirs.*

KEY DATES

JUNE 4–6 ★ *use your influence*

A powerful trine between active Mars and purging Pluto on **June 4** gives you the impetus to cut out unnecessary tasks and extraneous talk to operate at your highest level of efficiency. Your ability to motivate others is strong, too, since you know exactly what buttons to push to get the reactions you want. A stern Sun-Saturn square on **June 5** leaves no room for ambiguity, especially at work. Only take on responsibilities that are well defined and come with the authority you need to manage them properly. Vivacious Venus enters her sensual home sign of Taurus on **June 6**, sweetening your 9th House of Higher Thought and Faraway Places with images of spiritual comfort and island escapades.

JUNE 9-10 ★ *stuck inside a cloud*
Brilliant ideas spurred by a sharp Mercury-Uranus sextile may be difficult to explain when followed by a fuzzy square from Neptune to Mercury on **June 9**. It takes imagination to describe your insights, which aren't easily translated into ordinary language. Making your point could be frustrating on **June 10**, when extravagant Jupiter squares detail-oriented Mercury. Overflowing words and data obscure the message. More is not necessarily better now, so don't be impressed by someone else's inflated promises—and avoid making any of your own.

SUPER NOVA DAYS
JUNE 16-17 ★ *something in the air*
Mars and Uranus make a jumpy but innovative pair with their keyed-up semi-square on **June 16**. Spontaneity comes easily, but fast words and impulsive actions provoke unexpected responses. Experiments can produce amazing breakthroughs or blow up in your face, so be careful about where and how you take chances now. The Sun and Venus form tense aspects with rebellious Uranus on **June 17**, continuing to fill your life with electricity. Moods shift in an instant and your inclination to compromise can disappear, creating conflict with authority figures. Happily, the Sun forms peaceful trines with forgiving Neptune and Jupiter, giving you the faith to find common ground.

JUNE 21-23 ★ *seeds of love*
A sexy Venus-Mars conjunction on **June 21** jazzes up your Summer Solstice. This playful pair meets in your 9th House of Travel, raising your interest in exotic people and places. Harmonious trines from Venus and Mars to solid Saturn accompany the tender Cancer New Moon on **June 22**, turning creative ideas or romance into reality. However, Venus, the Sun, and Mars form tough aspects with "hard to please" Pluto on **June 23**, exposing gaps in a plan that will require cutbacks or additional resources. Resentment can rise with the pressure; dig deeper within yourself for answers rather than blaming others.

JULY

SHAKE IT UP

Two eclipses this month could lead you to a significant shift involving kids, self-expression, or friends. A Lunar Eclipse in responsible Capricorn on **July 7** falls in your 5th House of Romance, Children, and Creativity and could alter your plans in these areas. Discipline may fail and rules may be broken as your steady progress is interrupted. Still, with karmic Saturn, Capricorn's ruling planet, forming a supportive trine to this Full Moon, a change of routine may be exactly what you need. Instead of rigidly sticking to a fixed program as a parent, lover, or artist, it may be time to let go of your old methods and establish new ones to advance your personal interests. The New Moon in cautious Cancer on **July 21** is a Solar Eclipse in your 11th House of Groups that reflects changing patterns in teamwork. Reorganization at your job or within a volunteer organization is possible. A dependable old friend may no longer be available to you—yet you'll be experiencing more than enough new activity to make up for any sense of loss. Unique Uranus's trine to this Sun-Moon conjunction represents the stimulation that can come from new people or practices. Exploring fresh areas of interest or trying new tasks within the team should put some excitement back into your life.

Your level of inspiration rises with boundless Jupiter's conjunctions to spiritual Neptune and healing Chiron on **July 10 and July 22**, the second in a series of aspects that began in **May** and end in **December**. You may be motivated to offer your services to a worthy cause and refine skills that support those efforts.

KEEP IN MIND THIS MONTH

When you face a potential loss with a creative and confident spirit, you can transform a threatening situation into a golden opportunity.

KEY DATES

SUPER NOVA DAYS

JULY 1-2 ★ *crazy love*

On **July 1**, a romantic but unrealistic Venus-Neptune square nurtures your dreams of fascinating places and people. Your imagination is overfed by mental Mercury's trines to Neptune and Jupiter and a square with surprising Uranus. Brilliant thinking and clever words can be used to justify almost anything, so maintain a dash of skepticism to keep yourself grounded. Sensual Venus squares indulgent Jupiter and sextiles Uranus on **July 2**, intensifying your desire for more attention and affection. Opening yourself up to different kinds of delight, however, is an excellent idea, as long as the price you pay isn't too high.

JULY 11-13 ★ *subjective speech*
Your ability to multitask shines now as Mercury aligns in a well-organized sextile to serious Saturn while active Mars enters diverse Gemini on **July 11**. Following your instincts is likely to be more successful than sticking to a rigid plan. Mercury joins the Sun on **July 13**, helping you clarify your intentions. This conjunction in the sensitive water sign of Cancer also adds an emotional quality that tends to make all communication feel highly personal.

JULY 15-17 ★ *fix your focus*
You can waste your time with confusing conversations and imprecise information on **July 15**, so double-check details to avoid going off on a wild goose chase. A clear picture emerges on **July 16** as a clever Mercury-Uranus trine promotes original thinking. Yet chatty Mercury's tender semisquare with Venus adds vulnerability to personal exchanges; only gentle words will prevent wounded feelings. Mercury strides into bold Leo on **July 17**, stimulating grand ideas that you must analyze thoroughly before you make them public.

JULY 21-23 ★ *believe in yourself*
Moods are mixed on **July 21**, when a tense square between needy Venus and withholding Saturn forces you to work harder for approval and, perhaps, even doubt yourself. The Sun's entry into fiery Leo on **July 22**, though, could give you an inner glow, enhancing your self-confidence no matter what others say. Your mind can shoot off in new directions with a nervous Mercury-Uranus sesquisquare on **July 23**. Pressure to conform to someone else's vision could surface with a Sun-Pluto quincunx on **July 23**, suggesting that a powerful person doesn't appreciate your profound insights. If you're not being heard, wait for a more inviting moment to make your point.

JULY 30-31 ★ *not the doctor*
Mercury's oppositions to Jupiter, Chiron, and Neptune rouse your inner poet and compassion for others. Excessive optimism, though, may encourage you to take on more than you can handle. If you're unwilling to say no, do your best to delay any commitments until you can.

AUGUST

ANALYTICAL MIND

Your thinking grows sharper as intellectual Mercury enters discerning Virgo on **August 2**. The narrowing lens of perception helps you cut through complex issues to get at key points, increasing your efficiency and ability to influence others. Still, it's helpful to step back and widen your perspective occasionally to make sure that your precisely defined picture fits into the larger scheme of things. The Full Moon on **August 5** is a Lunar Eclipse in unconventional Aquarius that falls in your 6th House of Health, Work, and Daily Routines, reminding you that new ideas and systems aren't always better than old ones. Fortunately, active Mars in flexible Gemini trines the Moon to show you how to make adjustments without making waves.

Finding balance between tomorrow's potential and today's reality can seem challenging with a clumsy quincunx between positive Jupiter and pragmatic Saturn on **August 19**. This second in a series of three aspects—which began on **March 22** and finishes on **February 5, 2010**—requires you to play the role of a skeptic to overly enthusiastic believers as well as act as a source of inspiration for those stuck in doubt and fear. Connecting with your inner guides and having faith in your vision of a brighter future are possibilities with the New Moon in expressive Leo on **August 20**. This energizing event occurs in your 12th House of Privacy, where its flames of creativity may be hidden from view. Nourish your hopes quietly instead of sharing them too soon. The Sun's entry into hardworking Virgo on **August 22** will put some wind into your sails. This solar energy in your sign increases confidence and vitality to enrich your personal life and empower you in business.

KEEP IN MIND THIS MONTH

It's very easy to spot errors, but you must also know how and when to point them out if you hope to make a positive contribution.

KEY DATES

AUGUST 1-3 ★ *after the deluge*

An opposition between nurturing Venus in Cancer and manipulative Pluto on **August 1** agitates strong emotions. Speak honestly about your feelings, but leave room for responses from others. If all you're doing is venting, you are more likely to drive someone away than get satisfaction. Mercury's entry into Virgo on **August 2** leans toward logic. The communication planet's harmonious trine to Pluto on **August 3** helps you discuss difficult issues effectively and repair any recent damage.

AUGUST 10 ★ *slow down*

You may be feeling stressed at work as Mars in your 10th House of Career pushes toward a hard square with stringent Saturn. An aggressive boss or an overload of responsibilities weighs heavily on your shoulders. Concentrate on one task at a time—remember, going too fast may lead to mistakes. Be gentle with colleagues for whom a little nudge feels like a major shove.

AUGUST 13–14 ★ *all systems go*

An enormous release of energy is possible as dynamic Mars aligns in a friction-free trine with upbeat Jupiter on **August 13**. This powerful pair connects work-related houses, giving you enthusiasm for new projects. The Sun's opposition to Jupiter on **August 14** lifts the wave even higher, nourishing your creativity with confidence. Fortunately, your instinctive sense of practicality should keep you from overstating your case or promising more than you can deliver.

SUPER NOVA DAYS
AUGUST 17–18 ★ *mixed signals*

You can switch gears to match the moods of different colleagues and friends on **August 17**, for planets are firing off in several directions throughout the day. A sassy Sun-Mars sextile gets you support from unexpected sources, but mental Mercury and sober Saturn join up to demand concentration, leaving little margin for error. Nevertheless, a spacey Sun-Neptune opposition and unstable Mercury-Jupiter quincunx keep providing opportunities for confusion. Trust your intuition—a Mars-Neptune trine can guide your actions more effectively than planning out every move. Expect surprises at work on **August 18**, when Mars in your 10th House forms a volatile square with Uranus. Instead of blowing up at someone or running for the hills, use this high-frequency force to invent new ways to get a job done.

AUGUST 25 26 ★ *hard to swallow*

Anger and impatience could be ignited by a pushy Mercury-Mars square on **August 25**, just as Mars enters protective Cancer and Mercury enters polite Libra. A mild disagreement might grow into a serious conflict the next day, when both planets make hard aspects with passionate Pluto. If you can stay calm, however, the depth of your thinking and precision of your words could produce lasting breakthroughs of awareness and understanding.

SEPTEMBER

RELATIONSHIPS IN THE BALANCE

Examining relationships to adjust the balance between healthy self-interest and loving concern for others is a major theme for you this month. The Full Moon in psychic Pisces on **September 4** occurs in your 7th House of Partnerships, shedding new light on the subject. This compassionate water sign can wear down your self-restraint and open the way to richer emotional connections. Remember, however, that losing yourself in a co-dependent connection is not a recipe for long-term success. Objective thinking is challenged when Mercury the Messenger turns retrograde on **September 7**. Your orderly world can be skewed by miscommunication and difficulty with details until your ruling planet turns direct again on **September 29**. Its backward turn starts in Libra in your 2nd House of Resources, indicating a potential review of your financial situation. On **September 17**, Mercury returns to your sign, making you more conscious of your appearance and attitude. Your flaws may seem more serious than is really the case, so even minor changes will have greater impact than you imagine.

The ongoing planetary tug-of-war between strict Saturn and rebellious Uranus flares up on **September 15** when they oppose each other again. This long series of aspects falls in your 1st House of Self and 7th House of Others, putting a strain on relationships. The New Moon in fussy Virgo on **September 18** triggers both planets as it joins Saturn and opposes Uranus, making you itchy for change—or desperate to stay put while a partner or close ally is anxious to make a move. Attractive Venus enters Virgo on **September 20**, swinging the balance in your favor by helping you recognize your true worth. The Sun enters cooperative Libra on **September 22**, marking the Autumnal Equinox and illuminating gifts of beauty and harmony in your 2nd House of Resources.

> **KEEP IN MIND THIS MONTH**
>
> *You don't always have to be consistent to have integrity. Changing your mind is healthier than maintaining a position that no longer feels right.*

KEY DATES

SEPTEMBER 3–4 ★ *not ready to make nice*

Words pack an extra punch when Mercury squares pugnacious Mars on **September 3**. If you can't resolve a difference of opinion quickly, it's best to back off—Mercury is almost standing still just four days prior to turning retrograde. Any agreements you make now are likely to need renegotiation later. Interpersonal dynamics can take on an edgy tone on **September 4** with a shaky sesquisquare between Venus and Uranus. Unexpected changes in your social life or a relationship are best met with a flexible attitude, because trying to control the situation or denying your feelings only increases tension.

SEPTEMBER 11–12 ★ *tunnel of love*
Big waves are moving just below the surface as powerful Pluto turns direct on **September 11** in your 5th House of Self-Expression. The desires for romance, play, and participation in the arts that have been stewing inside of you may be ready to flourish. An emotionally expressive opposition between loving Venus and opulent Jupiter expands your appetite for pleasure. Have fun, but be cautious about overindulging yourself, overestimating someone, or spending more than your budget allows. A delicate semisquare between Mercury and Venus on **September 12** increases your sensitivity about personal matters. This is useful for intimate conversations, but tends to make any critical comments sound harsher than intended.

SEPTEMBER 17 ★ *pressure cooker*
This complex day is heated up by the Sun's explosive opposition to Uranus and constricting conjunction with Saturn. You can feel the pressure to hold your ground even when a part of you might want to run away from everyone and everything. It's best to take care of yourself and recognize that you cannot control what others do. Mercury squares unforgiving Pluto just before retrograding back into Virgo, which suggests that saying less is better than speaking out at this volatile time.

SUPER NOVA DAYS
SEPTEMBER 20–23 ★ *master the madness*
You are especially clear in your thinking as Mercury joins the Sun and feeling self-confident with Venus entering capable Virgo on **September 20**. The love planet's easy trine with intense Pluto helps you cut through relationship clutter to make your needs known. The winds shift with a spicy but dicey Venus-Mars semisquare on **September 21** that attracts both flirting and fighting. Mercury joins serious Saturn as the Sun enters Libra on **September 22**, a combination that favors careful deliberation over impulsive actions. However, Mercury's opposition to spontaneous Uranus and quincunx with imaginative Neptune on **September 23** is more intuitive and creative than concrete and careful. And the Sun's tense square with Pluto demands strength and self-control, especially if you're confronted by an adversary.

OCTOBER

Money matters steal the spotlight this month as the New and Full Moons fall in your houses of finance. The initiating Aries Full Moon occurs on **October 4**, stimulating ideas about investments and business partnerships in your 8th House of Shared Resources. Take the lead in a current economic union, or consider starting a new one. Friends or colleagues should be good sources of information about ways to get a greater return on your time, money, and energy. The New Moon in artistic Libra lands in your 2nd House of Possessions on **October 18**, providing a more objective picture of your financial situation. Saturn enters Libra on **October 29** to crystallize material issues during the next two years. Draw on the undeveloped gifts you already have within you. You have creative skills that can be honed with patience and discipline to upgrade your sense of self-worth—and perhaps your income as well.

Intelligent Mercury provides a sharp perspective to values and resources when it enters your 2nd House on **October 9**. You may tend toward indecisiveness with this thoughtful planet in the consensus-seeking sign of Libra. Consulting with others who recognize your talent can give you a boost, but don't let someone else's negative opinion overrule your best instincts. Auspicious Jupiter turns direct in your 6th House of Work on **October 12**, raising your hopes for more rewarding employment. If the vision of greater fulfillment on the job seems beyond your reach, don't give up. Your success will be a benefit to others. Once you take the next step, support is likely to come from unexpected sources.

> **KEEP IN MIND THIS MONTH**
>
> *Leisure activities that bring you joy could be critical components in creating a positive environment that attracts what you desire most.*

KEY DATES

OCTOBER 1–4 ★ *rapid response*

Mercury, just out of retrograde, is moving so slowly that it forms two sweet sextiles with Mars, one on **October 1** and the other on **October 4**. These compatible aspects align intellect and action to increase your efficiency. You could, however, misinterpret messages on **October 4**, when cloudy planetary conditions make for a mixed forecast that blurs your judgment. An electrifying Mercury-Uranus square accelerates your mind into hyperdrive to catch brilliant ideas . . . or maybe blow a fuse. Fortunately, protective Mars in Cancer creates an ingenious trine with fast-acting Uranus to help you make rapid adjustments if you veer too far off course.

SUPER NOVA DAYS
OCTOBER 8–10 ★ *controlled indulgence*
Hone your concentration: A Mercury-Saturn conjunction on **October 8** favors precision and leaves little room for error. If you feel down or doubtful, excitement should arrive soon with a lively Venus-Uranus opposition on **October 9**. Celebrate a sense of freedom by exploring new delights. Logical Mercury returns to reasonable Libra late in the day, enabling you to see another point of view and to let go of old grievances. A sociable Sun-Jupiter trine on **October 10** blends work and pleasure in a most rewarding way. Use the Mercury-Pluto square to challenge your thinking instead of closing down in fear.

OCTOBER 14–16 ★ *building a mystery*
The innocent romance of Venus entering lovely Libra on **October 14** is darkened by her square to controlling Pluto on **October 15**. Mistrust can be fed by confusion from Neptune's blurring square with Mercury. The current situation is only a trigger for an old issue, so don't take it personally. A spiritual Sun-Neptune trine on **October 16** brings you the grace and clarity to feel pain without suffering from it, and to use that intuitive awareness to change your life.

OCTOBER 20 ★ *smooth operator*
A divine trine between Mercury and Jupiter sweetly expands your mind. You can see how the smallest of facts are still part of a bigger picture. Life makes more sense. You deliver information effectively on the job or in any practical situation, combining logic with cleverness to find the easiest way to get around.

OCTOBER 28–29 ★ *watching the detective*
Your perceptions are especially keen on **October 28** when Mercury enters intense Scorpio in your 3rd House of Information and contacts penetrating Pluto. You can see through others' stories and work your way to the truth. Secrets may be exposed in intimate conversations. Joy and generosity are present, too, with a big fat Venus-Jupiter trine promising a really good time. Nevertheless, a combative Mars-Sun square on **October 29** can make you fight for what you thought was already yours.

NOVEMBER

STUDENT OF LIFE

Travel and education are key this month. The earthy Taurus Full Moon on **November 2** falls in your 9th House of Higher Thought and Faraway Places, inspiring you to seek peace in a belief system or comfort in a distant land. You need a break from the pressures of your regular routine. Whether you plan a trip to the Caribbean, take a meditation class, or schedule a daily iPod moment to tune out the world, be sure to create space for yourself. Assertive Mars in your 12th House of Privacy squares this Sun-Moon opposition, telling you that you may have to struggle to get what you want, so don't be timid in pursuit of your dreams. Your ruling planet, Mercury, enters restless Sagittarius in your 4th House of Roots on **November 15**. An urge to know the truth about your family and its past evokes questions that require honest answers. Blunt statements can clear away cobwebs of confusion at home, but could also drive others away if too abrasive.

The New Moon in passionate Scorpio on **November 16** falls in your 3rd House of Information and Education. Its message is that you need to learn more and communicate with greater force. The intensity of this lunation is amplified by a powerful Saturn-Pluto square on **November 15** that will return on **January 31, 2010,** and **August 21, 2010**. Both planets demand that you concentrate to avoid feeling over-whelmed by circumstances beyond your control. Eliminate distractions, dig in and do research to find key ideas, and apply what you discover with precision. The Sun's entry into adventuresome Sagittarius on **November 21** stokes the fire in your belly, encouraging you to step out of your comfort zone and aim higher in your life.

> **KEEP IN MIND THIS MONTH**
>
> *Moving gracefully from intense engagement to cool detachment allows you to play hard without wearing out your welcome or burning yourself out.*

KEY DATES

NOVEMBER 1-2 ★ *high-speed connection*

Mercury, in your 3rd House of Information, forms a sharp-edged square with aggressive Mars on **November 1** to rouse lively debate and instigate arguments. Expect aggravation when Mercury and Mars create irritable sesquisquares with shockingly brilliant Uranus on **November 2**. Quick thinking overtakes caution as the sensual Taurus Full Moon raises emotional tides, leading to breakthroughs in awareness—or breakdowns in communication.

SUPER NOVA DAYS
NOVEMBER 5–8 ★ *suspicious minds*
Astute leadership skills originate from your clarity of purpose, empowered by a Mercury-Sun conjunction on **November 5**. However, a stubborn Mercury-Saturn semisquare on **November 6** delays information and requires you to express yourself more slowly to be understood by friends and colleagues. The plot thickens when Mercury semisquares Pluto on **November 7** as Venus enters skeptical Scorpio. Suspicion is difficult to avoid, even with your most trusted allies. Your ideas about relationships, self-worth, and personal values may be challenged, perhaps unfairly. Yet your exploration reveals what is most important to you. Cutting out unessential activities, objects, and individuals may feel harsh, but it's your key to satisfaction. Too much talk and an overabundance of data could have you seeking sanctuary in a quiet place on **November 8**.

NOVEMBER 11 ★ *this magic moment*
A highly intelligent Mercury-Uranus trine supplies fresh insights and unconventional ideas. But apply them quickly, because an indefinite Mercury-Neptune square follows, making it easy to get distracted and lose track of the brilliant solutions you just discovered.

NOVEMBER 21 ★ *take it easy*
Romance could get rocky with loving Venus caught up in the unrelenting pressure of the Saturn-Pluto square. You feel the weight of the world on your shoulders, which can put the squeeze on relationships and up the cost of having a good time. Letting go of a plan that grows too complicated will reduce stress. Make this a no-frills day in which you can enjoy life's simple pleasures, relax, and recharge your batteries.

NOVEMBER 29–30 ★ *odds in your favor*
Expressing yourself skillfully is simple with a Mercury-Jupiter sextile on **November 29**. This super-smart connection between two mental planets makes it easy to absorb new ideas and information. Big concepts crystallize, and you recognize useful ways to apply them in your daily life. You share your knowledge effectively thanks to a well-organized presentation. The tone is quite different on **November 30** when Mercury crosses paths with bright but eccentric Uranus. Their tense square can put you on edge and provoke impulsive speech, yet stepping outside your usual mental box can provide flashes of genius that solve problems in unexpected ways.

DECEMBER

SURPRISE ENDING

You must regroup, adjust your plans, and reorganize your life, for this transitional month features two Full Moons (one of them an eclipse), retrograde turns by Mars and Mercury, and the last of Jupiter's three magical conjunctions with Neptune and Chiron. On **December 2**, the Full Moon in verbal Gemini lights up your 10th House of Career, strengthening your communication skills and helping you make new connections. The danger of overextending yourself is reduced by steady Saturn's supportive trine to the Moon, enabling you to skillfully manage a busy schedule. Philosophical Jupiter joins healing Chiron on **December 7** and spiritual Neptune on **December 21** in the last of a series of conjunctions that began in May. This inspiring trio adds vision to your 6th House of Health and Daily Routines, lightening your present load with imagination and idealism and pointing the way to more fulfilling work in the future.

Domestic matters take the spotlight with a free-spirited Sagittarius New Moon in your 4th House of Roots on **December 16**. A tense square from erratic Uranus may create sudden chaos on the home front, but shaking the family tree unhooks you from old unhealthy patterns and opens the way to bigger dreams for tomorrow. Militant Mars starts marching backward in your 12th House of Secrets on **December 20**, energizing you with inner motivation well into next year. Turning anger into a creative plan is imperative if you hope to avoid resentment that could simmer dangerously for weeks. Mercury's retrograde shift on **December 26** ends the year on an introspective note. The moody Cancer Full Moon on **December 31** is a Lunar Eclipse in your 11th House of Groups that could lead to a parting of the ways with a colleague or friend.

> **KEEP IN MIND THIS MONTH**
>
> *Keep your ambition and sense of duty in check to avoid overloading yourself with more responsibilities than you can comfortably handle.*

KEY DATES

DECEMBER 5-8 ★ *breaking the silence*

Serious thinking prevails as Mercury enters responsible Capricorn on **December 5**. This planet's presence in your 5th House of Self-Expression, however, suggests that you have something very important to say. Preparing for an important presentation, whether personal or professional, takes on additional urgency when Mercury joins relentless Pluto and squares demanding Saturn on **December 7**. Master your message to overcome inner doubt or external critics. Don't be intimidated into silence, even if it's difficult to speak your mind. An edgy Mercury-Mars sesquisquare on **December 8** may spark confrontation, yet when you focus on facts, you can be very convincing.

DECEMBER 10-11 ★ *truth or dare*
Enthusiasm allows you to be more open than usual due to a boundless Mercury-Jupiter semisquare on **December 10**. An energetic trine between the Sun and Mars could even dare you into revealing a secret. It's better to be frank and push some limits than to stifle communication. Besides, Mercury's semisquare with compassionate Neptune on **December 11** can bring either forgiveness—or so much confusion that whatever you say will be forgotten. The quality of feeling behind any idea is likely to have more impact than facts, so use your intuition to read between the lines and your emotions to send a compelling message.

DECEMBER 19-21 ★ *just out of reach*
You could be feeling antsy with a restless square from Venus to electric Uranus on **December 19**. Expect last-minute changes of social plans or sudden shifts of mood. Aesthetic improvements in your home can scratch your itch for new sources of pleasure. The reticence of Mars retrograde on **December 20** contrasts with a joyful Venus-Jupiter sextile. Use caution to avoid expensive excesses. Jupiter's conjunction and Venus's sextile with Neptune blankets **December 21** with clouds of hope and faith, reinforced by the Sun's entry into traditional Capricorn on the Winter Solstice. Mercury's quincunx with Mars stirs up disagreements that are best avoided—they can be difficult to resolve.

SUPER NOVA DAYS
DECEMBER 24-27 ★ *peaceful warrior*
Power struggles are possible when the Sun joins provocative Pluto on **December 24** and squares unyielding Saturn on **December 25**. An aggressive Sun-Mars sesquisquare increases your likelihood of frustration. Mercury's backward turn on **December 26** can mix up messages, while a hard-nosed Mars-Saturn semisquare on **December 27** turns up the heat. Peace is especially desirable during the holidays, but if you must fight, be clear and concise. Make your point with strength and focus to keep conflict to a minimum. Victory is not about winning over the other person, but stating your position with well-controlled passion and precision.

LIBRA
SEPTEMBER 23–OCTOBER 22

LIBRA

2008 SUMMARY

Taking more time to tend to your inner life is a good way to gain strength, heal old wounds, and reassess your life purpose. In fact, you might be ready for a rebound when it comes to love. The magic lies within you, so create through your own acts of art, style, and self-expression where you can direct the process and control the outcome.

AUGUST—*making magic*

When you like what you see in the mirror, others will as well. Trust your naturally good taste to determine the look that suits you best.

SEPTEMBER—*working it*

Short-term crises can lead to long-term opportunities when you are able to let go of your unnecessary fears and visualize future opportunities.

OCTOBER—*dollars and common sense*

Tame impulsive urges, but use the intent behind them to point you in the right direction so you can create a strategy to reach your goals.

NOVEMBER—*strategic planning*

Speaking the truth can ruffle someone's feathers—but it's a price you should be willing to pay to claim your power.

DECEMBER—*holiday cleanup*

The price of peace may be giving up on your own convictions. Consider this high cost before seeking compromise.

2008 CALENDAR

AUGUST

TUESDAY 5 ★ Miscommunications can trigger outbursts through the 6th

WEDNESDAY 13 ★ **SUPER NOVA DAYS** Change is in the air through the 17th

TUESDAY 19 ★ Begin a personal project that doesn't need support or approval

FRIDAY 22 ★ Social inconsistency can build nervous tension through the 24th

WEDNESDAY 27 ★ A struggle reveals your deepest desires through the 30th

SEPTEMBER

WEDNESDAY 3 ★ Keep your eyes on the prize through the 4th

TUESDAY 9 ★ Your personality can win friends through the 11th

SUNDAY 14 ★ Find the common ground to restore harmony through the 17th

SATURDAY 20 ★ **SUPER NOVA DAYS** Take steps toward self-empowerment through the 23rd

OCTOBER

SATURDAY 4 ★ **SUPER NOVA DAYS** Protect your interests through the 6th

FRIDAY 10 ★ Unique situations spark your social life through the 11th

SATURDAY 18 ★ You glimpse the great beyond; give yourself time to reach it

FRIDAY 24 ★ Make a power play for change

SUNDAY 26 ★ You're in the lead and others follow you through the 27th

NOVEMBER

MONDAY 3 ★ **SUPER NOVA DAYS** Emotions contradict through the 5th

WEDNESDAY 12 ★ Dig deep and face unresolved issues through the 13th

SUNDAY 16 ★ Fantasies can cloud your judgment through the 17th

THURSDAY 27 ★ Fresh perceptions and strong opinions embolden you through the 29th

DECEMBER

MONDAY 1 ★ Enjoy your quiet inner strength

FRIDAY 5 ★ A war of words lets you break tough news through the 6th

THURSDAY 11 ★ **SUPER NOVA DAYS** Fasten your seatbelt through the 13th

SUNDAY 21 ★ Make a descent into emotional awareness through the 22nd

FRIDAY 26 ★ Old disappointment dissolves through the 28th

LIBRA OVERVIEW

You may feel time is running out, but if you stay focused on what's real, you'll be ready for the significant changes heading your way. Somber Saturn entered critical Virgo and your 12th House of Destiny on September 2, 2007, signaling the beginning of an end. Saturn continues to remind you of what must be completed prior to its entry into your sign on October 29. **Don't wait until the last moment to finish old business**, for you might have backed yourself into a corner by then. Look over recent years and consider what can be pruned from your life as a fourteen-year growing season reaches culmination. Starting in November, Saturn in objective Libra will crystallize your successes and reveal your failures.

Maintaining regularity in your daily routine continues to be an issue for you as unpredictable Uranus journeys through your 6th House of Health and Habits. This phase started in May 2003, yet something is different now. Your desire for change became more intense when Saturn first opposed Uranus on November 4, 2008. This cosmic tug-of-war between the planets of constraint and release that began last year is exact again on February 5 and September 15, **raising tension as you try to balance your desire for increased freedom with karmic responsibilities that you accepted previously**. There is no quick solution to this profound life dilemma: The opposition recurs through July 26, 2010. It can take another year until you fully understand the ramifications of this shift and where your new path will take you.

You are a natural diplomat who's often ready to set your personal needs aside to make others happy. **You are particularly sensitive to the movement of Venus**, your ruling planet. She goes retrograde—as she does every year and a half—on March 6, turning your desires inward. Normally, Venus breezes though a sign in about a month, but this retrograde keeps her in impulsive Aries in your 7th House of Partnerships for most of February–May, making it easier than normal for you to charm others without sacrificing your needs.

But there's good news, too, as foretold by a rare super-conjunction among three spiritual planets—expansive Jupiter, healing Chiron, and intuitive Neptune—in your 5th House of Self-Expression. You have an opportunity now—perhaps even an obligation to yourself—to make the most of this year by saying yes to love, life, and the creative potential hidden in every moment. Of course, serious Saturn will prevent you from flying off a cliff without the proper wings, but your imagination is uncontainable and not restrainable. **Giving yourself permission to dream can reawaken your inner child and make anything seem possible**. It will, however, take a dose of common sense to manage such unbridled enthusiasm that knows no bounds. Encourage your creative visions, but keep your feet on the ground, especially while this buoyant trio coalesces on May 23–27, July 10–22, and December 7–21.

FANTASY ISLAND

You may need to revisit your past if you wish to move into your future, because two eclipses activate your 5th House of Romance early in the year. First, a wild Aquarius New Moon Eclipse joined by joyful Jupiter on January 26 foreshadows success in love. You must, however, be respectful of boundaries, or a wonderful opportunity could fall apart very quickly. Then a bold Leo Full Moon Eclipse opposed by wounded Chiron and spiritual Neptune on February 9 helps you move beyond your fears—if you're willing to forgive someone in your past. Your dreams of ideal love feel close, yet you could waste energy chasing unrealizable fantasies as Jupiter, Chiron, and Neptune dance around one another in your 5th House all year. A little common sense will go a long way when this cosmic super-conjunction is most active in May, July, and December.

FOLLOW YOUR BLISS

Taskmaster Saturn in your 12th House of Destiny tells the story about your professional success. You must be connected with your inner purpose, for if your soul isn't in your work, you'll be sent back to the drawing board when Saturn enters your sign on October 29. Don't wait until it's too late; begin the process of self-evaluation as early in the year as possible. Saturn's oppositions with impatient Uranus on February 2 and September 15 can reveal clues about what you should be doing, for you won't likely be able to suppress your true desires then. Keep in mind, however, that if a major career change is indicated, you may need until next year to complete the transition. If you're already on the right track, your extra-hard work this year could begin to show results by November.

CLEVER COLLABORATION

Your key planet, Venus, is associated with money, and her long-term visits to your 7th House of Others—from February 2 to April 11, and from April 24 to June 6—indicate that you can increase your income by networking with the right people and working as part of a team. Seek out a responsible business partner or establish a relationship with a colleague whom you admire, because this is not the best time to set out on your own. Action-oriented Mars, the ruler of your 2nd House of Money, is well aspected on February 17, May 26, June 3, June 22, and August 13—good days for dealing with financial issues or making investments. Exercise caution, however, on March 8; April 4 and 15; and August 10, 18, and 26.

MIND OVER MATTER

Your 6th House of Health is co-ruled by philosophical Jupiter and metaphysical Neptune, suggesting that your thoughts have extraordinary power over your physical body. The Jupiter-Neptune conjunctions on May 27, July 10, and December 21 fall in your 5th House of Play, suggesting that relaxation may be more important to your well-being this year than rigid exercise programs and strict diets. "Shake it up" Uranus's long-term visit to your 6th House further advises that change is healthier than being stuck in a rut and that breaking out of a routine can greatly improve your overall attitude.

METAMORPHOSIS

Transformative Pluto entered your 4th House of Home and Family last year, and now it settles in for a long visit as it slowly yet relentlessly begins chang-ing key aspects of your personal world. This transition will take years to unfold, but starts by revealing the weakest areas of your internal foundations. Domestic disagreements can flare on February 27, June 23, July 13, August 26, and November 29. But a deeper malaise could develop throughout the year, culminating when restrictive Saturn squares Pluto on November 15 and continues into 2010. Don't let negativity get the best of you, for you're being offered an opportunity to preemptively cut back on excess. Instead of frivolously wasting resources, get back to basics in preparation for bigger changes ahead.

JOURNEY OF THE MIND

You'll spend a lot of time thinking about traveling with communicator Mercury ruling your 9th House of Higher Education and Long Journeys, but you may have a harder time making it happen. Extra planning could be necessary to get out of town when Mercury turns retrograde on January 11, May 7, and September 7. Although each of these periods lasts about three weeks, the problematic effects can linger, so be as patient as you can if you face delays. Mercury's visits to your 9th House on April 30–May 13 and June 13–July 3 can create a flurry of activity around travel, but you might end up spinning your wheels without ever getting your trip off the ground. Energetic Mars's arrival in your 9th House, however, can be the real deal, so schedule your vacation adventure between July 11 and August 25, if possible.

PRACTICAL MAGIC

Opportunities abound this year with the metaphysical trio of Jupiter, Chiron, and Neptune urging you to see the good in everyone and perhaps blessing you with an important teacher or mentor. But there are no shortcuts to happiness, so you may need to resign yourself to a more traditional approach to personal growth. Lessons will be hard-earned as Saturn moves through your spiritual 12th House until October 29, challenging you to practice what you preach. Attending workshops and reading books can be useful, but you must apply what you learn to your everyday life or you'll miss out on the magic that's right in front of you.

RICK & JEFF'S TIP FOR THE YEAR:
Finish Old Business

The appeal of an ideal life can distract you from your real work this year. Judgmental Saturn will put you in position to reap what you've previously earned when it enters Libra on October 29, but only concentration and hard work will complete the process. Accordingly, this is not a year to scatter your seeds of inspiration. Instead of initiating new projects, wrap up what you've already started and eliminate anything that isn't directly related to your goals. You may not know exactly what lies ahead, but preparing for it sooner, rather than later, is the smartest thing to do.

JANUARY

CREATE BALANCE

Although your year begins on a rather serious note, you'll see things lighten up as you move away from the overwhelming holiday season. The rest of the world may be heading back to work, but cerebral Mercury and joyful Jupiter enter airy Aquarius on **January 1 and January 5**, respectively, setting the stage for an ongoing planetary party in your 5th House of Love and Creativity that recurs in a variety of forms over the next couple of months. Nevertheless, you're also looking forward to establishing a regular daily routine that will allow you to accept your professional obligations in good spirit as your key planet, Venus, enters your 6th House of Work and Service on **January 3**. It's your decision: You can choose happiness by graciously accepting the responsibilities placed upon you at this time.

The emotionally sensitive Cancer Full Moon on **January 10** falls in your 10th House of Career, exposing your vulnerability to those around you—whether you intend to or not. Issues that come to the forefront now will likely be up for review through the rest of the month because thoughtful Mercury turns retrograde on **January 11**, backs into cautious Capricorn on **January 21**, and doesn't turn direct again until **February 1**. The nonconforming Aquarius New Moon Eclipse on **January 26** falls in your 5th House of Self-Expression, and its conjunction to confident Jupiter can give you an advantage when you share your thoughts with others. Even if your actions appear irresponsible, remember that this eclipse strongly encourages interacting with children and playfully expressing your own inner child.

> **KEEP IN MIND THIS MONTH**
>
> *Even if you feel like you're just reevaluating decisions you've already made, you are progressing toward a possible breakthrough next month.*

KEY DATES

JANUARY 3–5 ★ *do the right thing*

You're attracted to the idea of self-improvement when sweet Venus enters dreamy Pisces in your 6th House of Daily Routines on **January 3**. Turning your fantasies into reality may take more than a good imagination, of course; fortunately, you're motivated to express your needs and work toward a more efficient life when Venus receives the support of passionate Pluto on **January 4**. Although you may not be able to logically explain your actions, trust your intuition on **January 5** as mental Mercury and physical Mars activate brilliant Uranus. You'll be rewarded for doing what comes naturally, because generous Jupiter enters your spontaneous 5th House on the same day.

SUPER NOVA DAYS

JANUARY 9-11 ★ *a sigh of relief*

The security-seeking Cancer Full Moon often brings the extra pressure of increasing responsibility. The weight is lifted, however, by the Sun's clever sextile to inventive Uranus on **January 9**, and its harmonious trine to stable Saturn on **January 11**. Your smart yet restrained response can alleviate unexpressed tensions, allowing everyone involved to find much-needed balance. Still, the underlying problems may not be fully resolved as you continue toward bigger changes next month.

JANUARY 18-20 ★ *don't fence me in*

A change in the cosmic weather is under way. Retrograde Mercury's collision with expansive Jupiter on **January 18** widens your perceptions and opens your mind to possibilities you previously ignored. Your confidence grows as you receive new information, along with incoming waves of excitement, when the Sun enters conceptual Aquarius and your playful 5th House on **January 19**. The Sun's alignment with cerebral Mercury on **January 20** fires your mind with all the right words, so reach out and communicate with others.

JANUARY 22-24 ★ *finding your groove*

Wide swings of emotion pull you one way and then the other **January 22-24**, as loving Venus first joins erratic Uranus and then opposes restrictive Saturn, making it difficult to find a comfortable position in relationships. Good fortune arrives in the form of a Sun-Jupiter conjunction on **January 24**. Energetic Mars trines Saturn on that same day, reinforcing your willingness to work hard, your ability to follow through, and your positive attitude.

JANUARY 27-30 ★ *lives in the balance*

You're challenged to keep your eccentric behavior in line as boundless Jupiter overstimulates unorthodox Uranus **January 27**. Paradoxically, you can feel restrained when austere Saturn enters the picture on **January 30**. Using your diplomatic skills can help you move through this phase gracefully by balancing your individual needs with the desires of those you love.

FEBRUARY

TOMORROW SEEMS SO FAR AWAY

Smart Mercury turns direct on **February 1**, and although it may take awhile before you believe you're moving forward, the review phase is temporarily over. You may not see results until Mercury enters independent Aquarius and your creative 5th House on **February 14**, where it joins a planetary party of the Sun, Neptune, Chiron, Jupiter, and Mars already in progress. You are pushed to the edge of your patience and may alter your position with respect to an ongoing relationship. Loving Venus's entry into your 7th House of Partners on **February 2** should add harmony to your alliances and increase your willingness to please someone—though you may instead expect too much too soon, because she spends most of the next four months in reckless Aries. And because Venus moves so slowly throughout the month, you may fear that your desires will never be fulfilled.

Your greatest challenge now is recognizing that you don't have all the answers, and there's no quick way to get what you want. Issues related to personal habits and work are raised as shocking Uranus in your 6th House of Self-Improvement is opposed by karmic Saturn in your 12th House of Destiny. Saturn isn't necessarily gentle when it shows you what you need to learn. Although this long-lasting opposition is exact on **February 5**, it's part of a longer process that began on **November 4, 2008**, and culminates on **July 26, 2010**, so don't be hard on yourself if you can't reach your goals yet. Instead, take a more detached stance, understanding that what you do now is only part of a series of events that can ultimately free you from current restrictions.

> **KEEP IN MIND THIS MONTH**
>
> *Although you can see your heart's desire, rest assured that impulsive action is not the best way to reach it.*

KEY DATES

FEBRUARY 5 ★ *wait out the storm*

You're tempted to push hard for what you want when Venus squares domineering Pluto. Although you may worry about your survival or about possible abandonment, there's no need to overreact. A tense situation is stretched even farther by strict Saturn's opposition to rebellious Uranus today, but keep in mind that your discomfort will ease over the days ahead even if you take no action at all.

FEBRUARY 9–12 ★ *ready to explode*

An overly dramatic Leo Full Moon Eclipse on **February 9** encourages you to demand recognition from your peers. You know the significance of your unique contributions, and this eclipse in your 11th House of Friends and Associates tempts you to toss your patience out the window to get the acknowledgment you need now. This may not be in your best interest, though, for Chiron the Wounded Healer can remind you of another time when your contribution wasn't noticed. Your anxiety increases through **February 11–12** when Mars, moving through your spontaneous 5th House, can provoke an outburst of anger as he tenses up against the lingering Saturn-Uranus opposition.

SUPER NOVA DAYS

FEBRUARY 16–18 ★ *mutual admiration society*

Recent relationship pressures dissolve into memories as beautiful Venus receives a boost of energy from Mars and Jupiter on **February 16–18**. Love is in the air, and getting what has eluded you for so long may be as simple as just saying yes. Actions will surely speak louder than words when physical Mars joins grandiose Jupiter on **February 17** in your 5th House of Self-Expression. Don't miss the opportunity to show your appreciation to your children, your spouse, or a new love. These pleasures may not last, yet they can provide soul-nourishing enjoyment. Figure out how to incorporate your dreams into everyday life when the Sun enters imaginative Pisces and your 6th House of Daily Routines on **February 18**.

FEBRUARY 24 ★ *creating a better you*

You are quite upbeat about the future and have little problem imagining how your life can improve when mental Mercury joins optimistic Jupiter on **February 24**—the same day that a psychic Pisces New Moon activates your fantasy life. But this magical Sun-Moon conjunction falls in your practical 6th House of Self-Improvement, so motivate yourself to turn your dreams into action. Do it now; don't wait for some ideal situation to manifest in the distant future. Additionally, intelligent Mercury's harmonious sextile with charming Venus enhances your ability to talk about what you want in a way that allows you to be heard by those you love.

MARCH

LESSONS FROM THE PAST

Take a stroll down Memory Lane this month as sentimental Venus turns retrograde on **March 6** in your 7th House of Relationships. Venus's journey through this house can turn up your love light—you may well become more attractive to others. While she's retrograde, however, Venus can also propel you back to the past for insight into what to do in the present. Fortunately, your 5th House of Love and Romance is still quite active, although mental Mercury leaves to enter your work-oriented 6th House on **March 8**, followed by Mars on **March 14**. You'll see yourself gradually shift away from activities that bring you immediate pleasure and toward those that are more practical, aimed at keeping your everyday affairs in order.

The perfectionist Virgo Full Moon on **March 10** falls in your 12th House of Fantasy, activating your dreams and encouraging you to escape from your responsibilities. Paradoxically, this Full Moon is conjunct realistic Saturn, anchoring your feet on the ground, even if your head drifts up into the clouds. Pitting the focus of Virgo against the dispersion of Pisces can reawaken recent dissatisfaction, reminding you that it's not too late to make overdue changes. The enthusiastic Aries New Moon on **March 26** is particularly bittersweet as it falls in your 7th House of Partners, while conjuncting loving Venus. But Venus's retrograde can put an uncomfortable spin on this otherwise joyous event if you don't take the time to stop, look, and listen to what's truly going on. Don't miss an opportunity to break out of a long-term negative pattern that's standing in the way of your happiness in relationships.

KEEP IN MIND THIS MONTH

Discussing delicate issues that normally remain hidden in the twilight of consciousness can help put a relationship back on track.

KEY DATES

MARCH 8 ★ *nothing but the truth*

You must work extra hard to get the respect you deserve today, for the Sun in your 6th House of Self-Improvement is making its annual opposition to authoritative Saturn. Unfortunately, positive feedback may not be forthcoming—assertive Mars's conjunction with elusive Neptune can make you feel disillusioned. The silver lining in this dark cloud, however, is that once you know the truth, you can do something to change your current circumstances. Don't wallow in disappointment. A more enlightened approach to a current failure will allow you to overcome it in the days ahead.

MARCH 11–12 ★ *the lightness of being*

Retrograde Venus forms a cooperative sextile with indulgent Jupiter on **March 11**, reminding you of a recent good time while perhaps holding present satisfaction just out of reach. Sudden breakthroughs are possible on **March 12**, though, when the Sun conjoins unrestrained Uranus to free you from the heaviness of the last few days.

MARCH 19–20 ★ *spring into action*

You may feel cold judgment from a loved one right now without necessarily knowing how to change the situation. Fortunately, you can quickly rebound when forceful Mars receives a potent push from Pluto on **March 19**. It's a whole new ball game on **March 20** as the Spring Equinox is heralded by the Sun's entry into enterprising Aries and your 7th House of Partners. Internal processes now reach the surface and spill out into your life, positively impacting your interactions with others and relationships of all kinds.

SUPER NOVA DAYS
MARCH 22–23 ★ *out of sync*

Waves of uncertainty wash over you, building to a crescendo on **March 22** when expansive Jupiter forms a crunchy quincunx with restrictive Saturn. Put your optimism to work in a way that's self-motivating, but don't inflate its potential so much that you invite disappointment. Although you benefit from being serious, you won't accomplish much if you can't also find time for fun. You receive a motivational kick as communicator Mercury joins electric Uranus on **March 22**, enabling you to cleverly share your needs in ways that encourage immediate responses from others. Meanwhile, the Sun's provocative square to dark Pluto on **March 23** can turn an exciting discussion into an intense disagreement.

MARCH 27–30 ★ *the ball's in your court*

Communicator Mercury's dynamic square to shadowy Pluto on **March 27** is followed by its conjunction with lovely Venus on **March 28** and with the bright Aries Sun on **March 30**. You have all the impetus you need to talk about a secret and push through the fears that can prevent you from reaching satisfaction. Still, it's up to you to take the initiative.

APRIL

CONNECTIONS AND DISTRACTIONS

Although slow-moving Pluto turns retrograde on **April 4**, strengthening your passions as they deepen over the months ahead, the effects are subtle when compared with the direct turn of your ruling planet, Venus, on **April 17**. You've spent considerable time reevaluating what you're willing to give in relationships—and what you want in return—ever since romantic Venus retrograded on **March 6** in your 7th House of Partners. You're more concerned with solidifying a personal connection when logical Mercury enters sensual Taurus and your 8th House of Intimacy on **April 9**, the same day that the lovely Libra Full Moon overwhelms you with a profound desire to take your relationships to a more meaningful level. But your agenda concerning others becomes less clear when Venus slips back into dreamy Pisces in your 6th House of Self-Improvement on **April 11**. You're eager to get it right, even if you aren't entirely sure how.

Your desire for consistency may shatter as pushy Mars—also in your work-oriented 6th House—joins unruly Uranus on **April 15**. A stabilizing countercurrent arrives, though, when the Sun shines its way into earthy Taurus on **April 19**. But alternating waves of spontaneous emotionality and restrained practicality turn hot again when feisty Mars catches up with Venus on **April 21**, heating up an old romance or kicking off a new one. You can be uncharacteristically forceful at work and at play on **April 22**, when Mars enters enthusiastic Aries. Oddly enough, Venus's reentry into impulsive Aries occurs on **April 24**—the same day as a back-to-basics Taurus New Moon, which instills you with enough common sense to prevent you from doing something you'll later regret.

> **KEEP IN MIND THIS MONTH**
>
> *Significant life-changing events won't appear to shake up your life, so watch for subtle signs that can let you know when progress is being made.*

KEY DATES

APRIL 3–4 ★ *running hot and cold*

Your strong desires can make you uneasy on **April 3**, when sexy Venus is stimulated by passionate Pluto. Expressing yourself, however, doesn't guarantee anything. With Venus still retrograde, it might actually be a smart idea to downplay your needs. You may be stymied for reasons you don't yet understand on **April 4**, when hot Mars in your 6th House of Habits is opposed by restrained Saturn in your 12th House of Secrets. Be patient; change won't happen overnight.

APRIL 9-11 ★ *no hurry, no worry*

The friendly Libra Full Moon on **April 9** falls in your 1st House of Personality, bringing your changing moods to the surface for all to see. Still, don't expect an overemotional day—Mercury the Messenger is doggedly reasoning its way into stubborn Taurus while tensely aligning with authoritative Saturn. Others will step up to encourage you instead of holding you back as the Sun cooperatively sextiles confident Jupiter on **April 10**. You'll be better able to express your feelings when communicator Mercury harmonizes with intense Pluto on **April 11**, so hold your tongue until you know exactly what you want to say.

APRIL 15 ★ *shake it up*

If you've been working too hard or burning the candle at both ends, you may be in for a shock today as you are reminded to cool your jets. Accidents are not accidental now; they only occur if you fail to pay attention to what is most important. There's no place for boredom in your life when action-packed Mars conjoins electric Uranus in your 6th House of Health, Work, and Daily Routines. Consider ways to preemptively make changes so no one has to make them for you. Remember, it's better to be the lightning than to be struck by it.

SUPER NOVA DAYS
APRIL 21-24 ★ *carpe diem*

It's been said that men are from Mars and women from Venus, but when this pair of cosmic lovers join—as they do on **April 21**—it can be a party, even if they are in your 6th House of Details. Make a list of all the traits you long for in your perfect partner. Or consider what works and what doesn't in a current relationship, and then do something about it. Either way, start while the cycle is at its peak so you can ride energetic Mars back into his home sign of Aries on **April 22**. Romantic Venus rams into Aries just hours prior to the determined Taurus New Moon on **April 24**, firing up your love life even more.

MAY

REACH FOR YOUR DREAMS

Just as you begin to make progress in the relationship arena, you must face yet another round of complications demanding attention. Venus's extended visit to your 7th House of Partnerships continues to sweeten your interactions with others throughout the month. You're motivated to go after what you want, because resourceful Venus now has assertive Mars for a traveling companion. This confident Venus-Mars combo occurs in brash Aries, allowing you to be uncharacteristically direct when you're creatively pushing into new territory—romantically or professionally. But your thoughts can bottleneck as Mercury grinds to a halt in your 9th House of Big Ideas on **May 7**, possibly unraveling your plans to take a trip or enroll in a course of study. The messenger planet's retrograde phase lasts until **May 30**, suggesting that you'll be untangling miscommunications and tying up loose ends. It slips back into your 8th House of Shared Resources on **May 13**, raising old issues about jointly held property or what someone else brings to your relationship.

The Scorpio Full Moon on **May 9** falls in your 2nd House of Self-Worth, revealing the people close to you who aren't supporting your values. The curious Gemini New Moon on **May 24** in your 9th House of Adventure has you wondering how to reinvigorate your life. Expressing your fantasies through artistic creation, romantic love, or activities with children can play a significant role all month, for joyful Jupiter joins caring Chiron and Neptune on **May 23–27** in your 5th House of Play. Make the most of these days: This long-lasting transit is the first of three such spiritually uplifting super-conjunctions that can deliciously flavor the rest of your year.

> **KEEP IN MIND THIS MONTH**
>
> *Your capacity to imagine is greater than your ability to integrate fantasy with reality, so be selective when you choose which dreams to pursue.*

KEY DATES

MAY 2–5 ★ *a walk on the dark side*

Relationships grow rocky when romantic Venus is dealing with the challenges presented by shadowy Pluto. You might prefer to indulge in sensual delight, yet the Venus-Pluto square on **May 2** can expose a darker side of Eros. Fears of abandonment or feelings of jealousy can turn a complicated situation into a crisis. Suppressed emotions can fuel a creative outburst, however, so instead of stifling them, bring the intensity to the surface without being too attached to the outcome.

Passions temporarily out of control will settle back down when the Sun in your 8th House of Intimacy harmoniously trines stable Saturn on **May 5**. Relying on your common sense can help smooth ruffled feathers, allowing you to move on comfortably.

MAY 11 ★ *caught in the middle*
Don't let frustration get the best of you, even if something or someone stands between you and satisfaction. With an irritating aspect between hot Mars and cold Saturn, it's difficult to know how hard to push your agenda when you first meet resistance. You could be left with resentment if you just walk away from the situation. On the other hand, you might make matters worse if you force the issue. Instead of feeling discouraged, recognize that your timing may be slightly off and that a little patience can go a long way.

MAY 16-20 ★ *hold that thought*
An unusual bout of stubbornness may interrupt the smooth flow of your days, but it's crucial for you to hold a position that allows you to act with integrity. The fantastic Jupiter, Chiron, and Neptune conjunction in your 5th House of Self-Expression is tensely squared by the Sun on **May 16-17** and by Mercury on **May 20**, pointing out exactly where your dreams depart from reality. This realization can be temporarily disillusioning, yet it also frees you from unrealistic expectations. Additionally, an irritating quincunx from sweet Venus to restrictive Saturn on **May 20** can require you to make adjustments with a partner who may not feel very supportive now.

SUPER NOVA DAYS
MAY 26-27 ★ *saving grace*
The rare joining of buoyant Jupiter, healing Chiron, and psychic Neptune is deeply inspiring—especially when Mars forms a supportive sextile with this spiritual trio. Mars, the planet of physical energy, is now at home in pioneering Aries, giving you the impetus to turn your visions into reality by taking the initiative often. Enjoying what you do can be a spiritual practice in itself, and the current emphasis on the fun-loving 5th House reminds you that even difficult tasks can have an uplifting aspect when you're in a positive frame of mind.

JUNE

INTO THE GREAT WIDE OPEN

Expect smooth sailing the first few days of the month while the dynamic duo of Venus and Mars harmonize with other planets, but the Sun's stressful square with authoritative Saturn on **June 5** can temporarily stop you in your tracks. You are challenged to keep your interest in travel or in a new philosophy from interfering with your obligations as stern Saturn maintains a grip on your life through the inspirational Sagittarius Full Moon on **June 7**. This Full Moon is strengthened by Venus's luscious trine to passionate Pluto, turning the volume up on your desires. Fortunately your key planet, Venus, entered her other home sign of earthy Taurus on **June 6**, so your needs are more practical now than discretionary.

On **June 9–10**, mental Mercury's square to the spiritual Jupiter-Chiron-Neptune super-conjunction will likely bother you with facts that cannot be ignored. Magical quintiles from go-getter Mars to the powerful trio on **June 11–13**, followed by quintiles from creative Venus on **June 14–15**, however, allow you to apply your skills in an artistic way or to bring your dreams closer to reality. The Sun's harmonizing trine to Jupiter, Chiron, and Neptune on **June 16–17** would normally show you the easiest path to your goals, but its electric square with unconventional Uranus can complicate your life while also making it more thrilling. The Summer Solstice on **June 21** is marked by the Sun's entry into cautious Cancer and your 10th House of Status, emphasizing your professional and community work. The protective Cancer New Moon on **June 22**, followed by the Sun's opposition to domineering Pluto on **June 23**, reveals an ongoing struggle between career and family responsibilities. Find a way to keep everything in balance.

> ### KEEP IN MIND THIS MONTH
>
> *You're still in the early stages of a long-term cycle that will continue to inspire your creativity and advance your spiritual development.*

KEY DATES

JUNE 2-5 ★ *one change at a time*

Supportive sextiles from Venus to compassionate Chiron, imaginative Neptune, and expansive Jupiter on **June 2** rekindle the spiritual fires of the three-planet super-conjunction. Your easygoing attitude can be quite disarming now, enabling you to get your way with minimal conflict. A subtle move sends a convincing message on **June 3**, when forceful Mars trines intense Pluto. You could be tempted to demand more than you need, but Pluto doesn't reward selfishness. The Sun's square to pragmatic Saturn on **June 5** can place obstacles in your path. Working to limit unrestrained growth can have positive consequences.

JUNE 7-10 ★ *talk is cheap*

The adrenaline-seeking Sagittarius Full Moon on **June 7** in your 3rd House of Information increases your overall curiosity. Its opposition to the loquacious Gemini Sun in your 9th House of Faraway Places can highlight your desires to travel in the outer world or journey through the spiritual realms within. Be careful about frittering away your time unproductively as chatty Mercury squares Chiron, Neptune, and Jupiter on **June 9-10**. Consider the practicality of any new idea before you embrace it as a worthwhile subject of exploration.

JUNE 15-17 ★ *surprise yourself*

You have another chance to regain the potential of recently missed opportunities if you make use of your creative imagination. Beneficent Jupiter's backward turn on **June 15** in your 5th House of Self-Expression reconnects it with conjunctions to healing Chiron and visionary Neptune next month. Take a bold step as the Sun harmoniously trines Chiron, Neptune, and Jupiter on **June 16-17** to help your dreams come true. Don't play it safe—the unexpected can happen when the Sun, Venus, and Mars form destabilizing aspects with "wild and crazy" Uranus during these days.

SUPER NOVA DAYS
JUNE 21-23 ★ *this magic moment*

Your senses are heightened as the cosmic lovers, Venus and Mars, come together in your 8th House of Intimacy on **June 21**, the same day as the Summer Solstice. Don't waste this magnetic conjunction on transient pleasures, for a smooth trine to serious Saturn enables you to create something of enduring value. The powerful Cancer New Moon on **June 22** can prompt an uncharacteristic display of emotionality fueled by nostalgia. Memories of your childhood may remind you of what you're currently missing in your life, while the Sun's yearly opposition to Pluto on **June 23** can drive you to overstate your case and upset the balance of power in a close partnership. Don't spoil the magic with something that's not essential.

JULY

FOLLOW YOUR BLISS

This month offers you a chance to reevaluate how you express yourself in life as expansive Jupiter retrogrades over Neptune the Dreamer and Chiron the Wounded Healer. This is the second of three such exceptional super-conjunctions this year—the first was in March, and the last will be in December—all of them activating your 5th House of Romance, Children, and Creativity. It can be helpful to remember what was happening during the previous coalescence of these three slow-moving planets on **March 22–27**. Now that you've had time to integrate what you learned, you'll be ready to open yourself up to the next level of opportunities when Jupiter conjuncts Neptune on **July 10**. The ambitious Capricorn Full Moon Eclipse on **July 7** falls in your 4th House of Roots and draws your attention to the support you need at home in order to have a more successful career. This can give you a stable foundation from which to grow into your creative potential—or it can reveal instability, thereby motivating you to focus on outer accomplishments.

With your current optimism showing you the silver lining in every dark cloud, you may be tempted to avoid dealing with possible pitfalls on your way. You aren't willing to let previous failures prevent you from reaching your goals, especially when lucky Jupiter conjuncts Chiron on **July 22**. But the lingering effects of the hypersensitive Cancer New Moon Eclipse on **July 21** can serve as a reminder that you cannot bury old emotional wounds without paying a price. Look for a workable balance between self-protection and blind optimism.

> **KEEP IN MIND THIS MONTH**
>
> *Exploring ways to enjoy yourself is a smart idea, for you'll be most productive when you're having fun.*

KEY DATES

JULY 1 ★ *don't take it personally*
The spiritual super-conjunction of Jupiter, Chiron, and Neptune receives a tense square from your key planet, Venus, and a harmonious trine from logical Mercury, blessing you with the ability to rationalize your feelings, even if your desires aren't fulfilled. Stick with reason for now and use your logic to manage your emotions.

JULY 3–5 ★ *no strings attached*
Your words become emotionally charged when irrational Mercury enters moody Cancer on **July 3** and then opposes passionate Pluto on **July 4**. Paradoxically, you are less attached to the outcome of events as flirty Venus enters carefree Gemini

on **July 5**. Temporarily accepting the duality of desire and detachment allows you to maintain a positive and friendly attitude.

JULY 6–7 ★ *free falling*
Confusion builds as you swing between heightened enthusiasm and increased uncertainty. It's likely that a romantic attraction is involved, for physical Mars in your 8th House of Intimacy is dynamically square nebulous Neptune and confident Jupiter in your 5th House of Love on **July 6**. Nevertheless, a result-oriented Capricorn Full Moon Eclipse on **July 7** indicates a sudden resolution. Mars gets zapped by electric Uranus the same day, provoking you to take immediate action.

JULY 17–18 ★ *just do it*
You begin a more social phase as communicator Mercury enters lively Leo and your 11th House of Groups on **July 17**. Nevertheless, a series of annoying quincunxes may complicate your interactions until the Sun harmonizes with brilliant Uranus on **July 18**, enabling you to break through the noise of your own uncertainty. Trust your instincts and don't try to justify your current actions.

SUPER NOVA DAYS
JULY 21–22 ★ *nothing ventured, nothing gained*
Building emotional walls won't necessarily protect you, although you still may choose isolation as your preferred relationship strategy on **July 21** when loving Venus squares cautious Saturn. The insecure Cancer Full Moon Eclipse the same day can magnify your fears and send you running to the imagined safety of your past. Optimistic Jupiter's conjunction with healing Chiron and the Sun's entry into outgoing Leo on **July 22** can be the perfect antidote to your defensiveness.

JULY 26–31 ★ *roller coaster of love*
Several easy days are followed by a couple of tougher ones as the idealistic Jupiter-Chiron-Neptune super-conjunction is activated again. Love is an adventure when sweet Venus in your 9th House of Big Ideas harmonizes with this trio on **July 26–28**. But chatty Mercury's opposition on **July 30–31** can bring on endless discussions, pulling you away from the satisfaction that seemed so close only a few days ago. Luckily, Venus's entry into patient Cancer on **July 31** can shift your focus away from the frustration.

AUGUST

RIDING THE SEESAW OF LIFE

Your struggle to gain control of certain aspects of your life may be a recurring theme this month, beginning on **August 1** as Venus, the Goddess of Love, engages in a standoff with potent Pluto. The month ends with Mars, the God of War, entangled in the same tug-of-war on **August 26**. Between this challenging pair of dramatic oppositions, you may attempt to carve out a balance between opportunities to enjoy yourself and your responsibilities to finish what you've already started. The Full Moon Eclipse in nonconformist Aquarius on **August 5** falls in your creative 5th House, suggesting a breakthrough in how you express yourself. If you're involved with any type of artistic endeavor, this is the time for a radical approach—you may discover exciting ways to advance your technique. The 5th House is also associated with children, so you could have a surprising interaction with a clever child who teaches you something you might not expect from a youngster.

Overconfident Jupiter in your 5th House of Love and Play forms an aggravating quincunx with serious Saturn in your 12th House of Endings on **August 19**—the second of three such aspects that began on **March 22** and culminates on **February 5, 2010**. You may be quite clear about what you want and what you need to do, yet executing your plan won't necessarily set things right. For now, accept the presence of unresolvable extremes in your life, even as you strive for more moderation. The fixed Leo New Moon on **August 20** falls in your 11th House of Goals, indicating your unwillingness to simply go with the flow. You have an agenda and are determined to stick to it, even if progress is temporarily elusive.

> **KEEP IN MIND THIS MONTH**
>
> *Difficult as it is to fully relax in times of heightened instability, do what you must—and then make time to replenish your reserves.*

KEY DATES

AUGUST 1–5 ★ *timing is everything*

You want to be appreciated at work now that sweet Venus is in your 10th House of Status, yet her opposition to shadowy Pluto on **August 1** suggests that your reputation could be in jeopardy. Jealousy may figure into the current drama, but it's challenging to bring the issue out into the open until talkative Mercury harmonizes with Pluto on **August 3**. Don't miss this opportunity to discuss your feelings—it'll only grow harder if you wait until the emotionally detached Aquarius Lunar Eclipse on **August 5**.

AUGUST 10–14 ★ *don't give up*

Your best efforts to make something happen hit a wall, and you could spin your wheels until you're exhausted and ready to retreat. The problem is that flighty Mars in Gemini encourages you to scatter your energy, yet his square to mature Saturn from your 9th House of Future Vision on **August 10** suggests that slowing down and narrowing your focus is a smarter approach. Fortunately, you overcome obstacles and see your confidence return when propitious Jupiter trines Mars on **August 13** and opposes the Sun on **August 14**.

SUPER NOVA DAYS
AUGUST 17–20 ★ *juggling act*

A few days of cosmic rock and roll can send you first one way and then another, again and again, hardly able to recover from one event before you're called on to handle the next. A sobering Mercury-Saturn conjunction in your 12th House of Secrets is offset by easy aspects from the Sun and Mars to escapist Neptune on **August 17**. Explosive Uranus arrives on the scene on **August 18** to shake things up, but a Venus-Saturn alignment on **August 19** graces you with enough common sense that you won't risk too much. The long-term Jupiter-Saturn quincunx that's exact on **August 19** demands constant attitude adjustments, although you may be convinced that your reactions are too little or too much no matter what you try. The fiery Leo New Moon on **August 20**, however, can clear the air with a heartfelt expression of your feelings, preparing you for changes just around the corner.

AUGUST 25–26 ★ *find a work-around*

Mercury and Mars are in an argumentative square when they each move into a new sign on **August 25**. Mercury enters objective Libra and Mars enters subjective Cancer, while both form harsh aspects with domineering Pluto on **August 26**, intensifying differences of opinion. Although Venus's entry into expressive Leo the same day can alleviate some of the pressure, it's hard to face your fears of failure. Tempted as you are to force an issue or overstate your case, patience may be the smarter strategy.

SEPTEMBER

DESTINY CALLS

If you have some trouble making decisions, it's because you so often see both sides of an issue better than other people do. This month finds you pressed to choose between taking a risk and following a more conventional path. Ultimately, this is a turning point, even if you're uncertain about your current choices. No matter what you do, you're nearing the end of a long-term cycle on **September 12** when karmic Saturn in your 12th House of Endings opposes radical Uranus. Remember the fork in the road you faced at the previous Saturn-Uranus oppositions on **November 4, 2008,** and **February 5** as you manage this transition. The conflict between holding on to your past and stepping into your future is significant enough that it will require additional time to resolve. The final recurrence of this stressful aspect is on **July 26, 2010,** yet the immediate sense of urgency is still great. Saturn's imbalanced quincunx to foggy Neptune on **September 12** further muddies what's happening, for Neptune's influence from your 5th House of Love and Play may deceive you into believing you can avoid serious issues. Additionally, Mercury the Messenger is in its trickster phase—retrograde from **September 4 to** September 29—urging you to revisit and revise previously made plans.

> **KEEP IN MIND THIS MONTH**
>
> *You can avoid being overwhelmed by the pressures mounting in your life if you keep your eyes on the distant horizon instead of any one current situation.*

The psychic Pisces Full Moon on **September 4** falls in your 6th House of Details, overloading you with more than you care to handle. The efficient Virgo New Moon on **September 18,** however, is conjunct unyielding Saturn, focusing your attention on the crucial issues and empowering you to push through these major changes.

KEY DATES

SEPTEMBER 3-4 ★ *true-blue friend*

All forms of communication take center stage on **September 3,** when logical Mercury tensely squares Mars. But problems may arise if you have to take care of others with dynamic Mars in nurturing Cancer in your 10th House of Public Responsibility. Mercury turns retrograde on **September 4,** indicating an internal struggle between your needs and your current responsibilities. Additionally, the sensitive Pisces Full Moon floods you with compassion, suggesting that you will come through for others, even if you'd rather be doing something else.

SEPTEMBER 11–12 ★ *life of the party*

Don't go overboard when indulgent Venus in your 11th House of Friends opposes opulent Jupiter on **September 11**. Pleasure is abundant, yet you may still want more than you have, as social temptations could be hard to resist. The pressures of your life seem easier to handle, though, as you kick back and relax. Nevertheless, strict Saturn's crunchy quincunx to imaginative Neptune on **September 12** will remind you that avoidance isn't a viable long-term strategy. Take a bit of time for yourself and then get back to work.

SUPER NOVA DAYS
SEPTEMBER 15–18 ★ *the truth will set you free*

You vacillate between taking responsibility for your present situation and wanting to escape into your fantasies. The weight of the world sits on your shoulders as the exact Saturn-Uranus opposition on **September 15** tries your patience. Separating reality from your dreams is difficult, for your key planet, Venus, opposes nebulous Neptune on the same day. You're eager to break through your resistance to the truth on **September 17**, when analytical Mercury confronts powerful Pluto and the Sun conjuncts authentic Saturn. The critical Virgo New Moon falls in your 12th House of Inner Peace on **September 18**, helping you discern fact from fiction in order to move on.

SEPTEMBER 20 ★ *straight and narrow*

Set aside transient pleasures so you can be clear about which desires to pursue now that sensual Venus is in practical Virgo. Simplify your relationships, eliminate distractions, and generally lighten your load in preparation for great changes ahead. Trust your instincts: Venus's harmoniously trine with survivalist Pluto empowers you to forgo immediate gratification in the name of long-term emotional balance.

SEPTEMBER 22–23 ★ *beyond all bounds*

The Autumnal Equinox on **September 22** heralds the Sun's entry into harmonious Libra, yet its difficult square to dark Pluto on **September 23** suggests that transition won't be simple. Dramatic breakthroughs are possible, for your mind is freed from the usual social restraints as Mercury opposes unorthodox Uranus on the same day. Thinking about unrealized potential is a great start, but remember that you'll need to follow up your brilliant thoughts with sensible action.

OCTOBER

BEFORE THE HARVEST

You're reaching the culmination of a two-year process clearing away psychic undergrowth from your subconscious mind. Expect challenges as you work to complete old business before serious Saturn leaves your 12th House of Soul Consciousness on **October 29**. It's difficult now to see what fruits your labor will bear over the next couple of years when Saturn the Tester moves through Libra. In any case, your efforts are better aimed at tying up loose ends while there's still time. Instead of focusing on any failures, remember that pruning back your tree of life will encourage healthier growth ahead.

The self-centered Aries New Moon on **October 4** falls in your 7th House of Partnerships, placing you in the middle of a passionate tug-of-war. On the one hand, you recognize what others want and are drawn to providing it, if you can. On the other, you may feel that it's high time you satisfied your own needs, rather than always being the gracious one who acquiesces to make everyone else happy. Luckily, you can juggle your personal yearnings with your thirst for pleasing others as the Sun moves through relationship-oriented Libra until **October 23**. You receive additional assistance from thoughtful Mercury as it enters diplomatic Libra on **October 9**, followed by your ruling planet, Venus, on **October 14**. You are very much at home playing on both sides of the fence now. The reflective Libra New Moon on **October 18** harmonizes with spiritual Neptune, blessing you with grace, adding inspiration to your artful pursuits, and gently reminding you to believe in your dreams.

> **KEEP IN MIND THIS MONTH**
>
> *There's no need to overreact. Instead of making arbitrary decisions, adapt and adjust to maintain harmony.*

KEY DATES

OCTOBER 4 ★ *truth or dare*

Normally an independent Aries Full Moon in your 7th House of Others could high-light irresolvable differences in a relationship, yet now you can overcome conflict through radical action. A rebellious Mercury-Uranus opposition releases a lightning bolt of awareness as harmonious aspects to assertive Mars empower you to convert your thoughts into action. Show your cards so everyone knows where you stand.

OCTOBER 8-10 ★ *face the music*

You must confront reality on **October 8**, when mental Mercury in your 12th House of Fantasy runs into unforgiving Saturn. But even bad news can be liberating once you know the truth. Lovable Venus gets zapped by an opposition from shocking Uranus on **October 9**, blasting through your resistance to change. Mercury's entry into rational Libra the same day allows you to do a mental balancing act to keep things in perspective. The Sun's expansive trine with upbeat Jupiter on **October 10** may guarantee a positive outcome, yet an intense Mercury-Pluto square won't let you move on until you've analyzed and processed your deepest feelings.

SUPER NOVA DAYS
OCTOBER 12-15 ★ *ambitious plans*

No matter how well organized your strategy may be, you'll need to be patient before you see any tangible rewards. A self-disciplined Venus-Saturn conjunction is supported by Mars in your 10th House of Career on **October 12–13**, improving your chances of success at work or in love. Forgo immediate compensation in exchange for long-term potential. Still, there are tough issues to face as Venus enters your sign on **October 14**, only to meet up with overbearing Pluto on **October 15**. Avoid covert manipulation; act with integrity.

OCTOBER 23-24 ★ *warped perspective*

Your emotions pick up additional intensity when the Sun enters passionate Scorpio on **October 23**, followed by its connective sextile with potent Pluto on **October 24**. But you could let your thoughts run away in fantasy without even realizing it as creative Mercury in artistic Libra receives visions from a trine with escapist Neptune. An annoying quincunx to Mercury from crazy Uranus makes it impossible to gauge the relative importance of any one idea.

OCTOBER 28-29 ★ *give and take*

One of the most beautiful aspects, a generous Venus-Jupiter trine, graces your world with abundance on **October 28**, yet the Sun's harsh square to feisty Mars on **October 29** can burden you with challenges that don't allow you to fully indulge. You may feel as if something lovely is being taken away when austere Saturn enters your sign for a two-year visit. Learning an important lesson about appreciating pleasure while you can proves to be a blessing as you accept new responsibilities in the weeks and months ahead.

NOVEMBER

DECONSTRUCTION ZONE

There's no room for laziness now that hardworking Saturn is in your sign, but rest assured that your extra efforts will be recognized and rewarded, even if it takes time. Having Saturn in your 1st House of Self for the next couple of years may mean significant adjustments, but the sooner you realize that this is serious business, the easier life will be. Saturn forms a dynamic square with transformative Pluto on **November 15**—the first of three such transitions that recur on **January 31, 2010**, and **August 21, 2010**. The stressful connection between these two tough planetary heavyweights can exhaust you, so manage your time and resources carefully. You may win battle after battle yet still lose the war if you're overconfident or in denial. Pluto is in your 4th House of Roots, indicating that the metamorphosis will affect the most stable and fundamental areas of your life, including your home and family. Nevertheless, this intense process continues through the rest of the year, leaving you stronger and wiser if you're up for the challenge.

The stubborn Taurus Full Moon on **November 2** falls in your 8th House of Investments and Shared Resources, tempting you to hold on to what you've already earned. Trust feelings over logical analysis and don't get bogged down with too many facts, for they could mislead you now. Then, on **November 16**, a complex Scorpio New Moon occurs in your 2nd House of Personal Resources. Like the earlier Full Moon, this one can be hard on your purse unless you pay attention. Even if financial pressure subsides toward the end of the month, don't let up on your diligence and determination.

KEEP IN MIND THIS MONTH

If you've been disappointed by a current setback, don't waste time wallowing in self-pity: Shore up your plans and get to work.

KEY DATES

NOVEMBER 2 ★ *be polite*

While the sensible Taurus Moon is usually a time for inner reflection, today's Full Moon offers no respite as it stressfully squares feisty Mars and opposes factual Mercury. Your inflexible logic could precipitate an unnecessary argument, especially since several planets are in fixed signs. Charming Venus, however, harmonizes with gentle Neptune, blessing you with an easygoing manner that makes you likable, even if you are more obstinate than usual. But unruly Uranus is awkwardly aspected, so watch your manners or you might needlessly offend someone who'd prefer to be your ally.

NOVEMBER 7-10 ★ *sex appeal*

Your ruling planet, Venus, enters seductive Scorpio on **November 7**, initiating a three-week period of intense desires. The love planet's visit to passionate Scorpio can raise the bar of excellence on intimacy—or drive your needs so deep that you're forced to settle for less. Either way, approach all your interactions with caution, for pensive Mercury—also in Scorpio now—squares overindulgent Jupiter on **November 8**. Exercising self-restraint is more challenging than usual, especially when a Venus-Pluto sextile on **November 9** heats things up another notch. The dynamic Sun-Jupiter square on **November 10** is the frosting on the cake, making everything overwhelmingly sweet.

SUPER NOVA DAYS
NOVEMBER 14-16 ★ *no quick fix*

Although the rugged Saturn-Pluto square is exact on **November 15**, it tests your stamina for weeks before and after the event. But an exciting Sun-Uranus trine on **November 14** dares you to break free from your routine. You're eager to experiment, but the Sun's square to psychic Neptune makes it tricky for you to know which of your contradictory instincts to trust. Save the biggest decisions until after the resourceful Scorpio New Moon on **November 16**, when you'll finally be feeling the mentally stabilizing effects of Mercury's cooperative sextile to conservative Saturn.

NOVEMBER 23-26 ★ *pleasant interlude*

You may be feeling much better now that your key planet, Venus, is back in the picture. Be careful or you could squander your emotional and fiscal resources when she squares excessive Jupiter on **November 23** and deceptive Neptune on **November 26**. Nevertheless, you're likely to thoroughly enjoy yourself as Venus, the planet of love, creates an easy trine with rebellious Uranus on **November 25**. You can express your needs easily now, for Mercury the Communicator receives a strong boost of energy from a trine with physical Mars, also on the 26th. Go ahead and treat yourself to a well-deserved vacation or a fun-filled gathering with friends and family.

DECEMBER

BEAUTIFUL DREAMER

A rainbow that vanished in a recent storm may reappear this month, tempting you to look again for the legendary pot of gold as benevolent Jupiter conjuncts healing Chiron on **December 7** and mystical Neptune on **December 21**. These idealistic conjunctions are the culmination of an ongoing pattern that began in May and July, and that continues to open your heart and mind to your own creativity. Now, as this magical super-conjunction coalesces for the third and final time, you mustn't miss the opportunity to actualize your dreams. Paradoxically, you cannot be greedy—if you try to grab too much, it will all just disappear like a mirage. Balance reality with your hopes as best you can. Fortunately, you receive cosmic assistance that enables you to keep your feet on the ground as messenger Mercury enters traditional Capricorn on **December 5**, followed by the willful Sun on **December 21** and sensual Venus on **December 25**. Be prepared to journey into the transformative shadows of change as each of these planets conjuncts dark Pluto—already in Capricorn—on **December 7, December 24, and December 28**.

Your confidence increases, and you might believe that your success is near on **December 16** as the enthusiastic Sagittarius New Moon supports the inspirational trio of Jupiter, Chiron, and Neptune. But everything may take longer than you wish, because action-hero Mars slows down and turns retrograde on **December 20**, followed by communicator Mercury's backward turn on **December 26**. You may feel weary or even defeated, but don't give up; you just need some time to relax. Your ambition will get a second wind after the self-protective Cancer Full Moon Eclipse clears the air on **December 31**.

> **KEEP IN MIND THIS MONTH**
>
> *Your dreams can motivate you to reach far, but don't be too hard on yourself if you fall short of your lofty expectations.*

KEY DATES

DECEMBER 1–2 ★ *close to home*

Venus's entry into friendly Sagittarius and your 3rd House of Immediate Environment on **December 1** amplifies your interest in people, places, and things. You want more than you can get as the distracting Gemini Full Moon on **December 2** falls in your 9th House of Adventure, luring you farther along your path of learning. Although you may desire something out of reach, your lesson is about finding satisfaction right where you are.

DECEMBER 7 ★ *against all odds*

You are relentless in your pursuit of happiness as the dramatic Leo Moon conjuncts aggressive Mars in your 11th House of Dreams and Wishes while opposing the hopeful Jupiter-Chiron conjunction. But problems may arise when analytical Mercury joins piercing Pluto, plunging your thoughts into the depths. Mercury also squares stern Saturn, so the obstacles may seem insurmountable. The uplifting Sagittarius Sun, however, creates a magical quintile with taskmaster Saturn, empowering you to stand up to authority as you learn to believe in yourself.

SUPER NOVA DAYS
DECEMBER 14–17 ★ *no holding back*

You can reach your goals if you step outside whatever box that contains you. The Sun's dynamic square to unconventional Uranus on **December 14** is a lightning bolt that floods your consciousness with insight. Rich Venus forms a brilliant quintile with Saturn on the same day, enabling you to skillfully apply your creativity to take advantage of the current situation. The visionary Sagittarius New Moon on **December 16** gives you a spiritual boost, while Venus's easy trine to Mars on **December 17** adds flair to your style.

DECEMBER 19–21 ★ *turning point*

Another surprise throws you for a loop on **December 19** when your ruling planet, Venus, squares astonishing Uranus. It may be hard for you to react quickly as active Mars turns retrograde on **December 20**. Nevertheless, your dreams are alive and well as beautiful Venus harmonizes with the idealistic Jupiter-Neptune conjunction on **December 20–21**. Be ready, however, for a more mundane perspective as the Sun enters dutiful Capricorn to mark the Winter Solstice on **December 21**.

DECEMBER 28–31 ★ *beyond the end of the road*

These few days take you on an emotional roller-coaster ride, testing your ability to maintain the holiday spirit. Loving Venus joins with forceful Pluto on **December 28**, pushing you past the bounds of logic, whether this passionate journey brings you to satisfaction or not. Venus's harsh square with austere Saturn on **December 29** can delay gratification in a relationship—or perhaps you're the one setting personal limits. Either way, the Cancer Full Moon Eclipse on **December 31** suggests that the New Year will be anything but boring.

SCORPIO

OCTOBER 23–NOVEMBER 21

SCORPIO

2008 SUMMARY

A big year lies ahead of you, complete with a few surprises that can complicate your life, yet fortunately you have the tools to integrate change with great ease. Although you are eager to test the ground in a new world, temper your optimism with reason and caution. Even if you feel a great sense of urgency about making sweeping changes to the fundamental underpinnings of your life, remember that you don't have to make them all at once.

AUGUST—*no holding back*

Growth is not painless, and you may be required to give up something dear to move into the next phase of your life. Even the best changes can be difficult at first.

SEPTEMBER—*spiritual renewal*

Taking care of your responsibilities must be a part of your spiritual practice. It's not just about finding deeper meaning; it's also about making your life work.

OCTOBER—*phoenix rising*

Become more engaged in every aspect of your life. Although the days may be getting shorter, your light is growing brighter and your actions now have major consequences for your future.

NOVEMBER—*present tense, future perfect*

Instead of worrying, keep one eye on the past, one eye on the future, and your feet grounded in the present circumstances.

DECEMBER—*after the deluge*

Managing your stress through the holidays is crucial. If you take care of each situation as it arises, you will have time to partake in the festivities as well.

2008 CALENDAR

AUGUST
TUESDAY 5 ★ Take a risk and deal with the consequences through the 6th

WEDNESDAY 13 ★ **SUPER NOVA DAYS** Consider the cost of battle through the 17th

THURSDAY 21 ★ If you're open to surprise, you'll have a wonderful time

WEDNESDAY 27 ★ Let go of old feelings and perspectives through the 29th

SEPTEMBER
WEDNESDAY 3 ★ You may feel the weight of the world on your back through the 4th

SUNDAY 7 ★ **SUPER NOVA DAYS** Be selective with your altruism through the 11th

MONDAY 15 ★ Trust your heart when emotional challenges rise through the 17th

TUESDAY 23 ★ Meditation and contemplation help you grow spiritually

OCTOBER
MONDAY 6 ★ Pull back the reins before you overcommit

FRIDAY 10 ★ Explore unusual interests through the 11th

SATURDAY 18 ★ Move beyond your comfort zone to become emotionally available

FRIDAY 24 ★ Don't succumb to paranoia during relationship struggles

MONDAY 27 ★ **SUPER NOVA DAYS** Don't look back now

NOVEMBER
MONDAY 3 ★ **SUPER NOVA DAYS** There's no easy solution in sight through the 4th

WEDNESDAY 12 ★ Trust your own thoughts over anyone else's through the 16th

FRIDAY 21 ★ Venture into the great wide open through the 23rd

THURSDAY 27 ★ The holidays are spiced with fun-loving intensity

DECEMBER
FRIDAY 5 ★ Trouble lurks if you don't answer to authority now

FRIDAY 12 ★ **SUPER NOVA DAY** True confessions pack a punch

SUNDAY 21 ★ Let go of grudges through the 22nd

SUNDAY 28 ★ Take a purposeful and powerful stand through the 31st

SCORPIO OVERVIEW

This is a year for you to dissolve painful links with the past. Forgiving yourself and your family members for any past mistakes will pave the way to a brighter future. A rare series of conjunctions among generous Jupiter, idealistic Neptune, and healing Chiron in eye-opening Aquarius illuminates your 4th House of Roots to expand your base and fuel visions of a better tomorrow. **Loosen the emotional grip of old wounds by broadening your horizons and recognizing that you have access to much more than your current individual resources.** You are connected to all humanity and filled with potential beyond your personal limitations that can benefit everyone. Life's challenges do not disappear, but you'll be able to see them from a much wider perspective, opening more options for you to meet them. There are useful answers to be found, even in your darkest moments. It's better to err on the side of optimism than to permit habitual cynicism or self-doubt to choke off your dreams before they can be realized.

Reliable friends and co-workers are critical to your success. With karmic Saturn residing in your 11th House of Groups until October 29, you can't afford to carry the load for those unwilling to do their fair share. Expect crises when Saturn opposes rebellious Uranus on February 5 and September 15, temporarily interrupting teamwork. A lack of cooperation or some unreasonable demands may tempt you to jump ship. It's smart to recognize when a situation has become unmanageable and move on, rather than permitting your sense of loyalty to keep you chained to an unrewarding project. **With dutiful Saturn in practical Virgo, garner all the knowledge you can about your tasks and the means by which you're expected to fulfill them.** A precise understanding of everyone's role assures efficiency and fair compensation for your efforts.

Your co-ruling planet Pluto is now in your 3rd House of Communication—a long-term transit that can make you an adept observer and more influential communicator. Thoroughly studying the subject at hand and applying your natural psychological instincts will allow you to convince others of your ideas' value. But don't waste words—critical concepts can be lost in a blizzard of facts and overly complex explanations. Disciplining your mind helps you set aside distracting doubts to focus on effective solutions. Demanding Saturn begins a series of tense squares to Pluto on November 15 that recur on

January 31, 2010 and August 21, 2010. These will either elevate your communication skills or force you into silence at critical moments. Taking a speaking or writing class can be invaluable, as will specific training associated with your work. **Investing in further development of your powers of persuasion may be one of the keys to your future success.**

IT'S MAGIC

There's definitely magic in the world of love for you this year: Jupiter and Neptune, the co-rulers of your 5th House of Romance, nuzzle up to each other on May 27, July 10, and December 21. Their conjunctions with Chiron the Wounded Healer should help you mend a broken heart and free yourself for richer romantic experiences. Inventive Uranus is already in the 5th House, so breaking new ground is an effective counterforce to your instinctive patterns of holding on to the past. Spontaneous self-expression shatters shyness and habits rooted in your need to remain in control. Love is not something to master now, but an experience of pure discovery able to surprise you with delight when you least expect it. Regression in relationships is possible when Venus, the ruler of your 7th House of Partnerships, is retrograde March 6–April 18. Yet this return to old issues may well incite you to make changes rather than remain in your rut.

SEEK THE SPOTLIGHT

Two significant eclipses this year foreshadow a reorientation of your professional life. When the Sun, ruler of your 10th House of Career, is eclipsed in your 4th House of Security on January 26, you may find yourself disconnected from your customary approach to work. Enterprising Jupiter conjunct the eclipse can stir ambition for more meaningful employment. Another strong signal for change is the Leo Lunar Eclipse on February 9 in your professional 10th House. With this transformational event, lack of recognition may trigger your desire to seek greener pastures. Even if you can't alter your course, though, taking risks to demonstrate your creativity and gain attention will help your career. Expect a potential reshuffling when your key planet Mars turns retrograde in your 10th House on December 20, leading to modifications of job tasks and duties through March 10, 2010.

CASH IN ON CREATIVITY

Finances work best when this year when you can interweave logic with your imagination. Jupiter and Neptune, co-rulers of your 2nd House of Income, join in brilliant Aquarius to open windows of opportunity for increasing the value of your assets. You must still be practical, of course, but keep it to a minimum to cash in on inspiring ideas that are sure to enrich your spirit, if not your bank account. Mercury, the ruler of your 8th House of Shared Resources, turns retrograde in this sector of your chart on May 6 and will drift back into your 7th House of Partnership before resuming forward movement on May 30. Avoid new investments or business alliances during this period, which is best used for revising any existing agreements to better fit your current needs.

 ## ATTITUDE IS EVERYTHING

Your mind is the ultimate key to your health with transformative Pluto, the modern ruler of your sign, settled in for a fifteen-year run in your 3rd House of Information. The power of negative thoughts to inhibit your physical well-being and of positive ones to enhance it will continue to grow. March 6 through April 18 is a particularly sensitive period when Venus retrogrades in your 6th House of Health. The deleterious effects of self-indulgence and lack of exercise can take the fun out of life. However, eating nutritious foods and finding enjoyable forms of physical activity can restore your vitality. The holidays are a potentially precarious time: Accountable Saturn forms its first demanding square with Pluto on November 15, and Mars, the traditional ruler of your sign, turns retrograde on December 20. Take time to stop and breathe deeply; self-awareness will make all the difference.

 ## SACRED SPACE

Your residence becomes a spiritual retreat with the conjunctions of joyous Jupiter, gentle Neptune, and sympathetic Chiron in your 4th House of Home and Family. Their unions in late May, July, and December encourage open-mindedness, optimism, and faith that you can easily share with loved ones. This is not a withdrawal from the world, but the creation of a little piece of paradise where you live that pours happiness into every area of your life. Explore nontraditional religions, humanistic philosophies, and modern metaphysical practices that are free of negative judgment to feed this virtual spring of inspiration.

BACKYARD CAMPING

Travel might not be a top priority for you this year, what with Jupiter—the planet associated with higher education and distant excursions—hunkered down in your domestic 4th House. Your greatest adventures and opportunities for learning may occur within the confines of your own property. A Solar Eclipse in your 9th House of Faraway Places on July 21 could interfere with summer travel plans. A desire to see the land of your ancestors or significant historical sites makes sense, but getting there and back may be much more complicated than you anticipate.

 AT YOUR FINGERTIPS

The close proximity of an enlightening trio—Jupiter, Neptune, and Chiron—within your residential 4th House reveals the spiritual power and wisdom already within you. You don't need an external authority; you can discover truth at home, among your friends and colleagues. Discussion or study groups in which everyone is heard equally can provide all the answers you need. Faith and friendship are bound together in a supportive community of open minds and hearts. Informative Mercury turns retrograde in your 12th House of Divinity on September 6, reconnecting you with old sources of inspiration during this three-week cycle.

RICK & JEFF'S TIP FOR THE YEAR:
Brave New World

The sensation of being in strange and unfamiliar territory is rarely reassuring to you. Yet this year's gifts often come in packages that initially appear unsuitable to your tastes. Try to pause before instinctively withdrawing from situations you find odd or even uncomfortable. As long as there's no real danger, give yourself time to acclimate—you may discover joy, friendship, and fulfillment in the most unlikely forms. Your world is expanding, so finding a solid place to stand may be difficult. Instead, allow yourself to float. You'll soon find yourself connected and recharged in this brave new world.

JANUARY

CHAOTIC CONTRASTS

A long-term tug-of-war between your obligations to others and your need for personal freedom intensifies again this month. The tense opposition between duty-bound Saturn in your 11th House of Groups and liberty-loving Uranus in your 5th House of Self-Expression that began last November is activated now by challenging aspects from chatty Mercury. The communication planet spins from impulsiveness on **January 5** to stagnation on the **8th** before turning retrograde on the **11th** in your 4th House of Security to repeat the pattern in reverse. It's quieted by Saturn's sobriety on **January 14** and electrified by impatient Uranus on **January 17**. This erratic behavior returns next month after mental Mercury goes direct on **February 1**. A flexible attitude helps you adapt to your internal oscillations between excitement and fear, as well as the conflicting signals you receive from others.

The Sun follows Mercury's path from wild Uranus on **January 24** to strict Saturn on **January 25**, a likely trigger for battles with authority figures. Optimistic Jupiter enters Aquarius on **January 5**, initiating a year of personal expansion. But it, too, will tangle with the Saturn-Uranus opposition on **January 27 and 30**, magnifying the extremes of these two planets. Still, the New Moon in progressive Aquarius on **January 26** can plant seeds of great hope. This event—a Solar Eclipse in your 4th House of Foundations that's closely conjunct Jupiter—is a reminder that your perception of reality may be limited by outmoded belief systems; it's now time to trade them in for a more hopeful vision of the future. The price of a more fulfilling life tomorrow is to surrender your cynicism today.

KEEP IN MIND THIS MONTH

You're unlikely to enjoy absolute control under this month's volatile conditions. Acclimate yourself to the waves of change, though, and you'll soon be surfing life like a pro.

KEY DATES
JANUARY 3–6 ★ *spellbound*

Vivacious Venus enters sweet Pisces in your 5th House of Romance on **January 3**, opening your heart with an innocence that invites love. The risk of delusion or self-sacrifice associated with this position is reduced when magnetic Pluto forms a supportive sextile with Venus on **January 4**. This gives you the power to attract what you want and repel what you don't. Compelling charm and creative skills help you weave magic to entertain yourself or enchant others. Unexpected news may arrive on **January 5** with Mercury's edgy semisquare to surprising Uranus. Avoid committing to major tasks on **January 6**: Active Mars forms a slippery semisquare with Neptune, making it easy to underestimate the effort required.

JANUARY 10 ★ *the space between*
Your instincts guide you to overcome obstacles with an emotionally illuminating Cancer Full Moon in your 9th House of Big Ideas, where it's supported by constructive aspects from Saturn and Uranus. The futuristic vision of Uranus in imaginative Pisces can take root in the fertile soil of Saturn in earthy Virgo, offering you peace in the midst of chaos—as well as creative solutions to delicate issues. You instinctively understand the conflict presented by the ongoing Saturn-Uranus opposition and can now bridge the gap between them.

SUPER NOVA DAYS
JANUARY 22–25 ★ *playing the odds*
You can successfully manage risk when methodical Mars sextiles innovative Uranus as it conjuncts loving Venus on **January 22**. Unconventional and edgy social situations fulfill your need for novelty and allow you to experiment with your appearance and behavior. Feelings grow with the Sun's conjunction to inflationary Jupiter on **January 24**, yet optimism is contained by Venus's restrictive opposition to Saturn. Relationships require you to be clear about your desires and what's needed to fulfill them. Mars is there to help you achieve results with his capable trine to Saturn and gallant sextile to Venus. Yet all is not certain given the Sun's unstable semisquare to Uranus later that day, followed by an awkward sesquisquare to Saturn on **January 25**.

JANUARY 27 ★ *a fresh approach*
Old disagreements may return thanks to an argumentative conjunction between mental Mercury and assertive Mars. Avoid the trap of getting caught up in endless conflict by bringing a new perspective to the conversation. Clever ideas can break the deadlock and get you and your adversary back to a productive mode. Compromise and cooperation work better than bullying, since even logical debates won by force can leave a trail of resentment, making it difficult to find your way back to harmony.

FEBRUARY

TAKE A CHANCE

The pace of life accelerates this month. Mental Mercury starts the action by turning direct on **February 1**, stimulating fresh thoughts. The communication planet's forward shift in your 3rd House of Information occurs in strategic Capricorn, so your initial steps may be cautious as you catch up on the unfinished business of the past three weeks. However, new events at work push you to react more quickly with artistic Venus's entry into impulsive Aries in your 6th House of Work and Service on **February 2**. There's no time for plodding along on the job; just jump in and react as fast as you can, relying on your intuition if you feel unprepared for the tasks at hand. Potential changes of responsibility are highlighted by the Lunar Eclipse in your 10th House of Career on **February 9**. This Full Moon in dramatic Leo can put you in the spotlight, where you can show off your creativity and leadership skills. Still, an opposition from spacey Neptune indicates the possibility of spreading yourself too thin or chasing phantoms from your past. Be bold, but keep it real.

Joy can fill your heart when the Sun enters whimsical Pisces and illuminates your 5th House of Love and Play on **February 18**. Its monthlong stay in this expressive sector of your chart is highlighted by the dreamy Pisces New Moon on **February 24**. This fertile event nourishes your taste for fantasy and allows you to stop worrying about the results long enough to appreciate the delight of every precious moment. The world is your stage; you get to make up your part as you go along and are limited only by your own vivid imagination.

> **KEEP IN MIND THIS MONTH**
>
> *You are free to give and receive without keeping score now. Letting go of accountability in relationships can make impossible dreams come true.*

KEY DATES

FEBRUARY 4-5 ★ *circuit overload*

The feeling is electric when your ruling planet Mars enters high-tech Aquarius on **February 4**. This aggressive planet in your 4th House of Home and Family could incite conflict within your household, but its higher purpose is to motivate you to explore new activities and attitudes. Solid Saturn makes its second opposition to revolutionary Uranus on **February 5**, increasing tension between safety and your need for stimulation. Challenging aspects among reactive Venus in Aries, the willful Sun, and dangerous Pluto can make offhand comments seem like major attacks. Don't force issues unless you're willing to tear a relationship down to its roots and start over from scratch.

FEBRUARY 11-12 ★ *tiger by the tail*

You may find yourself struggling with the sluggishness of friends or colleagues when Mars in free-spirited Aquarius forms a stubborn sesquisquare with rigid Saturn on **February 11**. But a sudden change of conditions or an explosion of anger provokes extreme movement when Mars makes an irritable semisquare with radical Uranus on **February 12**. The warrior planet's encounter with the ongoing stress of the Saturn-Uranus opposition makes this a volatile time; you must tame your temper and apply your passion constructively to avoid problems.

SUPER NOVA DAYS
FEBRUARY 16-20 ★ *horn of plenty*

Meetings with eclectic individuals who entertain you and enrich your life are likely on **February 16**, when active Mars joins the connective North Node and sociable Venus forms a free-flowing sextile with lucky Jupiter. Mars in futuristic Aquarius joins Jupiter on **February 17**, stirring a sense of adventure rooted in childhood dreams that are now ready to be reactivated. Bold ideas for business or expanding your home are supported by new technologies on **February 18**. The Sun's entry into your 5th House of Love reinforces romantic potential, artistic ability, and your capacity to amuse others. But all may not be smooth sailing: Nervous Mercury's hard aspects to Saturn and Uranus on **February 18-20** mix messages of caution with those that encourage risk.

FEBRUARY 27-28 ★ *cool, calm, and collected*

Dampen any impulses to rush through a job, for precision is essential now. The quirky activities of Mars in Aquarius are likely to be curtailed by his tense semisquare to punishing Pluto on **February 27** and awkward quincunx with stern Saturn on **February 28**. It's time to slow down and attend to every task with the highest degree of concentration possible. When you focus your full attention, you are capable of overcoming almost any obstacle. Frustrating individuals and situations should be treated with calm, self-control, and a maturity that demonstrates your ability to manage tough situations.

MARCH

Love, play, and self-expression continue to be major themes as alert Mercury and energetic Mars follow the Sun into your 5th House of Romance, Children, and Creativity on **March 8 and 14**. Their smooth moves in sensitive Pisces add to the charm, imagination, and sense of style you already possess. You can be a compelling performer in any environment, with an ability to mesmerize an audience of one or a thousand. Nevertheless, amorous Venus turns retrograde in your 6th House of Daily Routines on **March 6**, requiring some adjustments in your habits at work and at home. Group activities may grow more challenging when the Full Moon in fussy Virgo is joined by restrictive Saturn on **March 10**. Pressure in your 11th House of Community is intensified by a conjunction of defiant Uranus and the Sun opposite Saturn and the Full Moon, activating your ongoing struggle between freedom and responsibility.

Your enthusiasm for self-improvement is stoked when the Sun enters frontrunner Aries on **March 20**, the Vernal Equinox. This transition, which falls in your 6th House of Health and Habits is an excellent time to begin physical and emotional spring cleaning. The New Moon in Aries on **March 26** forms a demanding square with purging Pluto, a reminder to eradicate any behavior that keeps you from meeting your full potential. Normally optimistic Jupiter enters some rough territory with tough aspects to Saturn and Pluto on **March 22 and 27**. Encountering barriers to living your truth can be frustrating, but don't let external obstacles feed internal doubts. You have nothing to prove to anyone but yourself, and your primary task is to keep faith in a world of unbelievers.

KEEP IN MIND THIS MONTH

Maintaining enthusiasm for work or play comes from satisfying yourself. If others don't share in your joy, don't let them bring you down.

KEY DATES

MARCH 1 ★ *firing on all cylinders*

Sharp thinking stimulates bright ideas with a mentally active conjunction between Mercury and Mars. However, this union in your 4th House of Home and Family can also ignite arguments within your household. There may be more than one right answer to any given question. Exploring unconventional concepts without requiring commitment reduces stress and encourages creativity.

SUPER NOVA DAYS

MARCH 8-12 ★ *keep calm*

Staying on course can exasperate you during a slippery conjunction between pushy Mars and dreamy Neptune on **March 8**. Mental Mercury's shift into Neptune's fanciful home sign, Pisces, inspires you to pursue fantasies and romantic delights. An opposition between the Sun and strict Saturn, though, either burdens you with responsibilities or inhibits your play with the criticism of an authority figure. Follow your bliss rather than someone else's command. A pointed sextile of Mercury and Pluto on **March 10** deepens your perceptions and makes you a clear communicator in the midst of a high-intensity Virgo Full Moon. A juicy Venus-Jupiter sextile on **March 11** opens the door to pleasure under unusual circumstances, helping you make rapid relationship adjustments if chaos ensues with the explosive Sun-Uranus conjunction on **March 12**.

MARCH 14 ★ *soft touch*

Passions rise when a sexy semisquare between Venus and Mars is followed by Mars's entry into your romantic 5th House. A little impulse control will be helpful, especially if you're pushing someone too hard. If you're trying to repair a relationship or reconnect with an old flame, apply your powerful emotions with discretion to avoid scaring this person away.

MARCH 19-20 ★ *raise the bar of excellence*

Use your powers of concentration to handle tough issues on **March 19**. A rigid Mercury-Saturn opposition provides you with a singular focus as a capable sextile of energetic Mars and demanding Pluto helps you cut through clutter, seize the core of a problem, and resolve it with efficiency. The Sun enters go-getter Aries in your 6th House of Work on **March 20**, encouraging you to tackle fresh challenges on the job and develop new skills that increase your professional value.

MARCH 22-23 ★ *double vision*

Maintaining your balance may be tricky on **March 22**: An awkward quincunx between Jupiter and Saturn combines with a Sun-Jupiter semisquare to muddle your sense of proportion. An imaginative, but impractical, Venus-Neptune connection adds to the confusion. What you hear, see, or feel might not be an accurate measure of reality. Any illusions are crushed on **March 23** when a Sun-Pluto square can strike with a crisis of consciousness. Eliminate distracting fantasies and focus on making one essential dream real.

APRIL

SPRING FEVER

Finding creative outlets for your feelings is critical this month, because powerful surges of emotion are ready to emerge. The key planet in this passion play is impulsive warrior Mars, as he moves from a sluggish opposition with restrictive Saturn on **April 4** to a volatile conjunction with shocking Uranus on **April 15**. The frustration of the former can build pressure that leads to an explosion with the latter. However, this high-energy event is in your 5th House of Romance and Self-Expression, where you can release its force with creativity to free your heart and display your originality in both work and pleasure. Mercury's entry into sensible Taurus on **April 9** can provide you with practical information from realistic individuals, supplying much-needed stability. At the same time, the Full Moon in artistic Libra highlighting your 12th House of Spirituality contrasts the stresses of daily life with beautiful visions of peace and a desire to escape to a better place. Jupiter generously trines the Full Moon, revealing ways to find the harmony you seek.

Sweet Venus in empathetic Pisces goes direct on **April 17**, turning your attention away from old romantic memories and back toward making love come alive in the here and now. The Sun warms your relationship life when it enters sensual Taurus and your 7th House of Partnerships on **April 19**. You can find more com-

> **KEEP IN MIND THIS MONTH**
>
> *Taking a second look at some-one is likely to reveal that he or she is more complex and has more to offer than you think.*

fortable ways to share your life, reducing the stress of an unsatisfying connection or easing you toward a gentle new one. The possibility of developing intimacy with others is increased when the New Moon in Taurus falls in your 7th House on **April 24**. The slow simmer of this earthy Sun-Moon conjunction is spiced with a trine from pungent Pluto, adding enough intensity to keep you hooked.

KEY DATES

APRIL 4 ★ *pace yourself*

You may have to slam on the brakes as mobile Mars opposes authoritative Saturn. It's better to take it slowly, even though you feel compelled to go on with the show. Instead of trying to dazzle anyone with style, demonstrating self-control and competence will win you points and help you avoid frustration.

APRIL 10–11 ★ *profound perception*

You can stretch your capacities at work on **April 10** with the Sun in your 6th House of Employment, aligning with expansive Jupiter. If you're not getting enough stimulation from your job, you might be motivated to consider a change. Trust your instincts with a sharp Mercury-Pluto trine on **April 11** that directs your attention where it will do the most good. Your thinking is clear and deep; your communication is concise and compelling. Venus enters initiating Aries to pique your interest in trying a new hobby or seeking ways to mix work and pleasure.

APRIL 13–15 ★ *breaking free*

Words flash with intensity as your nervous system is tightened by mental Mercury's stressful semisquares to Mars on **April 13** and Uranus on **April 14**. Edginess can originate from your own excitement or impatience, or it might be triggered by someone else's stress. Brilliant insights are possible, yet speaking too quickly ignites an argument. Tension may peak with the unstable Mars-Uranus conjunction on **April 15** that puts you in a less-than-cooperative mood. If possible, take time off to play or explore your own creativity. Your urge for freedom of expression needs to be heard to keep the emotional kettle from boiling over.

SUPER NOVA DAYS

APRIL 21–23 ★ *sweetly seductive*

A sexy Venus-Mars conjunction in your 5th House of Romance on **April 21** signals you to take the initiative in matters of the heart. An artistic and creative application of this pair can make you an alluring and entertaining force in any situation. Active Mars enters fiery Aries in your 6th House of Employment on **April 22** to stimulate you with new challenges . . . or leave you bored and itching for change. Don't leap without looking, though—an unbalanced Mercury-Jupiter square may cloud your judgment. Happily, a Sun-Pluto trine on **April 23** revives your good instincts to help you appropriately measure risk versus reward.

APRIL 26 ★ *fight to the finish*

The two rulers of your sign, Mars and Pluto, cross paths in a difficult square that can spur a power struggle. Your deepest emotions may be pushing you to act in an uncompromising way. Use this incredible force constructively by eliminating what you no longer need while concentrating on what's most essential to you now.

MAY

SHARING THE MYSTERY

Relationships demand reevaluation this month, for Mercury, the planet of communication, turns retrograde in your 8th House of Intimacy on **May 7**. Issues that you thought were already settled may need another round of negotiations during the Trickster's backward cycle, which doesn't end until **May 30**. The focus on partnership matters is underscored by the Sun's opposition in your 7th House of Others to the Full Moon in emotional Scorpio on **May 9**. You may need to readjust your expectations, because excessive Jupiter's stressful square to the Sun and Moon forces strong feelings out into the open. But don't be in a hurry to settle matters: Retrograde Mercury suggests that you need more time to untie knots of miscommunication before you can move forward again with confidence.

Contrasts between the real and the ideal can stretch you in two directions as materialistic Saturn turns direct on **May 16**, followed by philosophical Jupiter's conjunctions to healing Chiron on **May 23** and spiritual Neptune on **May 27**. Don't let the demands of your responsibilities to others crowd out the time you need for dreaming about your own future. Provocative people can spice up your life when the New Moon in chatty Gemini occurs in your 8th House of Deep Sharing on **May 24**. The union of the Sun and Moon in this mobile sign sows seeds of possibility for connections with new people or intensifying existing relationships with friends or lovers. Your co-ruling planet Mars ambles into easygoing Taurus in your 7th House of Partners on **May 31**. The potential of tangling with stubborn individuals is balanced by the help you get—personally and professionally—when you share a common goal with someone you trust.

> **KEEP IN MIND THIS MONTH**
>
> *No matter how urgent a situation may seem, delay your response to give yourself more time to think, unless it's a true emergency.*

KEY DATES

SUPER NOVA DAYS
MAY 4–8 ★ *prepare in advance*
An overload of work or excess ambition reflects boldness and possibly poor judgment on **May 4** when superhero Mars in Aries aligns with enthusiastic Jupiter. Demonstrating your ability to manage resources and complete projects on schedule should be your goal, especially with the support of an efficient

Sun-Saturn trine on **May 5**. It's vital to get all your ducks in a row before Mercury turns retrograde on **May 7**, because it may be much more difficult to master details during the next three weeks. Resentment may surface with a disgruntled Sun-Pluto sesquisquare on **May 8**. Learning to share power and letting go of negativity are keys to maintaining cooperation under this potentially threatening aspect.

MAY 11–12 ★ *no need to struggle*
You're challenged to control the pace of your day on **May 11**, when assertive Mars runs into restrictions from a quincunx with slow-moving Saturn. Don't force issues when you encounter obstacles; working around them may seem time consuming but will be more efficient in the end. Tension continues on **May 12** due to conflicting facts, careless speech, or different approaches to handling problems. A Mercury-Mars semisquare can easily elicit anger, so back off when the heat rises and seek a clever solution that you can share calmly.

MAY 23 ★ *kindness counts*
Jupiter joins Chiron—a pattern that returns on **July 22** and **December 7**—to heal emotional wounds with wisdom and understanding. However, a cross quincunx between the Sun and insatiable Pluto can attract individuals who push your buttons. Don't accept abuse; instead, recognize the subtle difference between someone's attempt to control you and his or her desire to help. Be gentle when it comes to offering your opinions to others.

MAY 26–27 ★ *rainbow in the sky*
Your enthusiasm motivates others, making tough jobs easier to complete on **May 26** when physical Mars forms favorable sextiles to jovial Jupiter and Chiron. This is an excellent time to pitch an idea—you combine sincerity with an excitement that's hard for anyone to resist. Mars makes a sweet sextile to whimsical Neptune on **May 27**, inspiring creativity and allowing you to advance your interests with care and compassion. Boundless Jupiter joins Neptune, opening your mind and showing you a field of dreams.

MAY 31 ★ *strategic maneuvers*
You may be tempted to take the bull by the horns as Mars enters Taurus and forms a stubborn sesquisquare to Saturn. Yet being forceful now is likely to produce an explosive reaction. Seriously consider your long-term goals and find a less threatening way to make your needs known if you hope to avoid a head-on collision.

JUNE

AMIABLE ALLIES

Deriving more satisfaction from relationships is a key theme this month. Loving Venus enters your 7th House of Partnerships on **June 6**. The planet of attraction's presence, along with efficient Mars in sensual Taurus, gets you more admiration with less effort. Aligning with others for profit, public service, or pleasure is easier without tricky games or complicated plans. Be direct and honest to earn trust and ensure enduring alliances. Financial matters grab your attention with an extravagant Sagittarius Full Moon in your 2nd House of Resources on **June 7**, while a square to austere Saturn can put the brakes on free spending. Managing your money and further developing your talents both require discipline—but can pay off by increasing your income in the future. Visionary Jupiter turns retrograde in your 4th House of Security on **June 15**, cautioning you to slow down and reevaluate your long-term goals. Family issues from the recent past or even your childhood can return for further discussion. You may need to clean up unfinished emotional business and make sure everyone's on the same page before you can launch your next big project.

Summer arrives with the Sun's entry into watery Cancer and your 9th House of Adventure on **June 21**. Optimism from this event may be short-lived, however, because potent Pluto opposes the Cancer New Moon on **June 22**. Something must be eliminated before you're free to widen your horizons and follow your dreams. Look closely at your immediate environment to see what you can change to make this possible. Be wary of getting bogged down; details and distractions will disrupt the learning and traveling that ultimately enrich you.

KEEP IN MIND THIS MONTH

Pleasant relationships should be productive, but struggling with individuals indicates that you need to back away for the time being.

KEY DATES

JUNE 4–6 ★ *serious business*

A super-powerful Mars-Pluto trine on **June 4** lets you complete even the most difficult tasks. Take advantage of this opportunity by confronting tough jobs, either physical or emotional, instead of wasting this energy on trivial matters. Total concentration is essential on **June 5**, when a demanding square between the Sun and Saturn leaves little margin for error. Make a plan and stick to it even when others tempt you to alter your schedule. Sweet Venus strolls into your 7th House of

Partnerships on **June 6**, opening the way to more comfortable relationships with easygoing individuals. Look for creative alliances during the next month that can raise your public profile and, perhaps, even increase your income.

JUNE 8 ★ *the power of love*
Luscious Venus aligns in a harmonious trine with intense Pluto that allows you to apply your passion intelligently. You may feel strong desires, yet you're not so taken by emotion that you lose your good judgment. Sharp perception shows you the value in people and objects that others cannot see, while a profound awareness of what you need makes it simple to screen out distractions to get what you want. Repair a damaged relationship or deepen a healthy one to take intimacy to another level.

JUNE 16–17 ★ *short fuse*
Misunderstandings can have explosive consequences on **June 16**. Listen closely and speak slowly to avoid trouble. A quirky quincunx between Mercury and Pluto twists information so much, it's hard to read someone's intention. These planets like to keep secrets, but a high-octane semisquare between Mars and Uranus requires careful communication to avoid blowups or accidents. The urge for innovation and independence is further fueled by an unruly Sun-Uranus square on **June 17**. Fortunately, the impulse to separate yourself from others is tempered by a compassionate Sun-Neptune trine that can restore a spirit of cooperation.

SUPER NOVA DAYS
JUNE 21–23 ★ *passion play*
Your hopes run high when the Sun enters nurturing Cancer on the Summer Solstice, **June 21**. The exact conjunction of Venus and Mars energizes you physically, socially, and creatively. Express your enthusiasm with self-restraint, though, for a tense Sun-Mars semisquare provokes strong reactions. A gentle nudge is all you need to get someone's attention. Establishing trust is essential on **June 22**, when Venus and Mars trine responsible Saturn while suspicious Pluto opposes the Cancer New Moon. The dark Lord of the Underworld pushes well-hidden emotional buttons with challenging aspects to the Sun, Venus, and Mars on **June 23**. If you're not ready to deal with delicate relationship matters, it's best to sidestep conflict for now.

JULY

INCREASING YOUR BANDWIDTH

Two eclipses this month can radically change the way you gather information and the meaning you derive from it. A Lunar Eclipse in well-organized Capricorn in your 3rd House of Information on **July 7** opens your mind to perceive your environment differently. Eclipses break down old patterns, which may at first cause communication problems or a loss of credibility. However, stabilizing Saturn, Capricorn's ruling planet, forms a supportive trine to this Full Moon that should help you build new structures where old ones are falling. Furthering your education and developing your communication skills are potential rewards of this mind-shifting event. A Solar Eclipse in supersensitive Cancer on **July 21**, occurring in your 9th House of Higher Thought and Faraway Places, may alter your big-picture view of reality. Expect to reevaluate long-range goals, beliefs, and travel plans. You'll be compensated for any losses by a sudden and surprising gain when inventive Uranus makes a creative trine to this New Moon Eclipse that shakes open unexpected windows of awareness.

Expanding your vision and bringing spirit down to earth is supported by joyful Jupiter's conjunctions to intuitive Neptune on **July 10** and healing Chiron on **July 22**. This is the second in a series of conjunctions in your 4th House of Roots that began in May and finish in December and are an ongoing source of inspiration. Take time to cultivate your dreams, no matter how impossible they seem, for all have elements of truth that you can turn into reality this year. The Sun enters expressive Leo and your 10th House of Career on **July 22** to put you in a professional spotlight where you can really shine.

KEEP IN MIND THIS MONTH

Acknowledging your uncertainty and opening your mind to alternative views can teach you more than fixing on a single perspective and clinging to it relentlessly.

KEY DATES

JULY 3-4 ★ *choose your battle wisely*

Talkative Mercury moves into caring Cancer on **July 3**, turning personal conversations toward meaningful subjects. However, you may have a hard time being open-minded with those who think differently from you. When Mercury opposes unyielding Pluto on **July 4**, you could find yourself in a verbal showdown where neither side is willing to compromise. Acquiescing is not surrender, especially when it clears the air to allow you to get your main point across.

JULY 6-7 ⋆ *going too far*

Your enthusiasm may be high yet misdirected when action-planet Mars wanders off course on **July 6**. Disorienting squares with spacey Neptune and extravagant Jupiter can drain your energy if you overcommit yourself. A Venus-Pluto quincunx could find you struggling for approval; don't let guilt drive you to give more than you should. Happily, a savvy Mars-Uranus sextile on **July 7** helps you shift gears quickly and come up with clever solutions to remove yourself from awkward arrangements.

JULY 14 ⋆ *flashing yellow light*

You've been moving more quickly since energetic Mars entered mobile Gemini on **July 11**, yet his irritating quincunx with Pluto today can slow you down with a burdensome task. You can complete it more quickly and skillfully through deliberate action than by racing through it. Avoid getting caught in an old dispute that may not be ready for resolution.

SUPER NOVA DAYS
JULY 18-21 ⋆ *accidental enlightenment*

A quirky quincunx between chatty Mercury and secretive Pluto makes for complex communication on **July 18**. If you value a relationship, settle in for a long conversation to address issues that one of you has been avoiding. Honesty plus kindness will produce greater intimacy and trust. Exchanging ideas and managing data get easier thanks to a Mercury-Mars sextile on **July 20**. Trusting intuition to guide your actions can be more productive than following a fixed procedure. The Solar Eclipse in Cancer on **July 21** could shadow your highest hopes with doubt, yet the support of surprising Uranus cracks open your consciousness to reveal an even more inviting vision of the future. Stepping off the path of your current beliefs will free you to find more meaningful truth.

JULY 23-25 ⋆ *an appropriate show of force*

Watch out for power struggles when the willful Sun clashes in a quincunx with uncompromising Pluto on **July 23**. Disputes can escalate into serious problems thanks to a sarcastic sesquisquare between Mercury and Pluto on **July 25**. If you're going to fight to make a point or put your reputation on the line, be sure it's worth the effort.

AUGUST

SPIN CONTROL

Flexibility isn't your forte, Scorpio, and it's likely to be tested this month by the complicated comings and goings of optimists, pessimists, rule makers, and rule breakers. Your co-ruling planet Mars flits through flighty Gemini in your 8th House of Intimacy and Transformation until **August 25**, forming aspects with five planets along the way. Learning how to alter your responses to meet each situation will strengthen relationships and earn you support; otherwise your unyielding reactions can drive people away. The Full Moon in unorthodox Aquarius on **August 5** is a Lunar Eclipse in your 4th House of Family that may rattle cages on the home front. You might feel a strong drive for freedom and a desire to flee your obligations. Whether this itch for change is yours or belongs to someone close to you, clever Mars in Gemini forms a creative trine to the Full Moon, showing you ways in which contrasting needs can be met without undermining your emotional security.

Inner optimism clashes with outer reality on **August 19**, when overconfident Jupiter in your 4th House of Foundations makes a hard-to-manage quincunx with restrictive Saturn in your 11th House of Groups. Be clear about what kind of assistance you'll get from colleagues and friends before you even consider taking on new responsibilities. The New Moon in proud Leo on **August 20** falls in your 10th House of Career, perhaps earning you greater public recognition. However, nebulous Neptune's opposition to this Sun-Moon conjunction can tempt you to take a professional leap that may not be realistic. Ensure the viability of your dream with careful research and planning before you make your move.

> **KEEP IN MIND THIS MONTH**
>
> *Taking many small constructive steps may seem tedious, but it increases the likelihood that you can turn a grand vision into reality.*

KEY DATES

AUGUST 1–3 ★ *true believer*

Intense emotions can be triggered over matters of principle when sensitive Venus enters defensive Cancer and your 9th House of Higher Truth to oppose potent Pluto on **August 1**. Standing up for your beliefs is worthwhile, yet if you wish to maintain peace and harmony, it's important to avoid being judgmental. You easily see through lies, uncover vital information, and illuminate key points in a convincing manner when mentally sharp Mercury in Virgo trines piercing Pluto on **August 3**.

AUGUST 8–10 ★ *the big squeeze*

You may feel like you're entering hostile territory on **August 8**, when a testy Sun-Pluto sesquisquare attracts people who push your buttons and challenge your motives no matter how nice you are. But if you're unhappy with someone's behavior, remember that these are your issues, and it's up to you to control your reactions. Still, even the most cooperative attitude might not alleviate the pressure of a tense Mars-Saturn square on **August 10**. Reduce stress by concentrating patiently and precisely on one thing at a time.

AUGUST 13–14 ★ *high hopes*

Your enthusiasm grows with a jaunty Mars-Jupiter trine on **August 13**. This sense of confidence is enhanced by an outgoing Sun-Jupiter square on **August 14**, encouraging complete honesty and risk taking. It's appropriate to stretch your limits professionally and personally as long as you don't oversell yourself on a big idea that strays too far from reality.

SUPER NOVA DAYS

AUGUST 17–18 ★ *winds of change*

You can handle delicate matters with finesse on **August 17** as energetic Mars forms favorable aspects to a Sun-Neptune opposition. You may be an intermediary between realists and dreamers, enabling the two to work well together. A strict Mercury-Saturn conjunction requires careful calculations and unambiguous communication, especially if you lean toward exaggeration. Your smooth moves are likely to be interrupted by surprising events and explosive attitudes with a volatile Mars-Uranus square on **August 18**. Edgy individuals can blow your plans out of the water, so be prepared to make quick adjustments to remain on course.

AUGUST 25–27 ★ *fight the good fight*

It's crucial to handle conflict constructively as an argumentative Mercury-Mars square on **August 25** triggers a powerful Mars-Pluto opposition on **August 26**. Even the kindest comments can sound harsh under these stressful conditions, turning conversations into verbal combat. Stirring up deep issues can be productive, but only when done with a conscious intent to heal. You may want to strip away social niceties to reach the truth, yet a Venus-Pluto quincunx on **August 27** can destabilize relationships. Cooling the drama of wounded feelings should hasten a return to normalcy.

SEPTEMBER

Your heart may be opening with love, joy, and innocence this month, but the complexities of the world keep imposing themselves to pull you out of the little paradise you're creating. The curtain rises when an illuminating Full Moon in idealistic Pisces on **September 4** falls in your 5th House of Romance and Self-Expression. A spirit of play stirs your imagination and invites you to share your most hopeful feelings. Your key planets, Mars and Pluto, oppose each other and form tense squares with mental Mercury that can instigate arguments. However, Mars is harmoniously trine the Full Moon, showing you peaceful ways to convert the fire of disagreement into fuel for cooperative fun. Reason retreats with Mercury's retrograde cycle **September 7-29**, a time when messages may be muddled. This backward turn in your relationship houses, though, provides second chances to repair partnerships that have gone off track.

Pluto's direct turn on **September 11** marks a subtle shift toward expressing your power and desires more openly in the weeks ahead. Group activities may prove more demanding when Saturn, in your 11th House of Teamwork, forms very tough aspects to slippery Neptune and crazy Uranus on **September 12-15**. Unrealistic expectations from colleagues or friends can put you in a difficult position, so be direct about what you can and cannot do to avoid misunderstandings or wearing yourself out. The theme of team chaos continues with the New Moon in detail-oriented Virgo on **September 18**. This Sun-Moon conjunction is joined by sluggish Saturn and retrograde Mercury in your 11th House and is opposed by rebellious Uranus, signaling the stark contrast between your sense of duty and your desire for freedom.

> **KEEP IN MIND THIS MONTH**
>
> *Taking time to live in your own bubble is not a retreat from reality; it's a return to the delight and divinity that exist in your heart.*

KEY DATES

SEPTEMBER 2-3 ★ *alternate routes*

You may be stretched to your limit on **September 2**, when rash Mars rubs excessive Jupiter with an ungainly sesquisquare. If you feel the heat of tension rising, don't try to push through it. Step back and reassess your plan, which you may need to simplify. Impulsive words or an overload of details to manage may bring more pressure with a Mercury-Mars square on **September 3**. Using your imagination to address problems from different angles should bring bright ideas and fresh solutions.

SEPTEMBER 8-9 ★ *clear intentions*

Getting what you want from someone takes focus and persistence with a Venus-Pluto sesquisquare on **September 8**. This tense angle raises the stakes in relation-ships, requiring a more precise description of your desires. Learning how to reject an action without rejecting the person can help you maintain your integrity without wounding someone else's pride. Straightforward Mars skids into Neptune on **September 9**, possibly distracting you while wasting your time and energy. Gingerly pursuing your own dreams, though, and nudging others gently are useful applica-tions of this aspect.

SEPTEMBER 17 ★ *the power of words*

The skies rumble with change as the Sun illuminates the ongoing opposition of revolutionary Uranus and conservative Saturn in your 11th House of Community. Maintaining balance between those who resist change and those who insist upon it requires leadership, and the job might be yours. People are easily offended with Mercury's verbal power multiplied by a square with pungent Pluto. Every word counts, so choose yours carefully for maximum results with minimum damage. You also have the right to keep your opinions to yourself if you're convinced that expressing them won't be helpful right now.

SUPER NOVA DAYS
SEPTEMBER 20-23 ★ *labor of love*

You'll see relationships solidify on **September 20** when romantic Venus enters hardworking Virgo and forms a supportive trine with regenerative Pluto. Revisiting old issues shows you where you can still gain rewards and where you might have made mistakes. Go light on the criticism—of yourself or anyone else—since the point is to improve your capacity for love and pleasure, rather than meting out punishment. Grace is required on **September 21** when Venus and Mars clash, making it easy to rub someone the wrong way. Still, the difference between fighting and flirting is one of attitude, enabling you to transform anger into a friendlier sort of engagement. The Sun's entry into diplomatic Libra on **September 22** marks the Fall Equinox and is normally a harbinger of peace. However, its square to dark Pluto on **September 23** can agitate jealousy or resentment. Motivate yourself to take action rather than depending upon others.

OCTOBER

WAITING IN THE WINGS

You might feel like you're lurking in the shadows and watching carefully before your next move with the Sun in your 12th House of Endings. You probably won't receive all the recognition you deserve, but you can use a tactical retreat to regain physical and spiritual strength. A crisis could erupt if you feel rushed to complete a task with the fiery Aries Full Moon in your 6th House of Service on **October 4**. Yet this might also spark interest in a new hobby or an urge to make changes at work. Optimistic Jupiter turns direct in your 4th House of Security on **October 12**, rekindling hope. Then Mars, your ruling planet, strides into dramatic Leo and your 10th House of Career on **October 16**, initiating a period of professional boldness and creativity that will carry you into next year.

You can more easily find your pathway to inner peace with the creative Libra New Moon in your 12th House of Soul Consciousness on **October 18** receiving harmonious trines from the spiritual trio of Jupiter, Neptune, and Chiron. This burst of inspiration transforms into reality when the Sun moves into powerful Scorpio on **October 23**. The conscious use of your full potential allows you to take more control of your life. Mentally active Mercury follows the Sun into your 1st House of Self on **October 28**, helping you clarify and express your desires with greater conviction. Karmic Saturn shifts from Virgo to Libra and your 12th House of Spirituality on **October 29**; there it will test your convictions for most of the next two years. Put your faith to work by donating your time, resources, and heart to those in need.

> **KEEP IN MIND THIS MONTH**
>
> *Your most important work happens behind the scenes. Take all the private time you can to nourish your soul and inspire your imagination.*

KEY DATES

OCTOBER 4 ★ *think on your feet*

The Aries Full Moon intensifies now as Mars makes three significant aspects. A slick sextile with Mercury favors clever thinking and quick action. A clumsy quincunx with Neptune, however, may leave you slipping and sliding around your objectives instead of hitting the mark. Additionally, a brilliant Mars-Uranus trine allows you to quickly come up with alternative methods for achieving your goals.

OCTOBER 10–13 ★ *still waters run deep*

Silence is better than spilling secrets with a Mercury-Pluto square on **October 10** that rewards discretion and punishes gossip. Lead by example on **October 12** when assertive Mars supports authoritative Saturn, enabling you to demonstrate your efficiency. Relationships can be tense with a Venus-Pluto square on **October 13** that deepens feelings of dissatisfaction. Search harder for what you desire, rather than stewing about a loss.

OCTOBER 15–18 ★ *emotional triage*
You're cut deeply even by small slights on **October 15**, when a critical Venus-Pluto square can put your relationships on edge. High hopes fueled by Mars in romantic Leo and an excessive Venus-Jupiter sesquisquare on **October 16** dramatize the difference between great desire and fear of loss. The range of what's possible in love is being extended, yet going too far in either direction could damage a partnership. Aggressive Mars forms a complex quincunx with surgical Pluto on **October 18** that makes it all too easy to rely on anger or sarcasm to express dissatisfaction. However, well-focused feelings can pinpoint problem areas and make precise extractions that heal instead of harm.

OCTOBER 23–24 ★ *strut your stuff*
Your confidence grows with the Sun entering magnetic Scorpio on **October 23**. It's time to step up and show yourself proudly and loudly. A supportive sextile from passionate Pluto to the Sun on **October 24** reinforces your strength and increases your sense of purpose. You know how to cut through clutter to concentrate your efforts where they'll do the most good. You are a powerful motivator, so don't be shy about guiding others when necessary.

SUPER NOVA DAYS
OCTOBER 28–29 ★ *in command*
Your laser-like mind now sees through phonies and zones in on facts with increased mind power from Mercury. The planet of perception enters your sign on **October 28** to sharpen your focus—and then sextiles Pluto to turn it into an intellectual X-ray machine. Your words pack a punch that can get your ideas across to even the densest of individuals. An assertive Sun-Mars square on **October 29** can provoke a battle, but you're well equipped to come out on top. As long are you concentrate on your objective and aim your passion with precision, you'll be tough to beat.

NOVEMBER

THE SHAPE OF THINGS TO COME

You may finally be ready to overcome resistance and push forward for change both professionally and personally this month. The Full Moon in your 7th House of Partnerships on **November 2** is in stubborn Taurus, but challenging squares to it from energetic Mars and enterprising Jupiter are bound to create movement. It's better for you to be bold and take the initiative than to stand still and find yourself reacting from a defensive position. Expecting more rewards from life makes sense when attractive Venus enters your sign on **November 11**. The magnetic planet of love in your 1st House of Personality allows you to be more comfortable in your own skin as well as more alluring to others. This is a good time to replenish your wardrobe or update your appearance: Your sense of what makes you look best is sharp now.

A deep rumble below the surface arrives on **November 15** with the first of three formative squares between planetary heavyweights Saturn and Pluto. This slow-moving pattern recurs on **January 31, 2010**, and **August 21, 2010**, representing a profound shift in your sense of purpose and life direction. You should get a preview of this major turn as the New Moon on **November 16** lights up your sign with passion and desire. Boundless Jupiter and psychic Neptune square this Sun-Moon conjunction, opening your mind to inspiring visions of the future. The expectations raised by these planets are often unrealistic, yet radical Uranus forms a creative trine to this Scorpio New Moon that can show you a surprising way to fulfill your dreams. Money and resources come into the foreground when the Sun enters independent Sagittarius and your 2nd House of Finances on **November 21**.

> **KEEP IN MIND THIS MONTH**
>
> *The motivation you feel in your heart is stronger than material obstacles. Find that fire and follow it to your dream.*

KEY DATES
NOVEMBER 1–2 ★ *cool under fire*
You may be in a snappy mood with mental Mercury's stressful square to Mars on **November 1**, but don't let impatience get the best of you. Applying force to make your point or when tackling a tough task is fine when you keep it under control. A "wild and crazy" Mars-Uranus sesquisquare on **November 2** produces surprising behavior from an otherwise reliable individual. If you remain calm in the midst of a storm, you can manifest amazing results in unconventional ways.

SUPER NOVA DAYS
NOVEMBER 7–10 ★ *persuasive powers*
Potent words and passionate feelings give you a lot of influence over others on **November 7**. A tight Mercury-Pluto semisquare demands concise and precise communication. Seductive Venus entering enigmatic Scorpio can put a twinkle in your eye as you notice that people are watching you. You might feel like you're being judged harshly with a Sun-Pluto semisquare on **November 8**, but others probably aren't as critical as you think. A supportive Venus-Pluto sextile on **November 9** helps you ignore distractions to motivate others and make the most of your abilities. Overzealous Jupiter's square to the Sun on **November 10**, however, can provoke risky behavior. Don't make promises you can't keep.

NOVEMBER 19–21 ★ *games people play*
A sassy Venus-Mars square on **November 19** puts you in the mood to flirt, yet you might not appreciate being teased in return. If you can't control the game, you'll probably choose not to participate. It's healthy for you to be in charge, rather than feeling compelled to be polite or act like you care when you don't. This theme continues through **November 21**, when a Venus-Pluto semisquare raises the stakes in relationships. Whether you're pushing to get what you want or pushing someone away, it's vital that you exercise your own free will. Anything you give under duress will cause resentment and undermine trust. The Sun's entry into adventurous Sagittarius and your resourceful 2nd House is a time to be generous with yourself. Investing in your continuing education or treating yourself to something special can enhance your self-worth.

NOVEMBER 29 ★ *take no prisoners*
A no-nonsense sesquisquare between aggressive Mars and extreme Pluto can bring out your overly competitive side. Although you may not want to engage in open combat, little comments show that you aren't in an entirely friendly situation. Rather than going on the offensive or denying your feelings, concentrate on one specific issue at a time. The power of these planets enables you to dig deeply and uncover the root cause of a long-standing problem. Focus your intention wisely and you can make a positive, lasting change.

DECEMBER

FLIRTING WITH TIME

December is packed with two Full Moons, two retrogrades, and the last of Jupiter's inspiring conjunctions to Neptune and Chiron. The Full Moon in talkative Gemini on **December 2** falls in your 8th House of Deep Sharing, enhancing relationships and opening up communication on intimate subjects. Hopeful Jupiter makes its third and final conjunctions to healing Chiron and intuitive Neptune on **December 7 and 21** to complete a process of enlightenment that began in May. Rays of sunshine and hope can filter through the darkest clouds to guide you in confusing situations and reinforce your life's purpose. A bold new approach to financial matters and an expanding sense of self-worth are sparked by the philosophical Sagittarius New Moon in your 2nd House of Resources on **December 16**. Eccentric Uranus brings surprises with a hard square to this Sun-Moon conjunction, but harmonious aspects from your planet Mars in creative Leo and the super-conjunction of Jupiter, Neptune, and Chiron provide guidance, power, and passion that let you achieve your objectives.

Energetic Mars turns retrograde on **December 20**, and you'll have to backtrack and modify your actions until **March 10, 2010**, when it resumes direct motion. You can still advance during this time, but careful steps will help you avoid wasteful mistakes. The Sun's entry into ambitious Capricorn marks the Winter Solstice on **December 21**, emphasizing the need for more clarity in your 3rd House of Communication. This is underscored when Mercury, the planet of messages, turns retrograde on **December 26**, forcing revisions for the next three weeks. Expect a readjustment in long-range plans thanks to a Full Moon Eclipse in cautious Cancer on **December 31** in your 9th House of Truth, Travel, and Higher Education.

> **KEEP IN MIND THIS MONTH**
>
> *Bold ideas are best served by careful plans, patience, and a willingness to adapt your methods as needed.*

KEY DATES

DECEMBER 5–8 ★ *nowhere to run*

Avoid distractions to concentrate your energy on completing a tough job on **December 5**, when active Mars is challenged by a demanding semisquare from Saturn and calculating Mercury marches into disciplined Capricorn. Patience and tenacity can help you overcome stubborn obstacles. Mental pressure lingers on **December 7** as Mercury joins penetrating Pluto and squares Saturn, draining all your tolerance for bad judgment or uncertainty. Stick to the facts or stay silent to maintain credibility. An edgy sesquisquare between Mercury and Mars on **December 8** could spur verbal aggression with a friend or colleague; speak carefully to skirt conflict.

DECEMBER 10 ★ *natural-born leader*
Your physical vitality and efficiency are running at full throttle with a trine between the willful Sun in enthusiastic Sagittarius and physical Mars in creative Leo. It's a potent alignment that allows you to be a strong leader without using a heavy hand, or to work behind the scenes effectively on your own. If you can't catch this wave by yourself, encouragement from others may well propel you forward.

DECEMBER 17 ★ *the love you make*
Muscular Mars is slowing down three days before his long retrograde period begins, but he stops off today to create a friendly trine with lovely Venus. This harmonious aspect between the planets of action and attraction brings joy and playfulness that can transform routine activities into delightful experiences. Relationships are likely to take on a sweet sense of youthful innocence that revives romantic feelings.

SUPER NOVA DAYS
DECEMBER 24–28 ★ *accentuate the positive*
An intense conjunction between the Sun and uncompromising Pluto on **December 24** sets a serious tone for the upcoming holidays. Power struggles may crop up as conversations are spoiled by mistrust. Do your best to let go of the negative thinking that can undermine the spirit of the season. Venus enters traditional Capricorn on **December 25**, bringing an air of formality that's amplified by the Sun's stressful square with Saturn. This doesn't exactly symbolize lighthearted times, especially with a contentious sesquisquare late in the day between the Sun and Mars. Be restrained—Mercury's retrograde turn on **December 26** is likely to lead to renegotiations anyway. The heavy beat goes on with a harsh Mars-Saturn semisquare on **December 27** that's more about taking care of business than having fun. Venus conjuncts Pluto and sesquisquares Mars on **December 28**, blowing the lid off secrets and driving resentment out into the open. Still, when you can mix the maturity to address difficult issues with kindness, you can overcome disagreements, repair relationships, and recover resources, restoring hope to all involved.

SAGITTARIUS

NOVEMBER 22–DECEMBER 21

SAGITTARIUS

2008 SUMMARY

This is a transitional year, for Jupiter's entry into your 2nd House of Self-Worth can increase material wealth and your self-esteem. Instead of starting things anew, it's time to build on what you have already created. If you're worried that your options are limited, keep in mind that you are on an even greater adventure than you think. You are ready to make use of everything you've learned over the past eighteen years when powerful Pluto moved through your sign.

AUGUST—*listen to your dreams*

Even when your dreams are unrealistic, they infuse your soul with hope and focus your attention onto your long-term goals.

SEPTEMBER—*into the future*

No matter how eager you are to run up the mountain, you're better off slowing down, talking to others about your mutual goals, and working together for everyone's benefit.

OCTOBER—*mirror, mirror, on the wall*

You're standing between two worlds, with one foot comfortably planted on familiar ground and the other ready to step somewhere.

NOVEMBER—*ready to rock and roll*

Make necessary adjustments to lessen your anxiety while developing strategies to live with those circumstances that are currently unchangeable.

DECEMBER—*metamorphosis*

Your current transitions are profound, although it will take months before you fully appreciate what's happened and completely understand your new direction.

2008 CALENDAR

AUGUST

TUESDAY 5 ★ Take baby steps through the 6th

WEDNESDAY 13 ★ Look on the bright side to find potential in current situations

FRIDAY 15 ★ **SUPER NOVA DAYS** Take a journey of the soul through the 17th

SATURDAY 23 ★ Social norms frustrate you through the 24th

WEDNESDAY 27 ★ A critical disclosure now will prevent confusion

SEPTEMBER

THURSDAY 4 ★ The mission is not impossible, just sustain common sense

SUNDAY 7 ★ **SUPER NOVA DAYS** Play it cool through the 9th

FRIDAY 12 ★ An unpredictable storm clears the air of negativity

SATURDAY 20 ★ Find a spiritual solution to worldly problems through the 22nd

OCTOBER

SUNDAY 5 ★ You want to talk, talk, talk...just know when to stop

FRIDAY 10 ★ Keep your feet on stable ground through the 11th

TUESDAY 14 ★ Fun and games bring out your inner child through the 18th

SUNDAY 26 ★ **SUPER NOVA DAYS** You hit a turning point by the 28th

NOVEMBER

SATURDAY 1 ★ Don't push too hard for change through the 4th

MONDAY 10 ★ **SUPER NOVA DAYS** See life's infinite possibilities through the 13th

SUNDAY 16 ★ Ask before initiating controversial discussions

FRIDAY 21 ★ A window of opportunity appears through the 23rd

DECEMBER

MONDAY 1 ★ Receive your just rewards, but beware of overindulging

WEDNESDAY 10 ★ **SUPER NOVA DAYS** Don't withhold emotions through the 12th

MONDAY 15 ★ Patience is a virtue. Don't try to force an issue

WEDNESDAY 24 ★ Take the time to organize your life through the 26th

SATURDAY 27 ★ Let go of dreamy illusions as you ring out the old year

SAGITTARIUS OVERVIEW

The dynamic activity of your ruling planet, Jupiter, could make this an extraordinary year. Wise and generous Jupiter joins Neptune, the planet of spirituality and faith, on May 27, July 10, and December 21, opening your heart and mind to an inspiring vision of your future. **Your imagination grows, your spirit soars, and a greater awareness of the meaning of life nourishes your hunger for spiritual understanding.** Jupiter also conjuncts Chiron the Wounded Healer on May 23, July 22, and December 7, adding another layer of sensitivity and compassion to this memorable period of your life. Vulnerability can become a gift now, rather than a burden or source of embarrassment. The tenderness of your heart and the flexibility of your mind allow you discoveries that you couldn't make with intellect alone. **What you're seeing could appear to be beyond your reach, but it's not.** Jupiter, Neptune, and Chiron are present in your 3rd House of Immediate Environment, allowing you to perceive the many blessings in your daily life and reminding you that you *can* turn dreams into reality.

The heightened stimulation of Jupiter, Neptune, and Chiron in your 3rd House of Learning is likely to intensify your interest in sharing new ideas with others. Expressing yourself creatively through writing or teaching can be especially rewarding now. However, you may have intuitive experiences or psychic perceptions that aren't easily put into words and some people you know might not be open to such unconventional ideas. **Finding less literal forms of communication such as art, music, or dance may prove more satisfying**—these connect directly to the profound inspiration you're feeling. Letting go of one form of telling your story and replacing it with a new one may result from a Solar Eclipse in your 3rd House of Communication on January 26. A conjunction to the eclipse from visionary Jupiter empowers you to broaden your perspective and gives you the enthusiasm to effectively present it to others.

Staying on course professionally might be a challenge this year as Saturn, the planet of responsibility, passes through your 10th House of Career and opposes rebellious Uranus in your 4th House of Home and Family. Face-offs on February 5 and September 15—the second and third in a series of five that began in November 2008 and finishes in July 2010—divide you between your job obligations and an urge for personal freedom. These planetary struggles can make it difficult to concentrate on your career, perhaps even signaling that difficulties at home require your close attention. Ideally, strategic Saturn helps you chart a new course in your life that brings more excitement to your work, including the possibility of starting your own business. If you don't have that option, however, **make sure to take as many breaks from your responsibilities as you can to avoid burning out** or blowing up and making an impulsive move you could regret.

REWIND AND RESTART

Vivacious Venus turns retrograde this year on March 6, setting the tone for your relationships. This shift in the planet of love's direction, while always important, is especially significant now because it occurs in your 5th House of Romance, suggesting a major reevaluation of your heart's desires and the best strategy to attain them. Rein in your impulses, even if it seems tedious. What may be enjoyable in the moment might not produce the enduring satisfaction you seek. When Venus turns direct on April 18, you may have resolved a critical issue, freeing you to move in a more rewarding direction. A new approach to partnership opens the door for you to enjoy greater intimacy without feeling smothered thanks to a Solar Eclipse on July 21. This event in touchy Cancer falls in your 8th House of Deep Sharing, which usually indicates separation. Surprising Uranus makes a creative trine to the eclipse, however, reviving a fading relationship or helping you make new connections where closeness and freedom can coexist.

LOOK BEFORE YOU LEAP

Your patience with handling seemingly minor details may be critical to professional success this year, for exacting Saturn in Virgo is in your 10th House of Career until October 29. Sharpening the tools of your trade can maintain your interest in your job and even prepare you for a promotion. Saturn's opposition to restless Uranus on February 5 and September 10, though, builds tension in the workplace. An unreasonable boss or unruly underlings can spark your desire to make a radical change, yet an impulsive reaction is unlikely to be a long-term solution. Think things through carefully to provide a solid foundation for an unconventional idea or to be bold in managing your professional life. And be sure to create a place to land before you make a leap.

ROCKY RIDE

Stable Saturn, the ruler of your 2nd House of Resources, opposes eccentric Uranus on February 5 and September 15, setting the stage for fluctuations in income. Don't worry too much about these financial ups and downs, though—they can point to possible breakthroughs in developing new skills and earning more money. Misinformation may seem costly when a Lunar Eclipse in controlling Capricorn falls in your 2nd House on July 7. However, Capricorn's ruling planet, Saturn, forms a supportive trine to this Full Moon, providing maturity and guidance to show you a safe way out of a scary economic situation.

 INTUITIVE MEDICINE

The optimistic and forward-looking nature of your fiery sign sometimes leaves you less than sensitive to your own well-being. This year Jupiter, the ruling planet of your 1st House of Physicality, tracks closely with impressionable Neptune and healing Chiron to heighten awareness of your health and vitality. You needn't be frightened by mysterious symptoms—but you shouldn't ignore them, either. You're probably fine, but you are learning to tune in and listen more carefully to the state of your body. Working with subtle methods such as homeopathy, energetic healing, prayer, and meditation will make you more aware of the connections among mind, body, and spirit. A key period for self-care is the Mercury retrograde cycle of May 6–30, which hangs up in your 6th House of Health and Habits. Refining your patterns of diet and exercise, as well as reducing stress, can help resolve nagging issues.

 DIVINE DESIGN

Your living space may turn into a sacred environment this year as the two rulers of your 4th House of Home and Family, Jupiter and Neptune, conjoin. A return to the religious traditions of your childhood is possible, although you'll probably blend them with elements from other cultures. This pair of inspiring planets in intellectual Aquarius provides you with a cooler perspective to help untangle emotional knots from your past and within your present household. Progressive and shocking Uranus is also in your 4th House, spurring you to experiment with redecorating—or perhaps precipitating an unexpected relocation out of sheer boredom.

PRINCIPLES INTO PRACTICE

Life's greatest adventures and finest learning opportunities can pop up any-
where this year. You don't need to travel to the ends of the Earth to find won-
drous things with Jupiter, the Cosmic Guru, in your 3rd House of Immediate
Environment. Education without direct application has little value now. Higher
truths are not abstract concepts to be considered in principle, but concrete
ideas to be experienced in fact. You may see patterns of learning or plans for a
trip altered on February 9 with a Lunar Eclipse in your 9th House of Travel and
Higher Education. This event in prideful Leo is a reminder that you don't need
to keep up appearances if you decide it's time to change course.

 ## TRUTH IN THE SHADOWS

Complex issues such as fear, desire, and power may arise to challenge your
faith this year. Deep, dark Pluto, the ruler of your 12th House of Spirituality, is
making a long passage through your 2nd House of Self-Worth to make them
even more obvious. Matters may come to a head when demanding Saturn
squares Pluto on November 15. Facing your basest instincts without shame
allows you to clearly recognize where you can cut them loose and where to
take something of value from this emotional land of shadows.

RICK & JEFF'S TIP FOR THE YEAR:
You Are Not Alone

You can create a magical map to the future this year that takes your life beyond the boundaries separating spirit and matter. To do so, however, you must discern the difference between distracting fantasies and true inspiration. You have access to sources of intelligence that far exceed your experiences thus far. Listening with your heart and soul, as well as your mind, can plug you into a network of higher consciousness that reveals how the patterns of your individual life are woven into the fabric of the collective human story.

JANUARY

MIXED MESSAGES

Your mental gears may be turning in two directions this month as your ruling planet, Jupiter, expands your vision while data- and detail-oriented Mercury trips you up on the small stuff. Jupiter enters futuristic Aquarius in your intellectual 3rd House on **January 5** for a one-year stay that could make you more curious about life than ever. Your interest even in subjects that never attracted you before is piqued, and you're excited to share your knowledge. Yet Mercury's retrograde on **January 11** can slow you down with missed connections, faulty information, and communication breakdowns. Do your research carefully and double-check facts before making important statements. Delaying presentations until Mercury turns direct on **February 1** might be prudent. A sensitive individual may challenge you to be more responsive on **January 10** when the Full Moon in emotional Cancer falls in your 8th House of Intimacy. Thankfully, a creative trine to the Moon from radical Uranus reveals ways that you can get closer without losing your independence.

The Aquarius New Moon on **January 26** is a Solar Eclipse in your 3rd House of Information, creating yet another impediment to getting your message across now. Buoyant Jupiter is conjunct this Sun-Moon conjunction in strong-minded Aquarius, which can pump you up with a sense of certainty that may be ill founded. Your confidence runs high, but there are obstacles ahead that you'll want to meet with a bit more self-restraint. Jupiter forms a tense semisquare with reckless Uranus on **January 27**, speeding you up, then an equally stressful sesquisquare with restrictive Saturn on **January 30**, slowing you down. Finding a comfortable rhythm or the right proportion between risk and safety may be tricky, so it's best to avoid making dramatic moves or major decisions.

> **KEEP IN MIND THIS MONTH**
>
> *Turn your excitement inward by learning all you can now, rather than dissipating your energy interacting too much with others.*

KEY DATES

JANUARY 5–6 ★ *ahead of your time*

You're challenged to find the patience for routine tasks on **January 5**, when agile Mercury semisquares electric Uranus to stir up your restlessness. Yet others are unlikely to match your need for speed or catch on to your unconventional ideas. In any case, impulsive actions could lead to mistakes and wasted time with assertive Mars sliding into a semisquare with slippery Neptune on **January 6**. Forcing issues may only push you farther off course. Your desire to escape reality is understandable, so take some time to fantasize, if you can. The riches of your imagination might not be practical now, but ideas born from it can pay off in the future.

JANUARY 17-18 ★ *wake-up call*

Another snappy Mercury-Uranus semisquare prompts unorthodox thinking and unusual conversations on **January 17**, but it can also lead to an abrupt break in communications. Still, retrograde Mercury's passage over sagacious Jupiter on **January 18** brings a generosity of spirit that creates enough space to talk about conflicting beliefs in an open-minded way. Over-explaining yourself, though, may add more confusion than clarity. If you sense that you're not making headway, or don't understand where the other person is coming from, back off until you settle down emotionally; then start over in a cooler and calmer manner.

SUPER NOVA DAYS
JANUARY 21-24 ★ *all over the map*

You're feeling indulgent on **January 21** when sweet Venus semisquares expansive Jupiter. While pleasure is certainly desirable, you could find yourself spending or eating too much, as well as overestimating someone's worth. Venus and Mars, the planetary lovers, align with excitable Uranus in your 4th House of Roots on **January 22**, motivating you to make sudden changes at home. The sense of adventure continues with a Sun-Jupiter conjunction on **January 24** that can make everything in your life seem bigger. However, you may not be able to control the outcome of events. A constructive Mars-Saturn trine adds stability, but the Sun's spiky sesquisquare to Uranus ensures surprises. A sexy Venus-Mars sextile is another vote for fun, yet stern Saturn's opposition to Venus may leave you with feelings of rejection.

JANUARY 26-27 ★ *blast of brilliance*

You could experience major revelations about your life with the Solar Eclipse conjunct Jupiter on **January 26**. What you see clearly, though, may be quite different from what others perceive. An argumentative Mercury-Mars conjunction on **January 27** reminds you to present your ideas gently if you hope to avoid conflict. Jupiter's sesquisquare to Uranus will bring more lightning strikes of awareness, turning yesterday's truth into today's old news. Allow plenty of time for these brainstorms to settle before you take action.

FEBRUARY

INNER FAITH

Changing perspectives can bring you renewed hope this month. Mercury, the information planet, turns direct on **February 1** to put projects back on track and free up communication. Its shift to forward gear in your 2nd House of Resources could generate money-making opportunities and a clearer picture of your long-range financial goals. To maximize your return, though, be sure your pragmatism is stronger than your pride. The messenger planet's presence in earthy Capricorn rewards ambition backed up by strategic planning. Additionally, the Full Moon in ego-centered Leo on **February 9** is a Lunar Eclipse in your 9th House of Big Ideas that may require you to let go of beliefs not serving your current needs. It can feel great to be right, of course, but not when it's more about saving face than effectively managing your life.

The long-standing opposition between authoritative Saturn and rule-breaking Uranus returns on **February 5**, forming tense squares to your Sun. You can feel pulled between your responsibilities and the call of freedom, but fortunately you don't have to make a definitive choice immediately. This is just another chance to weigh the importance of security against your need for stimulation. Learning as much as you can about your own limitations now will lead to wiser decisions in the future.

You may shift to a more contemplative mood when the Sun enters intuitive Pisces in your 4th House of Home and Family on **February 18**. Redirecting some of your attention from the outer world toward personal needs can restore your faith in yourself and those closest to you. You may be touched by a profound revelation on **February 24** as the New Moon in spiritual Pisces plants seeds of faith in your fertile 4th House of Roots.

> **KEEP IN MIND THIS MONTH**
>
> *The most important events are not always those visible to others, but the private ones that heal your heart and inspire hope in the future.*

KEY DATES
FEBRUARY 2–5 ★ *into the briar patch*

Passion heats up as sassy Venus fires into go-getter Aries and your 5th House of Romance on **February 2**. Fresh forms of fun and spontaneous self-expression can revitalize an old relationship or make it easier for you to start a new one. Expect unusual behavior on **February 4**, when active Mars enters quirky Aquarius. However, you may find your trust shaken when the Saturn-Uranus opposition on **February 5** intensifies the conflict between commitment and freedom. It's hard to feel comfortable with personal matters when socially sensitive Venus forms diffi-cult aspects with the Sun and manipulative Pluto. Don't dodge awkward conversa-tions that evoke unpleasant feelings—facing scary issues is a key to emotional growth and future relationship success.

FEBRUARY 11–13 ★ *loose cannon*

Impulsive actions or careless words can trigger accidents or arguments when pushy Mars clashes with Saturn on **February 11**, then with Uranus on **February 12**. Your frustration may lead to a sudden release of energy that you find challenging to control. A conjunction of spacey Neptune with the Sun blurs the boundaries of authority and individual responsibility. While this should fuel your imagination, it also represents a dangerous potential lack of judgment. Fortunately, protection arrives on **February 13** as benevolent Jupiter joins the Moon's North Node and a wise and generous individual gives you valuable guidance.

SUPER NOVA DAYS
FEBRUARY 16–18 ★ *irresistible you*

You'll enjoy favorable reactions from others while having a lot of fun on **February 16** as magnetic Venus creates a favorable sextile with enthusiastic Jupiter. Your zest grows as energetic Mars joins Jupiter on **February 17**, making this an ideal period to take the initiative in personal or professional matters. Your original ideas and obvious passion for what you're doing make it tough for anyone to refuse you now. On **February 18**, Venus and Mars, planetary lovers, align in a smart sextile, showcasing your charm, enhancing your attractiveness, and demonstrating your creative skills. The Sun's entry into gentle Pisces, which can indicate shyness, balances your high-powered personality with a healthy dose of sensitivity.

FEBRUARY 24 ★ *receptive audience*

You don't have to shout to be heard today, because people will listen when you talk. Chatty Mercury joins your ruling planet, Jupiter, empowering you with words of wisdom that motivate others to pay attention. You have the facts to back up your beliefs and the big-picture perspective that gives data meaning, which is excellent for teaching or selling. You could, however, overwhelm yourself or others with too much information. Being selective in your presentation is more effective than presenting everything you know.

MARCH

RETURN TO THE HEART

Matters of the heart take a lead role this month with a great deal of activity in your 5th House of Romance, Children, and Creativity. The key event occurs on **March 6**: Venus, the planet of love, turns retrograde in the 5th House. Her backward cycle through **April 18** is an opportunity for you to review the ways in which you give and receive pleasure. If you have a partner, it's time to relight the flame that brought you together initially; if you're single, consider changing how you pursue romance. Reconnecting with old creative interests and the joys of parenthood can revive relationships that have lost their luster. Your attention turns to work and matters of daily routine with a Full Moon in practical Virgo on **March 10**. You may feel daunted to keep up with both your job and your regular tasks as stressful Saturn conjuncts this Full Moon in your 10th House of Career and Responsibility. Maintaining order and discipline is difficult with erratic Uranus opposite the Full Moon. If you can adapt quickly to changing conditions, however, you can follow the rules when it's possible—and make up your own when it's not.

The Sun enters spontaneous Aries on **March 20**, marking the Spring Equinox and illuminating your 5th House of Play. Communicative Mercury also enters this house on **March 25**, generating more ideas for self-expression and creativity.

Recreation and romance receive another boost with the New Moon in excitable Aries on **March 26**. It's best to temper your impulsiveness, however: Venus is still retrograde and Pluto, the planet of exclusivity, makes a threatening square to the New Moon. Be selective in where you give your heart and how you spend your playtime.

> **KEEP IN MIND THIS MONTH**
>
> *There are so many opportunities for delight; you don't need to jump at the first one that catches your eye.*

KEY DATES
MARCH 5–8 ★ *psychic radar*

Your intuition is on target on **March 5** when intellectual Mercury joins mystical Neptune in your 3rd House of Communication. Still, it can take some patience to translate this awareness into language that others can understand. Assertive Mars joins compassionate Neptune on **March 8**, giving you a gentle touch that's helpful for feeling your way through a delicate situation. An opposition between the Sun and unforgiving Saturn, though, doesn't leave much room for error. Your instinctive approach might not be appreciated by a rigid individual who requires a specific plan of action.

MARCH 10-12 ★ *saving grace*

You find calm in the middle of tension on **March 10**. The stressful Full Moon in critical Virgo could create headaches at work that make you want to run for the hills— but pleasant moments of escape are offered, too, as lucky Jupiter sweetly sextiles Venus. Your innate ability to find humor in a tense situation provides relief for you and your colleagues. The Sun's conjunction with volatile Uranus in your 4th House of Home and Family on **March 12** can stimulate new adventures—or threaten peace and tranquility. A restructuring of rules may fulfill your need for change.

SUPER NOVA DAYS
MARCH 22-23 ★ *heart of the matter*

Watch out for restless rumblings on the home front with a high-frequency Mercury-Uranus conjunction on **March 22** that can turn ordinary events into chaotic experiences. Try to get a grip before things get too crazy, because a challenging semisquare between the Sun and excessive Jupiter can turn small issues into major ones. A super-sensitive semisquare between Venus and Neptune increases vulnerability in relationships, further complicating matters. The first in a series of awkward quincunxes between optimistic Jupiter and pessimistic Saturn is yet another reminder to act cautiously now. Finding just the right balance between future vision and present reality is a theme that will repeat with this aspect on **August 19** and **February 5, 2010**. The situation intensifies when the willful Sun squares unyielding Pluto on **March 23**. Ideally, this will take you to the core of the matter, eliminating distractions and allowing you to work precisely where you can be most effective.

MARCH 27 ★ *consider both sides now*

Differences of opinion grow overdramatic today as articulate Mercury and potent Pluto form tough semisquares with self-righteous Jupiter. Yet emotions are tender with delicate Venus conjunct the Sun. Strength of conviction is important, of course, but not if it causes you to harden your position instead of keeping an open mind. Understanding both sides of an issue makes you more skillful at presenting yours.

APRIL

SYSTEMS MANAGEMENT

Taking care of your health and maintaining your regular routine require more attention than usual this month. These activities, associated with your 6th House of Habits, are emphasized by mental Mercury's entry into sensible Taurus on **April 9**. The importance of these practical issues is reinforced when the Sun enters your 6th House on **April 22**, followed by the Taurus New Moon on **April 24**. Fun will not disappear entirely, thankfully, but maintenance work takes priority now over adventure. Attending to the systems that make your life work effectively is always easier when it's preventive. Ideally, you can take pleasure in refining your work skills and developing healthier habits. Taurus is a sign of stubbornness and sensuality, which means you're often resistant to making necessary adjustments unless you're enjoying the process.

Look for action on the romantic front later this month when Venus, the planet of attraction, backs into imaginative Pisces on **April 11** and then ends her retrograde period on **April 17**. Passionate Mars races into Aries and your 5th House of Love and Creativity on **April 22**, intensifying desires and increasing your willingness to express your feelings openly. Venus then enters spontaneous Aries, joining her consort Mars in your 5th House on **April 24**, putting you in hot pursuit of romance and creative expression. This dynamic pair in fellow fire sign Aries adds spice to your life and inspires you with a sense of innocence and discovery. The potential for turning fresh ideas into useful projects is supported by the Sun's presence in earthy Taurus. Sparks of excitement, mixed with patience and fueled by the right resources, can warm your life for years to come.

> **KEEP IN MIND THIS MONTH**
>
> *Don't overlook the details: Getting the little things right allows great things to happen.*

KEY DATES

SUPER NOVA DAYS
APRIL 1–4 ★ *attitude adjustment*

Foolishness is possible when pleasure-seeking Venus forms an unreliable semisquare with opulent Jupiter on **April 1**, skewing your judgment. Be cautious with your spending—overestimating the value of an object or individual can be costly. Prepare to make adjustments on **April 3**, when Venus crosses paths with exacting Pluto. Modest expectations prevent resentment and disappointment in relationships. A clear picture emerges and communication skills soar with an intelligent sextile between Mercury and Jupiter on **April 4**. Precision is essential as active Mars opposes strict Saturn, which frustrates careless moves but rewards well-planned ones with positive results.

APRIL 10 ★ *the power of brevity*
You're ready to make a great impression, with your confidence high and your enthusiasm, infectious. The willful Sun forms a silver-tongued sextile with outgoing Jupiter that helps you sell your ideas and inspire others. Don't go overboard with information to make your point: Being strong but subtle is more powerful than pouring it on too thick.

APRIL 15 ★ *state of emergency*
Staying cool while it feels like there's a volcano exploding inside challenges you today. An impatient and intense conjunction of energetic Mars and nervous Uranus in your 4th House of Roots can produce a surprise at home and tempt you to act without considering the long-term consequences. Fortunately, a broader view is offered by a compassionate Sun-Neptune sextile, which can attune you to others' needs despite your sense of urgency. Instead of blindly striking out against authority or struggling solo, you can see where your interests intersect with those of a group, ensuring a more responsible expression of your desires.

APRIL 21–24 ★ *sugar and spice*
A sexy Venus-Mars conjunction on **April 21** provokes the playful side of your personality into creativity and flirtatiousness. You may be at ease teasing people, but can be surprisingly thin-skinned if others do the same to you. A tougher and more combative side of you emerges with macho Mars's entry into Aries on **April 22**, breaking down the door of your 5th House of Fun and infusing you with the courage to act in bold and different ways. Talkative Mercury's square with bountiful Jupiter can send ideas pouring through your mind and out of your mouth. While you could overwhelm others with words, your capacity to handle tons of incoming data is also great. Vivacious Venus joins the party in your 5th House with her return to fiery Aries on **April 24**, kicking creativity into an even higher gear and turning your charm up to full volume.

MAY

SPIRIT WORLD

Spiritual influences weave through the down-to-earth realities of daily life—including your personal relationships—to give greater meaning to this month. The super-conjunction of confident Jupiter, inspirational Neptune, and healing Chiron begins on **May 23–27** to return in July and December of this year. The union of these planets of higher wisdom in your 3rd House of Information of the connection makes you aware of all living things, stirring desires to learn about new and different subjects and heightening your ability to share your ideas with clarity and conviction. However, an intellectual contrast starts on **May 7** when Mercury, the messenger planet, goes retrograde in your 7th House of Relationships. This backward turn may require you to review plans with partners, colleagues, and friends to make sure that you're still on the same page until Mercury starts moving forward again on **May 30**.

On **May 9**, secrets and metaphysical matters are awakened by the Full Moon in complex Scorpio in your 12th House of Spiritual Mystery, drawing your attention away from the ordinary and directing it toward the deepest parts of your soul. A supportive sextile from stabilizing Saturn to the Full Moon allows you to take what you find in the realms of imagination and apply it in realistic ways. You gain a fresh angle on connecting with others on **May 24** with the New Moon in versatile Gemini in your 7th House of Partnerships. This conjunction of the Sun and Moon can give you a more flexible and nonjudgmental attitude about others and help you attract intriguing individuals who motivate you personally and professionally.

> **KEEP IN MIND THIS MONTH**
>
> *Take time away from your tasks for periods of reflection. The most important work you do now may be private and behind the scenes.*

KEY DATES

MAY 4–7 ★ *sweet escape*

You're all fired up on **May 4** when energetic Mars makes an excitable semisquare to overly optimistic Jupiter. A tendency to push too hard or take on too much can get you in trouble. Tame your desire to go all-out by first figuring out how to fit everything into your schedule. Mercury's retrograde period starting on **May 7** is another reason to temporarily lower your expectations so you can catch up on unfinished business. Mars forms a semisquare to idealistic Neptune that can distract you from your duties as you pursue delicious fantasies. An escape from reality can recharge your spirit as long as it doesn't waste time or create more pressure later on.

SUPER NOVA DAYS
MAY 14-17 ★ *relax and enjoy*

A shopping spree can tempt you with sweet delights of desire on **May 14** as sensual Venus semisquares avaricious Jupiter. The love planet's semisquare to diffusive Neptune on **May 15** and the Sun's misguided squares to Jupiter and Neptune on **May 16–17** continue this theme of more is better. It's fun to stop counting calories, ignore your budget, or be unrealistic in romance. The heart needs its days of freedom when no cost is too high to pay for pleasure. As long as you can do it without breaking the bank or making promises you can't keep, a little excess is unavoidable . . . and might even be good for you.

MAY 20-21 ★ *rapid response*

Bright ideas and captivating people stimulate you as the Sun enters curious Gemini and your 7th House of Relationships on **May 20**. Retrograde Mercury's stressful square with opinionated Jupiter, though, may bring an overload of information or exaggeration that doesn't build trust. If partners seem less reliable during the coming month, try adapting to changes instead of resisting them. Fortunately, a brilliant Mercury-Uranus sextile on **May 21** can provide clever answers and unexpected insights, allowing you to quickly correct your current course.

MAY 26-27 ★ *magic carpet ride*

This could be a magical period when you stretch the boundaries that limit your world. Assertive Mars in your creative 5th House forms cooperative sextiles with philosophical Jupiter on **May 26** and otherworldly Neptune on **May 27**, bestowing intuitive guidance when you need it most. Trust your ability to make spontaneous adjustments, even in pressure-filled situations. The faith you have in yourself empowers you to conquer fears, overcome obstacles, and inspire others. Putting your faith into action encourages you to pursue your dreams without slowing down to justify every move you make or having to prove that you're always right.

JUNE

IT'S YOUR CHOICE

Accountability is a key theme this month. Serious Saturn forms a hard square to the flamboyant Sagittarius Full Moon on **June 7**, perhaps reminding you to slow down and make sure you're fulfilling your present obligations before adding any more to your schedule. Another reason to reconsider plans for expansion or escape arrives on **June 15** when your ruling planet, Jupiter, turns retrograde. Its backward cycle, lasting until **October 12**, doesn't stop you from advancing your interests, but indicates how important it is to assimilate new activities and experiences at a more leisurely pace. If you push hard and fast without a plan, your chances of success will be greatly reduced. Distractions can readily throw you off track when verbose Mercury in Gemini enters your 7th House of Partnerships on **June 13**. This should enhance communication in relationships and refresh your thinking with a wide variety of ideas. Too many choices, however, can counteract the benefits of curiosity.

The Sun's entry into introspective Cancer on **June 21** forces you to boil down your options to the individuals and activities that serve you best. This Summer Solstice occurs in your 8th House of Deep Sharing, which can increase intimacy and strengthen financial partnerships. Yet it's clear that someone or something has to go if you are to make the most of these opportunities. You may feel compelled to respond to your partner's needs, provoking an emotional reaction. Still, purging Pluto's conjunction to the New Moon in sentimental Cancer on **June 22** is a reminder to narrow your focus, shut out extraneous demands, and concentrate your resources where they're most needed.

> **KEEP IN MIND THIS MONTH**
>
> *Taking smaller bites out of life helps you truly appreciate the little things and digest your experiences comfortably.*

KEY DATES

JUNE 2 ★ *satisfaction guaranteed*

A delicious Venus-Jupiter sextile sends pleasure and rewards your way. Friends are ready for fun, and colleagues may give you the recognition you deserve. Connecting with an altruistic individual through a group or organization rooted in a desire to change the world might also provide an opening to a personal relationship for you now.

SUPER NOVA DAY

JUNE 7 ★ *building your tomorrow*

The Full Moon in extroverted Sagittarius usually pours more fuel on the fire of your enthusiasm, but today you may feel a bit blue. Restrictive Saturn's tense square to the Full Moon can put work in the way of play and burden you with complex tasks that stand between you and your desires. Yet Saturn also represents the chance to make things real—if you're willing to put in the required effort. If you're frustrated with your life, making a real commitment to self-improvement is bound to give you more control over the shape of your future.

JUNE 10 ★ *too much information*

A flood of information can be more than you want to handle as detail-crazed Mercury is stretched by a square from loud Jupiter. If someone is talking too much or making outlandish claims, do your best to filter out the excess and focus on the key points. But if you're the one dealing out the data, avoid boring your audience with extraneous facts. Channel your mental intensity into the power, passion, and precision of your ideas to make the most impact.

JUNE 17 ★ *exceptional connection*

Relationships are rocking with three major aspects from the creative Sun in your 7th House of Others. Shared dreams grow with trines to imaginative Neptune and broad-minded Jupiter, encouraging you to initiate a new alliance or expand a current one. However, a destabilizing square from the Sun to unpredictable Uranus adds an element of uncertainty that can suddenly alter the course of a partnership. Excitement is likely, yet reliability may remain elusive until these burgeoning plans are tested over time.

JUNE 22-23 ★ *cut to the chase*

Expect to be highly efficient on the job and dealing with routine matters on **June 22**, when graceful Venus and energetic Mars create productive trines with methodical Saturn from your 6th House of Work and Service. Cutting out the fat can be the key to success as the New Moon in nostalgic Cancer opposes surgical Pluto. Addition by subtraction continues to be a useful guiding principle on **June 23** with tense aspects from Pluto, the planet of elimination, to the Sun, Venus, and Mars.

JULY

MONEY TALKS

Financial issues are highlighted by two eclipses this month. On **July 7**, a Lunar Eclipse in ambitious Capricorn falls in your 2nd House of Resources, concentrating your efforts on bringing up the bottom line. This isn't a one-shot deal, though, but rather a long-term project to increase your material worth that requires a sustained effort. Disciplined Saturn, Capricorn's ruling planet, forms a favorable trine to this Full Moon, giving you the staying power you need to upgrade your skills, develop a business plan, and get yourself into the kind of mental and physical shape it takes to make it to the next level. The role of your partners in both material and personal matters may be altered with a Solar Eclipse in self-protective Cancer that falls in your 8th House of Shared Resources on **July 21**. Fortunately, if you experience a loss, you're likely to make a rapid recovery—inventive Uranus's creative trine to this receptive Cancer New Moon quickly unveils unexpected ways to reach your goals.

Relationships are invigorated on **July 5** when attractive Venus enters your 7th House of Partnerships. Passionate Mars follows on **July 11,** multiplying your chances to connect with different kinds of people as well as revitalizing your present relation-ships. These socially skilled planets are moving into a public area of your chart, which should make it easier for you to gain attention with the freshness of your ideas and liveliness of your personality. Expansive Jupiter's conjunctions with fantastic Neptune on **July 10** and healing Chiron on **July 22** refresh the inspiration awakened by their initial contacts in May to continue supporting your faith in your dreams.

> **KEEP IN MIND THIS MONTH**
>
> *A slow and sure-footed approach up the mountain of success is much more likely to take you to the top than an impatient one.*

KEY DATES

JULY 1–3 ★ *insatiable appetite*

A normally reliable colleague could lure you astray on **July 1** due to an idealistic Venus-Neptune square that confuses illusion with reality. Temper your generosity with a dash of skepticism to bring a dream down to earth. Sharp thinking, though, helps you make quick adjustments as Mercury trines Jupiter. Still, an excessive Venus-Jupiter square on **July 2** can overinflate optimism that's further encouraged by a misaligned Sun-Jupiter sesquisquare on **July 3**. Being hopeful is fine as long as you look carefully before you leap.

JULY 6–8 ★ *out of bounds*

Action-planet Mars stubbornly pushes along in Taurus, but he can lead to a poor judgment with his squares to spacey Neptune and smug Jupiter on **July 6**. If you're swamped at work or overloaded with mundane tasks, though, Mars's smart sextile to unorthodox Uranus on **July 7** could surprise you with a brilliant shortcut. Staying within reasonable bounds is an issue on **July 8**, when a messy Mercury-Jupiter sesquisquare can turn molehills into mountains. The cure is to keep it simple now.

JULY 15–17 ★ *double-check your facts*

Take what others tell you with a big grain of salt on **July 15** as Mercury slips on a squishy quincunx with Jupiter and confuses opinions with facts. The Sun slides into the same aspect with zealous Jupiter on **July 17** before Mercury strides into proud Leo and your 9th House of Big Ideas. This gives you the ability to sell your ideas with so much passion that you may overlook important details.

JULY 21–22 ★ *tread lightly*

Tender feelings reveal vulnerability in relationships on **July 21** with a tense square between sweet Venus and disapproving Saturn. If you feel unappreciated, speak up about what you want. Express yourself gently, though—others are probably just as sensitive now. The tide turns with the Sun's entry into bighearted Leo on **July 22**, lifting your spirit as you look ahead to your next big adventure with growing confidence.

SUPER NOVA DAYS
JULY 27–30 ★ *your cup runneth over*

The arms of love can open wide with a prosperous Venus-Jupiter trine on **July 27**. Romance is a real possibility, but other forms of pleasure are also present. You're ready to give even more than you receive, earning much-deserved admiration. Venus's trine with psychic Neptune on **July 28** could make sharing feel like a spiritual experience, as you co-create magic with an imaginative partner. Delight could be interrupted, though, when unruly Uranus squares Venus, challenging you to remain steady in suddenly changing circumstances. A Mercury-Jupiter opposition on **July 30** might bring secrets out into the open or enable you to have a deeply intimate conversation.

AUGUST

WORK AND WANDERLUST

No matter how much fun others are having, your attention is drawn to work this month. Mental Mercury points in a professional direction by entering task-oriented Virgo in your 10th House of Career on **August 2**. Sharpening your skills and managing details with greater care will enhance your job status. The Sun's ingress into methodical Virgo on **August 22** puts you in the spotlight, where you can shine by demonstrating competence, confidence, leadership, and self-discipline. If your vocation is unfulfilling, though, your discontent is likely to become more obvious. It's clear that you need intellectual stimulation when a Lunar Eclipse in airy Aquarius illuminates your 3rd House of Information on **August 5**. This Full Moon is supported by an assertive trine from Mars that strengthens your communication skills and helps you transform complex ideas into innovative actions.

An intense pattern of stop and then go, go, go starts on **August 10** when mobile Mars gets snagged in a restrictive square from Saturn. The speedy Aries Moon in your freewheeling 5th House urges you to drive forward against whatever's holding you back. It's best, though, to cool your jets and take a cautious approach until **August 13**, when Mars is freed by an exuberant trine from joyful Jupiter and followed by the Sun's opposition to this giant planet on **August 14**. This puts wind in your sails, giving you the ambition and energy to work and play with power and passion. Enthusiasm rises again as the New Moon in expressive Leo on **August 20** falls in your 9th House of Travel. This dramatic union of the Sun and Moon opposes the Jupiter-Chiron-Neptune super-conjunction, over-activating your powerful faith, vivid imagination, and extreme taste for adventure.

> **KEEP IN MIND THIS MONTH**
>
> *Make a clear distinction between work and play so that you can be tightly focused on one and loose and relaxed with the other.*

KEY DATES

AUGUST 7 ★ *simple pleasures*

You may feel caught between your desire to play and the need to stay home and catch up on rest. It's definitely great to have a little fun, but with pleasure-seeking Venus overextended by Jupiter, limit how much time or money you spend so there's something left in reserve. There are very sweet experiences you can have in a low-key way that allow you to taste life's goodness without wearing yourself out.

AUGUST 13–14 ★ *energy to spare*

You could be chafing against the demands of your job and other mundane duties on **August 13**, when energetic Mars aligns in an enthusiastic trine with boisterous Jupiter. Your naturally restless nature is extra-hungry for adventure, so find a way to satisfy your body with physical movement or your mind with a big idea. If you believe it now, you can sell it, and when you commit you're ready to give it your all. That can-do attitude grows on **August 14** as the Sun opposes Jupiter, which should bring you encouragement from allies and the support you need to advance your interests. Still, a bit of caution is smart—individuals may be tempted to make promises to you that they just can't keep.

SUPER NOVA DAYS
AUGUST 17–18 ★ *fire to burn*

You have the force to overcome almost any obstacle on **August 17**, but directing it effectively takes concentration and discipline. A Sun-Mars sextile and Mars's trine to Neptune provide all the rocket fuel you need, yet mental Mercury can stall with a conjunction to stiff Saturn and slip off track with a quincunx to Jupiter. The Sun's opposition to nebulous Neptune inspires you, but may also attract unreliable partners. You need a very tight plan of attack and a focus sharp enough to avoid distractions if you want to maximize your potential now. There's no slowing down on **August 18** as a red-hot Mars-Uranus alignment electrifies your world. The urge to do things in your own way may overpower your willingness to compromise. Wounded feelings can provoke angry responses, reminding you to soothe tense situations to avoid conflict.

AUGUST 25–26 ★ *war and peace*

Sharp words, impatience, and edginess can be stirred by verbal Mercury's tense square to Mars on **August 25**. Mercury's square with pungent Pluto on **August 26**, along with Mars's opposition, can bring frustration to the surface. Addressing repressed feelings is healthy if you can accompany it with good-natured humor and a generous spirit. Happily, loving Venus entering heartfelt Leo can be a source of these essential ingredients.

SEPTEMBER

QUESTION AUTHORITY

Your on-and-off struggle between freedom and responsibility is triggered again this month by a Saturn-Uranus opposition that began in November 2008. These giants face off on **September 15** for the third time, and are sparked by the transiting Sun on **September 17** and the Virgo New Moon on **September 18.** The combination can incite conflict with authority figures and a desire to escape your responsibilities. Don't let fatigue or frustration dictate your actions—they can keep you from achieving your goals. A well-planned path to freedom, on the other hand, can provide you the excitement promised by wild Uranus without destroying Saturn's sense of order. Emotions are likely to sway you with the Full Moon in super-sensitive Pisces falling in your 4th House of Home and Family on **September 4.** Active Mars's cooperative trine to the Full Moon from your 8th House of Shared Resources suggests that you should clarify your expectations in close relationships to keep them growing.

Communications may become muddled when thoughtful Mercury turns retrograde on **September 7.** Its reversal in your 11th House of Groups through **September 29** increases the likelihood of confusion when you work with others; counter this by checking facts with friends and colleagues more frequently. Diplomatic Venus is in your 10th House of Career **September 20–October 14,** enhancing your reputation as you combine efficiency and grace on the job. On **September 22,** the Sun enters objective Libra—Venus's airy home sign—and marks the Fall Equinox. This solar force in your sociable 11th House allows you to demonstrate your abilities as a fair-minded leader, but may also attract supportive individuals who encourage your dreams directly or through the example of their actions.

> ### KEEP IN MIND THIS MONTH
>
> *Finding ways to meet your obligations while still allocating enough free time for yourself reduces frustration and helps you avoid explosive situations.*

KEY DATES

SEPTEMBER 1–3 ★ *when push comes to shove*

Your mind may be racing to absorb new ideas or to share a ton of information that isn't easily assimilated. A mentally active Mercury-Jupiter sesquisquare on **September 1** represents too much data, whether you're sending or receiving. Active Mars's sesquisquare with Jupiter on **September 2** feeds this trend and may also coerce anger to the surface. On **September 3**, mouthy Mercury clashes in a square with Mars that produces impulsive speech and aggressive words. Apply the intensity you're feeling to an intellectually challenging task, rather than arguing, to use your force productively.

SEPTEMBER 11 ★ *unbridled pleasure*
Your social life should be sweet today, for romantic Venus is opposing lucky Jupiter while the Moon lights up your 7th House of Partnerships. It's time to let loose and enjoy yourself with just enough excess to have fun without going too far. Opportunities to expand a current relationship or meet someone new abound. However, promises made now are more likely to represent best-case scenarios than solid commitments. High hopes should inspire you, but only time and effort will make them real.

SEPTEMBER 17 ★ *riders on the storm*
You could feel overwhelmed with pressure at work on this high-energy day. The Moon in your 10th House of Career and Responsibility lays additional weight on your shoulders. But the Sun's opposition to rebellious Uranus and conjunction with dutiful Saturn might put you right in the middle of someone else's battle or find you torn between sticking to a plan and breaking away to try something new. A grumpy Mercury-Pluto square adds to the intensity with words readily used as weapons. If you can concentrate, however, this aspect allows you to see past the surface noise, avoid distractions, and discover a key piece of information that places you in a powerful position.

SUPER NOVA DAYS
SEPTEMBER 22–25 ★ *leader of the pack*
The Sun enters peaceable Libra on **September 22**, yet its tense square with paranoid Pluto on **September 23** can undermine the trusting nature of this sign. Power struggles could replace understanding as you battle for control. An electrifying opposition between Mercury and Uranus, meantime, can stretch nerves tight. This pair ignites brilliant ideas but is equally likely to provoke disputes. Protective Mars's misaligned quincunx with Jupiter might also stimulate reactions that tend to separate opposing parties. A potential upside can be the clarity you gain by bringing hidden issues to light and coming up with original ways to address them. Still, a Sun-Jupiter sesquisquare on **September 25** is more inclined to over-exaggerate opinions than seek consensus. Exercise tolerance and self-control; you'll need them.

OCTOBER

THE JOY OF LIFE

Opportunities for spontaneous creativity and play are everywhere this month. The Full Moon in enterprising Aries on **October 4** falls in your 5th House of Romance and Self-Expression to punch up your fiery personality with even more sparkle than usual. It's time to take the initiative to bring more love and fun into your life for your own delight, as well as for the amusement of others. Your jovial mood receives a boost when your ruling planet, Jupiter, turns direct on **October 12**. The forward shift of the planet of optimism can help you take exciting projects off the back burner and start working on them again. Messenger Mercury enters social Libra on **October 9**, followed by magnetic Venus on **October 14**, opening your mind and heart to new people, while dynamic Mars moves into playful Leo on **October 16** to underscore the rising tide of joy in your life.

Expect group activities to take center stage on **October 18** with a friendly Libra New Moon in your 11th House of Teamwork. A constructive trine to this Sun-Moon conjunction from the spiritual super-conjunction of Jupiter, Neptune, and Chiron instills you with faith and idealism, motivating you to make positive changes in the world. A community of friends and colleagues urge you to pursue your dreams, yet you may notice a shift when the Sun enters mysterious Scorpio and your 12th House of Secrets on **October 23**. Your boundless sense of camaraderie may be tempered by a greater need for privacy and time to sort through issues you don't want to discuss with just anyone. Rebalancing relationships is a long-term project that starts when karmic Saturn enters Libra on **October 29**.

KEEP IN MIND THIS MONTH

Follow your natural instincts to be impulsive in the pursuit of pleasure. Partake in the joy that's abundantly available at this moment.

KEY DATES

OCTOBER 4 ★ *off target*

Your judgment suffers when value-conscious Venus creates an irritating quincunx with excessive Jupiter. You may play or spend too much or, perhaps, give people credit they don't deserve. Additionally, mental Mercury and energetic Mars form quincunxes with fuzzy Neptune that can blur your perceptions and misdirect your actions. It's best to avoid making any decisions with long-term consequences right now.

OCTOBER 10-12 ⋆ *a turn for the better*
A buoyant Sun-Jupiter trine on **October 10** enhances your ability to sell or teach—but thanks to a Mercury-Pluto square, only pinpoint accuracy will get your message across to listeners who don't share your enthusiasm. You may overload others with information as data-loving Mercury sesquisquares Jupiter on **October 11**. Be discerning in what you say and what you absorb; remember, extraneous details add clutter instead of clarity. Jupiter's direct turn on **October 12** kicks your sense of adventure into overdrive. Celebrate this positive shift by exploring new physical, mental, or emotional territory.

OCTOBER 14-16 ⋆ *let go and let grow*
The sweetness of Venus's entry into sensual Libra on **October 14** promises happier relationships, but there's some emptying to be done before you can refill your cup with love. A tense square between Venus and dark Pluto on **October 15** suggests that discontent may be brewing. Difficult issues arise, threatening harmony but also bringing emotional truth to light. Obsessive individuals and unhealthy habits block the way to future fulfillment. You cannot ignore differences with those closest to you without paying a higher price down the road. The rewards of letting go may appear as early as **October 16** when Mars marches heroically into Leo, igniting your 9th House of Future Vision.

OCTOBER 20 ⋆ *20/20 vision*
Your communication skills are keen as the mental planets Mercury and Jupiter align in a favorable trine. A clear sense of balance between minor details and major principles allows you to see patterns that make sense of situations previously difficult to understand. Use your current sharp perceptions and persuasive speech to describe complex matters with precision and motivate others to act.

OCTOBER 28-29 ⋆ *fire in the belly*
A luscious Venus-Jupiter trine on **October 28** enhances your awareness of your many blessings. This creative aspect between astrology's traditional benefics— lucky planets—attracts fascinating people who appreciate your social grace and generosity. Nevertheless, you might want to enjoy yourself at home where you can control the environment. On **October 29**, a tense Sun-Mars square heats up passion that can produce lust, conflict, or reckless behavior. Physical activity and plunging into a cause you believe in are healthy ways to express this energy.

NOVEMBER

WORK IN PROGRESS

Service, spirit, and self-awareness are three major areas of interest this month. The Full Moon in practical Taurus on **November 2** falls in your 6th House of Health and Work, drawing your attention to the ways you meet your daily obligations. This is an opportunity to develop positive habits that ensure your physical well-being and also increase your value on the job. Patience is essential—slow-moving Taurus will reward you for persistence in pursuit of excellence. Magical Neptune goes direct on **November 4**, a subtle shift that can turn spiritual ideals into action in the days and even weeks ahead. Magnetic Venus enters Scorpio and your 12th House of Soul Consciousness on **November 7**, another call to connect with higher meaning and dimensions beyond the ordinary. You may find yourself attracted to metaphysical subjects and individuals who help you open portals to other worlds, placing a greater focus on your inner life than does your usual whirl of adventure and activity.

A powerful transformation begins to take root when structuring Saturn squares potent Pluto on **November 15** in the first of three aspects that will return on **January 31** and **August 21, 2010**. These planetary heavyweights align in your 11th House of Teamwork and 2nd House of Resources, challenging you to clarify the boundaries between supporting your community and attending to your own needs. The New Moon in mysterious Scorpio on **November 16** is squared by the super-conjunction of Jupiter, Neptune, and Chiron, shining awareness and forgiveness into the dark corners of doubt and fear. This illuminating influence is reinforced when the Sun enters uplifting Sagittarius on **November 21**, pouring some new energy into your 1st House of Personality. Your self-confidence overflows and your intentions take on razor sharpness as you celebrate the season of your birth.

KEEP IN MIND THIS MONTH

Plunging into the darkness of doubt is not a step toward failure, but a journey to the heart of desire that will ultimately fuel your rebirth.

KEY DATES

NOVEMBER 1–2 ⋆ *untested waters*

Arguments are possible with talkative Mercury in a tight square with aggressive Mars on **November 1**. Choose your words carefully to avoid conflict. The edginess continues on **November 2** as erratic Uranus forms hard aspects with Mercury, Venus, and Mars. It's easy to be bored with the old routine, so explore new styles and unconventional methods on your own, without expecting others to follow your lead.

SUPER NOVA DAYS
NOVEMBER 8-10 ★ *less is more*
When it comes to ideas, more is not necessarily better as a Mercury-Jupiter square on **November 8** can overload you with data or provoke exaggerated claims. Filter out the noise of promises that won't be kept and facts that will only fuzz your brain. Overexpansion continues on **November 10**, when the willful Sun squares Jupiter. Embarrassing secrets might be spilled, but sometimes these awkward moments can relieve pressure—if you're not too judgmental. Avoid standing on the sidelines and criticizing others when the real aim is to broaden your own vision by letting go of an unrealistic goal and replacing it with one that you can reach.

NOVEMBER 15-16 ★ *look deep within*
Your current sense of buoyancy may mask the underground rumblings of a powerful Saturn-Pluto square on **November 15**. The wheels of change are slowly turning below the surface while chatty Mercury soars into Sagittarius to lift your spirits and turn your attention toward the future. An imaginative Sun-Neptune square feeds your fantasies—but can also allow you to deny unpleasant realities right in front of you. The New Moon in relentless Scorpio on **November 16** is best used to explore the deep recesses of your psyche; clean out old ghosts, uncover hidden desires, and prepare the way for further growth.

NOVEMBER 21-23 ★ *life of the party*
The Sun energizes you as it enters good-natured Sagittarius on **November 21**— an excellent time for making strong impressions. However, an indulgent square between Venus and Jupiter on **November 23** can lead to overspending, overeating, or outrageous promises. Common sense and self-restraint are the best preventive measures.

NOVEMBER 29 ★ *fast learner*
A mentally sharp sextile between detail-oriented Mercury and visionary Jupiter gives you a clear picture that's ideal for solving problems. You're able to communicate complicated matters in simple terms by breaking down big issues into easily understood pieces. Your capacity to learn is excellent now as you adeptly assimilate new concepts—no matter how strange they may appear at first.

DECEMBER

TIME TO SHINE

This month starts out with a bang but ends on a more serious note. Flirty Venus enters friendly Sagittarius on **December 1** to warm your 1st House of Personality with style and charm. Uranus the Awakener's direct turn on the same day cranks up the excitement with unexpected encounters. More social activity is promised by the Full Moon in chatty Gemini on **December 2** in your 7th House of Partnerships. Fortunately, stabilizing Saturn's trine helps you organize your busy schedule, which could otherwise get out of hand now. The last of the intuitive super-conjunctions between Jupiter, Chiron, and Neptune occur on **December 7 and December 21**, adding a spiritual dimension to the season and heightening your awareness of the magic that surrounds you every day. This inspirational trio in your 3rd House of Communication makes you a valuable source of stimulating ideas for everyone around you. The ability to give advice without coming across as a know-it-all will be appreciated and admired.

There should be added bounce in your step with the New Moon in thrill-seeking Sagittarius on **December 16**. This energy-rich event pumps up your personality with even more charisma than usual, but a forceful square to this Sun-Moon conjunction from independent Uranus suggests that moderation may be needed. Your enthusiasm has you moving at speeds that others can't match, and your interest in exploring unconventional activities may upset traditionalists. Assertive Mars turns retrograde on **December 20**, the Sun enters conservative Capricorn on **December 21**, and Mercury goes retrograde on **December 26**, each of which tends to further slow you down. The Full Moon in cautious Cancer on **December 31** is a Lunar Eclipse squared by Saturn, another warning sign that safety is more important than speed now.

> **KEEP IN MIND THIS MONTH**
>
> *Focusing on your long-term goals in the midst of the holiday season helps you turn its gifts into lasting treasures.*

KEY DATES

DECEMBER 1 ★ *laughter is contagious*

Treat this workday as an occasion to play, for vivacious Venus's entry into cavalier Sagittarius is bound to make your personality shine. A fresh approach to your appearance and attitude makes you more attractive in personal and professional matters. Attending to your own happiness is your first priority. When you feel good, everyone around you benefits from the joy you so generously share.

DECEMBER 9–10 ★ *critical thinking*
You can handle difficult people skillfully on **December 9** as diplomatic Venus forms a creative quintile with wise Jupiter. Trust your instincts for recognizing what others need—as well as your own desires—to derive satisfaction from a challenging situation. Your perceptions may be less accurate on **December 10**, when Mercury and Jupiter align in a stressful semisquare. You could give a minor detail more weight than you should, leave out a critical fact, or buy into someone's bogus story. Listen with an open mind, but apply a little skepticism to maintain balance.

DECEMBER 14 ★ *larger than life*
Your opinions are loud and you could be itching for action as the expressive power of the Sun is multiplied by an explosive square to Uranus and a sassy sextile to Jupiter. This can be a difficult time to settle down thanks to all the excitement you feel. Pushing back against an authority figure isn't smart, though, since a small dispute could quickly get out of hand. Instead, seek to vent your overabundant energy and imagination in playful and constructive ways.

SUPER NOVA DAYS
DECEMBER 17–21 ★ *put your talents to work*
You can charm the birds out of the trees with a delightful Venus-Mars trine on **December 17**. Even the most obstinate individuals see things your way when you use the persuasive power of your personality. You turn work into play, bringing lightness and joy to serious situations. On **December 19**, a nervous Venus-Uranus square may complicate relationships and provoke sudden changes of plans. There may be tension in the air with aggressive Mars turning retrograde on **December 20**. Happily, good cheer is present with a Venus-Jupiter sextile, putting you in a forgiving mood. However, the Sun's shift into responsible Capricorn on **December 21**, the Winter Solstice, may focus your mind on practical matters, including your ambitions for the future.

DECEMBER 31 ★ *reshaping relationships*
Ending the year with a Lunar Eclipse in your 8th House of Shared Resources is a not-so-gentle reminder to consider the cost of your relationships. Stern Saturn's unflinching square to this Full Moon in protective Cancer urges you to set sentiment aside if you want to make a significant partnership more meaningful.

CAPRICORN

CAPRICORN

2008 SUMMARY

There is no time to settle for less in your life, either personally or professionally. If the weight of responsibility or drudgery of routine is too great, you may need to force a break to find some breathing room and reassess your situation. You sense that there is so much more to be gained from life; Pluto's message is that letting go is a prerequisite for satisfaction.

AUGUST—*settling accounts*

You can't control the course of a relationship all by yourself—not even with compromise and communication. It takes two to make a partnership work.

SEPTEMBER—*on-the-job diplomacy*

Responding to the needs and desires of other people will help you enlist their cooperation—as well as promoting your own ambitions.

OCTOBER—*building a team*

Even if your efforts have failed in the past, you can do things differently this time and enjoy a rousing success.

NOVEMBER—*irrepressible change*

It is reasonable to feel secure in some ways and uncertain in others. You don't need to be a superhero to achieve your goals.

DECEMBER—*season of renewal*

Instead of just working hard out of habit, stop and consolidate your resources for a climb to heights you've never reached before.

2008 CALENDAR

AUGUST

WEDNESDAY 6 ★ Give yourself permission to be imaginative and unconventional

WEDNESDAY 13 ★ **SUPER NOVA DAYS** Flexibility is key through the 16th

FRIDAY 22 ★ A change of tune requires a sense of humor through the 23rd

WEDNESDAY 27 ★ Intense communications reveal the naked truth through the 30th

SEPTEMBER

WEDNESDAY 3 ★ Slow down to take stock—your future is calling now

SUNDAY 7 ★ **SUPER NOVA DAYS** Make only strategic commitments through the 8th

SUNDAY 14 ★ You adapt skillfully to unexpected news through the 15th

SATURDAY 20 ★ Work out tough and tender issues through the 22nd

SUNDAY 28 ★ Stay relaxed to have fun when social plans are up in the air

OCTOBER

SUNDAY 5 ★ **SUPER NOVA DAYS** Return to reason through the 7th

SATURDAY 11 ★ Let go of the past to heal even the harshest of wounds

FRIDAY 17 ★ Focus your quest inward through the 18th

SATURDAY 25 ★ Tension passes quickly when it's out in the open

TUESDAY 28 ★ Trust your feelings when words aren't clear through the 30th

NOVEMBER

MONDAY 3 ★ Wait out the storm of shifting feelings through the 4th

TUESDAY 11 ★ **SUPER NOVA DAYS** Trust your head over your heart through the 13th

SUNDAY 16 ★ Vision, logic, and originality empower your ideas

FRIDAY 21 ★ Your awareness is a guiding light to your objective

THURSDAY 27 ★ Practice restraint when you want to blab through the 29th

DECEMBER

FRIDAY 5 ★ Find a creative way to apply your ideas through the 6th

FRIDAY 12 ★ **SUPER NOVA DAY** Stay flexible when feelings fluctuate

MONDAY 15 ★ Integrity is essential, saving time and effort in the long run

SUNDAY 21 ★ Give all or nothing in relationships through the 22nd

SATURDAY 27 ★ Learn when to lead and follow in the dance of love

CAPRICORN OVERVIEW

It's time to settle down and stabilize your life after all the changes of last year, when opportunity knocked at your door. Jupiter, the planet of growth, moved through your sign, widening your horizons and showing you a new direction to success. This year expansive Jupiter visits your 2nd House of Self-Worth, offering you a chance to increase your bank account while also improving your self-esteem. Although it can be easy to acquire material possessions now, be careful about declaring what you want, for you might end up with more than you need—yet still lack happiness. **There's no reason to deprive yourself of physical pleasure, but make sure your metaphysical needs are also being addressed.** Jupiter is part of a rare triple planet conjunction occurring this year that includes Chiron the Healer and Neptune the Dreamer, peaking on May 23–27, July 10–22, and throughout the month of December. Letting go of blame and forgiving those who have wronged you in the past are parts of a process that will build your self-assurance.

Practical Saturn in your 9th House of Big Ideas is there to remind you that you cannot climb every mountain you see, however ambitious and determined you may feel. Grandiose thinking is exciting, but it can get in the way of accomplishing real goals by diluting your energy with unrealizable dreams. One of the basic planetary themes of the year—a struggle between responsible planning and spontaneous self-expression—is emphasized when restrictive Saturn opposes unruly Uranus on February 5 and September 15. This entire year and these dates, in particular, are turning points in a larger cycle that began on November 4, 2008, and completes on July 26, 2010. You can't get away with denying your true ambitions, for your suppressed feelings will leak into other areas of your life and wreak havoc. **Examining your unexpressed emotions can make the difference between a year of great accomplishment and one of frustration and failure.** You'll begin to see where your life falls on this spectrum when Saturn first squares evolutionary Pluto on November 15, the opening volley in a period of dynamic personal and career change that affects you through August 21, 2010. Pluto is still in the beginning of a long-term visit to your sign that will gradually change much of your life as you now know it. Eliminating nonessential activities can make the ongoing transformation easier, while holding on to old ideas of success will make it much more difficult.

A Full Moon Eclipse in calculating Capricorn on July 7 can reveal the flaws in your current plan for advancement. Rather than being a setback, though, this can show you exactly what you need to do to clear the path in front of you. Support from taskmaster Saturn suggests that **you can persevere and reach your goals as long as you're willing to learn from past mistakes**.

NOT SO FAST

Impulsively jumping into a new relationship isn't your usual style, but this isn't a typical year when it comes to matters of the heart. You're inclined to express your feelings without considering their impact as sensual Venus spends most of February–May in spontaneous Aries. Nevertheless, you'd be wise to monitor your involvement so you don't jeopardize your stability, especially as Venus retrogrades through your 4th House of Security from March 3 through April 17. Make the most of Venus's harmonious trines to indulgent Jupiter on July 26 and October 28 by revealing your romantic desires selectively, leaving others more likely to respond with enthusiasm.

WORKING YOUR WAY TO THE TOP

Your key planet, Saturn, tells the story this year as it moves through your 9th House of Future Vision, giving you a very pragmatic view of your road to success. Fortunately, you aren't easily discouraged, even if rapid growth through 2008—when excessive Jupiter was in your ambitious sign—raised your expectations to unrealistic levels. Now, however, you must reinforce your professional foundation and prepare for Saturn's entry into fair-minded Libra and your 10th House of Career on October 29. This is the beginning of a karmic phase that will last a couple of years—a time when you will be justly compensated for your previous efforts.

MORE THAN MONEY

Your 2nd House of Income is the stage for an action-packed year as it hosts benevolent Jupiter, blessing you with opportunities to accumulate wealth. In May, July, and December, Jupiter joins Chiron and Neptune—two planets related to nonmaterial concerns—so it's important to measure your prosperity in relationship to your spiritual well-being. Of course it's not enough to envision the universe as abundant; you must follow through with a solid action plan. Cautious risk taking will be rewarded as austere Saturn and radical Uranus—the co-rulers of your resourceful 2nd House—engage in a tug-of-war that intensifies on February 5 and September 15. Be willing to take a chance, but remember that this destabilizing aspect will continue to bring surprising twists and turns to financial matters through July 26, 2010.

THE POWER OF POSITIVE THINKING

Quicksilver Mercury rules your 6th House of Health, leaving your body very susceptible to the influence of your mind. Mercury's retrograde turn on January 11 in your 2nd House of Self-Worth marks the beginning of a three-week phase when you can strengthen your health by building your self-esteem. Activities that make you feel better about yourself also bolster your immune system. Improve your diet and exercise regimen when Mercury enters your 6th House on April 30. Career obligations could drain your energy and compromise your health when Mercury turns retrograde in your 10th House of Public Responsibility on September 7. Practice mind-body relaxation techniques such as yoga or meditation—anything that takes your mind off the stress at work.

LESS IS MORE

You can be rather reckless when it comes to domestic matters because energetic Mars rules your 4th House of Home and Family. The warrior planet's conjunctions with confident Jupiter on February 17 and with dreamy Neptune on March 8 are in futuristic Aquarius and fall in your 2nd House of Resources, inspiring you to upgrade your residence—possibly with the latest digital technology. Be careful, though, for your dreams could outpace reality, tempting you to turn a little project into a major money pit. Mars's opposition to Saturn on April 4 can be a reality check, requiring you to settle for less. This theme of overextension is again brought to the forefront when Mars turns retrograde on December 20, just before he makes contact with extravagant Jupiter. It's better to temper your high hopes with realism than to face disillusionment.

SURPRISING RESULTS

Serious Saturn forces you to fulfill your responsibilities before you escape to faraway places as it moves through your 9th House of Voyages. Physical or metaphysical journeys may be postponed this year—or they may demand extra planning. Whether you're taking a vacation to the South Seas or enrolling in a course at a local college, it's going to take work to make it happen. Saturn will reward your extra effort, though, making your wildest dreams possible—especially when breakthrough Uranus opposes it on February 5 and September 15. Your travels may not go as expected, but if you can let go of control you may see some wonderful surprises.

 ## DREAM WEAVER

Imagination and intuition are your greatest assets this year as the spiritual super-conjunction of Jupiter, Chiron, and Neptune shines the light of consciousness into your 2nd House of Values. Jupiter's conjunctions with healing Chiron on May 23, July 22, and December 7 are times to work on humility as a way to spiritual growth. Let your visions of an ideal future define your path when Jupiter conjuncts psychic Neptune on May 27, July 10, and December 21. It's easy to get distracted by the material side of the 2nd House, but remember that your most important possession is you. Allowing time to delve into your core beliefs can have practical ramifications, for acting in congruence with your spirit smoothes the flow of energy in everything you do.

RICK & JEFF'S TIP FOR THE YEAR:
Limit Your Choices

If you can dream it, then it's possible. Yes, you must manage whatever problems surface throughout the year—but you now have a rare opportunity to build the framework for tomorrow by imagining your ideal future. Naturally, your fantasies won't manifest exactly as you see them in your mind's eye, but this isn't a time to get hung up on the details. You must, however, narrow your focus. Don't spread yourself too thin; prune your opportunities so you have the resources to make the most of the ones that can truly change your life.

JANUARY

CONSERVATION OF ENERGY

You have what it takes to make things happen this month, and with persistence you'll be able to deliver the goods—even if a project takes longer than you expect. You receive an energetic boost from assertive Mars in your sign all month, helping you sustain a steady pace of production without wearing yourself out. Nevertheless, you should expect some complications during Mercury's retrograde phase from **January 11 through February 1**, and especially when the trickster planet backs into cautious Capricorn on **January 21**. Loose ends merely alert you not to relax just yet; the job isn't as finished as you think. Still, impulsive actions that aren't part of your plan will only waste valuable time and effort. Resist shortcuts, therefore, when erratic Uranus is activated by the Sun on **January 9**, by creative Venus and Mars on **January 22**, and by overconfident Jupiter on **January 27**. Additionally, the struggle between taking a risk and adopting a more conservative approach will slowly build as restrictive Saturn moves to oppose unconventional Uranus on **February 5**. Conceptual breakthroughs are possible and even valuable, but tempering your behavior will prevent you from burning out before you reach your goal.

> **KEEP IN MIND THIS MONTH**
>
> *Don't fall prey to your own enthusiasm or you'll exhaust yourself like the hare. To up your chances of winning, take the tortoise's slow and steady approach.*

The Sun is in ambitious Capricorn until **January 19**, adding power to everything you do. The super-sensitive Cancer Full Moon on **January 10**, though, opposes the Sun in your sign, flooding you with reminders to consider others' feelings, too. The quirky Aquarius New Moon on **January 26** is a Solar Eclipse in your 2nd House of Money, so be careful to avoid any "get rich quick" schemes presented to you at this time.

KEY DATES

JANUARY 3–5 ★ *beyond your comfort zone*

Loving Venus enters watery Pisces on **January 3** and is pushed over the edge of restraint by intense Pluto on **January 4**, releasing powerful emotions from deep within your subconscious. Your first reaction may be discomfort; nevertheless, you can have a transformative experience if you're willing to step beyond logic, because shocking Uranus zaps analytical Mercury and forceful Mars with insight on **January 5**.

JANUARY 9–11 ★ *be the change you seek*
Originality is your secret weapon when the Sun forms a supportive sextile with unorthodox Uranus on **January 9**. Your actions can be quite productive as the Sun then smoothly trines your key planet, Saturn, on **January 11**, stabilizing your long-term plans. The emotional Cancer Full Moon in your 7th House of Partners on **January 10** harmonizes with both Uranus and Saturn, suggesting that others will help you in unexpected ways rather than hindering your efforts. Don't be overly concerned if you need to alter your strategy or reconsider a recent decision when Mercury turns retrograde on **January 11**, temporarily slowing you down or throwing you off course.

SUPER NOVA DAYS
JANUARY 18–22 ★ *no risk, no gain*
Optimism overrules common sense when retrograde Mercury conjuncts buoyant Jupiter on **January 18** and the Sun on **January 20**. It's not enough to believe you're right; Mercury insists that you share what you know. But you're less sure of yourself on **January 21** when the communicator planet backs into somber Capricorn, prompting you to rethink your point of view. Your serious demeanor won't prevent you from taking a radical approach to problem solving on **January 22**, when assertive Mars sextiles brilliant Uranus. Fortunately, you have extra charisma and charm working, for sweet Venus is also aligning now with Uranus.

JANUARY 24 ★ *follow the signs*
The power of positive thought works in your favor when the Sun conjuncts bountiful Jupiter. But Venus and Mars align with responsible Saturn to give you the sensible guidance you desperately need—even if it's not what you want to hear. Your willingness to learn an important lesson today can make a big difference in the weeks ahead.

JANUARY 26–30 ★ *nervous nellie*
The high-frequency vibrations of the Aquarius Solar Eclipse on **January 26** can kick your energy out of whack. Jupiter's tense aspects to unstable Uranus on **January 27** and to inflexible Saturn on **January 30** encourage you to overreact one day, then fearfully withhold your intentions the next. Moderating extravagant or desperate behavior sooner rather than later can make your life easier in the end.

FEBRUARY

GREAT ESCAPE

When you make a promise, you deliver, for Capricorns typically take commitments very seriously. This month, however, you're in the midst of a long-term transition that sets irrepressible Uranus against dutiful Saturn, creating enough stress in your life that you're tempted to impulsively break out of a rut. Since Saturn is your key planet, its opposition to Uranus on **February 5** rattles the core of your being— a tense opposition between these slow-moving giants that first occurred on **November 4, 2008**, and will repeat on **September 15**. If you aren't happy in your current situation, this is an opportunity to alter the direction of your life—but real change will take time, because this alignment returns again next year. Nevertheless, the more you integrate your need for independence now, the easier the process will be later on. With Saturn in your 9th House of Future Vision, you must seriously consider your life's purpose and make a plan to accomplish it. Still, keep in mind that unpredictable Uranus will continue to shake things up, requiring you to adjust your tactics and perhaps even your goals.

Clever Mercury in your formidable sign turns direct on **February 1**, giving you the mental power you need to tackle complex issues. The dramatic Leo Full Moon Eclipse on **February 9** falls in your 8th House of Shared Resources and can highlight difficulties with money, forcing you to reassess your financial priorities. The compassionate Pisces New Moon on **February 24** is a turning point that can open channels of intuition, while Mercury's conjunction with broad-minded Jupiter the same day brushes away any doubts, enabling you to communicate your highest ideals clearly.

> **KEEP IN MIND THIS MONTH**
>
> *If you're tempted to run away from your responsibilities, remember that your real job is to improve your current life, not plan your escape.*

KEY DATES

FEBRUARY 2-5 ★ *shadows of the past*

Your spirits are lifted when loving Venus enters feisty Aries on **February 2** and assertive Mars enters futuristic Aquarius on **February 4**. But it's not easy for you to let go of the past when resistant Saturn is stressed by the opposition to erratic Uranus on **February 5**, agitating your fear of change. The emotional intensity can be overwhelming as Venus dynamically squares powerful Pluto, yet it's healthier to temporarily sink into the shadows than to avoid your unexpressed feelings.

FEBRUARY 9-12 ★ *a space for healing*
Life seems unsettled on **February 9** as the Lunar Eclipse in proud Leo opposes
Chiron the Wounded Healer and Neptune the Dreamer, blurring your sense of
reality and, perhaps, shaking your self-confidence. Forgiving someone who has
hurt you can diminish your attachment to the past and free you to move on, but
aggressive Mars's tense aspects to the lingering Saturn-Uranus opposition on
February 11–12 ignite your anger, even if there's no logical target for it. Guided
meditations or positive affirmations can lead you out of the negativity and into
a more spiritual frame of mind as the Sun conjuncts mystical Neptune on
February 12.

FEBRUARY 16-18 ★ *conspicuous consumption*
Everything feels possible to you as beautiful Venus creates a cooperative sextile
with overreaching Jupiter on **February 16**, followed by energetic Mars's conjunction with Jupiter on **February 17**. All this self-assuredness is great—but be careful
that your unbridled enthusiasm doesn't set the stage for trouble once you realize
what you've promised. Ride the wave of creativity offered by the Venus-Mars sextile
on **February 18**, the same day that the Sun slips into imaginative Pisces. But temper your excitement while staying aware of other people's feelings to make the most
of this opportune period.

FEBRUARY 27-28 ★ *uncontrollable passion*
You're running on adrenaline as quicksilver Mercury approaches a conjunction
with red-hot Mars in your 2nd House of Self-Esteem. You are ready to declare
your core values, even if you must aggressively defend your point of view. But
Mercury and Mars both form agitated semisquares to domineering Pluto on
February 27–28, making it hard for you to control your words. You can hit a blind
spot with a frustrating Mars-Saturn quincunx on **February 28**. Be prepared to
slow down and adjust your course of action instead of pushing straight ahead.
Going faster will cost you more time in the end if you're not flexible enough
to adapt to changing conditions.

MARCH

TWO STEPS FORWARD, ONE STEP BACK

This is a month of intense communication that begins with messenger Mercury conjuncting aggressive Mars on **March 1**, amplifying the power of your words. Take your time and learn your lessons well, especially when the Sun makes its annual opposition to judgmental Saturn, your ruling planet, on **March 8**. Still, the pace of your daily life will likely pick up when interactive Mercury enters your 3rd House of Immediate Environment on **March 8**, followed by go-getter Mars on **March 14**. Mercury's opposition to Saturn on **March 18** can present temporary obstacles as your best ideas run into strong resistance. Fortunately, the Sun's entry into spontaneous Aries at the Spring Equinox on **March 20**, followed by Mercury's conjunction to rebellious Uranus on **March 22**, will help you quickly get over your doubts. Still, expansive Jupiter's annoying quincunx to "hard to please" Saturn on **March 23** can make it difficult for you to know whether to be optimistic or pessimistic about your recent choices. This long-term cycle sits in the background all month, so don't put unnecessary pressure on yourself to figure out how you're doing now. This aspect recurs on **August 19** and **February 5, 2010**, and it could take you until then to get the perspective you need for a final judgment.

KEEP IN MIND THIS MONTH

Discouragement will plague you if you think you must reach your goals on schedule. Be gentle with yourself and others while allowing events to unfold naturally.

The critical Virgo Full Moon on **March 10** falls in your 9th House of Higher Truth, but its conjunction to Saturn reminds you of your shortcomings rather than your accomplishments. Mercury's entry into forward-thinking Aries on **March 25**, followed by the Aries Full Moon on **March 26**, can open an entirely new chapter in your life—but only if you have the courage to look ahead instead of focusing on the rearview mirror.

KEY DATES
MARCH 5-6 ★ *play it again, Sam*
Mercury joins psychic Neptune on **March 5**, increasing your intuition and enabling you to inspire others by sharing your visions. The forward movement of events, however, may be slowed when Venus turns retrograde on **March 6** in your 4th House of Foundations. Emotional satisfaction can be elusive as you review recent experiences. You can reinvigorate your love life by examining what you previously missed, instead of seeking satisfaction in something new.

MARCH 10-12 ★ *don't look back*

Although Saturn's sobering presence during the Full Moon in discerning Virgo on **March 10** could prevent you from going overboard, mental Mercury can nudge you beyond the limitation of language as it receives messages from your subconscious. The communication planet's supportive sextile to intense Pluto opens a data channel to your suppressed passions, overpowering your rational resistance. An extra boost of pleasure can bring an overdue smile to your face when delightful Venus aligns with jovial Jupiter on **March 11**. Let any lingering doubts fall away when the Sun conjuncts surprising Uranus in your 3rd House of Data Collection on **March 12**. Instead of worrying about what you should've done, do what you can in the present moment to make the most of what you now know.

MARCH 18-22 ★ *too much on your plate*

Thoughtful Mercury's tense opposition to stern Saturn on **March 18** can stop you in your tracks and show you where your logic has gone astray. Rigid thinking is a liability right now; use the fierce Mars-Pluto sextile on **March 19** to adjust your perspective rather than to defend an indefensible position. Fortunately, you can start anew at the Spring Equinox on **March 20**. Unorthodox ideas come quickly on **March 22**, when the lightning of a Mercury-Uranus conjunction blows your mind. Nevertheless, you have your work cut out for you—and the Jupiter-Saturn quincunx suggests that you cannot take shortcuts on your road to success.

SUPER NOVA DAYS
MARCH 26-30 ★ *resolute in the face of adversity*

Although the enthusiastic Aries New Moon in your 4th House of Home and Family on **March 26** can feel like a confirmation of your new direction, you may be forced to stand up to a powerful person when talkative Mercury forms a dynamic square with dark Lord Pluto on **March 27**. Be careful, for you can take things too far with self-righteous Jupiter halfway between Mercury and Pluto. It's challenging to maintain a healthy perspective when you feel your core beliefs are being attacked. Luckily, Mercury joins charming Venus and the Sun through **March 30** with just the right words to soothe everyone's nerves.

APRIL

STEADY CLIMB

Your primary challenge this month is to manage your need for independence without negatively impacting your domestic situation or jeopardizing your emotional security. And you could have a lot to handle now as reckless behavior runs rampant when a gathering of planets in impulsive Aries falls in your 4th House of Home and Family. You're uncharacteristically prone to talk before you think with Mercury in Aries until **April 9**. The Sun's visit to your 4th House through **April 19** shines even more light on your personal life and could temporarily shift the focus away from your career. Additionally, loving Venus is retrograde until **April 11**, circumventing your romantic drive; you'll have to wait for the right moment to ask for what you want. Reconsider your options while gathering more information when the love planet backs into your 3rd House of Data Collection on **April 11–24**. Don't get discouraged; you should begin to feel more hopeful as soon as Venus turns direct on **April 17**. Finally, physical Mars's entry into fiery Aries on **April 22** can boost your energy and tempt you to push yourself harder than ever. Extra effort is a good thing as long as you don't burn out before your work is done.

The even-keeled Libra Full Moon on **April 9** falls in your familiar 10th House of Career, but its opposition to the Sun in your private 4th House can uncomfortably stretch you between work and home. Luckily, easy aspects to propitious Jupiter suggest that you'll be able to juggle your dual responsibilities with grace. **April 24** marks a turning point when a sensual Taurus New Moon falls in your 5th House of Self-Expression, leading you into a more relaxing and playful stage.

> **KEEP IN MIND THIS MONTH**
>
> *Direct action may feel exhilarating, but patience will probably be more effective in the long run.*

KEY DATES

APRIL 2–5 ★ *fools rush in*

It's hard to find your groove when judgmental Saturn forms uncomfortable quincunxes with fast-talking Mercury on **April 2** and with the Sun on **April 5**. You say or do too much, requiring you to pull back and take another approach. Red-hot Mars opposes cold Saturn on **April 4**, stopping you in your tracks, especially if you're being too demanding. A dynamic square between sensual Venus and potent Pluto on **April 3** can overwhelm rationality by amplifying your romantic or sexual needs. Moderation combined with self-restraint is your best course in the current intensity.

APRIL 9–10 ★ *keep your options open*

Your emotional involvement at work increases with the socially conscious Libra Full Moon on **April 9**. Its smooth trine to generous Jupiter suggests that you're feeling better about yourself, prompted by a financial windfall or the recognition of your valuable contributions at work or at home. Still, you may be torn between taking care of your own needs and someone else's. Fortunately, a harmonious Sun-Jupiter sextile on **April 10** suggests a positive outcome to this dilemma, as long as you're open to learning something new.

APRIL 15–17 ★ *no place to hide*

Explosive feelings can suddenly turn a bucolic setting into a disaster area if you're too rigid to state your true intentions. A high-energy Mars-Uranus conjunction on **April 15** stresses you in unexpected ways. The more you try to prevent tension from coming to the surface, the more powerful the release. It's best to lean on the sensible Mercury-Saturn trine, but you don't need to wait until **April 17** when it's exact. Picking your words carefully to address your anxiety can be enough to settle your emotions and prevent additional upset.

SUPER NOVA DAYS
APRIL 23–26 ★ *constant gardener*

You can tap a deeper source of energy when the Sun trines passionate Pluto on **April 23**. The Capricorn-friendly New Moon in earthy Taurus on **April 24** reemphasizes the need for transformation, but this isn't only about what occurs today: You're planting a seed in the fertile soil of your subconscious that will take time to germinate. The New Moon's magical quintile to visionary Jupiter shows the power of your positive thinking, but an intense square from warrior Mars to Pluto on **April 26** can tempt you to get involved in an unnecessary battle with someone who may be trying to sabotage your good intentions. Don't allow your fear to rule your actions. Stay focused on your goals, not on doing battle with anyone who gets in your way.

MAY

FOLLOW YOUR DREAMS

Hopes of increasing your net worth multiply as a new wave of self-confidence tempts you to reach farther than ever before. Although this can positively affect your pocketbook, you could also talk yourself into spending more than usual, so be careful where you invest. Your optimism stems from bountiful Jupiter, healing Chiron, and imaginative Neptune as they coalesce into a triple planet super-conjunction on **May 23–27**. This slow-moving dance is a rare alignment that can brighten your world and elevate your self-esteem. You see yourself now through rose-colored glasses and may overestimate your capabilities or underestimate the resources required to complete a project. Reaching beyond your usual limits can be a thrilling experience, but extending your finances too far or promising more than you can deliver can have unfortunate consequences when this alignment recurs in July and December. Try not to get frustrated when your dreams slip away, for messenger Mercury turns retrograde on **May 7** to show you where your plans still need improvement, especially when the Sun and Mercury square the super-conjunction on **May 16–20**.

The passionate Scorpio Full Moon on **May 9** falls in your 11th House of Groups and Friends, indicating that you'd be wise to involve others in your current plans, even if this complicates your life and draws you into an emotional web of intrigue. The breezy Gemini New Moon on **May 24** highlights the contradiction between work and play, for it quincunxes relentless Pluto in ambitious Capricorn. Your tendency is to contract and act responsibly, but this New Moon reminds you to give yourself permission to relax and have some fun.

> **KEEP IN MIND THIS MONTH**
>
> *Indulging your daydreams and fantasies is not a wasteful pastime, especially if it motivates you to try something you've never experienced.*

KEY DATES

MAY 2–5 ★ *make love, not fear*

Don't be disconcerted by the feelings released when romantic Venus dynamically squares transformative Pluto on **May 2**; the emotional intensity calms on **May 5** with the Sun's smooth trine to realistic Saturn. Instead of avoiding vulnerability by acting tough, discuss your innermost fears to deepen intimacy with a current partner or establish the basis for sharing more of yourself in a new relationship.

MAY 11 ★ *hold your tongue*
Impetuous Mars in brash Aries is in your 4th House of Security, provoking you to react impulsively if you feel threatened. Your instinct is to strike back without considering the consequences. You'll create problems, however, if you lash out at the wrong target or apply too much force, for Mars forms a crunchy quincunx with authoritative Saturn today. Instead of fighting back, work off excess physical energy through healthy exercise first. Then you'll be able to have a productive encounter instead of one that escalates a misunderstanding.

MAY 16–17 ★ *the power of the present moment*
Your energy level is high, yet your actions may be blocked as the Sun in your 5th House of Self-Expression squares the powerful Jupiter-Chiron-Neptune super-conjunction on **May 16–17**. Luckily, you could experience a breakthrough, because the Sun also cooperatively sextiles radical Uranus on **May 16**. Karmic Saturn turns direct the same day, putting its weight behind your actions and assuring that your current decisions can endure the tests of time.

MAY 20 ★ *question, but don't doubt*
Your fantasies are challenged today by the practical realities of daily life. While your potential for success is great, logical Mercury—now retrograde in back-to-basics Taurus—squares blurry Neptune and extravagant Jupiter, unveiling sensible reasons to doubt yourself. And when Venus, the planet of love and money, slides into an irritating quincunx with restrictive Saturn, you may question the value of what you bring to any situation. Fortunately, the Sun's entry into versatile Gemini—combined with the upcoming Jupiter conjunctions—urges you to look at the possibilities rather than at your failures.

SUPER NOVA DAYS
MAY 27–31 ★ *at rainbow's end*
Joyful Jupiter's conjunction with intuitive Neptune on **May 27** can open your mind to an unlimited array of possibilities, and the Sun's magical quintile to unorthodox Uranus on **May 29** can overcome almost anything that stands between you and the fulfillment of your wishes. There's still a lot of work ahead, though, and Mercury's direct turn on **May 30**, combined with Mars's entry into dependable Taurus on **May 31**, reminds you to come back to earth to follow through on your plans.

JUNE

PLAYS WELL WITH OTHERS

Hardworking Saturn is your key planet, and it demands that ambitious Capricorns take life quite seriously. This month, however, you should be able to set aside ample time for fun and games as flirty Venus and animated Mars travel in tandem through your 5th House of Romance and Self-Expression. These cosmic lovers form rich trines to passionate Pluto on **June 3 and June 8**, deepening your feelings and awakening hidden desires. The generous Sagittarius Full Moon on **June 7**, however, falls in your 12th House of Secrets and Spirituality, so everything might not come out into the open just yet. You have the best of intentions for assisting others—but if they can't see your altruism, they may believe you have selfish reasons for helping. Don't let anyone's negative judgment keep you from doing good.

Although sexy Venus and Mars are very close to each other throughout the month, their creative conjunction is exact on **June 21**, making this the best moment to let your inner child out for an extended playtime. This is also the Summer Solstice—the day when the Sun enters nurturing Cancer and your 7th House of Relationships, illuminating other people's emotional needs. Fortunately, you can relax and enjoy yourself without avoiding responsibilities or letting anyone down, for Venus and Mars are anchored as they trine concrete Saturn on **June 22**. The nurturing Cancer New Moon, also on the **22nd**, reminds you that you can support those you love while still being true to yourself. This New Moon's opposition to resolute Pluto, though, suggests that you'll have to stand up for yourself if someone tries to marginalize your point of view.

> **KEEP IN MIND THIS MONTH**
>
> *You've earned the right to take some time off, so enjoy yourself without feeling guilty about what others might think.*

KEY DATES

JUNE 2-5 ★ *easy does it*

You tend to put a positive spin on your world as beautiful Venus cooperatively sextiles the imaginative Chiron-Neptune-Jupiter super-conjunction on **June 2**. Go ahead and ask for what you want—but be aware that assertive Mars's trine with controlling Pluto on **June 3** can raise the stakes by transforming your simple request into a forceful demand without you realizing what's happened. Tread lightly; if you've overextended yourself emotionally or financially, you could face a rude reality check when the Sun squares sobering Saturn on **June 5**. A gentle approach, combined with common sense, adds intimacy and meaning to a special relationship.

JUNE 7-10 ★ *better left unsaid*

The philosophical Sagittarius Full Moon on **June 7** is held in check by a restrictive square to Saturn. On the one hand, Venus's harmonious trine to Pluto reactivates the intensity of **June 3**; on the other, this moment is more about feeling the fullness of your emotions than about expressing them. You find it hard to explain what you truly want, for rational Mercury's stressful square to wounded Chiron, nebulous Neptune, and extroverted Jupiter on **June 9-10** can dissipate your thoughts and make you seem unfocused, especially if you don't know when to stop talking.

JUNE 11-15 ★ *romantic interlude*

Creatively expressing your desires fuels a new love affair or revitalizes a current relationship as physical Mars forms a charismatic quintile with the metaphysical Chiron-Neptune-Jupiter super-conjunction on **June 11-12**. Sweet Venus repeats this magical dance on **June 14-15**, tempting you to lay on the charm to get what you want. Fortunately, these magical quintiles are bolstered by a slowly culminating Venus-Mars conjunction in tactile Taurus, keeping your mind on sharing pleasure. Talkative Mercury's entry into interactive Gemini on **June 13** and its tense aspect to complex Pluto on **June 15**, however, suggest that too many words can diminish the power of your message.

SUPER NOVA DAY
JUNE 22 ★ *running a marathon*

You're intent on personal enjoyment on **June 22**, when Venus and Mars in your playful 5th House form smooth trines with self-disciplined Saturn. Thankfully, this gives you an unflappable sense of determination during an otherwise stressful New Moon opposite a powerhouse Pluto transit, which puts your emotions in direct conflict with someone else's. Avoid getting swept up in the urgency of the moment. Focusing on your long-term goals keeps you even-keeled during this dynamic time.

JUNE 26 ★ *keep an open mind*

Instead of stubbornly trying to hold on to an indefensible position, be flexible enough to learn from your previous mistakes. Analytical Mercury's square to authoritative Saturn can clarify a real difference of opinion. Don't avoid difficult discussions now, even if solutions are not readily forthcoming.

JULY

DÉJÀ VU

Opportunity knocks again this month as benevolent Jupiter retrogrades back over psychic Neptune and healing Chiron, tempting you to reach for the abundance you desire. Jupiter joined Neptune and Chiron to form a powerful super-conjunction on **May 23–27**. If you had a taste of a better life or started a significant project back then, you can now take it to the next level. If you were unwilling or even unable to extend beyond your present routine, you may get a second chance. Don't close off your dreams just because they seem unrealistic when Jupiter conjuncts Neptune on **July 10**. Judging yourself less harshly or forgiving someone else's hurtful behavior on **July 22** can clear the air of negativity and allow you to move forward.

The Capricorn Full Moon on **July 7**—a Lunar Eclipse—will flood your consciousness with powerful emotions. Luckily, it's harmoniously trine to stabilizing Saturn, giving you the skills and the common sense to integrate your own feelings with those of a close friend or partner. Although your relationship life may be more complex than you prefer now, you can set your heart on a destination and successfully figure out the best way to arrive there. The highly sensitized Cancer New Moon on **July 21** is a Solar Eclipse that can bring your unexpressed needs out into the open, changing the dynamics of a current partnership or suddenly presenting the possibility of a new one. Try not to be too critical, though, for sweet Venus's square to austere Saturn can temporarily cool off even the most passionate relationship.

KEEP IN MIND THIS MONTH

Even if a lucky break doesn't turn out to be all you want, pursuing it with gusto could teach you what you need to know for the next opportunity.

KEY DATES

JULY 1–2 ★ *analysis over intuition*

You're productive and able to motivate others to help you on **July 1**, when Mercury the Communicator in your 6th House of Work forms easy trines with the Jupiter-Chiron-Neptune super-conjunction in your 2nd House of Self-Worth. You would be feeling pretty good about yourself, but attractive Venus tensely squares this same trio of planets on **July 1–2**, tempting you to increase your self-esteem by overindulging your senses. Luckily, Venus receives a supportive jolt from electric Uranus on **July 2**, suggesting that taking a risk could bring satisfaction.

JULY 4–7 ★ *lost and found*
Someone questions your motives when inquisitive Mercury opposes dark Pluto on **July 4**. You probably won't be able to hold on to a grudge, for likable Venus slips into breezy Gemini on **July 5**. Still, your new lighthearted attitude isn't enough to calm your nerves when assertive Mars squares Jupiter, Chiron, and Neptune on **July 5–6**. You don't like being uncertain about your direction, yet the Full Moon Eclipse in calculating Capricorn on **July 7** is trine steady Saturn, enabling you to reset your compass and put yourself back on track if you get lost.

JULY 9–11 ★ *bring it down to earth*
You're clear about your intentions and express your feelings succinctly on **July 9–11**, when the Sun and Mercury in emotional Cancer cooperatively sextile mature Saturn. However, the powerful Jupiter-Neptune conjunction on **July 10** feeds your imagination's fantastic dreams. This can be a powerful combination: Your psychic powers are strong and your creative vision is unrestrained while your ability to communicate is highly focused.

SUPER NOVA DAYS
JULY 19–22 ★ *wild good chase*
Your key planet, Saturn, is under analytical attack from a tense Mercury semi-square on **July 19** and a sweet Venus square on **July 21**. Pessimism overpowers objectivity, making good news hard to find. The insecure Cancer New Moon Eclipse—also on the **21st**—encourages you to take the blame for whatever difficulties you face. Jupiter's conjunction with Chiron on **July 22** lures you with salvation and has you chasing rainbows, only to be frustrated by the lack of treasure. Letting go of previous expectations helps you recover from disappointment and frustration with grace.

JULY 26–31 ★ *follow your bliss*
You're in a familiar pattern—but with the tables turned. The month began with Mercury trines and Venus squares to the spiritual trio of planets congregating in your 2nd House of Money and Resources. Now rich Venus harmoniously trines Jupiter, Chiron, and Neptune on **July 26–28** while mental Mercury struggles in opposition to the super-conjunction on **July 30–31**. Following your heart's desires will bring more happiness at the moment than doing what is logical.

AUGUST

MIDCOURSE CORRECTION

The summer provides you with a healthy reality check, enabling you to integrate some of the most positive changes that have already begun to unfold in your life. You can take a fresh look at whatever opportunities you're considering, which are less overwhelming now as retrograde Jupiter in your 2nd House of Personal Resources backs away from the hopeful Chiron-Neptune conjunction throughout the month. Expansive Jupiter forms an irritable quincunx with repressive Saturn on **August 19**. This is a long-lasting aspect that can have you doubting yourself even when everything appears to be going well. The progressive Aquarius Full Moon Eclipse on **August 5** falls in your 2nd House and can tilt your fortune one way or another, bringing a financial surprise or an unexpected hitch to a current plan. But this Full Moon is opposite the generous Leo Sun in your 8th House of Shared Resources, signaling that it would be smart to work closely in business with a partner who has a stake in your current activities.

Unfortunately, your inclination might be to go overboard with enthusiasm just to demonstrate your competence when the Sun opposes excessive Jupiter on **August 14**, but its opposition to Chiron on **August 16** reminds you of your limitations. Even if your idealism leads you to deny the truth when the Sun opposes Neptune on **August 17**, analytical Mercury's conjunction to sobering Saturn the same day won't let you keep your head in the clouds of illusion. The fiery Leo New Moon on **August 20** in your 7th House of Partnerships can attract arrogant individuals, because its opposition to Neptune muddles your self-awareness. Still, a supportive sextile from assertive Mars can harness your energies and push you into action.

KEEP IN MIND THIS MONTH

It's hard to know how much you should pull back when something pops your bubble of enthusiasm. Don't give up; just readjust your plans as needed.

KEY DATES

AUGUST 1–3 ★ *true confessions*

You're tempted to air your emotional grievances now, and you could easily hurt a loved one's feelings unless you're extra careful. Romantic Venus in protective Cancer is in a tug-of-war with shadowy Pluto on **August 1**, motivating you to express deep fears that you've previously kept to yourself. Communicator Mercury centers your attention on what's most crucial when it steps into picky Virgo on **August 2**. Your words gain focus on **August 3** as Mercury trines intense Pluto.

Remember, this isn't about limiting what you say; it's about revealing yourself in a nonjudgmental way that doesn't offend others.

AUGUST 7–10 ★ *worth the effort*
Relationship magic is in the air when romantic Venus in your 7th House of Partnerships forms a creative quintile with reliable Saturn in **August 7**, strengthening the practical side of love. When the Sun then forms a tense sesquisquare with domineering Pluto on **August 8**, however, you might feel that someone else has too much control over your life. Active Mars's square to conservative Saturn on **August 10** places obstacles wherever you aren't facing the facts, but your willingness to do the hard work can produce long-term success.

AUGUST 13–14 ★ *free falling*
You're given a temporary reprieve from your responsibilities when impetuous Mars in carefree Gemini harmoniously trines jolly Jupiter on **August 13**. The Sun's opposition to Jupiter on **August 14** inflates your self-confidence even more. You're so sure of yourself that you might jump without a parachute, thoroughly enjoying your ecstatic descent . . . until you realize you're about to hit the ground.

SUPER NOVA DAYS
AUGUST 17–19 ★ *stay light on your feet*
There's no escape from your own rigid thinking when thoughtful Mercury conjoins dogmatic Saturn on **August 17**. An authority figure might confront you, giving you an opportunity to learn from a past mistake. Take advantage of energetic Mars's smooth trine to gentle Neptune, which can show you the course of least resistance if you're willing to soften your stance. Don't be too surprised, though, if everything goes awry as Mars squares erratic Uranus on **August 18**. You won't be able to go back and undo what's been done, but making the right adjustments on **August 19**—when cheerful Jupiter runs into sensible Saturn—can get you moving in the right direction again.

AUGUST 25–26 ★ *can't let go*
Intellectual Mercury, physical Mars, and passionate Pluto engage in a three-way power struggle that can unravel a personal or business relationship as anxious fears overwhelm cool logic. Any attempts you make to avoid the intensity are probably useless, but conscious kindness can prevent this meltdown from turning nasty.

SEPTEMBER

OVERCOMING RESISTANCE

The pressure to change the direction of your life is strong again this month as the long-lasting opposition between traditional Saturn and progressive Uranus reaches another peak on **September 15**. Your key planet, Saturn, is in your 9th House of Future Vision all year, weighing you down with serious responsibilities stemming from the commitments you've made to others and to yourself. But rebellious Uranus in your 3rd House of Communication began a tug-of-war with your practical self on **November 4, 2008**, that stretched you again on **February 5** by presenting exciting possibilities and tempting you to take an uncharacteristic risk. Small steps, however, may be better than bold action. You have more time to reach your goal than you realize, for this Saturn-Uranus opposition recurs on **April 26, 2010**, and **July 26, 2010**.

The enchanted Pisces Full Moon on **September 4** extends your imagination into your everyday life, diverting you with fairy tales. On **September 6**, Mercury turns retrograde in your 10th House of Career, reminding you of all the things that haven't worked out according to your plans. Saturn also forms the first of three annoying quincunxes with phantasmagorical Neptune on **September 12** to confuse your choices with enticing dreams that have little possibility of manifestation. You find it challenging to separate your fantasies from reality—a struggle that can sap energy from the real issues at hand. Fortunately, the sensible Virgo New Moon on **September 18** is aided by strict Saturn to get you back to work and back on course. If your approach to change is in balance with your innate common sense, Mercury's direct turn on **September 29** will allow you to put your plan into motion next month.

> **KEEP IN MIND THIS MONTH**
>
> *Resist turning your world upside down in a hasty attempt to alleviate your boredom and end your growing frustration with the status quo.*

KEY DATES
SEPTEMBER 2–4 ★ *a rising tide*
Venus's harsh semisquare to stern Saturn on **September 2** can bring you financial or emotional disappointment—and perhaps prompt a conversation about your goals on **September 3**, when rational Mercury squares assertive Mars. Nevertheless, your emotions can lead you into turbulent waters as the Moon in fanciful Pisces waxes full on **September 4**. This Full Moon can elicit vivid dreams that overflow into your waking life, reactivating a struggle between your fantasies and your professional commitments.

SEPTEMBER 11–12 ★ *let your hair down*

Capricorns typically obey the rules and know the limits—but it's tough to rein in your desires when delicious Venus opposes extravagant Jupiter on **September 11.** Dutiful Saturn's crunchy quincunx with fantastic Neptune on **September 12** makes it even harder to remember when to stop. Letting go of control, though, could be exactly what you need.

SEPTEMBER 15 ★ *alice in wonderland*

Although you're eager to make your move today as conservative Saturn opposes radical Uranus, it's truly better to wait. An idealistic opposition between beautiful Venus and spiritual Neptune enables you to gloss over any negativity and see the best in any situation. This can feel wonderful—but it's not conducive to rational thinking. Accepting the fact that your perceptions are currently distorted by your imagination can lessen the pressure you feel to sustain today's magic.

SUPER NOVA DAYS
SEPTEMBER 17–18 ★ *what goes around comes around*

Unexpected events at work require you to refocus your energy and take responsibility for what's happening, even if everything seems out of control. This paradoxical mix of expression and restraint on **September 17** stems from the Sun's opposition to surprising Uranus, followed by its conjunction to methodical Saturn—reactivating recent events from the ongoing Saturn-Uranus opposition. The practical Virgo New Moon on **September 18** is conjunct karmic Saturn, bringing you exactly what you deserve—for better and for worse. The quicker you can learn from any mistakes now, the easier it will be to move on.

SEPTEMBER 20–23 ★ *don't back down*

Communicating your intentions is essential on **September 20**, when retrograde Mercury in meticulous Virgo conjuncts the Sun to align your words with your will. You can become even more self-critical as Venus enters fussy Virgo on the same day. Your high level of focus is sustained by Mercury's conjunction with constrictive Saturn on **September 22**. This is also the Autumnal Equinox, the day when the Sun enters gracious Libra, relaxing the heaviness that has defined your month so far. But dynamic aspects on **September 23** advise you to stay aware of your feelings and stand up for yourself when necessary.

OCTOBER

GET DOWN TO BUSINESS

You're in your element this month as the planets stack up in your 10th House of Public Responsibility. The Sun's presence here until **October 23** illuminates your career and—when it's joined by communicator Mercury on **October 9** and social Venus on **October 16**—increases your involvement at work and in the community. As much as this supports your natural tendency to get ahead professionally, a deeper issue begins to brew now when your key planet, taskmaster Saturn, comes within range of a dynamic and life-altering square with transformative Pluto. This Saturn-Pluto square isn't exact until **November 15**, but your drive is already intensified, and you crave immediate success. Unfortunately, you can't move as quickly as you wish and may face a shortage of time or resources to pull off your ambitious schemes. Nevertheless, Saturn's entry into diplomatic Libra and your business-oriented 10th House on **October 29** sets the tone for the next few years as you take on more responsibility and are recognized for the work you've done since Saturn opposed your sign from **June 2003** until **July 2006**.

The reckless Aries Full Moon on **October 4** falls in your 4th House of Home and Family, stressing you with personal obligations that could interfere with your job the following week. Forceful Mars enters your 8th House of Shared Resources on **October 16** for a protracted visit of eight months, agitating disputes about joint investments or taxes. The socially astute Libra New Moon on **October 18** falls in your 10th House of Career to reemphasize your need to get ahead. Be careful, for its smooth trine with deceptive Neptune can trick you into believing that everything's okay, even if it's not.

> **KEEP IN MIND THIS MONTH**
>
> *Eager as you are to climb the ladder of success, it's important to stay put and fulfill your current obligations before taking on new ones.*

KEY DATES

OCTOBER 4 ★ *life out of whack*

Your hopes of relaxation can be shattered today as a series of unexpected events demand your full attention. The rowdy Aries Full Moon disturbs your regular Sunday routine, but feisty Mars's easy trine to irregular Uranus allows you to enjoy the surprising change of pace once you accept what's happening. You might get into an argument as outspoken Mercury in your 9th House of Higher Truth opposes Uranus. Additionally, several annoying quincunxes converge, emphasizing the need to repeatedly adjust your schedule. It should go easier if you don't insist on having your own way.

SUPER NOVA DAYS

OCTOBER 8–10 ★ *don't sweat the small stuff*

Analytical Mercury's conjunction with nay-saying Saturn on **October 8** can expose the limitations of your present plan, so be ready to spend additional time making improvements. Unfortunately, you must be willing to let go of your strategy if you discover that it just won't work. Venus's opposition to unorthodox Uranus on **October 9** can help you break free from a problematic attraction, but her unsettling quincunx to nebulous Neptune makes you less sure of yourself. Don't engage in verbal warfare to defend an untenable position when Mercury crosses paths with implacable Pluto on **October 10**. Instead, focus on the awesome opportunities ahead, revealed by the Sun's trine to propitious Jupiter.

OCTOBER 12–13 ★ *true love takes time*

A synergistic sextile between expressive Mars and stylish Venus on **October 13** stimulates your creativity and allows you to express your natural gifts. But this isn't just about flirting: These romantic planets are currently connected to serious Saturn, requiring you to be practical. Mars's sextile to Saturn on **October 12** helps you apply your organizational skills to reach your goal. Venus's conjunction to Saturn on **October 13** can slow you down, but you'll find satisfaction if you're willing to be patient and work diligently for your rewards.

OCTOBER 20–24 ★ *talk it out*

Interactive Mercury allows you to approach negotiation objectively while it's in equitable Libra. Make the most of this ability to see both sides of an issue by going out of your way to mediate a disagreement at work. The messenger planet harmoniously trines generous Jupiter on **October 20**, compassionate Chiron on **October 23**, and intuitive Neptune on **October 24**, creating a perfect moment to demonstrate your communication skills. The Sun's shift into passionate Scorpio on **October 23** and its hookup with potent Pluto on **October 24** add depth to your understanding and intensity to your words.

NOVEMBER

TRUE GRIT

This month you face demands that aren't likely to be satisfied by additional planning or more hard work. You need to look beyond the end of this year and well into 2010 to see the light at the end of this tunnel. Taskmaster Saturn is now in socially conscious Libra in your 10th House of Status, where it emphasizes your professional ambitions for the next couple of years. You're driven to fulfill your current obligations so you can climb higher on the ladder of success, but events may not unfold according to your plans. Life seems harder as resolute Saturn forms a tough long-lasting square to ruthless Pluto that's exact on **November 15**, lingers until **January 31, 2010**, and recurs on **August 21, 2010**. This aspect requires serious attention as it slowly and profoundly transforms the foundation upon which you've built your world. A lack of resources or time might keep you from executing your strategy and force you to adapt to present circumstances. This can be a test of your will; survival depends on your positive attitude, so don't let discouragement get the best of you. Instead, commit to the long haul and do what you can every day to stay on top of the changes.

> ### KEEP IN MIND THIS MONTH
>
> *This can be a challenging time as you realize how much you must accomplish to be satisfied with your own progress.*

The determined Taurus Full Moon on **November 2** reminds you that keeping things simple is a practical path to success, even when a situation may seem complex. The intense Scorpio New Moon on **November 16** falls in your 11th House of Dreams. Its problematic square to nebulous Neptune can tantalize you with the beauty of your fantasies, yet this is a distraction from the real work at hand.

KEY DATES

NOVEMBER 1–2 ★ *a tangled tale*

Words spoken in the heat of anger could meet a harsh response when messenger Mercury dynamically squares fiery Mars on **November 1**. Mercury, Venus, and Mars form difficult aspects with erratic Uranus on **November 2** to turn the energy of an otherwise easygoing and dependable Taurus Full Moon into an unsolvable labyrinth of mixed-up thoughts and feelings. For now, keep your turmoil to yourself while temporarily escaping into the sweet fantasies generated by beautiful Venus's smooth trine to illusory Neptune.

NOVEMBER 6-8 ★ *far from the maddening crowd*
You don't have the time or patience this weekend for social events that deflect you from more serious concerns. A harsh Saturn-Pluto square that's exact later this month is prematurely agitated by tense aspects from overthinking Mercury on **November 6–7** and from the willful Sun on **November 8**, prompting you to avoid group activities in favor of your own work. Mercury and the Sun are joined by attractive Venus's entry into magnetic Scorpio and your 11th House of Friends on **November 7**, indicating that others are likely to want your participation, even if you aren't willing to play. Although Mercury's effusive square to Jupiter dares you to reveal more than is necessary, discretion is wiser for now.

SUPER NOVA DAYS
NOVEMBER 14-17 ★ *acting in self-defense*
The powerful Saturn-Pluto on **November 15** is likely to provoke your ire by forcing you to suppress your dreams and ambitions. Thankfully, an illuminating Sun-Uranus trine on **November 14** indicates that heightened awareness can open your mind to unorthodox solutions. The Sun's square to surrealistic Neptune, however, confuses you by dissolving boundaries, while thoughtful Mercury's entry into opinionated Sagittarius encourages you to believe your fantasies. The emotional Scorpio New Moon on **November 16** reactivates a brilliant Sun-Uranus trine to clear the air of any lingering uncertainty. Mercury's favorable sextile with stabilizing Saturn on **November 17** restores your natural common sense. Trust your logic and take the most conservative course of action.

NOVEMBER 23-26 ★ *kid in a candy store*
Sexy Venus in passionate Scorpio squares opulent Jupiter on **November 23**, sympathetic Chiron on **November 24**, and dreamy Neptune on **November 26**. Although squares are often thorny, your greatest challenge now may just be to say no. The temptation of sensual enjoyment is too sweet to resist—and you may mistakenly assume that more is better, especially when the love planet also trines thrilling Uranus on **November 25**. Succumbing to your romantic fantasies can be very exciting and also provides you with a story to tell as chatty Mercury harmonizes with assertive Mars on **November 26**.

DECEMBER

BEYOND THE MATERIAL WORLD

You're reminded of the true meaning of the holiday season when boundless Jupiter conjuncts healing Chiron on **December 7** and mystical Neptune on **December 21** for the third and final time this year. The metaphysical Jupiter-Chiron-Neptune super-conjunction falls in your 2nd House of Resources, awakening your spiritual values. Although you may be tempted to overspend to express your feelings of abundance, the greatest gifts you can give or receive don't involve money. Since the 2nd House also symbolizes personal assets, this planetary party can raise your self-esteem as long as you don't fritter away your resources on meaningless purchases. Reconsider the opportunities presented by the previous conjunctions on **May 23–27** and **July 10–22** to better understand the potential of your current situation. Keep in mind that your goals may still be just beyond your grasp. This isn't about reaching a destination; it's about reaching toward it.

The flighty Gemini Full Moon on **December 2** falls in your 6th House of Work, overwhelming you with things to do. The philosophical Sagittarius New Moon on **December 16** occurs in your 12th House of Divinity, filling you with the holiday spirit. Don't allow frustration or discouragement creep into your life if your chances for success now seem to slip away. Energetic Mars slows throughout the month to turn retrograde on **December 20**, suggesting that your arrival at your destination will be delayed, even if the pace of life is hectic. Quicksilver Mercury also begins its retrograde phase on **December 26**, unraveling plans and details. The Cancer Full Moon on December 31—a Lunar Eclipse in your 7th House of Relationships—drags buried emotional issues out into the open just in time for the New Year.

> **KEEP IN MIND THIS MONTH**
>
> *Although the holiday season can be a lovely distraction, don't lose track of the important work you must do to make your dreams come true.*

KEY DATES

DECEMBER 2-5 ★ *play it straight*

The Full Moon in curious Gemini on **December 2** sidetracks you from your serious commitments. Fortunately, social Venus's sextile with strict Saturn on **December 4** can restore the self-discipline you need. Still, it's a frustrating lesson, for a tough Mars-Saturn aspect on **December 5** requires you to answer to your boss or another authority figure. Don't try to get away with any fast-talking schemes: You will pay the price for seeking the easy way out.

DECEMBER 7 ★ *change your mind*

Forgiving someone helps you let go of difficult feelings when good-natured Jupiter conjuncts compassionate Chiron. Communicator Mercury aligns with unyielding Pluto to expose your secrets or to drive them deep within, whatever the emotional cost. A Mercury-Saturn square tells you where your logic has gone astray. You can learn an important lesson, but you must be willing to adapt your thinking to new information or it will be of no lasting value.

DECEMBER 14-16 ★ *on a clear day you can see forever*

A liberating few days lead up to the inspirational Sagittarius New Moon on **December 16**. The Sun's dynamic square with explosive Uranus on **December 14** releases a torrent of pent-up emotions and crazy ideas. Chances are you'll be motivated by this sudden awakening, for the Sun also supportively sextiles lucky Jupiter and imaginative Neptune on **December 14-15**. Don't set limits on what you can do; the distant horizon is much closer than you realize.

SUPER NOVA DAYS
DECEMBER 19-21 ★ *hurry up and wait*

Your sense of adventure perks up as creative Venus in grandiose Sagittarius hooks up with the visionary trio of Chiron, Jupiter, and Neptune on **December 19-21**. You might go too far by expressing your needs unconventionally, though, thanks to Venus's stressful square with unstable Uranus on **December 19**. It's hard to follow through on projects, for aggressive Mars turns retrograde on **December 20**, delaying satisfaction. The Winter Solstice on **December 21**, marked by the Sun's return to cautious Capricorn, is just one more reminder that only extra patience will conquer your frustration.

DECEMBER 27-29 ★ *accepting limits*

Feisty Mars runs into Saturn's wall on **December 27**, reminding you that reckless actions won't bring the results you want. Your emotions intensify as sensual Venus joins potent Pluto on **December 28**, yet you may have to take no for an answer when the love planet squares Saturn on **December 29**. Once you know what doesn't work, however, you'll be better able to create a new plan and try again when the time is right.

AQUARIUS

JANUARY 20–FEBRUARY 18

AQUARIUS

2008 SUMMARY

Many new experiences are just around the corner, even if you aren't quite ready to meet them. Apply yourself diligently to strengthen your ties with others, both in business and personally. Remain open to what you still need to learn as you delve into the less-than-logical emotional realms during the year. The most extraordinary growth may come to you in ways that are not necessarily apparent to others.

AUGUST— *free bird*

Don't avoid your feelings just because you're more comfortable living in your head. Your life will be more meaningful when you also express what's in your heart.

SEPTEMBER—*sustaining growth*

Even if you can see amazing possibilities everywhere you look, you must first take care of your current obligations if you want more measurable results.

OCTOBER—*just around the bend*

Dig in your heels and concentrate on long-term change this month instead of immediate gratification.

NOVEMBER—*the road ahead*

Although certain aspects of your life may not meet your expectations, the changes you seek are big enough that they could take years to unfold.

DECEMBER—*romance and rebellion*

Thoughts moving at the speed of light do not require immediate expression. Digest this mental fast food before taking action.

2008 CALENDAR

AUGUST

TUESDAY 5 ★ Humble yourself to alleviate your anxiety through the 9th

WEDNESDAY 13 ★ Use isolation to reevaluate your partnerships

FRIDAY 15 ★ **SUPER NOVA DAYS** Don't take the easy way out through the 17th

THURSDAY 21 ★ Your impulses may discomfort others through the 23rd

WEDNESDAY 27 ★ Discuss, rather than bury feelings through the 30th

SEPTEMBER

WEDNESDAY 3 ★ Blend adventure and responsibility through the 4th when opposites will attract

SUNDAY 7 ★ **SUPER NOVA DAYS** Be the change you seek through the 12th

TUESDAY 16 ★ Find a way to compromise when complications abound through the 21st

WEDNESDAY 24 ★ Go back to the drawing board with current plans and ideas

OCTOBER

SATURDAY 4 ★ Ride the waves of your enthusiasm through the 6th

FRIDAY 10 ★ Risking real life gains for a dream is a dangerous gamble

SATURDAY 18 ★ You're the life of the party, so enjoy social situations

FRIDAY 24 ★ Shift your focus from the past to the future

THURSDAY 30 ★ **SUPER NOVA DAYS** Tension is relieved through the 31st

NOVEMBER

MONDAY 3 ★ **SUPER NOVA DAYS** Make no sudden moves through tomorrow

MONDAY 10 ★ It's time to regroup, restrain, and discuss through the 12th

SUNDAY 16 ★ Unleash a brilliant idea now

THURSDAY 27 ★ Happy days and positive energy rule through the end of the month

DECEMBER

FRIDAY 5 ★ Apply your spirit of innovation to new projects now

WEDNESDAY 10 ★ **SUPER NOVA DAYS** Enough is enough through the 12th

MONDAY 15 ★ Avoid a showdown through the 16th and stress will fade

SUNDAY 21 ★ Tap your hidden reserve of passion and potency through the 22nd

SATURDAY 27 ★ Do serious work constructing your dreams through the 28th

AQUARIUS OVERVIEW

This is a year of rare opportunity—the spiritually active planets Jupiter, Neptune, and Chiron join together three times in your sign. Expansive Jupiter, the planet of growth, opportunity, and wisdom, conjuncts mystical Neptune on May 27, July 10, and December 22, connecting your heart and mind and offering you a greater vision of yourself and humanity. **You are inspired by an understanding beyond words—one that stretches from the bottom of your soul to the heights of cosmic consciousness.** This perspective can make you a teacher and a leader in the pursuit of human potential. Jupiter conjuncts Chiron the Wounded Healer on May 31, July 22, and December 7, nourishing your faith with enormous compassion for yourself and others. It's a perfect antidote to intellectual arrogance, because it matches your high level of mental ability with emotional depth. Every day can be sacred now as you find meaning in the events of ordinary life, yet your challenges will not all disappear. However, even the most difficult ones will be less burdensome as you discover the magic of faith, which empowers you with a wider palette of possibilities than ever before.

The expanding perspective in your life doesn't eliminate your need to make major choices this year. Restrictive Saturn, the traditional ruler of your sign, opposes rebellious Uranus, its modern ruler, on February 5 and September 15. The stark contrast between responsibility and freedom represented by this pair first occurred on November 4, 2008, and returns on April 26, 2010, and July 26, 2010. You may be resentful of the limitations in your life and push hard against authority figures. Blaming others for your frustration is unlikely to be productive, though. **Success comes from clearly defining your desires, making a plan to satisfy them, and executing it with patience and precision.** The rewards for following this path are well worth the self-discipline that is required of you now. Furthermore, strict Saturn forms tense squares with powerful Pluto on November 15, January 31, 2010, and August 21, 2010. These aspects demonstrate that you must be more purposeful if you want to maintain control over your life. Securing your professional position or discovering a new career path more suitable to your long-range interests is essential.

Eclipses in your 6th House of Daily Routines on July 21 and December 31 demand changes in your habits. These influences, lasting up to six months each, remind you that there are healthier and more efficient ways to function. **Minor problems can grow into more serious complications unless you address them right away.** Don't allow nagging health issues to linger if you have the means to attend to them. You're not the type to baby yourself, but self-care is critical now. Even if the usual patterns of your day-to-day existence are interrupted, it's wiser to creatively develop new modes of operation than to hold tightly to those that no longer serve your needs.

GREAT EXPECTATIONS

You naturally expect more from your relationships this year: A growing awareness of your own potential arouses your desire for a partner equally interested in seeking more from life. Visionary Jupiter in your sign indicates that you're unwilling to settle for less than what you want. Additionally, serious Saturn in your 8th House of Intimacy until October 29 reflects the need to restructure your most important relationships. The limitations of others may force you to talk about making fundamental changes if you and a partner hope to remain close. If he or she is willing to work with you, there's no limit to how far you can go together. However, a lack of effort will lead to stagnation and a loss of trust that can permanently undermine your bond. A Lunar Eclipse in expressive Leo on February 9 falls in your 7th House of Relationships. Expect powerful longings to connect with someone new or to go farther with a current mate. Yet dreamy Neptune's opposition to the eclipse indicates that you may be projecting fantasies, so double-check your assumptions before you make any dramatic moves.

MAKE YOUR MOVE

Sitting still professionally isn't your best option given the rocking and rolling of an ongoing Saturn-Uranus opposition that's shaking your world. It's better to boldly take your job in an exciting new direction than to cling to a situation that's likely to change anyhow . . . whether you want it to or not. Pressure could mount to a breaking point on November 15 when Pluto, the ruler of your 10th House of Public Status, is squeezed by a square from Saturn in a power play, leading to a shift of your responsibilities. Head off potential problems by facing your work-related desires and fears directly when penetrating Pluto turns direct on September 8. Making a major decision public should be easiest after October 22, when the Sun enters soul-searching Scorpio and your 10th House.

VALUABLE INSTINCTS

With independent Uranus in your 2nd House of Finances opposing stingy Saturn in your 8th House of Shared Resources on February 5 and September 15, you may feel torn between staying with a situation of reliable but limited income and taking a chance to go solo. Lucky Jupiter is the ruler of your 2nd House, and its bountiful conjunctions to Neptune on May 27, July 10, and December 21 indicate that prosperity comes from trusting your intuition. If you feel inspired by what you do, the money will follow, while sticking to the so-called safe path may leave you coming up short.

ENERGY MEDICINE

The rare super-conjunctions of Jupiter, Neptune, and Chiron in your 1st House of Physicality may alter your body chemistry this year. While robust Jupiter's presence offers protection against serious illness, both Neptune and Chiron can produce complications. Nebulous Neptune could make you more sensitive and vulnerable to fatigue, allergies, or infection, while Chiron the Wounded Healer can draw attention to your weak points. A Solar Eclipse in quirky Aquarius on January 26 also suggests that stress can change how your body functions. You benefit by paying more attention to your energy level while maintaining a positive attitude. Utilizing subtle treatments such as homeopathy, medicinal herbs, and acupuncture, along with proper hydration and plenty of rest, is your best assurance of good health.

E.T., PHONE HOME

The down-to-earth matters of home and family may seem less significant as your spirit soars to higher dimensions with buoyant Jupiter and mythical Neptune in your sign. The realities of domestic life fall short of the high ideals and inspiring concepts that may dominate your thoughts. Yet keeping a solid foundation is essential, especially when sociable Venus—the ruler of your 4th House of Roots—is retrograde March 6–April 18. This is a good time to shore up your base by attending to your household with physical and emotional maintenance wherever it's needed.

STREET SMARTS

Aquarians are naturally inquisitive and interested in learning, but direct experience will probably take you farther than formal studies this year. The innate wisdom emerging from Jupiter the Guru in your sign can teach you more than any classroom. Still, if you don't live up to your principles, the lessons will come hard and fast. Minimize travel to reduce complications while Venus is retrograde in your 9th House of Voyages from March 6 to April 18 and when mobile Mercury is retrograde in this house September 6–29. The New Moon on October 18 in equitable Libra in your 9th House, however, is enriched with a trine from adventuresome Jupiter, making this a great time to hit the road or the books.

 GROUP MIND

Spirituality is more powerful when you can share it with others as structured Saturn, the ruler of your 12th House of Divinity, resides in your 8th House of Intimacy until October 29. However, balancing personal desires with your highest ideals can be a challenge at times. A sobering Capricorn Lunar Eclipse in your 12th House on July 7 might mark a turning point when your faith is tested. Fortunately, a harmonious trine from Saturn to this Full Moon reveals a concrete way to handle a difficult moment while also giving you the discipline to react responsibly.

RICK & JEFF'S TIP FOR THE YEAR:
The Joy of Sharing

This has the potential to be one of the most amazing years of your life. Dreams that have seemed out of reach may now be well within your grasp. Your sign is deeply connected to larger collective issues, so that more selfish desires will probably go unfulfilled. However, when your goals contribute to the community, you're more likely to reach them. This is not about sacrificing yourself and vaguely hoping that you'll be rewarded, but about recognizing how your happiness can be a gift to everyone.

JANUARY

PLANET SURFING

A rising wave of optimism comes into sight with generous Jupiter entering your sign on **January 5**, lifting your spirits and expanding your opportunities for the coming year. The contradictions of your life may start to make sense as your self-understanding increases and the patterns in your life come into clearer focus. Being able to visualize future possibilities and establish successful strategies will put you ahead of the game. On **January 10**, the moody Cancer Full Moon falls in your 6th House of Details, which can make a minor issue feel like a major problem. Fortunately, this Sun-Moon opposition aligns favorably with competent Saturn and brilliant Uranus to reveal effective solutions. Talkative Mercury turns retrograde on **January 11**, complicating the flow of information through **February 1**. The potential to be misunderstood or to lose data is strong since this cycle begins in your sign, so be extra vigilant with communication now.

You should feel the wind in your sails when the Sun enters airy Aquarius on **January 19**—and an even bigger boost with the New Moon in your sign on **January 26**. This Sun-Moon conjunction is a Solar Eclipse, which often corresponds with a loss or taking a step backward. However, while you're likely to let go of a position or attitude that no longer suits you, you stand to gain much more, for propitious Jupiter conjuncts the eclipse and inspires you with a new vision. The ongoing opposition of strict Saturn and rebellious Uranus is triggered by hard aspects from Jupiter on **January 27–30** that can dramatize their differences. A semisquare to Uranus on the **27th** evokes restlessness and excitement, while a sesquisquare to Saturn on the **30th** slams on the brakes.

> **KEEP IN MIND THIS MONTH**
>
> *You can see a long way, but you'll only get there by putting your head down and carefully marking each step along the path.*

KEY DATES

JANUARY 1 ★ *know thyself*

You welcome the New Year with eagerness as intellectually curious Mercury enters your sign. This normally focuses your attention, sharpens your thinking, and helps you express yourself more clearly. However, since the messenger planet is slowing down in advance of its upcoming retrograde cycle, you may spend more time looking inward to understand yourself than communicating with others.

JANUARY 5 ★ *wake-up call*
Jupiter's entry into progressive Aquarius today is a long-lasting change that may take time to register on you, but you can't overlook a spiky semisquare between chatty Mercury and electric Uranus. Flashes of brilliance spur innovative ideas and scintillating conversations, though an air of nervousness lends unpredictability to the day. Sudden shifts of mood, mind, or plans could make you jumpy, so be flexible and adapt quickly when necessary.

JANUARY 9-11 ★ *team player*
The creative powers of the Sun come into play on **January 9** with an inventive sextile to Uranus that shows you how to stand up for yourself without alienating others. Your natural ability to balance individual rights with collective obligations makes it easy for you to bring the two together in a harmonious way. Mercury's retrograde on **January 11**, though, is a more complicated story—one in which precise, simple, and clear communication is essential. The inner workings of your mind could grow more complex, yet these private thoughts are not that easily explained. A stable Sun-Saturn trine, on the other hand, provides you with quiet self-confidence and a feeling of solidity in a relationship.

JANUARY 19-20 ★ *a fresh start*
The Sun's entry into idealistic Aquarius on **January 19** puts more sparkle in your eyes and power in your personality. Your energy level may be rising, making this a good time to get plenty of exercise and push yourself harder physically. Retrograde Mercury's conjunction with the Sun on **January 20** is perfect for introspection. Quiet meditation can be a rich experience that will reward you with wiser decisions in the future.

SUPER NOVA DAYS
JANUARY 22-24 ★ *party central*
You're hot, sexy, and fun with magnetic Venus and passionate Mars dancing with your key planet, Uranus, on **January 22**. This is an excellent time to take the lead in discovering new forms of play, creativity, and romance. Your hunger for change can make you intolerant of the old routine as you seek stimulation in unfamiliar ways. Teasing and joking are all too easy now, but could unnerve insecure individuals. On **January 24**, the Sun joins Jupiter, infusing you with a sense of righteousness that makes you a powerful spokesperson for your beliefs. Yet selling others on your vision is less important than taking action on it yourself.

FEBRUARY

FORGING AHEAD

Your usually cool and collected personality heats up on **February 4** when aggressive Mars enters your sign, where he puts more steam in your engine until **March 15**. This is excellent for getting new projects off the ground and being more active physically. However, your ideas tend to be ahead of their time, which may require you to slow down and carefully explain what you're doing when others can't keep up. Trickster Mercury's shift to forward motion on **February 1** starts to get communication back on track, yet the transition may not be obvious until the messenger planet enters intelligent Aquarius on **February 14**. The contrary couple of staid Saturn and cutting-edge Uranus oppose each other on **February 5**—the second in a series of oppositions that began **November 4, 2008**, and finishes on **September 15, 2009**. You may be less willing to compromise when you're pressured to follow someone else's rules. Rebellion is tempting, but it's more constructive to consciously create your freedom in your own way than to resist boundaries set by another.

Relationships are highlighted on **February 9** with the dramatic Leo Full Moon shining in your 7th House of Partnerships. This is a Lunar Eclipse opposite imaginative Neptune, tempting you to project your fantasies onto others. But its deeper message is that mixing romance with realism can put an end to illusions that get in the way of enduring alliances. The New Moon in compassionate Pisces stirs dreams in your 2nd House of Resources on **February 24**. You can resolve the conflict between idealism and income as you recognize sensitive ways to do well for humanity and for yourself at the same time.

> **KEEP IN MIND THIS MONTH**
>
> *Never underestimate how inventive you can be when you step outside the box. Original thinking can provide solutions to almost any problem.*

KEY DATES

SUPER NOVA DAYS
FEBRUARY 4–5 ★ *tug-of-war*

Mars punches into independent Aquarius on **February 4** to bring out your feisty side, which comes at a potentially dangerous time. The tension of the exact Saturn-Uranus opposition on **February 5** may be frustrating and could agitate your anger. The willful Sun, socially sensitive Venus, and penetrating Pluto align in challenging aspects that can undermine your trust in others and confidence in yourself. If you're feeling edgy, it's wise to defer action until you have a clear plan. Follow your passion to dig deeply within and you can find hidden or underused resources that allow you to initiate constructive change.

FEBRUARY 11-13 ★ *controlled chaos*
Macho Mars bangs into the Saturn-Uranus opposition with challenging aspects on **February 11-12**. Self-control is necessary for channeling your intensity productively instead of engaging in exhausting skirmishes. Do your best to work around the limitations of others by concentrating your energies on tasks that you can manage yourself. A psychic Sun-Neptune conjunction may be inspirational but also signals hypersensitivity, making you feel more vulnerable. Fortunately, confident Jupiter joins the integrative North Node of the Moon on **February 13**, bringing good advice that sends you in the right direction.

FEBRUARY 16-18 ★ *light up the world with your smile*
Connections with others come easily for you as active Mars joins the North Node of the Moon on **February 16** while Venus sweetly sextiles good-natured Jupiter. New social contacts and friendly interactions help you handle pressure with style and grace. High energy and enthusiasm propel you to take on big challenges as Mars conjuncts Jupiter on **February 17**. Your excitement is contagious, and you're able to motivate others skillfully thanks to your passion and intelligence. A friendly sextile between Venus and Mars, the planets of attraction and action, should put you at your playful best on **February 18**. You can flirt easily and create a joyous atmosphere under almost any circumstances.

FEBRUARY 22-24 ★ *know your audience*
Inquisitive Mercury joins the karmically significant North Node of the Moon in socially conscious Aquarius on **February 22**, hooking you up with intelligent people and giving you a chance to show off your brilliance, too. On **February 24**, the communication planet joins outspoken Jupiter in your sign to kick your thinking up another notch. You can readily break down complex subjects into simple concepts, making you an exceptional student and a highly effective teacher. Routine tasks, though, may become especially boring as you seek the intellectual stimulation of innovative ideas. When you speak, others will listen—as long as you tailor your comments to their level of interest and ability.

MARCH

STEP BY STEP

Relationship issues shake and stir your world in several ways this month. Venus, the planet of attraction, turns retrograde in your 11th House of Groups on **March 6**, complicating your interactions with friends and colleagues. Competitiveness, care-less comments, and thin-skinned individuals may break down trust or reopen old wounds. You will, however, have many opportunities to heal divisions with others during the six weeks of Venus's backward motion—if you're able to overcome your initial impulses and calmly seek alternative ways to address problems. The Full Moon in overanalytical Virgo on **March 10** occurs in your 8th House of Intimacy, where it can instigate a crisis in a close connection. The Moon joins restrictive Saturn and opposes rebellious Uranus to suddenly bring this ongoing conflict between obligation and freedom back into focus. Pressure to change the structure of a partnership should be handled quickly to avoid an explosion and possible breakup. Financial matters are also affected by this event, suggesting a sudden shift in income flow or investments.

A burst of fresh energy for group activities arrives on **March 20**—the Spring Equinox—with the Sun's entry into enthusiastic Aries and your 11th House. You could be motivated to take on new projects, yet it's important to measure your commitments of time and energy carefully. The New Moon in spontaneous Aries on **March 26** spawns tons of ideas in your 3rd House of Information, but a square from purging Pluto is a stark reminder to narrow your focus and concentrate on one task at a time. Hard aspects between extravagant Jupiter and unforgiving Saturn on **March 22**, then demanding Pluto on **March 27**, reinforce the message that resource management is vital—overreaching is bound to prove costly now.

KEEP IN MIND THIS MONTH

Rushing ahead is likely to set you back this month. Stretch out your excitement to fuel slow growth, rather than burning it all up at once.

KEY DATES

MARCH 1 ★ *food for thought*

Conversations can swing from sluggish to scintillating as chatty Mercury passes from a clunky quincunx with serious Saturn to a speedy conjunction with fiery Mars. If you let resentment accumulate without expression, it may escape in a torrent of angry words. Seek a higher level of intellectual stimulation to give your mind a positive activity worthy of its impressive power.

MARCH 8 ★ *back to reality*
There's a strange mix of hard and soft today as aggressive Mars is tenderized with a conjunction to nebulous Neptune that gives you a desire to either slack off or take time for inspirational projects. Mercury's passage into Pisces, Neptune's home sign, can reinforce this dreamy attitude and your current imaginative perspective. The Sun's opposition to dutiful Saturn can interrupt your reverie with the demands of someone who insists that you attend to utilitarian tasks. This could, however, provide you with a practical partner who helps turn your fantasies into reality.

SUPER NOVA DAYS
MARCH 10-12 ★ *delightful diplomacy*
Lovely Venus aligns with cheerful Jupiter to bolster your good mood on **March 10**. This is a good day to charm a hard-to-please person or to bring joy to a stressful job. Repairing relationships with friends or associates comes more easily now as you combine a generous spirit with a sharp instinct for what others need. The Full Moon in focused Virgo intensifies everyone's feelings, but you can be the mediator who brings peace to warring factions. On **March 12**, the Sun opposes shocking Uranus, which often incites rebellions. However, you have enough common sense to present unusual ideas in ways that make others comfortable as you gently open their minds to unfamiliar territory.

MARCH 21-22 ★ *cliffhanger danger*
You may be feeling wired on **March 21** with a high-frequency conjunction between Mercury and electric Uranus. This brilliant pair sparks original ideas and unconventional perceptions that are exciting—maybe too much so. Words fly without inhibition and are easily misunderstood. A bit of self-restraint is a good idea, especially with excessive Jupiter overstimulated from tough aspects to the Sun and authoritative Saturn on **March 22**. The thrill of adventure and expressing yourself boldly is alluring, yet if you're not careful you could find yourself hanging off a ledge.

MARCH 27 ★ *truce or consequences*
Do your best to avoid debates today, because verbal Mercury, opinionated Jupiter, and "take no prisoners" Pluto are crossing paths in difficult aspects. Casual conversations can devolve into arguments; differences of perspective may grow into major battles. Spend your mental energy on deepening your understanding of your own beliefs rather than trying to convince resistant individuals to agree with you.

APRIL

OPPOSING FORCES

You swing from playing it safe to going for broke this month when active Mars triggers the ongoing opposition of conservative Saturn and wild Uranus. Mars opposes Saturn on **April 4**, requiring you to operate within strictly defined limits. It can be very frustrating for a free spirit like you, but taking it slowly and sticking to a plan will save you time and energy in the long run. On **April 15**, Mars joins nonconformist Uranus, stimulating your intuition and inventiveness. Brilliant moves arise spontaneously, yet your need to act quickly can stir conflict with authorities or allies who can't keep pace. The likelihood for misunderstanding increases while sociable Venus continues moving retrograde until **April 17**. It could be especially hard to avoid wounding fragile individuals when she reenters sensitive Pisces on **April 11**.

The urge to get away from it all is stoked when a leisure-loving Libra Full Moon on **April 9** lands in your 9th House of Faraway Places. Escaping from your daily routine may alleviate some of the pressure, and planning a trip with an educational or spiritual theme is ideal with inspirational Jupiter and Neptune trine this Full Moon. Your attention turns to domestic matters when the Sun enters comfortable Taurus in your 4th House of Home and Family on **April 19**. Relax and recharge by spending time with your loved ones or puttering around in the garden. The need to return to basics and reconnect with your roots is reinforced by the New Moon in easygoing Taurus on **April 21**. Shadowy Pluto's creative trine to this Sun-Moon conjunction may help you rediscover resources that you haven't used in a very long time.

> **KEEP IN MIND THIS MONTH**
>
> *It's fine for you to go to extremes when you're operating independently, but moderation is essential when others are involved.*

KEY DATES

APRIL 3-4 ★ *agree to disagree*

A tense Venus-Pluto square on **April 3** can evoke mistrust or jealousy, perhaps complicating your relationships. Allowing long-repressed feelings to surface may provoke conflict, but it's healthier than suppressing them. Although communicative Mercury's sensible sextile with opinionated Jupiter favors clear thinking on **April 4**, messages are mixed as an opposition from mobile Mars to stable Saturn produces a battle of wills. Find a way to work around differences instead of settling in for a protracted struggle no one can win.

APRIL 10 ★ *motivational coach*
Your wealth of information and passionate beliefs combine to make you a very powerful spokesperson and teacher today. The sparkling Sun in your 3rd House of Communication forms a clever sextile with outgoing Jupiter in clever Aquarius, putting you at ease in front of any audience and enabling you to sell your ideas to even the most resistant individuals.

SUPER NOVA DAYS
APRIL 14-15 ★ *boiling point*
A smart and sassy Mercury-Uranus semisquare on **April 14** gets your mind buzzing impatiently with bright ideas. Don't expect others to catch on quickly, especially when you're thinking outside the box. Communication breakdowns are possible as connections are missed and technology fizzles. Impulsiveness continues on **April 15** with a Mars-Uranus conjunction that increases your originality and reduces your willingness to compromise. Turn your restlessness in a constructive direction to avoid exploding at an authority figure and getting yourself in trouble. If you feel tension building up inside, some gentle exercise can help reduce it.

APRIL 21-24 ★ *speed dating*
A sexy Venus-Mars conjunction on **April 21** aligns attraction and action to fuel creative and romantic activities. Passionate Mars enters excitable Aries on **April 22**, picking up the pace, which climbs even higher on **April 24** when Venus also enters this fast-moving sign. Fortunately, your intellect can keep up with accelerating social dynamics that pop you in and out of love or lust in just an instant. Mental Mercury slides into a smart sextile with shocking Uranus, showcasing your snappy thinking with sharp conversation and unconventional ideas.

APRIL 30 ★ *pulling the lion's tail*
A sluggish partner or boring task can really annoy you today. The willful Sun forms a tense semisquare with explosive Uranus that makes it hard for you to tolerate stagnant thinking or repetitive tasks. You know how to get under the skin of a pompous person, but the fun of irritating such an individual may prove too costly. Taking yourself less seriously can lighten the mood and enable you to be playful without provoking an undesirable backlash.

MAY

FAITH AND FOLLY

The winds of inspiration blow strongly this month as ever-hopeful Jupiter rejoins compassionate Chiron on **May 23** and spiritual Neptune on **May 27** in your idealistic sign. These are the first in a series of three superconjunctions that weave through the fabric of the year, binding emotion and intellect to weave a grander vision of your life. Taking time to contemplate larger issues isn't an exercise in escapism now; it's an investment in connecting with your higher purpose. Your earthly interests, though, don't disappear: Mercury's retrograde turn on **May 7** in your 5th House of Love and Play may lead to complications in romance, in creative endeavors, or with children. Measure your words carefully to avoid misunderstandings, and be prepared to repeat yourself to get your message across. On **May 9**, the emotionally intense Scorpio Full Moon falls in your 10th House of Career, forcing you to make a tough choice between advancement on the job and saving quality time for your personal life.

Karmic Saturn's direct turn on **May 16** in your 8th House of Intimacy could lead to a showdown in a relationship, but it can also connect you to a critical thinker who helps you weed out unrealistic ideas. The Sun's entry into carefree Gemini and your romantic 5th House on **May 20** arouses playful feelings. The innocence of your heart may bring moments of foolishness, but it's also a surefire way to have fun. It's better to be naive and awkward now than to protect yourself by avoiding mistakes. The flirtatious Gemini New Moon in the 5th House on **May 24** may give you more opportunities for pleasure than time to enjoy them.

KEEP IN MIND THIS MONTH

Spiritual development accelerates rapidly when you take yourself less seriously and express your inner child more freely.

KEY DATES

MAY 4 ★ *power to burn*

Energetic Mars is pushed by a semisquare with exorbitant Jupiter that may be hard to handle. Impatience and aggression can lead you to do too much, too fast. If a conversation turns edgy, that's your signal to back off before an explosion occurs. Channel the force you're feeling with cool precision to avoid wasting it in conflict or frittering it away on impractical pursuits.

MAY 11–12 ★ *don't panic*
Friends or colleagues could lead you astray when rash Mars makes a misguided quincunx with loyal Saturn on **May 11**. Your desire to support others is noble, but not when it distracts you from meeting more important commitments. Narrow your focus and stick to your plan as much as possible. Retrograde Mercury backs into a stressful semisquare with Mars on **May 12** that can create a false sense of urgency. Crises are best met with a cool demeanor that enables you to react quickly without losing your head.

MAY 16–17 ★ *reality-based faith*
The Sun in practical Taurus makes tough squares to Jupiter and Chiron on **May 16** that contrast present circumstances with long-range goals. This mismatch of the real and the ideal can skew your judgment and encourage exaggeration or disappointment. Recognizing that both views have value allows you to shift from concrete to conceptual without losing hope or contact with reality. The Sun squares whimsical Neptune on **May 17**, tilting you toward fantasy and faith and away from facts. Compassion and inspiration are wonderful gifts when they enhance a grounded perspective.

MAY 20–21 ★ *data deluge*
You could be headed for mental overload on **May 20**, when the Sun enters curious Gemini while cerebral Mercury squares philosophical Jupiter. It's fine to browse through a torrent of ideas, but you're not required to buy into any of them. On **May 21**, retrograde Mercury slides into a smart sextile with unorthodox Uranus that offers fresh perspectives, enabling you to make sense of a crazy situation. Trust your intuition to give you quick answers that work well but may not be easily explained.

SUPER NOVA DAYS
MAY 26–27 ★ *stairway to heaven*
Put your ideals into action as macho Mars sextiles wounded Chiron on **May 26** and the boundless Jupiter-Neptune conjunction on **May 27**. Don't let the demands of your daily routine squeeze out this chance to seed your dreams. Giving generously, caring for those in need, and allowing yourself to be guided by inspiration ensures that your highest hopes won't dissipate in a cloud of neglect. Applied enthusiasm anchors lofty thoughts in reality and builds a platform that can take you as far as your mind can stretch.

JUNE

SUSTAINABLE GROWTH

Managing your activities can be a challenge this month: Your involvement in groups can overload your busy schedule. On **June 7**, the Full Moon in fun-loving Sagittarius arrives in your 11th House of Friends and Wishes to stimulate your social life and fire up your taste for adventure. However, hard-nosed Saturn's restricting square to this Sun-Moon opposition is likely to impose additional responsibilities. You might recognize how the demands of teamwork are already stretching you to the limit. If you're not getting the support you need from colleagues or pals, it may be time to put your foot down and change the nature of your relationships. Mental Mercury buzzes into Gemini and your 7th House of Partnerships on **June 13**, attracting chatty people and increasing the flow of information from others. Temper your curiosity with a dose of practicality to avoid intellectual overload. The retrograde turn of overextending Jupiter on **June 15** is a reminder to narrow your vision and focus on the ideas that are most vital to you now.

Impulsiveness, rebellion, and an irrepressible itch for change run amok when active Mars aspects wired Uranus on **June 16**, followed by tense connections to your eccentric ruling planet from sweet Venus and the Sun on **June 17**. You may be compelled to control these desires on **June 21** when the Sun enters security-conscious Cancer, marking the Summer Solstice, in your 6th House of Health, Work, and Daily Routines. Even small changes can rock your emotional boat and provoke strong reactions from those around you. The New Moon in defensive Cancer on **June 22** is opposed by ruthless Pluto, which can turn a minor difference of opinion into a major power struggle.

> **KEEP IN MIND THIS MONTH**
>
> *Before you add a single new activity to your calendar, figure out how to save enough time for it.*

KEY DATES

JUNE 2 ★ *the joy of learning*

You're in a buoyant mood as fun-loving Venus forms a compatible sextile with jolly Jupiter. Indulging in a stimulating conversation over dessert or a culturally enriching outing can fill you with joy. An open mind and heart attract you to individuals from a diversity of backgrounds. Don't cajole someone who's not in the mood to play: An irritating square from Mars in stubborn Taurus to the Moon's Nodes can trigger angry reactions, warranted or not.

JUNE 9-10 ★ *information overload*

Thoughts are firing in all directions on **June 9**, when intellectual Mercury forms a brilliant sextile with Uranus and stressful squares with Chiron and Neptune. Mercury is in your 10th House of Career, so most of your bright ideas will apply to work. However, it's possible that signals will get crossed thanks to the fuzziness of Neptune, making it easy to misconstrue messages. Bring your concepts down to earth for practical application—it's tempting to be mesmerized with lofty concepts that will never be utilized. The data flow might even increase on **June 10** when detail-oriented Mercury squares grandiose Jupiter. Too much input and too many words can muddy the waters of logic. Exaggeration can take you totally off track, so focus on a key idea and don't be distracted by the fluff.

SUPER NOVA DAYS
JUNE 16-17 ★ *pivotal moment*

This can be an explosive time as a stressful semisquare between passionate Mars and untamed Uranus on **June 16** leaves you averse to following the rules. In fact, your need to do things your way may overrule caution and spur conflict with anyone who tries to control your actions. If you can stay cool, though, sparks of intuition reveal new methods that are surprising in their efficiency. Your urge for freedom and innovation continues on **June 17** with a Sun-Uranus square that's ideal for leading a revolution. A Venus-Uranus semisquare urges you to to break social patterns and seek fresh forms of pleasure. Relationships—both personal and professional—can be shaken by recklessness, so be careful unless you want something to break.

JUNE 21-22 ★ *the art of persuasion*

A sensual conjunction between Venus and Mars in your 10th House of Public Responsibility on **June 21** makes you a natural for hosting social events. This compatible pair of planets aligns in an easygoing trine with steady Saturn on **June 22**, turning your creativity and social skills into professional assets. Use your charm to graciously guide people where you want them to go—you'll be pleasantly surprised how well it all turns out.

AQUARIUS

JULY

REACH FOR THE SKY

The retrograde turn of your ruling planet, Uranus, on **July 1** shifts the field of significant change from your outer environment to your inner thoughts and feelings. You
are again reminded that freedom comes from within; altering your beliefs and attitudes is more liberating than anything you do in the external world. Additionally,
this action-packed month features two eclipses and the second magical conjunction
of Jupiter, Chiron, and Neptune. The Full Moon in industrious Capricorn on **July 7** is
a Solar Eclipse falling in your 12th House of Inner Peace that reveals the importance of the private work you do away from prying eyes. While disappointment can
lead you to question your beliefs, sturdy Saturn's uplifting trine to this Full Moon
rewards you for reestablishing a spiritual practice as part of your daily life. You're
strengthened by your ongoing commitment to rooting yourself in a higher power,
whether it's through prayer, meditation, or communing with nature.

A Solar Eclipse in security-conscious Cancer on **July 21** in your 6th House of
Employment can rattle things at work. However, electric Uranus's creative trine to
this New Moon can spark a sudden solution that replaces uncertainty with excitement. Jovial Jupiter rejoins inspirational Neptune on **July 10** and compassionate
Chiron on **July 22**, repeating the conjunctions that first occurred on **May 23–27**.
This gathering of planetary forces in your sign
elevates your spirit and expands your vision for
a more meaningful life. A profound sense of
purpose and connection to the cosmos can
make the most ordinary day feel special. Take
time out from your usual routine now to soak in
the metaphysical knowledge and you'll be newly
motivated to pursue loftier goals.

KEEP IN MIND THIS MONTH

*Don't let the drudgery and
drama of daily life diminish
the spiritual growth in store
for you now.*

KEY DATES

SUPER NOVA DAYS

JULY 1–2 ★ *intermittent brilliance*
Intellectual Mercury's imaginative trines with Jupiter and Neptune on **July 1**
give words to your dreams and help you rouse others with expressions of
compassion and wisdom. Your expanding awareness, though, may be interrupted by unexpected events or odd thoughts when Mercury squares irrever-
ent Uranus. Magnetic Venus enters the fray with a square to Jupiter on **July 2**

that can spur you to self-indulgence or overestimating others, yet her slick sextile to snappy Uranus helps you quickly change course socially or financially if you're heading in the wrong direction.

JULY 6 ★ *flights of fancy*
Sure-footed Mars in Taurus stumbles into squares with Jupiter and Neptune that can waste your time with misplaced efforts. Stretching your boundaries and exploring new activities and methods are helpful as long as you don't lose touch with your basic goals. If you're on the edge of frustration or anger, take your foot off the gas until you regain emotional equilibrium.

JULY 15–18 ★ *down but not out*
Sometimes you have to get lost to find yourself. Mercury skids off course with clunky quincunxes to Chiron, Jupiter, and Neptune on **July 15** before the lights flash on with a bright trine to Uranus on **July 16**. The Sun repeats the same slippery quincunxes that can have you flailing about on **July 17**, followed by a spontaneous correction with a Uranus trine on **July 18** to produce a sudden turnabout in your favor. Mercury's entry into dramatic Leo and your 7th House of Others on the **17th** attracts outspoken partners and encourages you to make bold public gestures.

JULY 22 ★ *double or nothing*
Your confidence rises as the Sun enters your 7th House of Partnerships and big-hearted Leo, beginning a month when it's better to express the heat of your passion than to play it cool. Showing your feelings more openly can warm up others, even if it feels like you're going too far. Taking chances, both personally and professionally, can be risky, but it's ultimately more rewarding than not even getting into the game.

JULY 27–30 ★ *divine delight*
Pleasure is yours when Venus creates sweet trines to opulent Jupiter and healing Chiron on **July 27** and to dreamy Neptune on **July 28**. Heaven and earth can meet as you bask in the company of intelligent and idealistic individuals. Still, the love planet's square to Uranus on **July 28** could signal a sudden break from someone or, at best, a breakthrough to new forms of love and delight. Oppositions from Mercury to Jupiter and Chiron on **July 29** and Neptune on **July 30** complicate communication around practical matters yet can inspire you with conversations about spiritual subjects.

AUGUST

EASY COME, EASY GO

It's easy to let go of expectations, attitudes, habits, and individuals that no longer fit in your life with the Lunar Eclipse in emotionally detached Aquarius on **August 5**. Usually, losses associated with eclipses in your sign can be painful, but flexible Mars in Gemini makes an efficient trine to this Full Moon, allowing you to effort-lessly release what you don't need. Jupiter forms a quincunx with strict Saturn on **August 19**, delaying your expansion plans—or forcing adjustments. This is the sec-ond in a series of challenging aspects that began on **March 22** and finishes on **February 5, 2010**. The high hopes and grand visions fed by Jupiter in your sign are countered by Saturn in methodical Virgo, forcing you to handle mundane matters on the way to making your dreams come true. This might feel like a detour, but carefully managing specific details is essential to reaching your long-term goals.

Dramatic people can spice up your life with the New Moon in lively Leo in your 7th House of Partners on **August 20**. Because this Sun-Moon conjunction opposes Jupiter, Chiron, and Neptune, you may have an accomplice as you hatch imagina-tive schemes. The potential to miss the mark with too much optimism is countered by the New Moon's sextile to Mars in versatile Gemini, enabling you and your new cohort to make adjustments on the fly. The practical aspects of relationships, both personal and professional, come into sharp focus with the Sun's entry into discerning Virgo and your 8th House of Shared Resources on **August 22**. Fortunately, mental Mercury enters your 9th House of Big Ideas on **August 25** to keep alive a spirit of adventure.

> **KEEP IN MIND THIS MONTH**
>
> *The most stubborn problems can be resolved when you're flexible enough to seek alter-native solutions.*

KEY DATES

AUGUST 3–5 ★ *impulse control*

You may not be inclined to compromise on **August 3** as the willful Sun forms a testy sesquisquare with erratic Uranus. If you're convinced that a relationship is no longer tenable, keep that thought to yourself—it's not quite the moment to show your cards. The Lunar Eclipse in Aquarius on **August 5** will allow you to make a more gracious exit or discover an ingenious way to improve the situation.

AUGUST 13–14 ★ *actions speak louder*

You have more than enough energy to launch new projects, line up the support of others, and pick up an extra job on the side when dynamic Mars trines opportunistic Jupiter on **August 13**. Still, it may be wiser to think about all these things rather than actually do them. Jupiter's opposition to the Sun on **August 14** puts more wind in your sails, but don't waste its power by making big promises or cooking up schemes with someone who's all talk but no action. Doing something small but substantial is worth more than mere words.

SUPER NOVA DAYS
AUGUST 17–18 ★ *dream a little dream*

Fantasy can fill your day with the Sun's opposition to surreal Neptune on **August 17**. Imaginative individuals weave tales of wonder that inspire or deceive you. Fortunately, active Mars's trine to Neptune can give you a way to make the magic really happen. An experienced person could give you a tip that brings your vision down to earth. Sticking to a schedule, though, may be tough on **August 18**, when Mars crashes into Uranus with a volatile square that can interrupt your plans. Internal stress or external pressure builds to an explosive point. If you feel jittery or jumpy, back away from conflict and apply that force creatively to transform danger into an opportunity.

AUGUST 21–22 ★ *creative juice*

Fascinating thoughts and fast talk are stimulated on **August 21** by a high-speed opposition of Mercury and Uranus. You may be filled with bright ideas, but adapting them to the slower pace around you requires patience. Lovely Venus's trine to surprising Uranus on **August 22** enlivens relationships, reveals new forms of pleasure, and helps you let bygones be bygones.

AUGUST 26 ★ *king of the jungle*

A mix of style and struggle is possible when Mercury and Mars align with dark Pluto in hard aspects that can incite resentment and harsh words. However, peacemaking Venus enters brave Leo in your 7th House of Partnerships to bring courage and grace into your life. Pride may be the key issue—when you wear it with confidence, you can minimize conflict, but using it as a mask to cover weakness leaves battles almost inevitable.

SEPTEMBER

FOLLOW YOUR INSTINCTS

Money matters may come to a head this month with both the Full and New Moons falling in the financial houses of your chart. The Full Moon in spacey Pisces on **September 4** occurs in your 2nd House of Resources. The sensitive nature of this sign could rattle your economic cage with uncertainty. Its message, though, is to be more intuitive in developing your talents and managing your cash flow. On **September 18**, the New Moon in pragmatic Virgo plants seeds of possibility in the 8th House of Shared Resources that could stimulate growth in business or personal partnerships. Allying yourself with competent and hardworking individuals is important—but with radical Uranus opposing the Sun, Moon, and rigid Saturn, you may feel stifled by an overly controlling relationship.

Saturn and Uranus make the third in their long series of oppositions on **September 15**, reactivating the conflict between order and freedom that began on **November 4, 2008**, and returned on **February 5**. This ongoing struggle to solidify a position of greater liberty in your life won't happen overnight. Even if you make a major breakthrough against old limits and fears this month, patiently secure your gains because this face-off between Saturn's status quo and Uranus's futuristic vision will reappear on **April 26, 2010**, and **July 26, 2010**. Another key factor this

month is Mercury's retrograde turn in your 9th House of Voyages on **September 7**. The communication planet's backward transit may require you to alter plans associated with travel or education. The urge to expand your horizons grows with the Sun's entry into your adventurous 9th House on **September 22**, yet you may have to adjust to minor delays until tricky Mercury turns direct on **September 29**.

> **KEEP IN MIND THIS MONTH**
>
> *Consistency may be an unreachable goal, but your awareness of the extremes makes it possible to successfully manage them.*

KEY DATES

SEPTEMBER 1–2 ★ *hold your horses*

Your exuberance and breadth of knowledge make you a very persuasive teacher and motivator now. Yet tough aspects to Jupiter from chatty Mercury on **September 1** and from assertive Mars on **September 2** can wind you up so tightly that you say or do too much. Overwhelming others with information or overpowering them with your passion might cost you their support or even provoke conflict, so try to tone your energy down.

SEPTEMBER 4 ★ *taste test*

A daring Venus-Uranus sesquisquare encourages you to experiment with your appearance and the ways you connect with people. If you don't get the reactions you want, try not to take it too personally. Moods can shift quickly, and your sense of self-worth will fluctuate. Think of this as a time to explore possibilities rather than taking a stand about what's right or wrong.

SEPTEMBER 11 ★ *extravagant living*

The excessive traits of untamed Jupiter can make this an expensive day of poor judgment. Sensual Venus in luscious Leo opposes the giant planet to expand your desire for pleasure and increase your expectations of others. Enjoying the company of warmhearted people is a reward you deserve—but try not to splurge. The Sun's ungainly quincunx with Jupiter can also mar your sense of proportion and encourage aimless conversations or encounters with egotistical people. By all means, stretch your boundaries of love, pleasure, and self-esteem with high hopes and new experiences, but do it within a range that you can sustain.

SUPER NOVA DAYS
SEPTEMBER 16–17 ★ *breaking away*

A wobbly Venus-Uranus quincunx on **September 16** makes it hard to know where you stand with others. Tension is growing, so tread lightly unless you're ready to make a dramatic change. On **September 17**, the Sun opposes wired Uranus and joins uptight Saturn, putting you right in the middle of this ongoing struggle between freedom and duty, excitement and safety. You may react to any restrictions with fierce resistance, but the real conflict is within yourself. Instead of blowing up at someone else, consider this a reminder to apply your genius toward creating more freedom in your life.

SEPTEMBER 22–23 ★ *shades of light and dark*

The Sun enters peaceable Libra and your 9th House of Higher Truth on **September 22**, heralding the Autumn Equinox and a more harmonious vision of your future. However, its tense square to insatiable Pluto on **September 23** can quickly lead to power struggles that pull you back to reality. Facing fears, manipulators, and your own primal desires today can clear the way to a nobler tomorrow.

OCTOBER

INTELLECTUAL PURSUITS

You have plenty of opportunities to share your love of ideas this month: Several planetary patterns prompt a high level of mental activity. It all starts with a Full Moon in go-getter Aries on **October 4** that falls in your 3rd House of Information. Fresh data, fast thinking, and sparkling conversations keep you intellectually entertained and, perhaps, challenged by unfamiliar concepts. Brainy Mercury enters diplomatic Libra and your 9th House of Higher Education on **October 9** to open your mind through course work, personal studies, or travel. The communication planet's presence here makes you a successful teacher or salesperson thanks to an ability to listen just as skillfully as you speak. On **October 12**, philosophical Jupiter turns direct in your sign, which should make you a bit more comfortable expressing yourself. Hopes for a more rewarding future that have been circulating inside your head will be more easily translated into positive action now.

Sweet Venus enters your educational 9th House on **October 14** to make acquiring knowledge a pleasure. Dynamic Mars moves into heartfelt Leo and your 7th House of Partnerships on **October 16**, where he's bound to enliven relationships. Forceful individuals could be exciting and intimidating; the lesson is that it's time to express your passion more openly. The sociable Libra New Moon on **October 18** arrives in your 9th House to increase opportunities for travel and advanced education. Idealism, however, is tempered with professional responsibilities when the Sun enters Scorpio and your 10th House of Career on **October 23**. Nevertheless, the long-term value of study and serious thought is underscored on **October 29** when ambitious Saturn enters objective Libra and your 9th House, where it will reside for the better part of the next two years.

> **KEEP IN MIND THIS MONTH**
>
> *Despite the material demands of your daily life, exploring ideas for the sheer joy of it is still a wise investment of your time.*

KEY DATES

SUPER NOVA DAY
OCTOBER 4 ★ *overloaded circuits*
Today starts with an awkward Venus-Jupiter quincunx that leads you to misjudge the value of people or products—or of your own capacity for self-indulgence. A high-speed Mercury-Uranus opposition zaps your mind with strange ideas

and brilliant insights that can also complicate ordinary conversations and scramble your schedule with unexpected events. Fortunately, active Mars forms a creative trine with innovative Uranus, blasting you with a flash of awareness that makes sense of the oddest situations.

OCTOBER 9–11 ★ *rocky road ahead*

A Venus-Uranus opposition on **October 9** upsets you with unexpected shifts in social plans or relationships. Normally, you can go with the flow, but an opposition from irritable Mars to the Moon's North Node may evoke fear and conflict. It's easier to defuse a tense situation before it gets out of hand than to put out a fire once it's taken hold. A more generous spirit gives you a philosophical perspective with a Sun-Jupiter trine on **October 10** that reduces tension. Yet a stubborn Mercury-Pluto square, followed by a Mercury-Jupiter sesquisquare on **October 11**, makes it difficult to let go of little details that tend to keep things off balance.

OCTOBER 16 ★ *give peace a chance*

Clashing with an authority figure is likely to rub both of you the wrong way today, because a Sun-Uranus quincunx reveals differences that aren't readily resolved. However, a spiritual Sun-Neptune trine brings a more compassionate perspective that makes it easier to forgive and to be forgiven.

OCTOBER 20 ★ *clear channel*

Good news arrives with an open-minded trine between detail-oriented Mercury and auspicious Jupiter. Information that's been stuck in transit flows easily now, as do bright ideas, stimulating conversations, and clever remarks. You know how to make a point with grace, presenting your opinions rationally with a friendly smile that gives you credibility without coming across too seriously.

OCTOBER 28–29 ★ *skillful leader*

Your words become more intense, especially related to work, when verbal Mercury enters emotional Scorpio in your 10th House of Career on **October 28**. A bighearted Venus-Jupiter trine brings pleasure as you get back twice as much as you give. Small acts of kindness or competence earn you more praise than you might expect. Mental acuity is present with a sharp Mercury-Pluto sextile that reveals secrets through research or private conversations. Self-control may become critical on **October 29**, when an angry square between Mars and the Sun attracts a competitive person who attacks your authority. Calmly standing up for yourself is the best way to minimize trouble.

NOVEMBER

TAKING CARE OF BUSINESS

Down-to-earth issues draw your attention this month, as practical concerns about the present leave you less time to fantasize about the future. A Full Moon in functional Taurus on **November 2** falls in your 4th House of Home and Family, reminding you to shore up your material and emotional foundations. Time spent with your loved ones deepens trust and heads off potential problems; preventive maintenance of your physical environment is another worthy investment. Active Mars and presumptuous Jupiter square the Full Moon, tempting you into home improvement projects that require more resources than you might expect. It's wiser to make minor modifications to what you already have and manage your money carefully than to take on major remodeling that could grow exorbitant.

The New Moon in transformational Scorpio on **November 16** can reshuffle the deck in your professional life. This Sun-Moon conjunction in your 10th House of Career squares the idealistic Jupiter-Chiron-Neptune trio, motivating you to bring a sense of spirituality or community service to your work. Unless you can meet your other obligations with greater efficiency, however, you may be taking on more than you can handle. You might start thinking about altering your employment situation, too—especially with inventive Uranus, your ruling planet, making a creative trine to this New Moon. Magnetic Venus's entry into passionate Scorpio and your 10th House on **November 7** can intensify relationships on the job while also revealing ways to work with colleagues more effectively. Your focus on survival issues is sharpened by a fertile square between austere Saturn and prioritizing Pluto on **November 15**. This powerful event recurs on **January 31, 2010**, and **August 21, 2010**, foreshadowing a long process of eliminating distractions that inhibit your potency.

> **KEEP IN MIND THIS MONTH**
>
> *Take direct action on practical matters even if your methods don't correspond with your favorite theories.*

KEY DATES

NOVEMBER 2 ★ *erratic encounters*

You're likely to encounter someone who surprises you with unconventional behavior today, as assertive Mars and stylish Venus clash with shocking Uranus to undermine your sense of security and disrupt your schedule. Yet if you're willing to explore new experiences without expectations, this could be an exciting time to discover new friends and forms of fun.

NOVEMBER 8–11 ★ *unnecessary force*
Any plans you have for a quiet Sunday on **November 8** may be shattered with an overload of information and a potential power struggle. Recognize when someone won't budge so you can save yourself wasted explanations and entreaties. A more benevolent mood prevails on **November 10** when the Sun squares giant Jupiter, yet this could lure you into making commitments you'll have a hard time keeping. Bright ideas can save the day with an intuitive Mercury-Uranus trine on **November 11** that spawns unconventional solutions to seemingly intractable problems. Thinking outside the box is your best way out of a bind.

NOVEMBER 14 ★ *ingenious solution*
An edgy Venus-Uranus sesquisquare makes it hard to control social events as an uncooperative partner or sudden shift of mood rattles relationships. Fortunately, an innovative Sun-Uranus trine gives you the flexibility and imagination to turn an awkward situation into an enjoyable adventure where everyone can have fun.

NOVEMBER 25–26 ★ *a softer side of you*
Your playful side is showing on **November 25**, when a Venus-Uranus trine encourages you to seek pleasure in unusual forms. An unconventional look attracts attention, even if you're only doing it for your own amusement. You feel vulnerable on **November 26** as super-sensitive Neptune squares self-conscious Venus. One careless comment or look of annoyance can be enough to trigger your insecurities. A gentle gesture, however, can draw you closer to someone to share a tender moment in which all will be forgiven.

NOVEMBER 29–30 ★ *bouncing all over the place*
You could be cracking lots of jokes with a witty Mercury-Jupiter sextile on **November 29**. The harmonious hookup of these two mental planets is ideal for clear thinking and communication, making it easy to shift from serious to silly and back again in a flash. The Moon's presence in earthy Taurus helps you take your brightest ideas and apply them in practical ways. High-frequency thoughts on **November 30** are triggered by an electric Mercury-Uranus square that's better for sudden hits of intuition than patient problem solving. Conversations are likely to be interrupted, and there's a sense of urgency that's very stimulating but can wear on your nerves. Slow down at the first sign of stress to keep from losing your emotional equilibrium.

DECEMBER
·

VISION QUEST

The month starts off at a rapid pace. Uranus initiates the excitement by turning direct on **December 1**. The forward shift of your ruling planet while pleasurable Venus enters adventurous Sagittarius incites impulsiveness and a taste for new experiences. Restlessness continues with the Full Moon in flighty Gemini in your 5th House of Fun and Games on **December 2**. The rising wave created by the third and final conjunctions of expansive Jupiter with compassionate Chiron that occurred on **May 23 and July 22**, and with imaginative Neptune on **May 27 and July 10**, returns on **December 7 and 21**. Your spirits are infused with hopes and expectations for the future. You're tempted to drop your present obligations to pursue a vision that takes you far from your current circumstances. It may take longer than you think to turn your dream into reality, though, no matter how beautiful the view.

Physical Mars and mental Mercury both turn retrograde this month. The backward turn of the energetic warrior planet on **December 20** starts in your 7th House of Partners, where you're likely to encounter delays when others cannot stick to schedule. You may have to go over the same issue several times before your team functions effectively. Reconnecting with old friends, colleagues, or an ex-lover is likely before Mars goes direct on **March 10, 2010**. Messenger Mercury's retrograde begins on **December 26** in your 12th House of Secrets and Spirituality, adding complexity to conversations and difficulty with details until its forward turn on **January 15, 2010**. This is, however, a favorable period for deep reflection that reveals the source of blockages or fears. Take time to explore the shadowy aspects of your personal history, untying the knots that have inhibited your growth.

> **KEEP IN MIND THIS MONTH**
>
> *A life-changing vision inspires you to greatness. Nevertheless, don't expect major changes to happen overnight.*

KEY DATES
DECEMBER 2 ★ *playfully productive*
You can be as playful as a puppy with the curious Gemini Full Moon in your 5th House of Love and Creativity. Any conversation can be a source of flirting and fun as your wit sparkles and shines. And even if you seem to be just shooting the breeze, with serious Saturn's supportive trine to the Full Moon you're actually getting some work done.

DECEMBER 10 ★ *charisma in action*
Passion can make you a great leader and innovator today. The creative Sun forms a free-flowing trine with energetic Mars in Leo to rev you up with enough force to overcome any obstacle—and enough charm to do it without ruffling feathers. Aligning yourself with those who share your enthusiasm is the key to making the most of your personal and professional relationships.

SUPER NOVA DAYS
DECEMBER 14–16 ★ *give it time*
Expect fireworks with authorities when the Sun squares unruly Uranus on **December 14**. The Sun's supportive sextiles to visionary Jupiter and Neptune on **December 14–15** can balance your immediate need for autonomy with a long-range perspective, enabling you to relax and watch events unfold at their own pace. On **December 16**, tension rises again with a spunky Sagittarius New Moon in your 11th House of Teamwork square impatient Uranus. Battles with friends or associates are possible, but Mars's trine to the Sun-Moon conjunction from creative Leo shows that a playful attitude and a little imagination can transform a struggle into a fresh new way of working together.

DECEMBER 19–21 ★ *count your blessings*
Relationships are rocked by a volatile Venus-Uranus square on **December 19**, but adapting to changing tastes and social conditions gets easier with the love planet's adaptable sextiles to Jupiter and Neptune on **December 20 and 21**. Additionally, on **December 21**, the Winter Solstice is marked by the Sun's entry into traditional Capricorn and your 12th House of Inner Peace. Fight or flight turns to delight as a generous mood opens you and those around you to enjoy the finer things of life.

DECEMBER 31 ★ *to feel it is to know it*
Serious thinking about your job shows you its limits and what you can do to overcome them. A Lunar Eclipse in your 6th House of Work in self-protective Cancer helps you recognize whether your needs are being met in your daily life. Realistic Saturn's tense square to this emotional Full Moon makes it impossible to deny your feelings, even if facing them presents you with practical challenges. Whether you decide to reapply yourself in your current position or look elsewhere for greener professional pastures, trusting your instincts is the first step toward success.

PISCES

FEBRUARY 19–MARCH 20

PISCES

2008 SUMMARY

You're ready for more responsibility and higher achievement, but ultimately your success depends on the quality of relationships you create with others. Carrying the load of a less-than-capable partner can wear you down in your personal life or hold you back in your career. Two eclipses in the 12th House, though, turn this into a critical year of letting go of old metaphysical concepts and religious beliefs, preparing you for new dimensions of awareness.

AUGUST—*partnership potential*

Thoughtless and unkind remarks tend to undermine trust, but constructive criticism can be a major asset for building stronger relationships.

SEPTEMBER—*rider on the storm*

If you keep a light hand on the wheel, the road will tell you which way you need to turn to avoid accidents and safely reach your destination.

OCTOBER—*hunger to learn*

Tune in carefully to what others are saying and you'll discover the best way to satisfy their needs while also fulfilling your own desires.

NOVEMBER—*endings and beginnings*

No matter how irritated you are by an obstinate person, gentle persuasion will be more effective than an emotional eruption.

DECEMBER—*serious about getting ahead*

You can achieve great things if you focus on yourself and let your ambition fuel the fire in your belly.

2008 CALENDAR

AUGUST

FRIDAY 1 ★ Conversations can go in circles through the 2nd

WEDNESDAY 6 ★ Be creative when there are no expectations to follow

WEDNESDAY 13 ★ **SUPER NOVA DAYS** Don't give up on love through the 16th

THURSDAY 21 ★ Stay on your toes through the 23rd. Surprises are in store

THURSDAY 28 ★ Sharing your feelings can heal a relationship through the 29th

SEPTEMBER

WEDNESDAY 3 ★ Decisions made through the 8th have a lasting effect

FRIDAY 12 ★ **SUPER NOVA DAYS** Chaos fuels change through the 15th

WEDNESDAY 17 ★ Indulge in a healthy escape

SATURDAY 20 ★ Supportive friends can help keep you centered through the 22nd

OCTOBER

SATURDAY 4 ★ **SUPER NOVA DAYS** Be clear about your needs through the 6th

SATURDAY 11 ★ Avoid your tendency to sacrifice for the happiness of others

TUESDAY 14 ★ Set realistic limits now

TUESDAY 21 ★ Your actions are fueled by quiet strength through the 22nd

SUNDAY 26 ★ Heartfelt intensity charges your beliefs through the 28th

NOVEMBER

MONDAY 3 ★ Break free from restrictive patterns through the 5th

MONDAY 10 ★ **SUPER NOVA DAYS** Apply discipline and diligence through the 13th

SUNDAY 16 ★ Your sense of strategy is heightened through the 17th

FRIDAY 21 ★ Hope helps you make long-term constructive change

THURSDAY 27 ★ Don't take in more data than you can digest through the 28th

DECEMBER

FRIDAY 5 ★ Choose words carefully when thoughts race through the 6th

WEDNESDAY 10 ★ **SUPER NOVA DAYS** Restlessness boils over through the 13th

MONDAY 15 ★ Breathe a sigh of relief now

SUNDAY 21 ★ Stay on top of business through the 22nd

SATURDAY 27 ★ Make a total commitment to lasting change through the 28th

PISCES OVERVIEW

Although Pisces is symbolized by two fish swimming in opposite directions, they are linked by a mystical thread that is the real key to understanding your sign. These opposing forces will test you this year in ways that can alter the fabric of your life—yet you have a rare opportunity to grow if you can focus on the connection instead of the differences. At times, you may feel as if you're spinning wheels without making progress, for task-master Saturn in hardworking Virgo opposite your sun sign until October 29 places your goals out of reach. To better understand this long-term success cycle, consider what obstacles you had to overcome when Saturn was in your sign from January 1994 until April 1996. You may have started on a pathway back then and are now at a decisive moment—for your journey may not be turning out just as expected. Therefore, Saturn's visit to Virgo, which began in September 2007, can be rather discouraging. Keep in mind that this is a natural part of the cycle; **it's a great time to prune what you no longer need, creating room for new growth ahead.**

Normally, you are at ease in the midst of contradictory currents that would disturb others. Your ability to go with the flow is legendary and enables you to adapt to the needs of those around you. Since unconventional Uranus entered your sign in 2003, though, you've been on a quest to reclaim your sense of self and express your individuality—even if it means shattering other people's expectations of you. This process of self-realization will continue until Uranus leaves Pisces in 2011. However, its long-term opposition with traditional Saturn this year sets you in the middle of an irresolvable tug-of-war between your need for independence and the inescapable responsibilities of your life. The stressful Saturn-Uranus opposition began on November 4, 2008, and recurs this year on February 5 and September 15 to push you to the edge of your patience. **You are ready to break free from unacceptable restraints or break out of boring routines—yet too many impulsive actions can wreak havoc on your stability and security.** Since this aspect repeats twice more through the spring and summer of 2010, it's best to make smaller adjustments now while you work toward the bigger changes ahead. If you don't begin to take charge of your own destiny this year, unexpected events are likely to alter your current landscape whether you like it or not.

A once-every-thirteen-years conjunction of your co-ruling planets—visionary Jupiter and imaginative Neptune—is joined this year by Chiron the Wounded Healer in your 12th House of Destiny. This rare and inspirational super-conjunction can bless your year with hope for a better future, soothe old emotional pains, and rejuvenate your spirit. **It's up to you, however, to reach beyond your old comfort zone to receive these benefits**, especially on May 23–27, July 10–22, and December 7–21 when the alignment is exact.

MAKE OR BREAK

Dutiful Saturn in your 7th House of Others suggests that you might be pressured to make a commitment to someone, but this isn't a smart idea if you're harboring doubts. The Saturn-Uranus oppositions on February 5 and again on September 15 can push a relationship to its breaking point unless you're willing to address your need for freedom within the established boundaries. Your desires are stronger than usual when sensual Venus is in your sign January 3–February 2 and again April 11–24. You could reunite with an old love or revitalize a current partnership during the love planet's retrograde March 6–April 17. She visits your 5th House of Romance on July 31–August 26, followed by Mars on August 25–October 16, increasing your chances to get involved with someone special. Eclipses on July 7, July 21, and December 31 activate your love houses, bringing into the open issues that can stress an unhappy relationship—or solidify a good one.

DREAM BIG

An idealistic yearning for more meaningful work can motivate you to make significant professional changes. Even if you can't dramatically alter your career path, though, there are other things you can do to increase the possibilities for growth on the job. Expansive Jupiter, the ruler of your 10th House of Status, aligns with super-sensory Neptune on May 27, July 10, and December 21. Trusting your intuition during these times can allow you to make the most of any opportunity that comes your way. Don't be afraid to fantasize about your long-term success, for your imagination can illuminate the future in ways that your rational mind cannot yet grasp.

PLAY IT SAFE

Be careful about making risky investments this year, for they may not turn out as you expect. You're driven by your hopes—great for self-motivation, but not as useful when dealing with money. Instead of relying on metaphysical laws of abundance, then, you need to focus on a more direct approach to financial stability. Fortunately, valuable Venus spends most of February through May in your 2nd House of Money, increasing your income potential. Her retrograde March 6–April 17 can indicate a financial setback if you aren't willing to reduce your expenses, but it can also show you where you might develop your earning power by reworking an old plan. Realistic Saturn enters your 8th House of Investments and Shared Resources on October 29, motivating you to work with others, especially to ensure your long-term security.

 VISUALIZE PERFECT HEALTH

Your susceptibilities reach an extreme as Neptune the Mystic and Chiron the Wounded Healer remain closely conjunct throughout the year in your 12th House of Destiny. More than ever, your health depends on your mental state, so it's crucial to maintain a positive attitude and visualize yourself in an ideal state of well-being. The Moon's karmic South Node is in your 6th House of Health until July 26, indicating that a chronic condition could return if you don't address its root cause. Opportunistic Jupiter's conjunctions with the Moon's North Node on February 11 and with Chiron on May 23, July 22, and December 7 are excellent days to focus on preventive health care.

 A ROOM OF YOUR OWN

With chatty Mercury as the planetary ruler of your 4th House of Home and Family, your place of residence can be busy with friends and relatives sharing precious memories and fine conversation. This year, however, your home becomes a place for retreat and renewal as planets pile up in your 12th House of Privacy. You need time away from the hectic demands of your life, so you may use your living quarters as a sanctuary. Don't take on any major domestic projects during Mercury's retrograde phases January 11–February 1, May 7–30, and September 7–29.

SOMEWHERE OVER THE RAINBOW

Your dreams carry you far and wide this year, which is dominated by the boundless Jupiter-Neptune conjunctions on May 27, July 10, and December 21. Get ready for adventure, both physical and mental. This is just the beginning of a long odyssey that will gradually transform your expectations of the future over the next couple of decades as evolutionary Pluto, the ruler of your 9th House of Faraway Places, visits your 11th House of Long-Term Goals. Don't take on too much, too fast or restrictive Saturn's square to Pluto on November 15 will be a reality check that could take the wind right out of your sails.

PRACTICAL MAGIC

If you open your mind, you could discover spiritual truths this year that change your life forever. The metaphysical Jupiter-Chiron-Neptune super-conjunction activates your 12th House of Soul Consciousness all year to enlighten you about the mysteries of the universe. Bringing these cosmic lessons down to earth can be challenging, however, for even the most profound teachings are wasted unless you can apply them to your everyday life. Fortunately, you can utilize karmic Saturn's magical biquintiles with wise Jupiter on March 1 and September 13, and with intuitive Neptune on October 26, to convert theory into practice.

RICK & JEFF'S TIP FOR THE YEAR:
Start Small

Your business and personal relationships reflect your success this year at balancing your own desires with the needs of those who depend upon you. You can't escape your obligations—even trying to do so could have disastrous results. But neither can you ignore the inevitable transitions that must occur for you to reestablish lost integrity, rekindle the sparks of excitement, and re-create a life of purposeful action. Being vigilant in your interactions with others is a great place to start, but remember that small changes with lasting impact are better than dramatic gestures that quickly fade into the past.

JANUARY

WRAP IT UP

A gathering of planets in your 12th House of Endings makes the beginning of the year feel more like the belated completion of last year than a fresh start. Mental Mercury joins the farewell party on **January 1**, followed by generous Jupiter on **January 5** and the confident Sun on **January 19**. Jupiter remains in your mysterious 12th House for the entire year, bringing opportunities to connect with your subconscious mind in a variety of ways, including spiritual practice, psychotherapy, dream work, and music. You long to retreat from the hectic pace of life, and Mercury's presence here emphasizes your current need to be alone. The Winged Messenger turns retrograde on **January 11**, helping you review recent events and tie up loose ends. Sweet Venus enters your compassionate sign on **January 3**, accentuating loving relationships throughout the month. Her alignment with wild Uranus on **January 22** and reserved Saturn on **January 24** may reveal a fundamental problem with self-esteem that will gain significance next month.

The receptive Cancer Full Moon on **January 10** falls in your 5th House of Self-Expression as you embrace the paradox of needing attention while simultaneously avoiding the spotlight. Grandiose ideas flow quickly when big-thinking Jupiter is joined by quicksilver Mercury on **January 18**, and you're ready to swing into action when the willful Sun makes its annual conjunction with Jupiter on January 24. The futuristic Aquarius New Moon on **January 26** is a Solar Eclipse that can instantaneously transport you where you want to be thanks to its conjunction to benevolent Jupiter. Still, eclipses have a way of shifting the energy in unexpected ways. Be careful what you wish for, as it may not turn out the way you imagined.

> **KEEP IN MIND THIS MONTH**
>
> *Minimize your frustration by remembering that even the simplest things may take longer than you expect.*

KEY DATES

JANUARY 3–5 ★ *love is in the air*

Stylish Venus visits impressionable Pisces **January 3–February 2**, enhancing your charm and making you more approachable. But your desires deepen when the Goddess of Love creates a cooperative sextile with Pluto, the Lord of the Underworld, on **January 4**. Your comfort with this high level of passion is short-lived when erratic Uranus snaps you out of your emotional intensity into the realm of logic on **January 5**, and you must figure out what to do with your recent attractions.

JANUARY 10-11 ★ *believing is seeing*

You can seamlessly combine nonconformity with a hearty respect for authority on **January 10**, when the gentle Cancer Full Moon is supported by ingenious Uranus and structured Saturn. You have the strength of your convictions now; Mercury's retrograde turn on **January 11** can slow your progress, but it's unlikely to change your mind. The Sun-Saturn trine reinforces your beliefs and enables you to follow through on whatever you start.

JANUARY 22-24 ★ *instant karma*

Relationship issues are likely to overwhelm you as you push limits one day, then make amends the next. It can be both thrilling and upsetting when loving Venus is awakened by her conjunction to shocking Uranus on **January 22**. You may express yourself now in ways that surprise those close to you, especially when assertive Mars aspects unconventional Uranus on the same day. Your actions elicit quick retribution, though, as Venus and Mars bump into authoritative Saturn on **January 24**. The cosmic lovers may be working harmoniously with each other, yet their confrontation with responsible Saturn won't let you get away with wild behavior now. You must play by the rules, and although you may feel lonely or even rejected for your previous antics, sensible actions will be justly rewarded.

SUPER NOVA DAYS
JANUARY 26-30 ★ *on the horizon*

Your life is about to leap forward again. On **January 26**, a progressive Aquarius New Moon Eclipse releases enough tensions to turn everything upside down. Jovial Jupiter's conjunction to this eclipse in your 12th House of Destiny is likely to make you feel optimistic about the future. You aren't willing to be a bystander, though, as talkative Mercury joins impatient Mars on **January 27**. It's time to put your words into motion. Nevertheless, your awareness of a chronic issue is activated on **January 27 and 30**, when giant Jupiter forms tense aspects to the brittle opposition between staid Saturn and revolutionary Uranus that's exact on **February 5**. You won't find resolution now, but at least you can think more freely about your options.

FEBRUARY

THE TEMPTATION OF ESCAPE

A long-lasting opposition from Saturn the Taskmaster to Uranus the Awakener that began on **November 4, 2008**, requires you to work harder than ever this month. On **February 5**, these two slow-moving planets align for a second time, reminding you of everything you want to change but can't. You're ready to explode, convinced that you're destined to be either a prisoner chained to a life you no longer want, or a free spirit following your cosmic destiny. Caught in the polarity, you may be overwhelmed by frustration unless you remain vigilant. Impulsively trying to escape responsibility is not a viable option, but neither is denying your true nature. Compromise is difficult—yet it's your job right now to moderate these extremes until circumstances let you make your move. Don't expect immediate solutions, for you will revisit these issues when the Saturn-Uranus opposition returns on **September 15, April 26, 2010**, and **July 26, 2010**.

You can make a great deal of progress this month, because Mercury the Communicator turns direct on **February 1**, and Venus's entry into courageous Aries and your 2nd House of Money on **February 2** can excite you about your financial prospects. Additionally, assertive Mars enters idealistic Aquarius on **February 4** to fire up your dreams, especially when he conjuncts confident Jupiter on **February 17.**

The proud Leo Full Moon on **February 9** is a Lunar Eclipse in your 6th House of Details. You prefer to live in a dream world and not the minutiae, so anything that makes you focus your attention closely can feel limiting. Trust your intuition when the Sun returns to your sign on **February 18**, followed by a supernatural Pisces New Moon on **February 24** that inspires you to make your dreams come true.

> **KEEP IN MIND THIS MONTH**
>
> *Rising tensions make it difficult to stay positive right now—yet in fact you're closer to your ideal life than you realize.*

KEY DATES

FEBRUARY 5 ★ *play nice*

Focus on managing stress today, as restrictive Saturn in your 7th House of Relationships opposes unrestrainable Uranus in your 1st House of Self. Your need for autonomy conflicts with other people's dependence on you. You may be convinced there's no way out when congenial Venus squares ruthless Pluto. Your fears could drive you to lash out—possibly at the wrong target. Avoid manipulative schemes and try a more temperate approach that focuses on long-term solutions rather than a quick fix.

FEBRUARY 11-12 ★ *safety first*

Your energy builds as "go for it" Mars in your 12th House of Fantasy continues to approach extravagant Jupiter, yet you may be stopped in your tracks on **February 11** when the God of War meets Saturn the Boss in less-than-encouraging circumstances. Instead of adapting a more mature approach and heeding the warning, you might try to break through the resistance—Mars's tense semisquare to rebellious Uranus on **February 12** won't let you take no for an answer. Additionally, the Sun's conjunction with your key planet Neptune the Dreamer can mesmerize you with your own illusions, seducing you into ignoring any danger signs. Accepting wise counsel is smarter than learning a lesson the hard way.

SUPER NOVA DAYS
FEBRUARY 15-17 ★ *optical illusion*

Beautiful Venus creates a tense semisquare with deceptive Neptune on **February 15**, painting your desires in rose-colored hues. Meanwhile, Venus cooperatively sextiles overreaching Jupiter on **February 16**, encouraging you to ignore any potential problems ahead. It's difficult to maintain your sense of proportion when action-hero Mars conjuncts Jupiter on **February 17**, further exaggerating your ability to perform like Superman. If you can't restrain your enthusiasm, at least apply it to a worthwhile cause.

FEBRUARY 27-28 ★ *collateral damage*

Even if you're just standing around minding your own business, trouble finds you when feisty Mars crosses swords with take-no-prisoners Pluto on **February 27**. These two combative planets now use your imagination as a stage for their battle. Clever Mercury steps into the action on **February 28**, persuading you to talk tougher than you feel to fend off a perceived attack from a friend. But your mind may be working overtime, and your defensive words could actually provoke aggression you only imagined. Nevertheless, you may have some cleaning up to do on the **28th** when hot Mars forms an irritating quincunx to cold Saturn in your 7th House of Others.

MARCH

ELUSIVE SATISFACTION

This is not an easy month for you. Venus begins her retrograde cycle on **March 6** in your 2nd House of Self-Worth, putting your desires on the back burner. The planet of love and money, Venus can be spontaneous in Aries, yet her backward movement through **April 17** may actually slow you down. You doubt yourself and wonder what others see in you—a lack of confidence that can diminish your income unless you consciously decide to guard against your excessive modesty and self-deprecation. On the other hand, Venus in your financially sensible 2nd House could turn you into a successful negotiator who can revisit a recent opportunity and bring it back to life.

Retrograde Venus isn't the only planetary influence that can delay prosperity and postpone love now. Zealous Jupiter forms a long-lasting quincunx with pragmatic Saturn on **March 22** to skew your judgment into underestimating the resources needed to complete a job. Additionally, Jupiter's tense semisquare to forceful Pluto on **March 27** can intensify your discontent with your current rate of progress. An exacting Virgo Full Moon on **March 10** falls in your 7th House of Partners to reactivate last month's relationship issues and possibly turn you into a harsh judge of yourself and others. The Sun enters pioneering Aries on **March 20**, the Spring Equinox, enticing you with enterprising ventures. The Aries New Moon in your 2nd House of Money on **March 26** continues the "newness" theme. Indeed, its conjunction with friendly Venus can attract a fresh source of money or love into your life.

> **KEEP IN MIND THIS MONTH**
>
> *Your heart's desires are intense now . . . but they may remain just out of reach. Avoid frustration now by acknowledging how much you already possess.*

KEY DATES

MARCH 5–6 ★ *express yourself*

You can tap a deep creative well when the Sun forms a transformative quintile with intense Pluto on **March 5**. Communicator Mercury conjoins otherworldly Neptune to add spiritual vision to your words. Still, you may feel blocked by memories of a difficult or hurtful situation, for assertive Mars joins wounded Chiron on the same day. Poetic Venus turns retrograde on **March 6**, tempting you to retreat rather than interact. Take a chance and ride the expressive tide instead of holding everything in because of unsubstantiated fears.

MARCH 8 ★ *lost in space*
You may lose direction today as go-getter Mars conjuncts foggy Neptune. Logical Mercury's entry into intuitive Pisces cautions you not to trust the facts. Instead of relying on your natural instincts, though, the Sun's annual opposition to exacting Saturn leaves you temporarily paralyzed by fear of doing the wrong thing. Putting off any major decisions is a smart idea now; wait until after the Full Moon, when your confidence will return.

MARCH 10-12 ★ *it's getting better all the time*
Your mind is sharp thanks to analytical Mercury's supportive sextile to piercing Pluto on **March 10**—the same day the critical Virgo Full Moon joins austere Saturn. But keep your emotions in check so they don't interfere with your objectivity. Allow yourself to be joyful on **March 11**, when rich Venus receives the support of bountiful Jupiter. Just be careful, for it's tempting now to be overly generous with your heart, or spend too much on something beautiful that you don't really need. An electric Sun-Uranus conjunction can shock you with an amazing idea or surprising experience on **March 12**. Don't say no simply because you're afraid of what others might think. An exciting new jolt of energy may be exactly what you need.

MARCH 22-23 ★ *emotional exposure*
Your indecision grows when an annoying Jupiter-Saturn quincunx wedges you into a difficult position on **March 22**. Mental Mercury's alignment with unorthodox Uranus can reveal an original solution, but other aspects diminish your certainty. Ultimately, a tough Sun-Pluto square on **March 23** can force you to take a stand; just don't overcompensate for your insecurity by acting tougher than you feel.

SUPER NOVA DAYS
MARCH 26-30 ★ *happy ending*
The courageous Aries New Moon on **March 26** can clear the air of unresolved feelings that have been holding you back. Mercury dynamically squares shadowy Pluto on **March 27** to uncover the motives of someone blocking your progress. And although far-reaching Jupiter's involvement might widen your horizons, it's Mercury's conjunctions with the Sun and Venus **March 28–30** that offer compassionate communication—indicating a sweet outcome to these intense few days.

APRIL

HOT TO TROT

Spring fever can set your blood on fire this month as impetuous Mars moves through your sign until the **22nd** and sensual Venus backs into emotionally vulnerable Pisces on **April 11-24**. But all is not rosy: Venus's tough square to dark Pluto on **April 3** and Mars's tense opposition to cold Saturn on **April 4** may have you slamming on the emotional brakes to avoid a relationship wall. Fortunately, paying attention to your feelings and slowing down enough to acknowledge those of someone else can be just what you need to make the most of the possibilities ahead. Mars's conjunction with high-voltage Uranus on **April 15** electrifies your nervous system. If you can find a way to express this energy, it will lead to thrilling experiences; if you can't you may be left with a free-floating anxiety that's hard to manage. Venus turns direct on **April 17** to start the relationship wheels moving forward again after a period of review or maybe even regret. The cosmic lovers, Venus and Mars, kiss on **April 21** in your 1st House of Personality, increasing your charisma and magnifying your sex appeal. It may be time for a spring makeover or an upgrade to your wardrobe.

The socially astute Libra Full Moon on **April 9** is your green light for intimacy, for it falls in your 8th House of Deep Sharing and is further bolstered by a harmonious trine from opulent Jupiter. On **April 24**, a practical Taurus New Moon in your 3rd House of Communication trines shadowy Pluto to intensify your life. This is an opportune time for talking about things that matter, even if you must raise a difficult issue.

KEEP IN MIND THIS MONTH

Start slowly and methodically and your patience will be rewarded. No matter what, don't try to force anyone to keep up with your schedule.

KEY DATES

APRIL 2-4 ★ *no easy fix*

You could be in a serious funk on **April 2** when analytical Mercury forms a crunchy quincunx with concrete Saturn, turning a simple problem into an unsolvable mystery because you can't trust your own logic. Innocent Venus squares potent Pluto on **April 3**, deepening your emotions and making them very difficult to manage. Although a positive Mercury-Jupiter aspect on **April 4** encourages you to talk about your feelings, an opposition between energetic Mars and resistant Saturn leaves you dissatisfied. Don't take out your frustrations on others; instead, learn from a past mistake and change your attitude.

APRIL 9-11 ★ *from the bottom of your heart*

Look for a kinder and gentler approach to love thanks to cerebral Mercury's entry into sensual Taurus on **April 9**, and romantic Venus's retrograde return to your sensitive sign on **April 11**. Positive aspects to optimistic Jupiter on **April 10** grace you with an uplifting attitude. Although Full Moons are often overwhelming, this one in relationship-oriented Libra on **April 9** provides you with a much-needed sense of balance. Be careful what you say on **April 11**, when Mercury receives a passionate blast from incisive Pluto to give your words tremendous power.

APRIL 15-17 ★ *hurry up and wait*

Your impatience drives you to make quick decisions now, even if you'd be better served by taking more time to think. Fiery Mars joins erratic Uranus in escapist Pisces on **April 15**, encouraging risky behavior. The Sun's supportive sextile to intuitive Neptune can foster an illusory sense of certainty, even when you don't yet have all the substantiating data. Instead of lighting the fuse without thinking about what will happen next, take a few deep breaths and wait for the sensible support you'll receive from Mercury's trine to stabilizing Saturn on **April 17**.

SUPER NOVA DAYS
APRIL 22-26 ★ *blind faith*

You are all fired up and raring to go as aggressive Mars and the needy Moon both enter rowdy Aries on **April 22**. You receive a go-ahead from an uncompromising Sun-Pluto trine on **April 23** and Venus's direct reentry into Aries on **April 24**—the same day as a New Moon in determined Taurus. If you feel unstoppable, though, remember that this can be dangerous. Mercury's square to nebulous Neptune on **April 25** confuses reality with illusion, while Mars's square to ruthless Pluto on **April 26** can intensify any situation to the point of meltdown. You may be right, but is it worth a fight to the finish? Conscious negotiation combined with flexibility is much smarter than unconscious conflict fueled by fearful rigidity.

MAY

ONCE UPON A DREAM

You are increasingly challenged to distinguish fact from fiction as your dreams escape the nights and overflow into your days. This is a tremendous opportunity for creative expression, but it may be difficult to turn the jewels of your imagination into tangible products. Visionary Jupiter's sweep across compassionate Chiron on **May 23** and ethereal Neptune on **May 27**—as Chiron and Neptune draw close together—drives your spiritual quest. This rare triple-planet conjunction occurs in your 12th House of Soul Consciousness, luring you away from your mundane responsibilities and exposing you to nonphysical dimensions of the mind—the realms of myth and symbol. But this is not a ticket to dodge responsibility; in fact, you may be confronted with hard work to assimilate all you're learning as your soul deepens and your spirit grows. Don't try to get closure on whatever happens now, for this pattern repeats on **July 10–22** and **December 7–21** to awaken your dreams again and again.

Interactive Mercury turns retrograde on **May 7–30**, confirming your inward journey this month and sending you back to the drawing board to rework old plans before you can transform your ideas into action. The mysterious Scorpio Full Moon on **May 9** is stressed by shady Pluto, compelling you to change your perspective when you realize what you accidentally missed. Integrating previously suppressed feelings, though, can help you rediscover your true purpose and give you the strength you need to reach your goals. The curious Gemini New Moon on **May 24** falls in your 4th House of Roots, enticing you to delve even deeper into the origins of your current feelings.

> **KEEP IN MIND THIS MONTH**
>
> *Exploring your fantasies does not mean you must take any specific action to make them come true. For now, just watch your Technicolor dreams unfold.*

KEY DATES

SUPER NOVA DAYS
MAY 2–5 ★ *personal conviction*
You have an opportunity on **May 2** to revisit an issue that can alter your core beliefs or impact your earning potential as beautiful Venus in your 2nd House of Self-Worth creates a stressful square with relentless Pluto. You may have to struggle with your passions or resist someone else's. An enthusiastic

Mars-Jupiter semisquare on **May 4** can encourage you to go for broke and get your feelings out into the open. Thankfully, a stabilizing Sun-Saturn trine on **May 5** provides additional strength as long as you're true to yourself.

MAY 8–11 ★ *pushing buttons*
The Sun's stressful sesquisquare to demanding Pluto on **May 8** can incite disagreements with friends. On **May 9**, you may be uncharacteristically stubborn when the simplistic Taurus Sun in your 3rd House of Communication is opposed by the complex Scorpio Full Moon. Instead of closing down to the possibility of change, try to anticipate the relief you'll feel once the current resistance dissipates. Still, you could have a challenging time finding the the right amount of force to apply—a tough aspect between aggressive Mars and strict Saturn on **May 11** makes it difficult to know where the limits are until it's too late.

MAY 16–17 ★ *runaway train*
Reckless schemes explode like fireworks thanks to a brilliant Sun-Uranus sextile on **May 16**. Dynamic squares to Jupiter, Chiron, and Neptune on **May 16–17** can make your dreams seem real—but be careful, for your imagination is running wild. Although this stimulates creative visualization, practice keeping one foot on the ground so you don't end up wasting time and energy on an impractical plan.

MAY 20 ★ *back to the drawing board*
Mental Mercury squares the tightening Jupiter-Chiron-Neptune super-conjunction, making you less certain of your ability to turn your dreams into reality, for when you lose focus you can be overwhelmed by these mystical planets. Your options are limited, though, if an authority figure rejects your innovative plan, as indicated by a frustrating Venus-Saturn quincunx. Luckily, the Sun's entry into adaptable Gemini allows you to pursue other possibilities without too much discouragement.

MAY 24–27 ★ *magical mystery tour*
An inquisitive Gemini New Moon on **May 24** turns you into a data scavenger as you gather the information you need to make a crucial decision. Fortunately, action-hero Mars comes to your aid when he cooperatively sextiles the spiritual Jupiter-Chiron-Neptune trio on **May 26–27**, illuminating a practical way through an otherwise mysterious journey. Still, the grand conjunction of your two planetary rulers, Jupiter and Neptune, on the **27th** could scatter your energy to the winds.

JUNE

HEAD IN THE CLOUDS, FEET ON THE GROUND

Your spiritual growth continues this month, inspired by the otherworldly Jupiter-Chiron-Neptune super-conjunction in your 12th House of Destiny that was exact last month. The 12th House is a secret and sacred place where magic can unfold beneath the radar of everyday life. Although the metaphysical planetary trio is separating now, your co-ruling planet Jupiter turns retrograde on **June 15** to keep your hopes alive all month. Your forward progress may be suspended as you are given additional time to allow reality to catch up with your plans. Sweet Venus sextiles the super-conjunction on **June 2**, making everything seem quite rosy. Stressful squares from analytical Mercury on **June 9–10** reveal shortcomings in your logic, while creative quintiles from energetic Mars and indulgent Venus on **June 11–15** enable you to magically turn your desires into decisive action. The Sun's easygoing trines to Jupiter, Chiron, and Neptune on **June 16–17** bolster your confidence, even as you realize that everything will take longer than you expect.

Your unrestrained idealism is countered by a series of reality checks beginning **June 5–6**, when pragmatic Saturn is tensely aspected by the Sun and Venus. The normally adventurous Sagittarius Full Moon on **June 7** falls in your 10th House of Career; its square to Saturn in your 7th House of Others suggests that you need to convince an unsupportive boss or partner before taking your preferred course of action. The Summer Solstice on **June 21** can also slow you down as the Sun enters cautious Cancer just a day before the Cancer New Moon on **June 22**. Thankfully, the lazy mood of summer can bring more stability to your life, because Venus and Mars harmonize with solid Saturn the same day.

> **KEEP IN MIND THIS MONTH**
>
> *Your dreams are important enough to keep cultivating—even if they seem unrealistic next to your present circumstances.*

KEY DATES

JUNE 2–5 ★ *don't judge a book by its cover*

You may be overly concerned with your appearance on **June 2**, when stylish Venus in your 2nd House of Self-Worth receives the support of your two ruling planets—abundant Jupiter and responsive Neptune. But there's more to it than your looks when energetic Mars harmonizes with penetrating Pluto on **June 3**, connecting you to intense passions. Delving beneath the surface is tricky, but if you attempt to avoid the issues, the Sun's stressful square to authoritative Saturn on **June 5** will surely stop you in your tracks until you acknowledge the serious work that must be done.

JUNE 7-10 ★ *beyond language*

The aspiring Sagittarius Full Moon on **June 7** convinces you that you deserve more, but its harsh square to "stop sign" Saturn suggests that obstacles still stand in your way. Nevertheless, you aren't willing to accept no for an answer on **June 8**, when sensual Venus's smooth trine with demanding Pluto strengthens your desires. Unfortunately, it may be difficult to handle these intense feelings as thoughtful Mercury dynamically squares the metaphysical Jupiter-Chiron-Neptune super-conjunction **June 8–10**, confusing your logic with fantasy. Ride the wild waves of your imagination now without trying to justify yourself to anyone else.

JUNE 16-17 ★ *let loose*

Your behavior might seem erratic to others now, yet you should be able to get away with it more easily than usual. Rebellious Uranus is fired up by action-planet Mars on **June 16** and by the Sun on **June 17**, suddenly releasing previously buried tension. Luckily, the Sun's sympathetic trine with benevolent Jupiter and spiritual Neptune on **June 17** is like a visit from your guardian angel, smoothing over the rough spots and clearing a path to your goals. As long as you respect the boundaries of everyone involved, you're likely to get what you want.

SUPER NOVA DAYS
JUNE 22-23 ★ *stand by me*

You may be overly protective of someone you love on **June 22** when the super-sensitive Cancer New Moon increases your empathy, making it difficult to distinguish your feelings from those of the people around you. But the Sun's stressful opposition to domineering Pluto on **June 23** can indicate a real threat; your defensive tactics may fend off an emotional attack before it actually occurs. You gain additional strength from the cosmic lovers, Venus and Mars, as they harmoniously trine unflappable Saturn, also on **June 22**, giving you the ability to firmly stand up to someone else's power play. Secure a safe haven for yourself and your family. Remember, you needn't be swept up in any drama that isn't yours.

JULY

DREAM INTERRUPTED

You're tempted to wander off into dreamland this month, but there's too much to do at work and at home to take any long breaks from reality. Your attraction to other worlds is rekindled by visionary Jupiter's conjunctions to mythical Neptune on **July 10** and healing Chiron on **July 22**. Your consciousness can be raised to a higher level by this second occurrence in a series of super-conjunctions that began **May 23–27** and will end **December 7–21**. Take note of your moments of inspiration and store them deep in your memory as an ongoing source of hope and faith. Sociable Venus in Gemini waltzes into your 4th House of Roots on **July 5**, followed by animated Mars on **July 11**, increasing playful activities at home. Visitors are likely to interrupt the tranquility of your abode, so make it a party and just invite them in. Joyous times with lively individuals will lift the spirits of your entire household.

The Full Moon in responsible Capricorn on **July 7** is a Lunar Eclipse in your 11th House of Groups that could alter your relationships with friends or colleagues, perhaps via a change of duties. Still, a constructive trine from hardworking Saturn to the Full Moon reveals that you may wind up with even more on your plate. Make sure that you have a solid support system and a clear understanding of what's expected of you before signing on. The New Moon in caring Cancer on **July 21** is a Solar Eclipse in your 5th House of Romance, Children, and Creativity. A trine to this Sun-Moon conjunction from innovative Uranus unveils surprising ways to adapt to crises in any of these areas.

> **KEEP IN MIND THIS MONTH**
>
> *Maintaining a playful spirit isn't immature or irresponsible; it's a healthy release from the daily pressures of dealing with reality.*

KEY DATES

SUPER NOVA DAYS
JULY 1–3 ★ *take it to the limit*

Your attention may be pulled in so many directions on **July 1** that it's wise to prioritize. Mental Mercury buzzes through aspects with Neptune, Jupiter, and Uranus that can light up your mind with bright ideas, but an unconditionally loving Venus-Neptune square makes you so sensitive to the desires of others that you can easily forget yourself. Giving more than your fair share is further encouraged with an excessive Venus-Jupiter square on **July 2**, when passion can overrule common sense. The Sun's squishy sesquisquares to diffusive Neptune and excessive Jupiter on **July 2–3** continue the trend of going too far or giving too much. Stretching your capacity for love and joy is fine as long as you don't overdo it.

JULY 6–8 ★ *do your research*
Anger or enthusiasm can take you over the top on **July 6**, when dynamic Mars forms stressful squares with ungrounded Neptune and giant Jupiter. Be sure you have all the facts before supporting a friend. Fortunately, a clever Mars-Uranus sextile on **July 7** lets you make a rapid course correction if needed. Still, mental Mercury's edgy aspects with Jupiter and Neptune on **July 8** flood you with information that may be faulty. Check and double-check the facts before speaking out.

JULY 17–18 ★ *hold your ground*
Your will may wobble as the Sun slides off slippery quincunxes with Jupiter on **July 17** and Neptune on **July 18**. Even if you're absolutely right about an important issue, you may find it difficult to hold your ground. It's best not to waste your time talking with those who lack your sincerity; they only distract you from the truth you know in your heart.

JULY 21 ★ *keep it real*
Be realistic about relationships today as a Venus-Saturn square signals that it's time to take a stand. You don't need to be negative—or accept negativity from others—yet if you're not happy with a situation, it's time to commit to making a change. Today's Solar Eclipse may sadly end one chapter, but it also empowers you to turn the page and start a new one.

JULY 27–28 ★ *hooked on a feeling*
Spoiling yourself is called for with a luxurious Venus-Jupiter trine on **July 27**. You can sense that change is coming but are likely to feel positive about the outcome. Venus trines compassionate Neptune on **July 28**, sprinkling magic dust on your relationships, yet the love planet's highly charged square to wild Uranus encourages reckless reactions that suddenly break the mood. You're traveling in uncharted territory of the heart, where caution and courage are your strongest allies.

AUGUST

ONE STEP AT A TIME

Minor adjustments done well are much more valuable this month than dramatic moves. An awkward quincunx between expansive Jupiter and contractive Saturn on **August 19** requires you to scale back an idea that's running away with itself. The reappearance of this aspect—which began on **March 22** and finishes on **February 5, 2010**—is not meant to quash your dreams but to bring them down to a scale where you can shepherd them into reality. Consider constructive input from others, yet don't pull back because of someone else's doubts or fears. Combining small but positive steps with the magic you feel is the winning formula. The Full Moon in unconventional Aquarius on **August 5** is a Lunar Eclipse that falls in your 12th House of Escapism, tempting you to run away from your responsibilities. However, active Mars in multitalented Gemini trines the Full Moon to provide alternative ways to meet your obligations.

A spacey Sun-Neptune opposition on **August 17** could bring unreliable partners whose promises lure you into giving more than you'll receive in return. There is a positive potential for spiritual opening and shared idealism, but without a solid plan they're likely to go up in smoke. The brash Leo New Moon in your 6th House

> **KEEP IN MIND THIS MONTH**
>
> *Mastering even minor details in your daily life builds a web of competence and confidence to support your long-term goals.*

of Work and Service on **August 20** should spark your enthusiasm for learning new skills or seeking more fulfilling employment. A growing desire for greater recognition or creativity on the job can inspire you to take bold action. The Sun's entry into dependable Virgo on **August 22** can attract competent support in your 7th House of Partnerships. It's time to set aside fantasies and take a more realistic view of relationships.

KEY DATES

AUGUST 1–2 ★ *don't take it personally*

You may feel emotionally threatened by disagreements over significant principles thanks to a tense Venus-Pluto square on **August 1**. If you sense a destructive tone, back away unless you're willing to risk a relationship. Thoughtful Mercury's entry into discerning Virgo and your 7th House of Others on **August 2** spurs critical conversations that are worthwhile when the focus is on fixing faults rather than simply finding them.

AUGUST 9–10 ★ *work for your dreams*

With an overly idealistic Venus-Neptune sesquisquare on **August 9**, even a broken-down piece of furniture or undesirable individual looks promising to you. If your heart can't help it, then spend your time or money on a reclamation project, but it probably won't be a bargain. Consequences for carelessness come quickly with a stern Mars-Saturn square on **August 10**. Make your priorities, stick to them closely, and don't back down.

AUGUST 13–14 ★ *pushing the envelope*

An overenergetic Mars-Jupiter trine on **August 13** invites you to exceed your normal limits by being more physically active and intellectually assertive. Sharing your secret desires can feel risky, yet it's probably safer than you think. The courageous Sun's opposition to Jupiter on **August 14** is another day of supersizing when crossing the threshold of your comfort zone can be rewarding. If an ambitious work project seems daunting, break it down into simple steps.

SUPER NOVA DAYS
AUGUST 17–18 ★ *genius potential*

Inspiration supported by clear thinking can produce miraculous results on **August 17**. An intellectually intense Mercury-Saturn conjunction focuses your mind as aspects from the Sun and dynamic Mars to fanciful Neptune flood you with creativity. You're riding a wild wave of energy that could spin out of control if you don't apply it purposefully. On **August 18**, a high-frequency Mars-Uranus square delivers surprises that can upset your daily routine. Reckless reactions against restraint could be destructive, but experimenting with a fresh approach of your own choosing can be brilliant.

AUGUST 20–22 ★ *agitated atmosphere*

A Mercury-Neptune quincunx on **August 20** can prompt a misunderstanding with a normally reliable individual. Listen carefully and don't be shy about asking for clarification if you have the slightest doubt about the meaning of his or her message. Tension builds with a Mercury-Uranus opposition on **August 21**; one careless word can provoke an irrational response. Your mind may be racing with bright ideas, but it's wiser to slow down and respond thoughtfully rather than speaking too quickly. A super-sensitive Venus-Neptune connection on **August 22** could undermine your confidence in a relationship. Forgiving others for their shortcomings is noble—as long as you aren't burying your true feelings.

SEPTEMBER

BE TRUE TO YOURSELF

Your ongoing struggle between personal freedom and committed partnership heats up this month and could push a relationship to the limit. Self-interest—something you too often sacrifice to please others—is ignited by the Full Moon in subjective Pisces on **September 4** and an energetic trine from reactive Mars, motivating you to take more control of your life. On **September 18**, the New Moon in analytical Virgo falls in your 7th House of Relationships, where its opposition to disruptive Uranus is almost certain to trigger changes in the way you connect with others. You don't like to ripple tranquil waters, but it's healthier to make the first move than to sit back and react to what's thrust upon you.

You're in the midst of a remarkable period of redefining yourself that began when rule-making Saturn opposed liberty-loving Uranus on **November 4, 2008**, and **February 5**. This aspect recurs on **September 15** and will return on **April 26, 2010**, and **July 26, 2010**. This month's transit may be the most potent of the series since the willful Sun joins Saturn and opposes Uranus on **September 17**, adding fuel to the fire and urging you to act now. Your instinct to try to hold together an alliance that's not working is reflected by responsible Saturn's awkward quincunx with elusive Neptune on **September 12**. Control can easily slip from your grasp—another reason to release yourself from this impossible task. Expressive Mercury retrogrades through your relationship houses **September 7–29**, stirring up old issues, yet the Sun's passage into objective Libra and your 8th House of Intimacy on **September 22** marks the Autumn Equinox and, perhaps, a new chapter in your relationship life.

> **KEEP IN MIND THIS MONTH**
>
> *Putting yourself first now is not an act of selfishness; it's an essential step to getting your life in order.*

KEY DATES

SEPTEMBER 1–2 ★ *too much, too little, too late*

Runaway enthusiasm could get you in trouble on **September 1**, when communicative Mercury makes a clunky sesquisquare to extravagant Jupiter, followed by hyperactive Mars on **September 2**. It's a potential double dose of excess, impatience, and poor judgment—but you can counter it with self-control. A strict semisquare from Saturn to loving Venus sets clear limits that take the air out of your overinflated balloon.

SEPTEMBER 9–11 ★ *find your way*

A clash between mobile Mars and mushy Neptune makes it tough for you to get in gear on **September 9**. If you focus on one task at a time, your attention is less likely to wander and you can correct your course more quickly. Going too far may feel just about right with flamboyant Venus in Leo opposing over-the-top Jupiter on **September 11**. The Sun's quincunx with Jupiter increases the danger that you'll spend, promise, or expect too much. Broaden your horizons, but don't lose your bearings and fall off the edge of the map.

SUPER NOVA DAYS
SEPTEMBER 15–17 ★ *the cost of freedom*

The hard edge of the Saturn-Uranus opposition on **September 15** is softened by a kindhearted Venus-Neptune opposition. The Sun continues this caring, if not entirely realistic, trend with a quincunx to Neptune on **September 16**. But the tone changes radically on **September 17** when the Sun joins controlling Saturn and opposes unruly Uranus, provoking battles with authority figures. A harsh Mercury-Pluto square is profoundly perceptive; however, callous comments can undermine a relationship, so be aware of the wounding power of words.

SEPTEMBER 20–23 ★ *give peace a chance*

You can repair damaged partnerships on **September 20** with loving Venus entering your 7th House of Others. The romance planet's creative trine to intense Pluto brings passion without the loss of control. A sexy Venus-Mars semisquare on **September 21** adds even more heat before it's time to get down to brass tacks. The Sun entering gracious Libra on **September 22** suggests compromise—but it's in your 8th House of Intimacy, where it's critical that you know the score. A hard-headed Mercury-Saturn conjunction underscores the importance of maintaining clarity in the midst of an emotional merger. However, the messenger planet's opposition to unpredictable Uranus on **September 23** can signal a sudden change of mind or unexpected news that alters a previous agreement. You may find yourself panicking, especially with confusing quincunxes from Mercury to Neptune and Mars to Jupiter. Misunderstandings can lead to regrettable actions or misplaced anger. Take a slow, deep breath before pushing ahead on assumptions that might not be accurate.

OCTOBER

KNOW WHAT YOU WANT

You're not the most materialistic person, Pisces, but money is on your mind this month. The Full Moon in enterprising Aries falls in your 2nd House of Finances on **October 4**, which can spur a spending spree, panic about resources, or some fresh ideas to increase your income. On **October 18**, the New Moon in friendly Libra enlivens your 8th House of Shared Resources with the potential of new personal or business partnerships. Opportunistic trines from generous Jupiter, caring Chiron, and sympathetic Neptune can attract an open-minded individual who could help you out with a financial fix. Being fair with someone who treats you with respect is a positive step toward creating a healthy alliance. Hope rises as your co-ruling planet Jupiter turns direct on **October 12**, which can help you put into action a plan that's been simmering below the surface during the previous four months.

Optimistic visions of the future can reveal your goals, but only careful calculation will enable you to clear away obstacles and gather the resources you need to reach them. The Sun's passage into powerful Scorpio on **October 23** strengthens your intentions, so set aside distractions and pursue your desires with controlled passion. Your emotions are a great asset as long as they stay within the bounds of your own desires, rather than leaking out in response to everyone else's needs.

> ### KEEP IN MIND THIS MONTH
>
> *Being vague with others may be your way of not seeming pushy, but an honest expression of your needs is a truer sign of trust and love.*

Mental Mercury's shift into Scorpio on **October 28** reinforces the narrow but necessary perspective you need to advance your interests. Crystallizing Saturn enters cooperative Libra and your 8th House on **October 29**, initiating a two-year period during which it will be vital to bring more balance into your relationships. Clearly state your expectations if you want to minimize the control that others exert over you.

KEY DATES

OCTOBER 4 ★ *running in circles*

Physical Mars and intellectual Mercury slip on a banana peel quincunx with spacey Neptune, leading to wasted effort and unclear communication. You can be incredibly efficient at getting lost or doing a task that doesn't need to be done. Double-check your information before diving into a project that feels energizing—but might just be taking you for a joyride.

OCTOBER 8–11 ★ *measured speech*

You may have to take no for an answer with a restrictive Mercury-Saturn conjunction in your 7th House of Partnerships on **October 8.** There is potential for clear communication if you carefully consider your words and express them with precision. Still, it may be impossible to prevent the unexpected when Venus opposes volatile Uranus on **October 9** while also skidding off a quincunx with peace-loving Neptune. Relationships may be shaken by impulsive attractions that undermine security. Avoid overreacting; take whatever you're feeling and cut it in half for a more realistic picture of the situation. A Sun-Jupiter trine on **October 10** widens your perspective, allowing you to step back for a more strategic view of a partnership. Too much talking could confuse matters thanks to a Mercury-Jupiter sesquisquare on **October 11**, turning a minor detail into a major issue.

OCTOBER 16 ★ *gentle persuasion*

A sweet Sun-Neptune trine fills you with kindness, compassion, and forgiveness, enabling you to overcome your differences with a partner or close friend. You may act as a leader now, but with such a gentle touch that no one feels pressured. As long as you're treated with the same respect you give others, harmonious connections will be yours.

OCTOBER 20–21 ★ *out of proportion*

Your words have more influence than you think on **October 20** as a visionary Mercury-Jupiter trine makes you a convincing speaker. Listening to the ideas of others without losing track of your own leads to enriching discussions in which you can learn as much as you teach. Undeserved enthusiasm for someone or something on **October 21**, however, could skew your judgment. Take off your rose-colored glasses to make a more realistic evaluation that won't cost you so much.

OCTOBER 24 ★ *insight beyond words*

Your intuition is right on target as brainy Mercury aligns in a wise trine with mystical Neptune. Even if you can't put your thoughts perfectly into a format that a friend or lover might understand, don't let go of the vision you're holding in your mind. Creativity flourishes when you have to prove yourself to others, so seek an outlet where you can apply your special talents.

NOVEMBER

THE POWER OF THE MIND

Serious conversations and deep thinking are on your agenda this month, starting on **November 2** with the Full Moon in sensible and determined Taurus in your 3rd House of Communication. Your usually adaptable attitude can harden in this fixed sign, especially as opinionated Jupiter and aggressive Mars square the stubborn Taurus Moon. It's helpful to hold firm when you encounter intimidation; just don't confuse your resistance with being right while refusing to consider new information that's outside your comfort zone. Dreams that have been on the edge of your consciousness begin to come into focus when illusory Neptune turns direct on **November 4.** This is unlikely to create immediate changes, yet it marks a subtle shift that gives new life to your desires and allows you to be more comfortable expressing them openly. Total discipline is critical if you hope to achieve your goals as exacting Saturn aligns in a tough square with driven Pluto on **November 15** that will recur on **January 31, 2010,** and **August 21, 2010.** Distancing yourself from individuals who don't respect you can be difficult, but it may determine whether you gain more control over your life.

Your vision for the future and dedication to your beliefs reach the next level of commitment with the New Moon in your 9th House of Truth, Travel, and Higher Education on **November 16.** Tense squares to the Moon in extreme Scorpio from Jupiter, Chiron, and Neptune might cause you to overreach, yet the hope you feel may carry you farther than you expect if you mix in the right dose of practical thinking. On **November 21,** the Sun enters fun-loving Sagittarius in your 11th House of Groups, enabling you to let go and be the life of the party.

> **KEEP IN MIND THIS MONTH**
>
> *When you're sure of yourself, you can be open to the ideas of others without worrying that you'll be overly influenced by them.*

KEY DATES

NOVEMBER 2 ★ *unconditional love*

Life is sweet with a romantic Venus-Neptune trine bringing magic to your day. You're aware of love's presence without any effort required. This free feeling of connection can happen within a partnership, with a passing stranger, or even alone through music, art, nature, or spiritual practice.

SUPER NOVA DAYS
NOVEMBER 8-11 ★ *fantasy island*

Don't try so hard to justify yourself to others **November 8-10**, when stressful squares from Mercury and the Sun to Jupiter can provoke you to say or promise more than you should. Focus on key concepts for maximum impact instead of spreading yourself thin with a wide-ranging discussion that wanders off course. Mental clarity may be hard to come by when Mercury drifts into a square with dreamy Neptune on **November 11**. Facts can be lost in the mists of your imagination as fantasy is so much more interesting than reality. This is wonderful for creative thinking and intimate conversations, but not ideal for handling important details.

NOVEMBER 14-15 ★ *avoid pressure*

An expressive trine between the Sun and unorthodox Uranus on **November 14** allows you to be comfortable in unfamiliar situations. Your intuition helps you adjust to changes that might upset others, putting you in the position of being a guide, counselor, or peacemaker. But don't stray too far from home base on **November 15**, when a Sun-Neptune square may skew your judgment. Stay away from folks who try to control you no matter what their justification. You don't have to prove them wrong to have the right to be left alone.

NOVEMBER 21-23 ★ *play between the lines*

A sense of abundance brings out your generous side when the Sun enters bountiful Sagittarius on **November 21**. This placement illumines your 10th House of Public Responsibility, where belief in yourself or your cause is crucial. Sensual Venus and opulent Jupiter cross in a high-powered square on **November 23** that can lead you right into overindulgence. Spending, eating, or playing too much may empty your wallet and wear out your body. Going a little farther in the pursuit of pleasure is fine if you respect your financial, physical, and emotional limits.

NOVEMBER 26 ★ *spiritual gifts*

Romantic foolishness and divine discontent arrive with an idealistic Venus-Neptune square that can make your feelings hard to manage. You may be especially sensitive to criticism and quick to sacrifice yourself to please others. However, the magic you seek is in your heart and soul, so you needn't go elsewhere to find it. What you desire most is given to you freely when you look within and give yourself permission to receive it.

DECEMBER

SPIRIT RISING

Your long process of spiritual growth and intuitive awakening that began in May culminates this month. Benevolent Jupiter conjuncts healing Chiron on **December 7**, as it did on **May 23** and **July 22**, and compassionate Neptune on **December 21**, repeating the conjunctions of **May 27** and **July 10**. The profound connection you naturally have with the divine is expanding into a wider web of awareness that nourishes your soul and inspires your dreams. Support comes from unexpected sources if you're willing to aid others while asking nothing in return. A quiet confidence grows inside you because you know that in the cosmic sense, you are never completely alone.

You can stabilize a shaky domestic situation on **December 2** when the Full Moon falls in your 4th House of Home and Family. Solid Saturn's constructive trine to this jittery Gemini Moon clarifies your priorities, enabling you to act decisively. Surprises at your workplace can be disturbing on **December 16**, however, as the New Moon in outgoing Sagittarius squares wired Uranus. A desire to seek more interesting employment or a sudden change of status stirs restless feelings, yet it's best to act with caution no matter how quickly your mind is moving. Action-hero Mars turns retrograde on **December 20**, which is another signal telling you to manage growth carefully. His reversal in your 6th House of Health and Work suggests the value of reorganizing your daily routine to reduce waste and increase efficiency through better nutrition, exercise, and refinement of your professional skills. Talkative Mercury goes retrograde on **December 26**, which can complicate teamwork with friends and associates in your 11th House of Groups; make an extra effort to ensure that you're all on the same page in the same book.

KEEP IN MIND THIS MONTH

The highest truth is something you can find inside yourself; it does not have to be validated by anyone else.

KEY DATES

DECEMBER 1 ★ *sixth sense*

A clever sextile between mental Mercury and receptive Neptune strengthens your innate psychic powers. You have the ability to sense things others don't and to communicate with such sensitivity that you can be very persuasive without seeming the least bit pushy. This allows you to be an excellent leader who uses finesse rather than force to solve problems.

DECEMBER 10–11 ★ *wishful thinking*

Thoughts ramble and messages grow muddled when messenger Mercury forms stressful semisquares with excessive Jupiter on **December 10** and nebulous Neptune on **December 11**. Be alert for a person who means well but can't master details. It's easy to buy into a beautiful story because it fulfills your idea of how things should be, yet even a normally reliable partner can be sloppy with facts and make empty promises. Relying on fantasies to come true could be disappointing.

SUPER NOVA DAYS
DECEMBER 14–15 ★ *danger equals opportunity*

A crisis can quickly turn into an opportunity on **December 14** when the Sun travels from a calamitous square with shocking Uranus to a supportive sextile with wise Jupiter. Unmet responsibilities or a blowup with a boss may open your mind to more inventive ways to take care of business. Stay cool if you're hit by a shock wave; you can recover more quickly than you think when you're flexible enough to consider alternative approaches. Gentler winds waft through your life on **December 15** with a Sun-Neptune sextile that's rich in empathy and forgiveness. This may be a day of work-related endings, but your compassion makes it easier to let go graciously.

DECEMBER 20–21 ★ *many hands make light work*

Your mood is mixed on **December 20**. The delight of a joyous Venus-Jupiter sextile—the perfect warm-up for the holiday season—may be diminished as Mars's retrograde turn piles up tasks that won't be finished quickly. The Sun's entry into traditional Capricorn on **December 21** marks the Winter Solstice in your 11th House of Friends and Associates. Your obligations to others can weigh heavily, but a graceful Venus-Neptune sextile helps you lighten the load by turning work into play.

DECEMBER 30–31 ★ *face the music*

A soft Sun-Neptune semisquare encourages distraction on **December 30**, but an intense Lunar Eclipse in emotional Cancer on **December 31** is sure to grab your attention. This Full Moon Eclipse in your 5th House of Fun and Games receives hard aspects from deadly serious Pluto and Saturn. Careless social behavior can prove costly, so don't fall prey to New Year's Eve foolishness. A hard decision about a romance or a creative project lies ahead; taking charge of the situation is better than trying to duck it.